MW01601826

PRINCIPLES

OF SERVOMECHANISMS

PRINCIPLES
OF SERVOMECHANISMS

Dynamics and Synthesis
of
Closed-Loop Control Systems

GORDON S. BROWN

PROFESSOR OF ELECTRICAL ENGINEERING
DIRECTOR, SERVOMECHANISMS LABORATORY

DONALD P. CAMPBELL

LATE ASSISTANT PROFESSOR
OF ELECTRICAL ENGINEERING

BOTH AT MASSACHUSETTS INSTITUTE OF TECHNOLOGY

John Wiley & Sons, Inc., New York
Chapman & Hall, Limited, London

Preface

This book takes up a number of ideas and concepts that are important to the understanding of closed-loop control systems, explains them in simple terms, and shows how they are used in control system synthesis. Its writing has been prompted by such factors as the great engineering and scientific interest that exists today in the principles of closed-loop control, by the recent increase in the diversification of control applications and the exacting revisions to their performance demands, by the recent sharpening up of some engineering practices and the obsolescence of others used for development and design, and finally by the unique pedagogic aspects of the general subject of closed-loop control which aid the engineering teacher in holding the interest and broadening the viewpoint of his students. We believe the book will have interest for the scientist, the practicing engineer, the engineering teacher, and the student.

Closed-loop system design has often been based on a static philosophy. Sometimes it has been based on mere analysis which, in itself, is only a means of understanding the behavior of an existing mechanism. Frequently, cut-and-try procedures for altering existing mechanisms to meet specifications have been used as substitutes for design. None of these practices copes adequately with the dynamics problem of closed-loop control. . Each fails to take account of the fact that the system is a dynamic one. Each also fails to give an explicit or even a direct solution to the problem and contributes little to the need for design practices that will open up unexplored aspects of control engineering. Because present-day applications impose many exacting performance criteria, and many physical limitations on systems, the only approach to an explicit design involves what might be called guided conception or dynamic synthesis. We have made dynamic synthesis the central theme of the book.

Our approach to the synthesis problem is along two main avenues of mathematics. Both emphasize dynamics. One involves the transient response; the other the sinusoidal response. Each furnishes useful data, each has significant obstacles, and each illuminates the subject

v

differently. A transient response is familiar to everyone because it presents dynamics in terms of time-varying signals that our senses can interpret. It gives data that are necessary but insufficient for the synthesis of even elementary systems. A sinusoidal response is not easily interpreted by our senses because the individual frequencies are merged into a frequency spectrum. However, the frequency spectrum defines the dynamic properties of the equipment in a manner that is highly effective for the synthesis of complicated systems.

An acceptable transient response is one of several performance criteria that a design must fulfill, and is therefore an inherent aspect of synthesis. The book begins with a formulation of the closed-loop problem in terms of elementary differential equations for which transient solutions are given and evaluated. It then extends the treatment to utilize features of the Laplace transform applicable to more complicated dynamics problems and to give the basis for a transfer function representation of the system. It next develops the transfer function into an effective tool in synthesis in terms of loci plots that define system behavior as a frequency spectrum. It ends with the presentation of approximate methods for determining the transient behavior from the frequency function.

Much of our text material stems from an educational program in which we acted mainly as catalysts by stimulating students to make contributions in uncharted areas. Our viewpoint has developed largely by our work with these students, who, while primarily interested in servomechanisms, were studying in related fields. This student association has cross-fertilized various specialized branches of engineering and continues as thesis investigations and seminars are conducted on the subject.

We believe the treatment given the subject matter of the book can help a teacher unify the contrasting viewpoints of students and engineers. We note that many students make only isolated analyses whereas practicing engineers frequently create components for integration into a system. That is, engineering involves practices in which system synthesis overshadows analysis. Although the teacher can illustrate many principles of engineering by the treatment of specific electrical or mechanical problems, the viewpoint of the student is broadened by the intermingling of electrical, electronic, mechanical, or hydraulic mechanisms and associated types of equipment encountered in automatic control. A real challenge is offered the student or the engineer by the fact that closed-loop systems known as servomechanisms, regulators, and governors, while similar in many ways, differ in many important aspects of synthesis. Theoretical studies can be conducted and confirmed by laboratory experiment and thereby serve as a medium for integrating into a balanced whole the many varied engineering problems and help increase the value students will place on the various topics of a curriculum. For these reasons, we have emphasized dynamic synthesis as contrasted with dynamic analysis, have introduced a dimensionless treatment to avoid the mention of analogues and equivalents and to simplify the mathematics, have included the chapter on experimental studies, and have given diverse problems for student exercise. While we do not expect the book alone to make a student expert in the synthesis of closed-loop dynamic systems, we believe it can broaden his viewpoint. We think also that it can help to make a designer into a student of dynamic synthesis.

Our book is intended for the use of both senior and graduate students. Our experience indicates that Chapters 1, 2, part of 3, 4, and 5, and all of 6 serve as a connected treatment for use at the senior level. We use the book in its entirety, supplemented by excursions into related subjects, in a one-semester graduate course. The subject attracts students from Electrical, Mechanical, Aeronautical, and Chemical Engineering.

Our book is not a compilation of components, hardware, or even isolated design tricks. It does not treat systems with distributed or nonlinear parameters, nor does it treat the power and energy aspects of closed loops, although extension of the work into these areas presents no insurmountable problem. It is not intended as an advanced mathematical treatise. Since a subject as broad as this one inherently involves pitfalls when only a portion of it is treated, we hope the purist will not be critical if we have stumbled into many of them.

We appreciate the valuable assistance given us by our colleagues in the Department of Electrical Engineering and in the Servomechanisms Laboratory at Massachusetts Institute of Technology. In particular, we gratefully acknowledge the encouragement of Professor Harold L. Hazen and the contributions of Professor Harold I. Tarpley, Messrs. H. Tyler Marcy, George C. Newton, Jr., William M. Pease, Ernest W. Therkelsen, and Robert B. Wilcox, made while teaching all or part of the academic courses. Thanks are especially due George F. Floyd for permission to include the material of Chapter 11 and Robert B. Wilcox for his valuable criticism and for his help in preparing the manuscript.

GORDON S. BROWN
DONALD P. CAMPBELL

Wellesley Hills, Massachusetts
Cambridge, Massachusetts
April 1948

Contents

Contents   xiii

1

Outline of Subject

1 Introduction

This book tells about closed-loop control systems. It tells how certain of them operate and it establishes a theoretical basis for their design. The particular closed-loop control systems are those servomechanisms * or regulators which, during the past few decades, have become important in manufacturing, the process industries, the steering of ships or aircraft, scientific research, and a host of other applications.

Servomechanisms and regulators, or robots as they are often called, relieve man of drudgery in many of his menial daily tasks. They also serve as intelligent substitutes for the human in many explorations into the unknown. At the flick of a pointer, they control great masses. In response to signals no greater than the light from a star or the radio reflection from a body they can control hundreds of horsepower.

As the applications of control systems have been increased in number, the demands imposed on their reliability, precision, and speed of operation have also increased. Fortunately, many of these demands have been satisfied because of developments in the various branches of engineering and physics that have taken place simultaneously with the growth of automatic control. At the same time the complexity of the mechanisms has often been increased. The result of all this has been that the design of servomechanisms and automatic regulating systems has now become a science in itself. For the skillful and straightforward design of a high-caliber system the designer requires, first, a clear appreciation of the fundamental principles involved in the functioning of automatic control systems; and, second, an accurate knowledge of the properties of the mechanisms of which it is composed.

The specific objective of this book is to set forth in fairly simple terms a procedure for understanding the complexities involved in the system

* For numerous references on servomechanisms and regulators refer to the bibliography at the end of the book.

1

behavior and a technique for the direct approach to system design as a substitute for the approach through experimentation. An aim of the book is to establish in the mind of the designer a concept of synthesis as contrasted with mere analysis. Synthesis means the direct approach to the problem of putting together particular amplifiers, motors, gears, and so forth, which when interconnected will accomplish a prescribed function. Experimentation may become a trial and error selection of amplifiers, motors, gears, based only on hunches or intuition. In other words, the approach in this book is toward a statement of an explicit solution to the problem rather than an intuitive or experimental one. In establishing the technique much use is made of organized analysis.

Unfortunately the objective of the general problem is not fully realized. However, as scientific and mathematical work in the field is continued, it is hoped that the goal of complete synthesis will eventually be achieved.

2 The Elements of Control

As knowledge of automatic control advanced, two general classes of control gradually emerged. One class is called open-loop control; the other, closed-loop control. In the former, which is not the principal subject of this book, the control acts in accordance with the dictates of some arbitrary quantity, and the fidelity of action is dependent wholly on the linearity of the mechanism, or on calibration. In the latter, the control acts in accordance with the dictates of an arbitrary quantity *and* in accordance with what happened as a result of the control operation. Linearity of the mechanisms and calibration occupy only a secondary role.

Time-operated traffic lights are one example of open-loop control, since what the lights do or even what the traffic does cannot affect the time mechanism that actuates the lights. A conventional automatic home laundry is another example of open-loop control, for the degree of dirtiness of the clothes does not affect the time they remain in the washer. On the other hand, when Mother washes the clothes by hand, she functions as a closed-loop system because the time she takes at the task and the vigor of her action are functions of the effectiveness of the washing operation.

It is often desired to control a force or a motion, a hydraulic pressure, or some physical quantity in accordance with another physical quantity. For example, a light flux may be used to control voltage, or the weight of an object to control the intensity of sound. The agreement between the responding or controlled quantity and the signaling quantity may here be accomplished by means of an open-loop or open-ended control as shown in Figure 1. Notice that the disturbing or input quantity enters a calibration or scaling mechanism which sends information to another mechanism; this second mechanism then produces forces, deflections, pressures, or any number of different physical quantities in accordance with its command.   Many examples of open-loop control devices

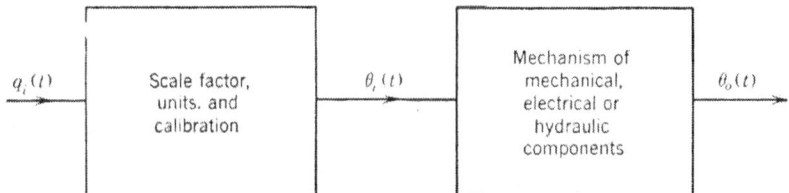

FIGURE 1.   Open-ended control.

may be found throughout industry and experimental laboratories.   They require careful attention to insure their correct continued performance. They must be calibrated and maintained in calibration against wear and changes in environment such as temperature, humidity, friction, or vibration.   There are many factors which can alter their performance as precision instruments.   This whole class of controls is termed open-loop, because there is nothing in the mechanism that actually measures the result of the control operation and does something about it if the result is not what is desired.   The essential requirement of closed-loop control, on the other hand, is that the error between the state desired and the

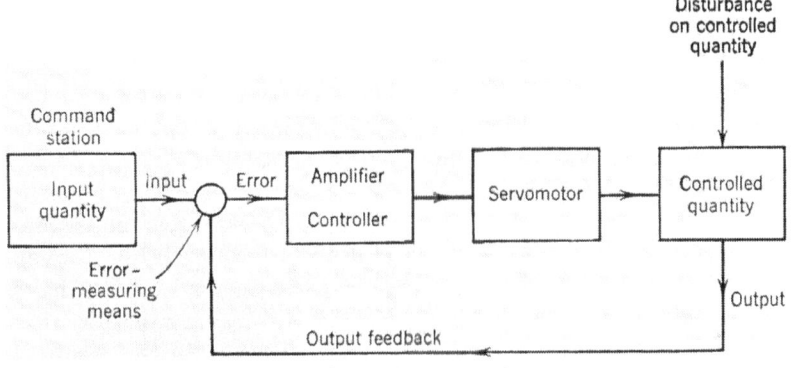

FIGURE 2.   Closed-loop control system.

state existing is constantly measured and if there is an error something is done about it.   A closed-loop control system is thus an error-sensitive system and, being such, it acquires certain peculiarities and idiosyncrasies which, in large measure, are the reasons for this book.   Figure 2 is a diagram of a closed-loop control system.

Open-loop systems are easier to build than closed-loop systems. However, the improved performance of the closed loop makes it greatly superior because it can nullify or counteract imperfections and non-linearities of component parts. The contrast in the principle of operation between the open loop and the closed loop is important in explaining this superiority. The open loop must be calibrated first to perform some specific task, and the perfection of operation depends upon the maintenance of this calibration. In other words, the open-loop system operates without a knowledge of the precision it attains during operation. In contrast, the closed-loop system operates in terms of an error and tends to minimize the error in the closed loop at all times. Thus, such a system knows the accuracy of its performance at all times during operation and continually tends to keep its output in agreement with its command. Only closed-loop or error-sensitive control systems and *specifically that class that are linearly and continuously error-sensitive are treated in this book*. However, it will be noted that many open-loop phenomena of closed-loop systems are considered because they help us understand the operation of the closed-loop system.

The specification of continuous control eliminates from discussion the often-encountered contactor or on-off type of error-sensitive system. Mechanisms of this kind are used a great deal where an insensitive band of operation, or a so-called dead zone, and jerkiness in operation may be tolerated in the interests of simplicity. Many references to these mechanisms and their analyses exist in the literature.*

3   Servomechanisms and Regulators

Early examples of closed-loop control systems are encountered in the control of temperature, pressure, voltage, speed, position, and the like. Many systems are called servomechanisms,† others are called regulators.‡

Servomechanisms were first successfully applied to industry and science for the automatic control of machines and processes several decades ago. Basically, their sole function is to control automatically a given quantity or process in accordance with a given command. They have three predominant features. (1) They are closed-loop systems in that the control is actuated by a quantity that is affected by the result of the control operation; (2) they can establish control throughout a wide range of command that may vary in a random manner; and (3) they permit the control of high-power operations at a remote point from low-

---

* References 1, 3, 4, and 5 of the bibliography at the end of the book give extensive treatments of this subject.

† References 1, 4, 6, 7, 8, 32, and 65.

‡ References 2, 9, 10, 11, and 70.

power operations at a local point.   In other words, the servomechanism is an error-sensitive, follow-up, amplifying system permitting wide range of the input command remotely located from the element being controlled.

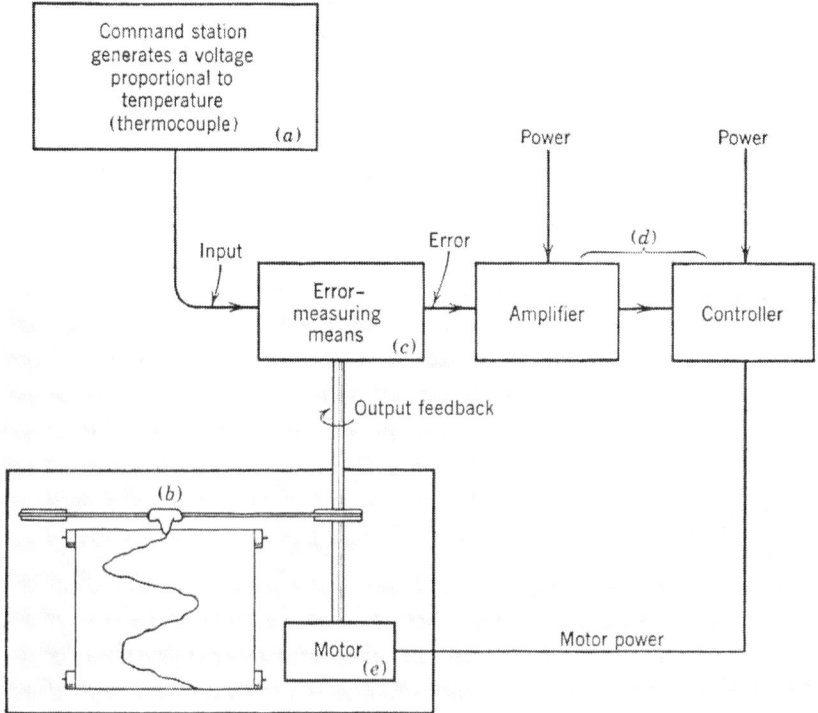

FIGURE 3.   Elementary servomechanism.

Figure 3 is a diagram of a closed-loop control system, and specifically a servomechanism, showing the generally recognizable principal functional components.   They are:

1. A remotely located command, or input station designated as a in the figure.   The symbol for the command is $\theta_i(t)$.
2. An output member or process designated as b in the figure.   The symbol for the controlled quantity is $\theta_o(t)$.
3. An error-measuring means capable of measuring the difference between command and output, designated as c in the figure.   The symbol for the error is $\mathcal{E}(t)$.
4. An amplifier or controller designated as d in the figure.   It actuates a servomotor in accordance with some function of the error $\mathcal{E}(t)$.
5. A servomotor designated as e in the figure.   It operates the controlled member or output.

That a servomechanism is a *system* and not merely a collection of components is a matter of great importance. The system behavior is continuously a function of the difference or *error* between the state or condition existing at the controlled point, and the state or condition desired as indicated by the command point. The closed-loop condition results from this error-sensitive feature since, as noted from Figure 2, a signal established at the input to the amplifier affects the controlled member, the output, and eventually the input to the amplifier itself by the feedback through the error-measuring means. It is the time sequence of these events that must be recognized by the designer as he evolves his servomechanism.

During the late 1930's, the meaning of the term "servomechanism" was gradually clarified. The distinction between the servomechanism and the regulator then became a subject for debate. It is often noted that persons will classify regulators as servomechanisms or vice versa. To a certain extent, this is understandable because, when viewed as dynamical systems, they have many properties in common. Also, when viewed merely as power-amplifying systems in which the amplifier element driving the output is actuated by the difference or error between the state existing and the state desired, they are indistinguishable. They are often distinguished in practice by virtue of the function which each is normally called upon to perform. The generally accepted meaning of the word regulate leads to a mathematical distinction. For example, in the commonly accepted elementary regulator, the steady-state difference between the command and the output, that is, the error, need generate merely the output; whereas in even the elementary servomechanism, the steady-state error must generate the rate of change of the output, not merely the output.

The servomechanism accomplishes the more general task. It can cope with a random variation of its command as well as with random disturbances applied to its output. The command or control level may vary over a very wide range, and the servomechanism functions to hold the controlled quantity at the value desired by the command anywhere within this range. A servomechanism is a follow-up system. On the other hand, the regulator usually functions to maintain the controlled quantity at a fixed control level. Its command has a relatively fixed value. For example, the mechanism for the control of voltage of an electric generator used to furnish regulated voltage at a load is a regulator. It tends to hold a preset terminal voltage,[12, 13, 14] in spite of the disturbing effects of the application of load to the generator. The controlled quantity is voltage, and the condition that tends to change the voltage is the application of load to the generator. Figure 4 illustrates

a system of the kind used to regulate voltage. Figure 5 illustrates a
system used to regulate speed.[14, 15, 16]

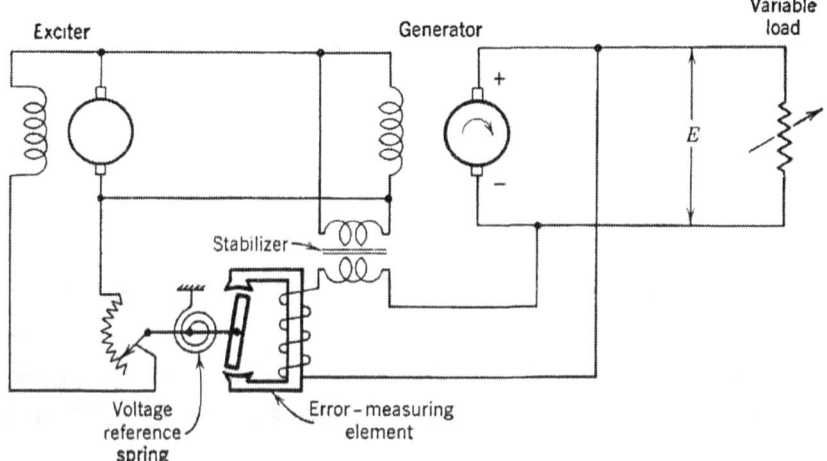

FIGURE 4.   Essential components of a voltage regulator.

On the other hand, the mechanism for the control of the pointing of a
radar located at an airport is a servomechanism. The supervisor in
the control tower may select any aircraft in the sky by means of his
radar, but to locate it with respect to plan coordinates of the airport he

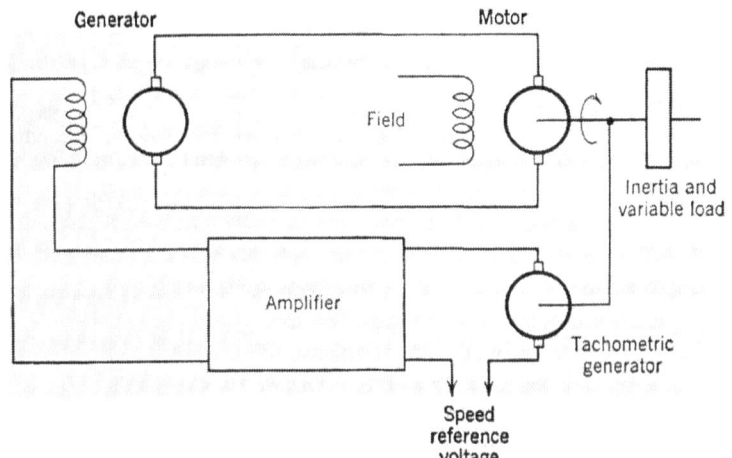

FIGURE 5.   Essential components of a speed regulator.

must use his servomechanism.   Here the random time variation of position of the aircraft over the airport calls for a mechanism that can control
the motion of the radar antenna to point it at the aircraft regardless

of the position of the aircraft. The controlled quantity or output is antenna direction. Any random position of the antenna direction is a possible direction. The command is the direction desired by the supervisor, and it has random time variation because of the random flight of the aircraft. Furthermore, the antenna may be exposed to the wind, which may tend to turn it away from the desired direction. The torque applied by the wind is a random load or disturbance on the controlled quantity that the servomechanism must counteract.

As a further illustration, consider a mechanism used for the control of an automatic die-cutting or replica-cutting machine,[20] as shown in

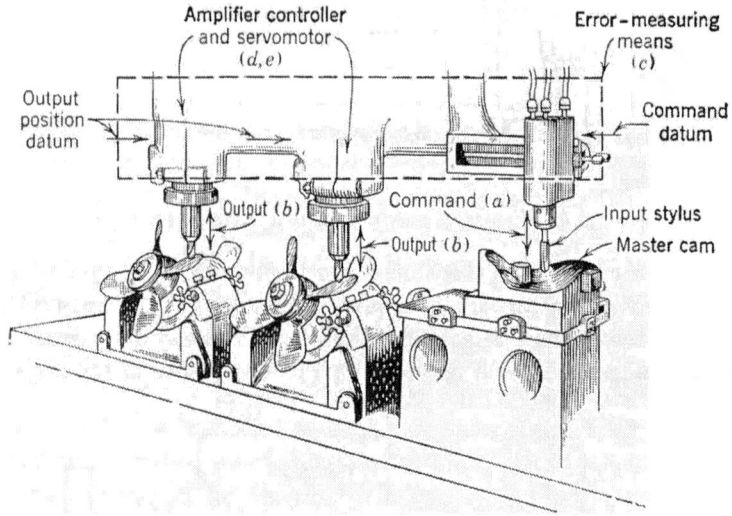

FIGURE 6. The industrial use of a servomechanism for contour reproduction. (Drawn from photograph furnished by Cincinnati Milling Machine Co.)

Figure 6. The cutting head is required to follow automatically a contour laid out on a master pattern or the contour of an existing member, as in a replica production. An application such as this could possibly result in maintaining the angular position of a shaft operating at a high-power level automatically in synchronism, or in step, with the angular position of a shaft as established by a low-power mechanism. The input signal might be the angular position of a cam-operated shaft. The controlled quantity or output would be the angular position of the lead screw carrying the cutting head. The cam-operated shaft may have any random variation of position established by the master pattern. In practice the angular positions of the two shafts are compared by one of several means common in the art; a measuring device detects the error in the position of the output and establishes a control signal, and a controller is actuated by this control signal and operates either directly on the shaft of the high-power member or through some accessory device to bring the output shaft into the desired position. Such a device must possess the follow-up property of a servomechanism in order to fulfill its function.

Figures 3 to 6 illustrate many varieties of and similarities between servomechanisms and regulators. The point which may not be apparent in this early part of the discussion is that whereas all servomechanisms can meet the specifications for an elementary regulator, not all regulators can meet the specifications for an elementary servomechanism.

The fields of application of these automatic control devices are very extensive. To cite merely a few, servomechanisms or regulators, without distinction, are found performing such functions as the control of position, pressure, speed, strain, or flow in mechanical problems; the control of frequency, voltage, or power in electrical systems; the control of combustion, density, humidity, temperature, or flow in chemical systems. More specifically, one finds such applications as the control of the speed of wind-up reels for receiving steel strip stock in a steel mill and quickly winding it on a reel for shipment; or the control of the flow of paper through the printing press where, with speed and precision, the multi-color pages of magazines are printed. The list is almost without end.

4   Recent Historical Development

The regulator, or governor as it is also called, established its place in industry and science about a century ago. The servomechanism is somewhat younger in years since inception. It ranks with the regulator in its assignments in society.

A number of applications of servomechanism systems had been made by the early nineteen hundreds, several in industry. Others were made in connection with scientific researches. Many more were made by the armed services for restricted use in military applications. The mathematical analysis that would substantiate the dynamic behavior of these systems and permit their synthesis directly was, however, only partially organized at this time. A philosophy of synthesizing elements or components to give desired control properties to the overall system was only beginning to take shape. It might be said that by 1940 the development of rigorous methods of analysis and synthesis had reached the stage of adolescence when suddenly the work was blacked out by the fog of military security. Since 1945, a wealth of technique of analysis and synthesis has emerged from this blackout. Those who knew the field in the 1930's and see it at present note many changes. It has grown from the state where mechanisms were devised using awkward, cumbersome methods of "gadgeteering" to the state where the analytical approach to the analysis, synthesis, and development of a mechanism proceeds along well-established scientific lines.

The specific effects of the activity of the last decade on the developments of the subject may be summarized as follows:

1. Highly skilled scientific talent was called upon to formulate and to analyze the basic dynamical problem. Its expression in terms of differential equations was clarified. Its solutions, using the mathematical techniques of Heaviside, Fourier, Laplace, Cauchy, and Routh, were extended. Criteria relating to the analysis and synthesis of networks following the work of Nyquist, Bode, Wiener, and Guillemin in the field of feedback amplifiers and communication systems were phrased in the form that made them directly applicable to the servomechanisms synthesis problem.* The understanding of the basic mathematical problem was carried from the stage where it was expressed in awkward and loose terms to where it is clearly understood and expressible in analytical principles that are simple, straightforward, and rigorous.

2. The reduction of ideas to practice was stimulated to a high degree. On all fronts, control principles or techniques were reduced to practice, and such hardware as motors, valves, or similar circuit elements was developed rapidly to accomplish the control. Weird and wonderful electronic, electric, hydraulic, electrohydraulic, pneumatic, and mechanical elements were devised, manufactured, and successfully used.

3. The wide application of servomechanisms served to introduce the principles and the elements themselves to thousands of persons.

5 The Wide Versatility of Closed-Loop Control

It is perhaps their wide versatility that makes the servomechanism, the regulator, and the process control of such great public interest. They are versatile because a wide selection of control functions can be carried out using a wide selection of control elements. Furthermore they are fascinating machines.

Because they involve (1) the transmission of intelligence from command point to a remote controlled point, (2) the measurement of the difference between the existing and desired conditions of the control, (3) the control of power to establish the output, it is apparent that all the known methods of data transmission, measurement, and control of power receive consideration in their design. Hence electrical, hydraulic, mechanical, pneumatic, optical, thermal, and numerous other physical

---

* Many of the contributors to this work are specifically mentioned in later chapters. The contributions of many others exist only in unpublished memoranda and cannot be referenced.

components are found in closed-loop systems. The reason for this is made clearer by the following more detailed consideration of the function of the principal components.

6 Functional Components

Command Station. The command station is usually located remotely from the point where the control is eventually to be effective. It is usually a low-power-level point because many control phenomena must result from signals generated by the command at a power level frequently of the order of 10^{-15} watt. The information provided by the command station is usually called the *input signal* or input quantity. Thus input quantity, input, command, and set point are often considered to be synonomous.

The command or input quantity may exist in a number of physical forms expressing its information in a wide number of physical quantities. For example, the command may originate from:

1. The pointing of a compass needle or a gyroscope for indicating the desired direction of a ship [17] or an aircraft; [18] or the position of a delicate roller,[19] cam, or index in an industrial process; [20] or the pressure of a force exerted by a spring for indicating the position or speed desired of some controlled member.
2. The directive property of a radio wave reflected from a body moving in space. The command here calls for a direction.
3. A light flux whose magnitude is a measure of an integration or multiplication, as in a calculating machine.[21, 22, 23]
4. A voltage or a current from a thermocouple used to measure temperature,[24] or any one of several other physical quantities.

An essential feature is that the command is eventually indicated in terms of a physical quantity capable of actuating other mechanisms.

Controlled Quantity. The controlled quantity or output also exists in a wide variety of forms. It need not be the same quantity or have the same physical form as the command or input. For example, the command may be a light flux and the controlled quantity may be the position of a mechanical shaft.[21] However, as explained below, the closed-loop system must contain those elements that will convert information about the magnitude of the controlled quantity and the command into physical quantities that the error-measuring means can use. Examples of controlled quantity or output and the elements often encountered in controls that involve these outputs are:

1. *Position or speed* of members such as a ship, airplane, automobile, gun turret,[25] roller in a printing operation,[26] drum or cutting tool

in an industrial operation, conveyor in a plant.   In these instances
the control quantity may be either position, speed, or the like, and
the controlled member is the body whose position or speed is controlled in accordance with the command.
2. *Temperature* of a house or process. The element controlled may
   be either the valve regulating the flow of heat or the fuel consump-
   tion necessary to establish the temperature desired by the command.
3. *A volume* or quantity as encountered in the process industries or
   the dairy industry. The element controlled would be the valve
   regulating the flow of fluid necessary to establish the volume or
   flow rate desired by the command.
4. *An electromotive force* of a power supply. The element controlled
   would be the exciter furnishing the excitation necessary to give the
   voltage desired by the command.

The particular choice of the quantity used to express the command
and the quantity used to indicate the state of the control is frequently
a function of the particular circumstances of the specific control application.   However, the data must be transmitted to the error-measuring
means from the command and controlled stations in such a form that
the error between control and command is measurable.

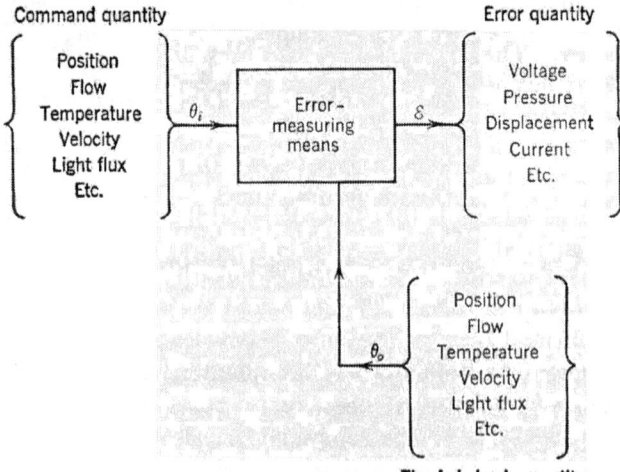

FIGURE 7.   Generalization of the error-measuring means.

Error-Measuring Means. The error-measuring means has no standard form. It is difficult to distinguish it from the data transmission
equipment that interconnects the input or controlling quantity with the

controlled quantity. It constantly monitors the controlled quantity. It is made to indicate the difference between the input and the output and to give an error signal as a function of time by appropriate design. It is sometimes called a summing device. Its form varies widely with the application, as is illustrated by the diagram of Figure 7.

Amplifier Controller. The amplifier controller receives the error signal and supplies the necessary quantities or signals to the servomotor or controlled member. This unit serves as the brain of the system and, if considered as a human being, takes the error signal and decides what the servomotor should do in order to establish the desired state of the output as is indicated by the diagram of Figure 8. The amplifier portion

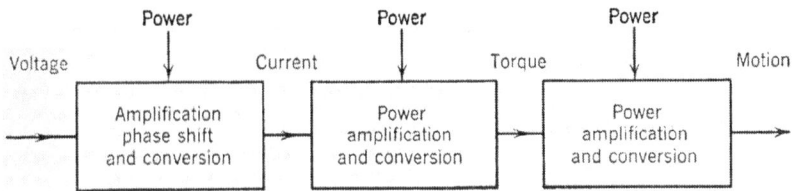

FIGURE 8.   Sequence of conversions of physical quantities in an amplifier controller.

usually raises the power level from the extremely low values usually encountered in the error-measuring process, for example, from as low as 10^{-15} watt to a few watts. At this power level of a few watts the controller amplifies the signal further and converts it from perhaps voltage to position, or from pressure to voltage, or from displacement to pressure, or any convenient conversion in order to control the servomotor or final process. As later chapters of this book show, the controller is made to introduce a phase advance or phase delay to the amplifier signal in accordance with the control procedure desired. The kind of equipment involved and the functional relationships existing between the input and the output of the amplifier controller are dependent on the specific application encountered and the specific technique being applied to the control of the particular problem. Basically the controller is a modulator of power.

Servomotor or Control Element. The servomotor, where used, is generally the element that operates the controlled member, quantity, or process. It is often an electric motor, frequently an hydraulic motor or a piston, but it may be a regulating valve, rheostat, or a clutch. It is, in general, energized by the amplifier controller, and its response determines the future state of the controlled quantity. It may be required to overcome a friction or an inertia load or both as in gun drives or industrial machine control. Frequently it must work against an hydrodynamic pressure as in automatic pilots or flow control. Often it may actuate a valve or a rheostat to control power flow to a furnace or vat.

Frequently a servomotor, as such, does not exist. The control element may then be a generator which furnishes control power as heat or as current to an output member. The fact of the matter is that it is not always easy to identify a specific element as a servomotor.

7 Desirable Operating Characteristics

The characteristic often desired of an ideal control is that the error be maintained absolutely zero at all times.* This characteristic follows from the fact that the purpose of a servomechanism or regulator is to establish the state of the controlled quantity in accordance with the dictates of the command. They do this by making the error or difference between the actual state and the desired state of the controlled quantity approach a minimum. Because of the presence of stored energy throughout various parts of the system and because of the random nature of time variation of command or load, it is never possible to maintain the error continuously zero in the dynamic state. Also, because of the complexities normally encountered in mechanisms as the degree of perfection of control is extended, it is rarely feasible to make the error zero even in the steady state. However, the error is frequently made negligibly small without the introduction of excessive complexity.

For purposes of comparison it is customary to speak of the characteristics of a servomechanism in terms of (1) its error under steady or sinusoidally varying commands or load disturbances, (2) its error during a transient following a sudden command or load disturbance, and (3) its error under a random continuous time variation of command or load.

Examples of the so-called steady-state error can be illustrated by reference to the control of the pointing of the radar search antenna. Consider that the master mechanism in the control tower is operating to transmit a command signal which would require the antenna merely to sweep around the sky at a constant rate, or to sweep back and forth cyclically. If the command calls for a constant angular velocity of the antenna structure, the system is said to be operating with a steady velocity input and output. A misalignment between the antenna direction desired by the master command and the actual mount direction is said to be an error in position caused by the constant velocity operation. In an abbreviated way, this is spoken of as the *steady-state velocity error*. Such an error could be caused by resistance to motion of the antenna as it moves against the wind force or the resistance to

---

* Complicated interconnections of servomechanisms frequently impose specifications on the characteristic of error as a function of frequency.

motion caused by bearing friction, or it could be because error signals are required to make the servomotor operate at a given speed. The basic requirement for a small steady-state error is that the system have high static sensitivity; that is, that a small steady-state error in the desired position of the antenna bring about a large change in the control effort or cause a large velocity of the output. If, in the limit, the steady-state position error for a rate input is to be zero, the sensitivity of the system must be infinite as will be shown by the treatment given in later chapters. Figure 9 illustrates a steady-state error condition for a closed-loop system having a linearly varying command or, specifically, a positional servomechanism operating with a constant input velocity.

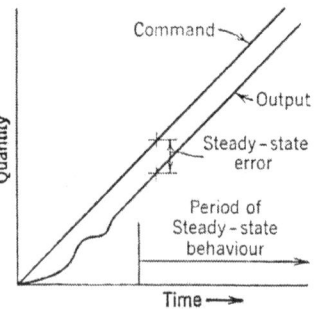

FIGURE 9.   Steady-state error.

When a sinusoidally time-varying command is applied to a linear control system, the output response must be sinusoidal with time; that is, the angular frequency of the response sinusoid must be identical with the angular frequency of the disturbing sinusoid. However, the magnitude and the phase of the response may not agree identically with that of the command because of the dynamical properties of the components contained in the closed loop. Figure 10 illustrates a sinusoidally time-varying command with possible output responses plotted to the same

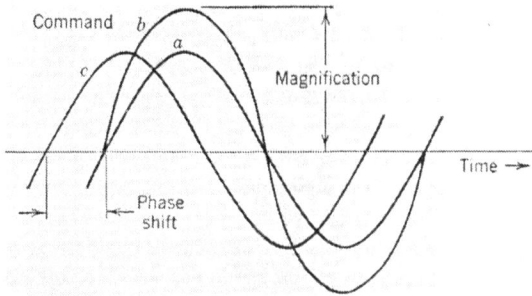

FIGURE 10.   Sinusoidal command and response.

time scale. Note particularly the possibility of phase shift in the response (curve a) or magnification of the response (curve b) with respect to the command (curve c). Much significance attaches to this phenomenon of phase shift and magnification as is discussed in Chapters 4, 6, and 7.

Transient errors occur whenever the system is called upon to correct for a sudden variation in the command or the load. A typical time variation of command that represents sudden changes is shown in Figure 11. Immediately following the sudden change in command a transient error condition exists while the control tends to wipe out the error. Performance considerations generally require that the error or deviation be corrected in a minimum of time. The so-called transient response of the system then becomes a significant characteristic. It is apparent that the system must have the characteristic of being able to bring about a large rate of change in the controlled condition for relatively small

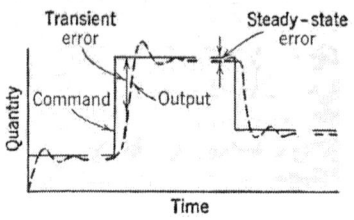

FIGURE 11.   Response to sudden change   FIGURE 12.   Degrees of tran-
of command.   sient stability.

errors in order that the transient response should be fast and the transient error should be kept small. However, as is shown in Figure 12 and discussed in later chapters, this characteristic may introduce the problem of transient stability which is the tendency of a system to oscillate about its final steady-state condition following the correction of a transient. The design problem then becomes one of synthesizing a control that will maintain the smallest steady-state error with the smallest dynamic error consistent with a satisfactory degree of stability. Curve 1 of Figure 12 represents a system whose response is overdamped. The time required for correction is long, however, by comparison with curves 2, 3, or 4 which represent a system whose response is oscillatory or underdamped. The *degree of stability* represented by curve 1 is probably sufficient, but the response time may be too great. On the other hand, the response time of the system of curve 4 may be sufficient, but the degree of stability may be too small.

As a rule, the designer is permitted only to synthesize the characteristics of the controller. The characteristics of the process or element being controlled are generally beyond his jurisdiction. His working data are only knowledge of the input, the error, the output, and probably certain of their time derivatives. He must decide how to use these data in order to establish the control. His problem becomes one of *synthesis* of dynamic elements into a connected whole to accomplish certain objectives.

Errors under random dynamic operation are difficult to establish quantitatively. For a time variation of command as shown in Figure 13, it is seen that the error is large when the rate of change of the command is large. Also, if the command undergoes a sudden change, the control is likely to hunt or oscillate about the desired value. One approach that a designer can make to a study of the performance of his system under random conditions is to make a frequency spectrum representation of his input for a certain interval of time and then determine

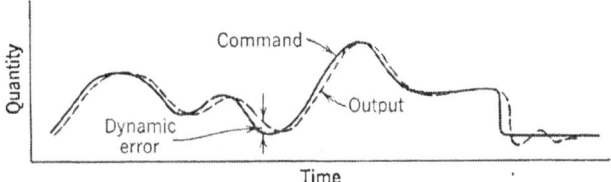

FIGURE 13.   Random variation of command.

how his system will respond at each individual frequency of the representation. As shown in later chapters, much use is made of this information in the analysis and synthesis of closed-loop systems. Another approach is to determine the response of the system to an impulse command, and then by the techniques shown in Chapter 11 determine the response to any arbitrary command.

8   Summary of Techniques of Analysis and Synthesis

The analysis of the dynamic behavior of a closed-loop linear control system is a straightforward problem to persons familiar with the formulation of differential equations and the techniques of arriving at their solution. The importance of a dynamic analysis, however, comes not from the mere results of analysis but from a foundation of *dynamic behavior concepts* that come from an evaluation of these results and can guide the synthesis of components that will give more desirable closed-loop characteristics.

For the types of control usually under discussion, two forms of preselected input are used. The first one is represented by a sudden change of the command or load, either as a step or an impulse. The controlled quantity then behaves in accordance with the characteristics of the system. The performance of the system is described by a time relationship between the output and the input quantities. An illuminating technique is often to describe the difference between input and output, or error, as a function of time following the disturbance rather than to describe the output itself.

The analytical treatment of the system following a step or an impulse disturbance, which is generally called a transient study,[28, 29, 30, 31] gives a direct indication of how the system behaves. It is treated in detail in the next two chapters. It results in the formulation of the characteristic equation of the system which for the error $\varepsilon(t)$ is of the form

$$\left(a_o \frac{d^n}{dt^n} + b_o \frac{d^{n-1}}{dt^{n-1}} + \text{etc.} \right) \varepsilon(t) = 0 \tag{1}$$

and has as roots r_1, r_2, etc., giving a transient solution of the form

$$\varepsilon(t) = \varepsilon_{ss} + A e^{r_1 t} + B e^{r_2 t} + \text{etc.} \tag{2}$$

Whenever roots of Equation 1 exist as conjugate complex pairs, the pairs of roots establish a principal oscillatory mode of behavior for the system. If the roots have the form

$$\left. \begin{aligned} r_1 &= -a + j\omega = -\zeta\omega_n + j\omega_n\sqrt{1 - \zeta^2} \\ r_2 &= -a - j\omega = -\zeta\omega_n - j\omega_n\sqrt{1 - \zeta^2} \end{aligned} \right\} \tag{3}$$

it is possible to define a damping ratio ζ, an undamped angular frequency ω_n, and a damped angular frequency ω for the particular mode defined by the roots. The damping ratio ζ (see Chapter 2) defines the exponential attenuation envelope for the particular mode of oscillation.

The second type of preselected input used to study closed-loop controls is a sinusoidal time variation of the command or load.* It is sustained over a considerable period of time to insure elimination of all transient effects in the response. Again, the performance of the system is described by a time relation between the response and disturbing sinusoidally varying quantities. This relation is readily converted into a vector equation from which all time-varying quantities are eliminated. The relative amplitude and phase of the output response when compared to the input amplitude and phase completely describe the system's behavior. (See Tables 1 and 2.) Obviously, the amplitude and phase of the output sinusoid relative to the input sinusoid vary with the frequency of the input. In the manner shown in Chapter 6, the system behavior may be represented in terms of *transfer functions* $KG(j\omega)$, which are complex functions of the frequency variable ω. The value K is frequency invariant and $G(j\omega)$ describes the magnitude and phase relationship of the transfer function in terms of complex numbers. This technique introduces an abstraction in the sense that these complex

* See References 6, 8, 32, 33, 34, 35, 65.

functions of frequency, $KG(j\omega)$, cannot be vividly appreciated as can the transient time functions, $\theta_o(t)$ of Figure 12, for example.

To design in terms of differential equations and their transient solution requires detailed knowledge of all the system parameters. Also a reliable linear approximation to these parameters should be available. In complicated systems the work leads to high-order differential equations with the attendant considerable amount of labor in getting their solutions. Correlation between transients as calculated and transients as observed in practice can be accomplished. A sudden disturbance is merely applied to the physical apparatus, and its subsequent behavior is observed. However, a transient method of analysis is not, of itself, especially effective when the problem of synthesis is being attacked because of the relative obscurity surrounding the identification of the particular parameter whose magnitude must be changed to yield the performance desired of the system. That is, when ζ and ω_n of the transient components of the solution do not meet the requirements, the change that must be made to a specific component in the system is not readily apparent because ζ and ω_n depend on heterogeneous groupings of the system parameters in a manner that makes system synthesis difficult.

Simulators [36] or analyzers [37] have received much attention in recent years in order to overcome the complexity of analysis. In some instances, electronic devices or networks are assembled in a manner that makes them represent the behavior of the elements of the system over a reasonable frequency band. In other instances, inductance, capacitance, resistance, and electronic amplifiers are used as analogues of mass, springs, and dampers in a so-called transient analyzer. One limitation of this approach to the problem is that the simulator or analyzer cannot be used until a lot is known about the components of the system. Unless a long study is to be made on a single system and the equipment is flexible and well instrumented, the direct analytical method may, in the long run, take less time. Furthermore, not everyone has a simulator.

The sinusoidal method, which is treated extensively in Chapters 6 through 8, requires a knowledge of the frequency characteristic of the equipments under consideration over a reasonable frequency band. The method then followed is to insert phase-correcting networks either in cascade or in parallel in the loop in order to yield (1) a desired stability as indicated by a transient study and (2) a dynamic performance dictated by error specifications. As shown in Chapters 6 through 8, this work leads to studies in terms of Nyquist diagrams as commonly applied to feedback amplifiers and to studies in terms of complex functions plotted as contours in the complex plane to linear or logarithmic scales.

The view held by the authors at the present time is, briefly, that dynamic stability specifications are more easily based on transients following a sudden disturbance than on the behavior following sinusoidal disturbance of varying frequency. However, the design of conventional systems to fulfill the majority of performance specifications is more easily accomplished by studying the response to a sinusoidal disturbance of varying frequency. It should be mentioned, however, that both transient and sinusoidal studies are needed to guarantee satisfactory designs. No single mathematical method should be given undue preference or emphasis. Each gives certain clarity to the problem, and used together they lead to a well-integrated understanding of behavior and design.

One important reason for the interest in the sinusoidal procedure comes from the relative ease with which the dynamic properties of a piece of complicated apparatus can be represented by an experimentally determined frequency function, whereas representation of its properties in terms of a differential equation is almost unattainable. To illustrate, consider the ease of making a frequency measurement at a small amplitude on the plant in a process industry as it actually operates, and compare this effort with the task of defining numerically every parameter in the plant for the preparation of its differential equation.

The effectiveness of the sinusoidal procedure involves correlation between frequency functions and time functions. Correlation to a degree useful for engineering work is made (1) by noting salient features of a transient such as *speed of response*, frequency of oscillations, degree of stability, and steady-state error and (2) by noting salient features of the frequency response such as resonance conditions indicated by peaking of the ratio of output to input at certain frequencies, the angle by which the error is related to the output at low frequencies, and the frequency range wherein the output magnitude stays less than a specified magnification of input; that is, $\left| \dfrac{\theta_o(j\omega)}{\theta_i(j\omega)} \right|$ does not exceed a specified constant M_p. These salient features are paired in their significance and used as the basis for the estimation of transient response from frequency response data and vice versa. These matters are treated in detail in Chapters 3 through 11.

The behavior of a system following a sudden disturbance may be expressed as functions involving system parameters or as functions involving certain nondimensional ratios of parameters. The ratios are selected in a manner that has physical significance or may make the analysis more compact. The technique of expressing the solution in terms of dimensionless parameters generalizes the solution to apply to all systems having the identical dimensionless form. However, when working with the sinusoidal inputs, it is more convenient to draw upon the techniques which have been largely developed in electrical engineering whereby the properties of a group of elements, mechanical or electrical, are characterized by an impedance (or admittance) function of the complex variable $j\omega$. The study of servomechanisms becomes somewhat unique with respect to many communication problems because, in terms of communication engineering terminology, it involves low "Q" rather than high "Q" networks, which is another way of saying that servos are nearly critically damped systems. Large amounts of circuit theory used in communications engineering are applicable to the study of the closed-loop controls even though they are highly dissipative systems. They are like negative feedback amplifier systems, which operate in a frequency spectrum from zero to only a few cycles per second and for which certain steady-state characteristics, such as their response to a continuous load torque, are specified. It is because the designer of the control system has a specific interest in the steady-state requirements and in the degree of stability that his design viewpoint takes a different emphasis from that of the communications engineer.

Table 1 attempts to show an organization of the techniques discussed above for the study of servomechanisms. A detailed treatment of the formulation of the differential equation, requirements for stability, methods to determine the roots of the characteristic equation, transient solutions, frequency response techniques of analysis and synthesis using linear or logarithmic contours are discussed in detail in later chapters. Table 2 gives a summary of analysis and synthesis techniques.

9 Summary of Analysis and Synthesis Procedure

Table 2 supplements the information given in Table 1. It outlines briefly the following series of steps that might be used in conducting a quantitative synthesis and design study of a typical control problem.

1. Write the differential equation. Express it in the form to show the dynamic system response in terms of the output quantity $\theta_o(t)$, or error quantity $\varepsilon(t)$, as a function of the initiating disturbances, $\theta_i(t)$, or load disturbance $T_L(t)$. (See Chapter 2.)

2. Form the steady-state complex relationship expressing the ratio of the variables $\theta_o(j\omega)$ to $\varepsilon(j\omega)$ on the assumption that the system is excited by an error signal $\varepsilon \sin \omega t$. This relation defines the system transfer function $\theta_o/\varepsilon = KG(j\omega)$. The quantity $KG(j\omega)$ is the complex form of the transfer function. It is derived or measured when the loop is opened at the error-measuring means and excited by the signal $\varepsilon \sin \omega t$ applied to the input terminals of the amplifier. (See Chapters 3, 4, and 10.)

TABLE 1

SUMMARY ORGANIZATION OF TECHNIQUES USED TO STUDY AND TO SYNTHESIZE CLOSED-LOOP SYSTEMS

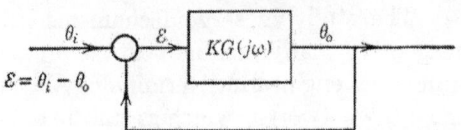

$$\mathcal{E} = \theta_i - \theta_o$$

$KG(j\omega)$ is a complex transfer function of compensating networks, devices, and basic servo elements.
$KG(j\omega)$ is derived from the differential equation relating $\theta_o(t)$ to $\mathcal{E}(t)$.

$$\frac{\theta_o}{\mathcal{E}}(j\omega) = KG(j\omega)$$

$$\frac{\theta_o}{\theta_i}(j\omega) = \frac{KG(j\omega)}{1 + KG(j\omega)}$$

$$\frac{\mathcal{E}}{\theta_i}(j\omega) = \frac{1}{1 + KG(j\omega)}$$

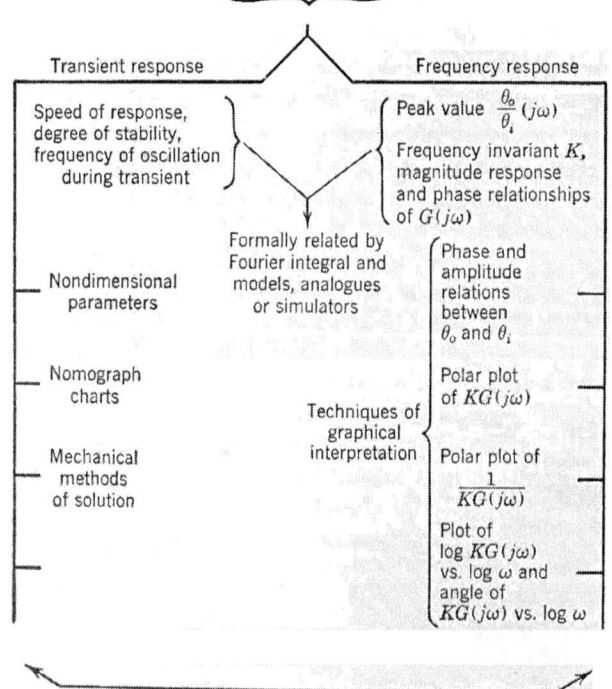

Transient response   Frequency response

Speed of response, degree of stability, frequency of oscillation during transient

Peak value $\frac{\theta_o}{\theta_i}(j\omega)$

Frequency invariant K, magnitude response and phase relationships of $G(j\omega)$

Formally related by Fourier integral and models, analogues or simulators

Nondimensional parameters

Phase and amplitude relations between θ_o and θ_i

Nomograph charts

Polar plot of $KG(j\omega)$

Techniques of graphical interpretation

Mechanical methods of solution

Polar plot of $\frac{1}{KG(j\omega)}$

Plot of $\log KG(j\omega)$ vs. $\log \omega$ and angle of $KG(j\omega)$ vs. $\log \omega$

Absolute stability criteria

3. Factorize $KG(j\omega)$ in a form where only single-order and quadratic factors appear. The coefficients of $j\omega$ in these factors become, in the nondimensional form of the transfer function $KG(j\omega)$, time constants τ, damping ratios ζ, and angular frequencies ω_n. (See Chapters 5 and 6.)

4. Form a new variable u by dividing ω by a reference frequency ω_n or time constant τ to reduce the number of variables in the analysis. Plot the complex function $G(ju)$ as a contour in the complex plane. Several sets of coordinates for the plot may be used, namely, polar coordinate to a linear scale or the logarithm of the absolute value of $|G(ju)|$ and the phase of $G(ju)$ plotted as a function of $\log u$. (See Chapters 6, 7, and 8.)

5. Interpret these plots in terms of design practices treated in Chapters 6 through 8. When the preliminary design using the initial complex transfer function $KG(ju)$ does not meet the desired specifications, modify the system dynamics by the introduction of compensating circuits in cascade with $KG(ju)$. Alternatively place auxiliary loops around a portion of the equipment included in the function $KG(ju)$. The choice of compensating techniques depends upon the specific problem under consideration and is discussed quantitatively in Chapters 6, 7, and 8.

6. Calculate the transient behavior of the proposed system using the differential equation, Chapter 3, or the graphical inverse transform techniques using the transfer functions as shown in Chapter 11.

10   Physical Components

The broad application of servomechanisms makes it impractical to give in a book of this kind a detailed or complete discussion of physical components. However, because of the general interest in positional control, certain of the more frequently used components are briefly described below.

Data Transmission and Error-Sensing Components. The data transmission and error-sensing elements are usually the first to receive consideration in any control problem. This occurs because there will be no control unless the command intelligence can be transmitted and the errors can be measured. In positional systems the command station generates input data either as mechanical motion or as a voltage. Elements often used to accomplish the transmission and error sensing are synchros or selsyns. The reader is referred to the extensive literature [38] for a discussion of the various functions that synchros can perform, their methods of interconnection, and a number of their more general characteristics. Other error-sensing elements are E magnet pickoffs, strain

TABLE 2

Summary of Analysis and Synthesis Procedure

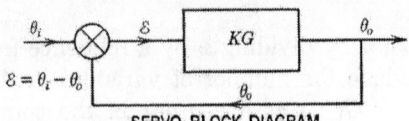

SERVO BLOCK DIAGRAM

Differential Equation

$$\left[a_n \frac{d^n \varepsilon}{dt^n} + a_{n-1} \frac{d^{n-1}\varepsilon}{dt^{n-1}} + \cdots\cdots\cdots\cdots a_0 \varepsilon \right] = \left[b_m \frac{d^m \theta_i}{dt^m} + \cdots b_0 \theta_i \right]$$

$$\varepsilon(t) = \theta_i(t) - \theta_o(t)$$

Complex Form of Equation, d/dt Replaced by $j\omega$ for Sinusoidal Steady State

$$[a_n(j\omega)^n + a_{n-1}(j\omega)^{n-1} + \cdots\cdots\cdots\cdots\cdots a_0]\varepsilon(j\omega) = [b_m(j\omega)^m + \cdots]\theta_i(j\omega)$$

$$\varepsilon(j\omega) = \theta_i(j\omega) - \theta_o(j\omega)$$

Symbolic Transfer Function

$$\frac{\theta_o}{\varepsilon}(j\omega) = \frac{c_p(j\omega)^p + c_{p-1}(j\omega)^{p-1}\cdots}{d_q(j\omega)^q + d_{q-1}(j\omega)^{q-1}\cdots} = KG(j\omega)$$

Nondimensional Form

$$\frac{\theta_o}{\varepsilon}\left(\frac{j\omega}{\omega_n}\right) = \frac{\left(j\tau_1 \dfrac{\omega}{\omega_n} + 1\right)\text{ (etc.)}}{\left(-\dfrac{\omega^2}{\omega_n{}^2} + j2\zeta \dfrac{\omega}{\omega_n} + 1\right)\left(j\tau_2 \dfrac{\omega}{\omega_n} + 1\right)\left(j\tau_1 \dfrac{\omega}{\omega_n} + 1\right)\text{ (etc.)}}$$

Change Variable ω/ω_n to u Giving

$$\frac{\theta_o}{\varepsilon}(ju) = K_u G(ju), \text{ to plot locus}$$

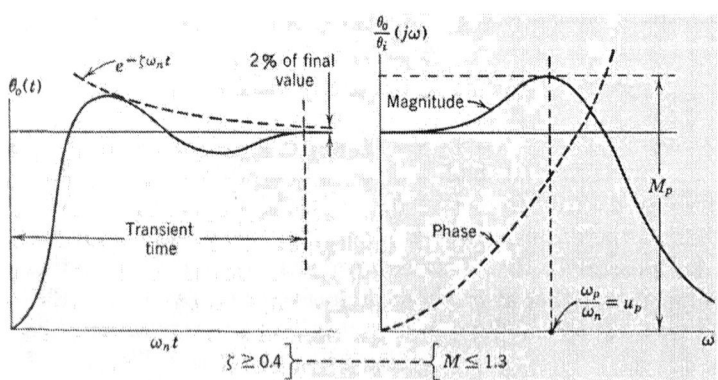

Transient response   Frequency response

RESPONSE CORRELATION

TABLE 2 (*Continued*)

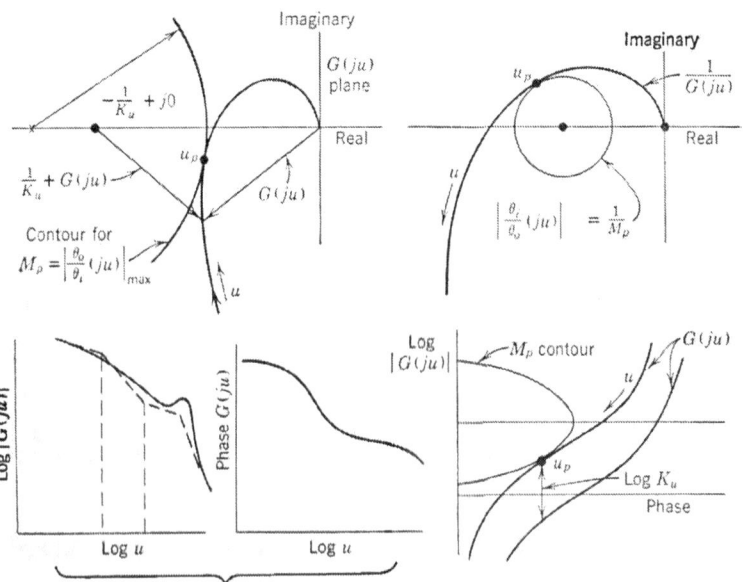

Log vector contour chart

CONFIRMATION OF TRIAL DESIGN WITH RESPONSE CORRELATION CRITERIA

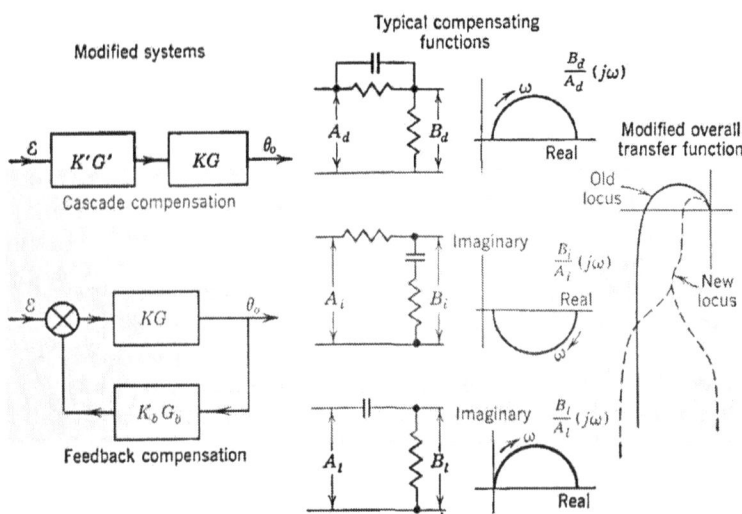

MODIFICATION OF TRANSFER FUNCTION FOR IMPROVED PERFORMANCE

gages, nozzles, diaphragms, gyroscopes, and so forth.[39]   Each application
is a specialized one.

Amplifier Controller.   The choice of amplifier is dictated by the form
in which the error signal is established.   If voltage or current is the
physical quantity representing the error, electrical or electronic methods
are used for amplification.   Error signals in the form of direct or alternating voltage modulate [40, 43] the power to the servomotor.   Whenever
the error indication is available as a mechanical motion, one of several
kinds of hydraulic or pneumatic amplifiers [27, 44] may be used.   They
comprise a small pilot valve whose motion opens ports at lands connected
to an oil or air supply.   Oil or air under high pressure is admitted to a
motor or piston or some other element in accordance with the pilot
valve motion.   These devices exhibit a surprisingly large amount of
amplification although their sinusoidal response following small input
signals shows sharp attenuation above frequencies greater than perhaps
20 cycles per second.

Frequently, phase lead or phase lag compensation circuits mentioned
in Table 2 are introduced into the amplifier controller.   The ingenuity
of the mathematician and designer has already produced a wide variety
of amplifier controllers with inherent compensation features.   They are
used in an assortment of ways.

Servomotors or Power Output Elements.   Servomotors of the electrical, hydraulic, or pneumatic type have found application to about an
equal extent in servomechanisms during the past decade.   In an electrical system using a control generator such as an amplidyne [41, 42] or a
Ward-Leonard [32] machine, the servomotor is a conventional direct
current machine using constant field excitation.   A variety of adapta-
tions of the generator motor assembly has been used.   Vacuum tubes
or thyratrons have been used to control a d-c motor or a polyphase
induction motor.   Other methods of motor control will naturally sug-
gest themselves to designers as their problems receive appropriate
investigation.

Hydraulic motors are the conventional gear type or the multi-piston
constant stroke type.   In these latter cases the pump-motor assembly
is called an hydraulic transmission.[27]   Their properties closely parallel
those of electrical machinery, except for the fact that the amount of
inertia inherent in the servomotor rotor is generally considerably less
in the case of an hydraulic or pneumatic machine than in an electric
motor of comparable rating and speed.   Furthermore, an hydraulic
transmission tends to have output speed as a function of control rather
than output torque related to control as do electric motors.

Frequently the output elements do not involve rotational energy. They may involve energy in the form of heat, flow, or pressure. Output elements in the form of generators, furnaces, or vats are commonly encountered.

11 Conclusion

In the subsequent chapters the details of the formulation of the problem, its analysis and synthesis, and typical servomechanisms investigations are given.

2

Dynamics of Elementary Control Systems

1 Introduction

Closed-loop dynamic systems may comprise relatively few individual dynamic elements arranged in cascade or groups of dynamic elements interrelated among themselves and then grouped in a closed-loop concatenation. Furthermore, these loops may comprise a wide variety of electrical, electronic, electromagnetic, hydraulic, pneumatic, and mechanical components, to say nothing of the possibilities of optical, chemical, or thermal members.

Closed-loop systems made up of components that possess the property of energy storage, for example, inductance in electrical systems, inertia in mechanical systems, or capacitance in thermal systems exhibit transient modes of behavior when excited by discontinuous external disturbances. Also transients may arise when disturbances occur internally in the system. During the transient, oscillations of an undesirable form may occur and may even be sustained. To identify the causes for this condition, it is desirable to be able to state accurately the dynamic behavior of various elements which appear in the closed loop. The mathematical equations which describe these physical elements are then written in the form of an integro-differential equation defining the closed-loop properties. Solutions to these equations for known physical conditions are then compared to actual physical system behavior. This procedure is basically one of analysis.

The analysis of complicated systems may be accomplished with an ease comparable to that found when working in elementary mechanics or elementary circuit theory in spite of nonlinearities and the complex nature of the system. The nonlinearity of the elements, which is a property of nearly everything in nature, often may be minimized by studying small departures or variations of the signals from a reference point. Linear behavior for each element is then assumed for all operation within a narrow range of variation from this reference point. Complications are reduced by representing components as lumped assemblies, in contrast with distributed assemblies, following the technique used for lumping elements in electric circuits. Basic circuit analysis techniques commonly used by electrical engineers are then directly applicable to the solution of many aspects of closed-loop problems regardless of the many varied physical forms of apparatus. Clearly the linearizing assumption must be applied with discretion.

The material which follows in this chapter endeavors to present a mathematical study of elementary closed-loop mechanical and electrical systems. It introduces the elementary problem of transient analysis and one method of selecting disturbances by which closed-loop properties may be examined. The mathematical findings are explored to focus attention on the behavior of closed loops as found in regulators and servomechanisms. Chapter 3 presents a general discussion of mathematics which may be used to analyze the performance of more complicated systems. Certain properties of the Laplace transform and functions of a complex variable are introduced in Chapter 3. This advanced material includes a discussion of the limitations of a transient-analysis method for establishing the synthesis of complicated systems. Later chapters extend the techniques of analysis and synthesis.

2   Elementary Positioning System (Open-Ended)

Consider as a basis for an elementary study, the problem of positioning the shaft to which an opposing torque T_L is applied. From the practical standpoint, a rigid shaft would meet the requirements. However, an actual shaft is only rigid to a relative degree. Furthermore, if it has lubricated bearings a viscous drag will oppose its motion. Thus the system of Figure 1 may be considered to represent the problem with merely exaggeration of the lack of rigidity by substituting a spring for the shaft, and a viscous drag unit to represent the bearing friction.

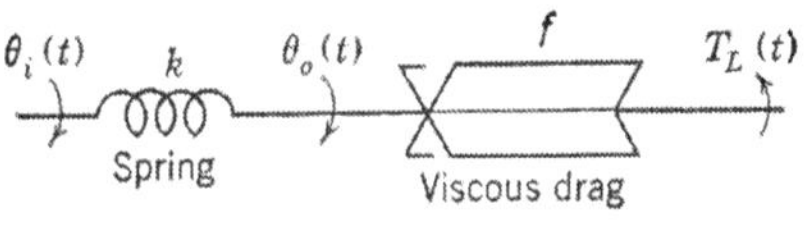

FIGURE 1.   Elementary positioning system (open-ended mechanical).

In Figure 1, the input end of the system is identified in position by the quantity $\theta_i(t)$, and the output by $\theta_o(t)$. The subscripts i and o herein designate input and output respectively. The elastance coefficient of the shaft is k. It is the torque per unit angular twist and is represented by the relation

$$\text{Torque} = k \text{ (angular twist)}$$

$$= k(\theta_i - \theta_o) \tag{1}$$

The viscous drag is lumped into a single viscous element whose behavior is expressed by the relation

$$\text{Drag torque} = f\frac{d\theta_o}{dt} \tag{2}$$

where f is termed the viscous friction coefficient.

If a torque is applied to the shaft at the input $\theta_i(t)$, the spring will tend to wind up. The torque resulting from angular winding up of the spring will be exerted on the damper. The torque available to rotate the damper is the algebraic sum of the torque exerted by the spring and any torque T_L applied at $\theta_o(t)$ by external means.

Thus, when a positive displacement is given to $\theta_i(t)$, the equation expressing the equilibrium of torques on the system is

$$k[\theta_i(t) - \theta_o(t)] = f\frac{d\theta_o(t)}{dt} + T_L(t) \tag{3}$$

which may be rewritten as

$$k\theta_i(t) = f\frac{d\theta_o(t)}{dt} + k\theta_o(t) + T_L(t) \tag{4}$$

If both sides of Equation 4 are divided by k,

$$\theta_i(t) = \tau\frac{d\theta_o(t)}{dt} + \theta_o(t) + \frac{T_L(t)}{k} \tag{5}$$

where $\tau = f/k$ and has the dimensions of seconds, since dimensionally,

$$\tau = \frac{f}{k} = \frac{\text{torque per angle per second}}{\text{torque per angle}} = \text{seconds} \tag{6}$$

Equation 5 may be rewritten as

$$\left(\tau\frac{d}{dt} + 1\right)\theta_o(t) = \theta_i(t) - \frac{T_L(t)}{k} \tag{7}$$

or alternatively, in quasi operational form,* as

$$\theta_o(t) = \frac{1}{\left(\tau\dfrac{d}{dt} + 1\right)}\theta_i(t) - \frac{1}{\left(\tau\dfrac{d}{dt} + 1\right)}\frac{T_L(t)}{k} \tag{8}$$

Equation 8 as formulated relates a dependent variable $\theta_o(t)$ to two independent variables, namely $\theta_i(t)$ and $T_L(t)$. Since linearity is assumed, the variation of $\theta_o(t)$ resulting from the application of $\theta_i(t)$ or $T_L(t)$ is the linear sum of the contribution from each variable acting alone.

* Some writers might make the substitution $d/dt = p$ in Equation 8, and use Cauchy-Heaviside operational calculus. We do not because we prefer to use the Laplace Transform method as given in Chapter 3. Functions of time are then transformed into algebraic functions of the complex variable s. See also Equations 15, 16, 26, 49, 69, and 70.

Any examination of the behavior of the system given in Figure 1 requires a solution to the differential equation in Equation 8. Throughout this chapter the step-by-step procedure for determining the solution is omitted. This is done in order to place full emphasis on the interpretation of the solution rather than divide attention between techniques of arriving at the solution and the meaning of the solution.

For purposes of illustration, assume that T_L is zero and the system is at rest. If an angle change $|\theta_i|$ is suddenly applied to the system at rest, the solution for $\theta_o(t)$ is

$$\theta_o(t) = |\theta_i| [1 - e^{-(t/\tau)}]\Big|_{T_L=0} \tag{9}$$

In dimensionless form Equation 9 is

$$\frac{\theta_o(t)}{|\theta_i|} = [1 - e^{-(t/\tau)}]\Big|_{T_L=0} \tag{10}$$

Likewise if θ_i is zero and a torque $|T_L|$ is suddenly applied when the system is at rest, the solution for $\theta_o(t)$ is

$$\theta_o(t) = -\frac{|T_L|}{k}[1 - e^{-(t/\tau)}]\Big|_{\theta_i=0} \tag{11}$$

Since the angle $|T_L/k|$ in this instance is the eventual or steady-state value of the output, it will be expressed symbolically as θ_{oss}. Equation 11 in dimensionless form is

$$\frac{\theta_o(t)}{\theta_{oss}} = -[1 - e^{-(t/\tau)}]\Big|_{\theta_i=0} \tag{12}$$

If the system of Figure 1 is viewed as a positioning device, the extent to which it falls short of the objective is given by

$$\mathcal{E}(t) = \theta_i(t) - \theta_o(t) \tag{13}$$

where $\mathcal{E}(t)$ is the positional error between the input and the output at any time during operation. Rewriting Equation 7 to eliminate $\theta_o(t)$ gives

$$\left(\tau\frac{d}{dt} + 1\right)[\theta_i(t) - \mathcal{E}(t)] = \theta_i(t) - \frac{T_L(t)}{k} \tag{14}$$

which, if solved for error $\mathcal{E}(t)$, is

$$\mathcal{E}(t) = \frac{\tau\dfrac{d\theta_i(t)}{dt}}{\left(\tau\dfrac{d}{dt} + 1\right)} + \frac{\dfrac{1}{k}}{\left(\tau\dfrac{d}{dt} + 1\right)}T_L(t) \tag{15}$$

If the input variable is a velocity $\omega_i(t)$, then $d\theta_i(t)/dt$ may be replaced by $\omega_i(t)$. The error is then given by

$$\mathcal{E}(t) = \frac{\tau}{\left(\tau\dfrac{d}{dt} + 1\right)}\, \omega_i(t) + \frac{\dfrac{1}{k}}{\left(\tau\dfrac{d}{dt} + 1\right)}\, T_L(t) \qquad (16)$$

The time solution of Equation 16 for a suddenly applied input velocity $\left|\,\omega_i\,\right|$ when T_L equals zero is

$$\mathcal{E}(t) = \tau[1 - e^{-(t/\tau)}]\,\left|\,\omega_i\,\right|\Big|_{T_L=0} \qquad (17)$$

Since $\tau\left|\,\omega_i\,\right|$ is the magnitude of the steady-state misalignment $\mathcal{E}_{ss}$ between input and output when the input moves at a steady velocity $\left|\,\omega_i\,\right|$, Equation 17 may be written in dimensionless form as

$$\frac{\mathcal{E}(t)}{\mathcal{E}_{ss}} = [1 - e^{-(t/\tau)}]\Big|_{T_L=0} \qquad (18)$$

The time solution of Equation 16 for $\omega_i(t) = 0$, and a suddenly applied load $\left|\,T_L\,\right|$ is merely the negative of Equation 11, as is seen by inspection of Equations 8 and 16.

The time constant τ of the system of Figure 1 is of much interest to the present discussion. Reference to Equations 10, 12, and 18 shows

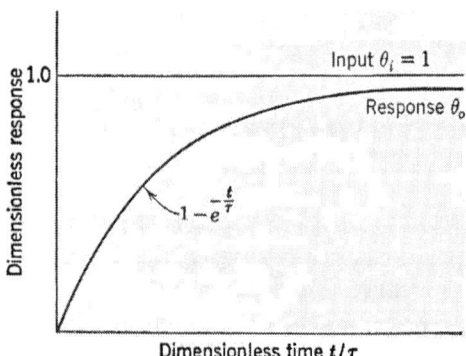

FIGURE 2.   Response of elementary system.

that the time required for the output to reach its steady-state position following a disturbance is a function of $e^{-(t/\tau)}$. The larger the value of τ, the longer the transient persists. Figure 2 shows a dimensionless plot of the response of the system following either a sudden application of position θ_i to the input, or torque T_L to the output. The ordinate is the dimensionless ratio $\theta_o(t)/\theta_{oss}$ or $\mathcal{E}(t)/\mathcal{E}_{ss}$, and the abscissa is a dimensionless ratio t/τ. Notice that a single dimensionless curve of Figure 2 represents all possible variations of the system. Plotting solutions in this manner [45] is a process that will be followed extensively in this book.

A simple guide to the determination of the time required for transients to disappear follows from a recognition of the fact that $e^{-4} = 0.018$. Therefore the transients of all systems represented by the differential equation 7 will be attenuated to approximately 2 per cent of their initial value in a time $t = 4\tau$ regardless of whether the system is electrical, mechanical, or hydraulic. Since, for the illustration, τ is equal to f/k, the response can be made faster only by decreasing f or by increasing k. In other words, the output always more nearly corresponds to its final position as k is increased or f is decreased, regardless of whether the input is at rest, or moving, or whether the output carries a load.

An examination of the system of Figure 1 shows that it lacks many features desired in a positioning system. For example:

1. The torque applied at the input or the work done at the input on the average is equal to or greater than the work expended at the output. There is no torque amplification.
2. The dynamic behavior of the system is a function of the constancy of k and f. That is, whenever they vary, the system needs recalibration.
3. The input and output are directly connected and must be coaxial. Therefore, negligible flexibility exists for locating the input at one place and the output at another. There is no opportunity for remote location of one with respect to the other.

It is of interest, therefore, to consider means that will eliminate the above undesirable features and provide thereby a system in which (1) the torque or work done by the output is a considerable amplification over that needed at the input, (2) the operation of the system is substantially independent of any variations in k and f, (3) in which the output station may be located remotely from the input with a high order of flexibility.

As means to accomplish the features (1), (2), and (3) are studied, the technique of constantly comparing the input with the output and using the difference or error as a control emerges as one that is well suited to the problem. The comparison involves the process of measurement. The use of the error quantity comprising the difference between input and output as a primary control quantity becomes the basis of closed-loop-control practice.

Closed-loop systems of widely different physical form may have many properties in common for certain modes of operation but may be very different with respect to others. In order that these matters can be given adequate consideration, an elementary problem involving an open-ended electric speed control will be considered before closed-loop practices are discussed.

3 Elementary Speed-Control System (Open-Ended Electric)

Consider now that it is desired to control the speed of a shaft in accordance with a given signal. A means often suggested for doing this is shown in Figure 3. An electric motor is used to drive the shaft, and

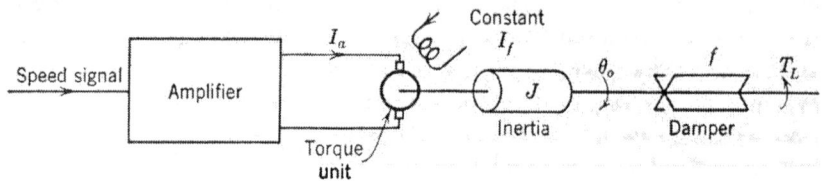

FIGURE 3. Elementary speed control system (open-ended electric).

the motor is operated by an electric current supplied to its armature.

For purposes of analysis, let the motor be represented by an inertia J and a viscous drag coefficient f. Let the external load torque be $T_L(t)$. Assume that the motor develops a torque proportional to the armature current I_a, such that

$$\text{Torque} = kI_a(t) \tag{19}$$

Thus for a steady armature current there is a steady torque and a steady speed, $d\theta_o/dt$. The equation of motion of the system is then

$$kI_a(t) = J\frac{d^2\theta_o(t)}{dt^2} + f\frac{d\theta_o(t)}{dt} + T_L(t) \tag{20}$$

If the armature source of power is a current source, and if proportionality exists between current I_a and desired speed denoted by ω_i, the relation between the input velocity ω_i and I_a is

$$I_a = \mu\omega_i \tag{21}$$

Then Equation 20 becomes

$$k\mu\omega_i(t) = J\frac{d^2\theta_o(t)}{dt^2} + f\frac{d\theta_o(t)}{dt} + T_L(t) \tag{22}$$

Since

$$\frac{d^2\theta_o(t)}{dt^2} = \frac{d\omega_o(t)}{dt}$$

Equation 22 may be written and nondimensionalized as

$$A\omega_i(t) = \tau \frac{d\omega_o(t)}{dt} + \omega_o(t) + \frac{T_L(t)}{f} \tag{23}$$

where $\tau = J/f$, and $A = k\mu/f$ is dimensionless. If the speed error of the system is denoted by

$$\mathcal{E}_\omega(t) = \omega_i(t) - \omega_o(t) \tag{24}$$

and $\omega_o(t)$ is eliminated from Equation 23, the result is

$$\left(\tau \frac{d}{dt} + 1\right)\mathcal{E}_\omega(t) = \left(\tau \frac{d}{dt} + 1\right)\omega_i(t) - A\omega_i(t) + \frac{T_L(t)}{f} \tag{25}$$

giving

$$\mathcal{E}_\omega(t) = \frac{\tau \dfrac{d}{dt} + (1 - A)}{\left(\tau \dfrac{d}{dt} + 1\right)}\omega_i(t) + \frac{\dfrac{1}{f}}{\left(\tau \dfrac{d}{dt} + 1\right)}T_L(t) \tag{26}$$

The transient solution to Equation 26 has the same form as the solution to Equation 16. Again the correspondence between input and output, or the command and the response, is made faster as τ is decreased. A low value of τ requires a small inertia or a large viscous drag. In the presence of a load T_L, the speed error $\mathcal{E}_\omega$ is a function of the magnitude of the viscous coefficient f as shown by the second term of Equation 26.

An examination of the uniformity of the steady-state control properties of the open-ended systems of Figures 1 and 3 shows each to be completely dependent on the calibration of the components. For example, the steady-state errors $\mathcal{E}_{ss}$ for the positional system, and $\mathcal{E}_{\omega_{ss}}$ for the speed system, from Equations 16 and 26, respectively, are

Positional system

$$\mathcal{E}_{ss} = \frac{f}{k}\omega_i + \frac{T_L}{k} \tag{27}$$

Speed system

$$\mathcal{E}_{\omega_{ss}} = \left(1 - \frac{\mu k}{f}\right)\omega_i + \frac{T_L}{f} \tag{28}$$

Thus the quality of the control depends on the permanency and linearity of the spring and damper in the mechanical system; and the viscous drag, the current source, and the motor in the electrical system. Although springs may be permanent to a high degree, viscous forces are not. Furthermore, a glance at the energy dissipation shows that the system of Figure 3 would have a power loss proportional to the viscous drag. But without the drag this system would not exhibit the property of speed control. Clearly a more attractive system would not depend upon the viscous drag. Offhand, a direct-current motor with adjustable armature voltage might appear to be one. Such an arrangement exhibits the property of speed regulation because of the internal back emf of the armature. From the mathematical viewpoint back emf is analogous to viscous drag, although heat loss is not involved. However, armature control of a direct-current motor is hardly any better than the use of viscous drag for speed regulation.

As is shown in a later section, the procedure of measuring the output speed, comparing it with the desired speed, and using the speed difference or speed error ε_ω as a control signal makes possible the removal of many of the undesirable properties of the elementary speed system treated above. This procedure again leads to a closed-loop control system. Even the improvement obtained by closing the loop is limited unless skillful selection is made of particular physical elements.

4 Elementary Closed-Loop Positioning System (Mechanical)

A closed-loop substitute for the system of Figure 1 is shown in Figure 4. It is here assumed that the connection of Figure 1 between the spring

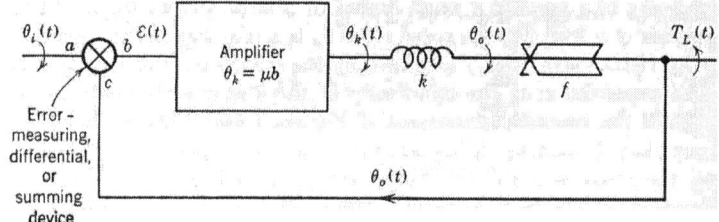

Figure 4.   Elementary closed-loop positioning system (mechanical).

and the input is opened, and a mechanical differential or mechanical summing device and amplifier are inserted. This device, also called the error-measuring means, compares the input or command with the output and indicates the difference as an error. Its behavior is represented by the relation

$$\varepsilon(t) = \theta_i(t) - \theta_o(t) \tag{29}$$

In Figure 4, the input quantity $\theta_i(t)$ is assumed to be applied to the summing device at the point a. The connection to the spring is made at the output from the amplifier whose input is the member b of the summing device. The third member c is connected to the output quantity $\theta_o(t)$. The arrangement of the shafts is such that the quantity b is equal to the quantity $a - c$. This means that in terms of a positional control system, the quantity b is the error between the input $\theta_i(t)$ and the output $\theta_o(t)$. The error is identified by the symbol $\mathcal{E}(t)$.

At this stage of the discussion, the amplifier between b and the spring merely amplifies the motion at b by the ratio μ. Thus the motion $\theta_k(t)$ at the input to the spring is $\mu\mathcal{E}(t)$. The load on the output shaft $\theta_o(t)$ is $T_L(t)$.

If the procedure used for the analysis of Figure 1 is followed, the equations relating the motions and forces of Figure 4 are:

$$\theta_k(t) = \mu\mathcal{E}(t) \tag{30}$$

$$\mathcal{E}(t) = \theta_i(t) - \theta_o(t) \tag{31}$$

$$k[\theta_k(t) - \theta_o(t)] = f\frac{d\theta_o(t)}{dt} + T_L(t) \tag{32}$$

These equations may be manipulated to form the response equations which predict either the output motion, or the error in terms of the parameters of the system and the time behavior of the disturbances $\theta_i(t)$ and $T_L(t)$. The substitution of Equations 30 and 31 in Equation 32 gives

$$k[\mu\theta_i(t) - \mu\theta_o(t) - \theta_o(t)] = f\frac{d\theta_o(t)}{dt} + T_L(t) \tag{33}$$

which may be written as

$$f\frac{d\theta_o(t)}{dt} + k(1 + \mu)\theta_o(t) = k\mu\theta_i(t) - T_L(t) \tag{34}$$

or, if $\theta_o(t)$ is eliminated in favor of error $\mathcal{E}(t)$, by substituting Equations 30 and 31 in Equation 32,

$$f\frac{d\mathcal{E}(t)}{dt} + k(1 + \mu)\mathcal{E}(t) = f\frac{d\theta_i(t)}{dt} + k\theta_i(t) + T_L(t) \tag{35}$$

The left-hand sides of Equations 34 and 35 contain the dependent variables $\theta_o(t)$ or $\mathcal{E}(t)$, whereas the right-hand sides contain the independent variables $\theta_i(t)$ or $T_L(t)$. For constant disturbances θ_i or T_L, the steady-state values of $\theta_o(t)$ and $\mathcal{E}(t)$ are given by

$$\left.\begin{array}{l} \theta_{oss} = \lim_{t \to \infty} \theta_o(t) = \dfrac{\mu}{1 + \mu}|\theta_i| \\[4mm] \mathcal{E}_{ss} = \lim_{t \to \infty} \mathcal{E}(t) = \dfrac{1}{1 + \mu}|\theta_i| \end{array}\right\} \text{for } T_L = 0 \tag{36}$$

and

$$\theta_{oss} = \underset{t \to \infty}{\text{limit }} \theta_o(t) = \frac{-1}{k(1 + \mu)} \left| T_L \right|$$

$$\varepsilon_{ss} = \underset{t \to \infty}{\text{limit }} \varepsilon(t) = \frac{1}{k(1 + \mu)} \left| T_L \right|$$

$\left.\begin{array}{l}\\ \\ \\ \\ \\\end{array}\right\}$ for $\theta_i = 0$ (37)

Equations 36 and 37 indicate that the final position of the output member of the closed loop will not be in agreement with the command. For the moment the explanation of the disagreement will be deferred, and the equations will be solved for their time response.

By following the procedure used in Equation 6, the time constant τ for the closed loop described by Equations 34 and 35 is obtained by dividing both sides by $k(1 + \mu)$. This gives

$$\tau \frac{d\theta_o(t)}{dt} + \theta_o(t) = \frac{\mu}{(1 + \mu)} \theta_i(t) - \frac{1}{k(1 + \mu)} T_L(t) \qquad (38)$$

and

$$\tau \frac{d\varepsilon(t)}{dt} + \varepsilon(t) = \tau \frac{d\theta_i(t)}{dt} + \frac{1}{(1 + \mu)} \theta_i(t) + \frac{1}{k(1 + \mu)} T_L(t) \qquad (39)$$

where

$$\tau = \frac{f}{k(1 + \mu)} \qquad (40)$$

These equations when solved for their time solution for a sudden constant disturbance θ_i or T_L give

$$\frac{\theta_o(t)}{\left| \theta_i \right|} = \left[\frac{\mu}{1 + \mu} \right] [1 - e^{-(t/\tau)}]$$

$$\frac{\varepsilon(t)}{\left| \theta_i \right|} = \left[\frac{1}{1 + \mu} \right] [1 + \mu e^{-(t/\tau)}]$$

$\left.\begin{array}{l}\\ \\ \\ \\\end{array}\right\}$ for $T_L = 0$ and disturbance $\left| \theta_i \right|$ (41)

and

$$\frac{\theta_o(t)}{\theta_{oss}} = [1 - e^{-(t/\tau)}]$$

where

$$\theta_{oss} = -\frac{T_L}{k(1 + \mu)}$$

$\left.\begin{array}{l}\\ \\ \\\end{array}\right\}$ for $\theta_i = 0$ and disturbance $\left| T_L \right|$ (42)

and

$$\frac{\varepsilon(t)}{\varepsilon_{ss}} = [1 - e^{-(t/\tau)}]$$

where

$$\varepsilon_{ss} = \frac{T_L}{k(1 + \mu)}$$

$\left.\begin{array}{l}\\ \\ \\\end{array}\right\}$ for $\theta_i = 0$ and disturbance $\left| T_L \right|$ (43)

The result of using one form of closed-loop system instead of an open-ended system is illustrated by comparing the performance indicated by Equations 10 and 12 with that indicated by Equations 41, 42, and 43. For example, in the presence of a load torque, the open-ended system has a misalignment between input and output inversely proportional to the spring constant k.   On the other hand, in presence of the same load, the closed-loop system has a misalignment inversely proportional to $k(1 + \mu)$.   The closing of the loop has the effect of increasing the overall stiffness of the system in the ratio of $(1 + \mu):1$.

The speed of response of the system with the closed loop differs appreciably from that with the open loop.   The time constant τ, equal to f/k in Figure 1, has been reduced in the ratio $1:(1 + \mu)$ for Figure 4. Therefore, if the positional amplifier has a gain of 10, for example, the closed-loop system is eleven times as stiff as the open-ended one and its speed of response is eleven times greater.

It is logical at this point to inquire whether the system as shown in Figure 4 would qualify as a servomechanism or as a regulator.   The answer to this question does not depend upon any universally established law, or term, or definition.   It is only partially answered by commonly accepted engineering terminology.   In the opinion of the authors, the system of Figure 4 does not qualify as a servomechanism, but does qualify as an elementary regulator.   The mere presence of a closed loop does not automatically make a system a servomechanism.   When called upon to function as a regulator, a system would be subjected merely to the disturbance T_L.   The input θ_i would be held constant at a set point. Equation 42 shows that the deviation in the quantity $\theta_o(t)$, from the set point to which it would correspond when θ_i is zero, equals $-T_L/k(1 + \mu)$.   Many regulators have this characteristic.   They are spoken of as regulators with load droop.   Parallel operation of certain prime movers or generators calls for load droop in their regulation.

A characteristic that, in the opinion of the authors, distinguishes the servomechanism from the regulator relates to behavior with respect to the independent variable $\theta_i(t)$.   Equation 41 shows that any finite deviation of θ_i from the initial set point results in the output θ_o being equal only to a fraction of that value, specifically $\theta_o = \left(\dfrac{\mu}{1 + \mu}\right)\theta_i$.

Likewise the error ε or deviation between θ_i and θ_o is equal to $\theta_i/(1 + \mu)$. As μ is increased, the output more nearly corresponds with the input, and the error is made correspondingly small.   However, it is always possible to make the input deviation large enough to cause an error between output and input greater than can be tolerated for any finite value of μ.   It is generally accepted that one property of the servomechanism, and specifically a positional servomechanism, is that for any constant value of input angle θ_i, regardless of its magnitude from a set point, the output angle in the absence of a load will correspond exactly with the input angle. This phenomenon is sometimes expressed by applying the name "follow-up system" to a servomechanism because it follows up unlimited variation of its input. All regulators are not subjected to such unlimited variation of the input, whereas all servomechanisms may be. In the absence of load disturbances the steady-state output of a servomechanism always follows up into exact correspondence with the input. Figure 5 shows that the system described in Figure 4 would fulfill the servomechanism requirement only in the limit

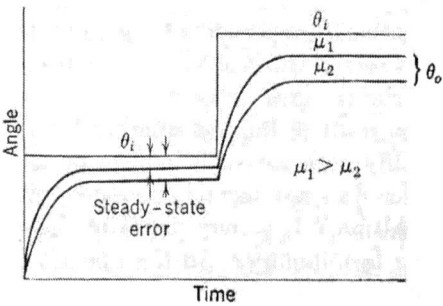

FIGURE 5. Steady-state positional error in a closed-loop positional system (not a servomechanism).

when μ is infinite. Under such conditions, the loop gain would be infinite and the system time constant would be zero. Neither of these conditions is physically realizable. The system of Figure 4 is not a servomechanism.

Application of the above test excludes the conventional negative feedback electronic amplifier from the category of a servomechanism. Although it may have the property of droop in output voltage when the load is increased, the output voltage is only a fraction of the input voltage, never exactly in correspondence with it; that is,

$$E_2 = \frac{\mu}{1 + \mu} E_1 \qquad (44)$$

where E_1 = input volts, E_2 = output voltage, μ = amplification factor.

It may be argued that a servomechanism frequently shows an error in the presence of a fixed load torque. This is true, and in this respect servomechanisms and regulators are often alike. It is herein shown that techniques of design exist that will zero the error for this condition in either system. It is with respect to the steady error behavior for un-

limited variation in the input quantity or unlimited variation in the
set point that servomechanisms and regulators differ.   In other words,
regulators are not necessarily follow-up systems.   Since they often do
not need to be, their design need not apply criteria always applied for
servomechanisms.

Section 6 illustrates the property desired of the elements in the loop
in order to permit operation as a servomechanism.

5   Elementary Closed-Loop Speed Control System (Electrical)

Now consider that the electric motor speed control system treated
in Section 3 is converted to a closed-loop system as shown in Figure 6.

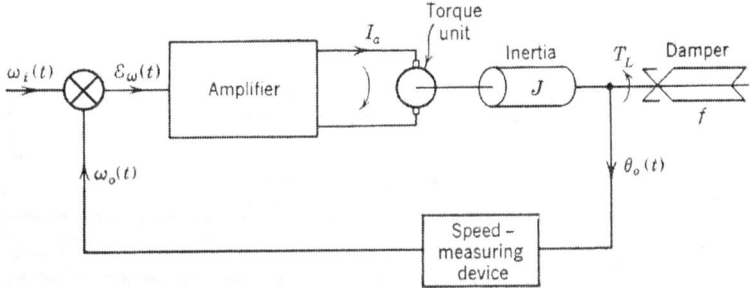

FIGURE 6.   Elementary closed-loop speed control system (electrical).

Assume that a measuring device such as a tachometer is attached to the
output shaft of the motor and gives a signal that is a measure of the output speed $\omega_o = d\theta_o/dt$.   Consider that the signal is a voltage and that
it is compared by the error-measuring means with a reference voltage
whose magnitude is a measure of the speed desired, ω_i.   The output of
the error-measuring means is then a speed error, $\mathcal{E}_\omega$, which is applied
to the input terminals of an amplifier whose output applies a torque
to the motor proportional to the speed error.   On the assumption that
the motor is characterized by inertia J, and viscous damping f, and that
the load torque is $T_L(t)$, the equation of motion of the system is

$$\mathcal{E}_\omega(t) = \omega_i(t) - \omega_o(t) \tag{45}$$

and

$$k\mathcal{E}_\omega(t) = J\frac{d\omega_o(t)}{dt} + f\omega_o(t) + T_L(t) \tag{46}$$

where k is the torque per unit speed error.   Eliminating $\omega_o(t)$ from Equation 46 gives

$$J\frac{d\mathcal{E}_\omega(t)}{dt} + (k + f)\mathcal{E}_\omega(t) = J\frac{d\omega_i(t)}{dt} + f\omega_i(t) + T_L(t) \tag{47}$$

If Equation 47 is divided by the coefficient $(k + f)$ and if $J/(k + f)$ is defined as the time constant τ, the result is

$$\tau \frac{d\mathcal{E}_\omega(t)}{dt} + \mathcal{E}_\omega(t) = \tau \frac{d\omega_i(t)}{dt} + \frac{f}{k + f} \omega_i(t) + \frac{T_L(t)}{k + f} \qquad (48)$$

which may be written in the form shown in Equation 26 for the open-ended speed control system as

$$\mathcal{E}_\omega(t) = \frac{\left(\tau \dfrac{d}{dt} + \dfrac{f}{k + f}\right)}{\left(\tau \dfrac{d}{dt} + 1\right)} \omega_i(t) + \frac{\dfrac{1}{k + f}}{\left(\tau \dfrac{d}{dt} + 1\right)} T_L(t) \qquad (49)$$

The steady-state condition for this system is

$$\mathcal{E}_{\omega_{ss}} = \frac{f}{k + f} |\omega_i| + \frac{|T_L|}{k + f} \qquad (50)$$

An examination of Equation 50 with Equation 28 shows a very important result of closed-loop operation. For example, the viscous drag, so essential to the operation of the open-ended system of Figure 3, could be eliminated entirely from the system of Figure 6. The performance would then be improved. There would be no dissipation of energy in the system incidental to the speed regulation. The time constant is now $J/(k + f)$ contrasted with J/f for the open loop. The viscous drag in the closed loop can now be merely incidental friction and should be small. Since the limit imposed on the magnitude of k is only one of practical expediency, k may be made relatively large. The speed errors under steady variations in input ω_i or load torques T_L are thereby decreased. Furthermore, the speed of response steadily improves with increasing k. Closed-loop operation for a speed control such as the one considered, therefore, offers many attractions.

6 Elementary Servomechanism (Mechanical)

Since the system of Figure 4 is not a follow-up system, or positional servomechanism, some alteration must be made to the components of the closed loop if it is to become one. The clue may not be obvious, but in closed-loop positional systems permitting correspondence between input and output for any value of the input there must be an integrating element in the closed loop. It is the phenomenon of integration inside the loop that makes possible steady-state one-to-one correspondence between the input and the output following displacements of the input regardless of magnitude. Stated another way, the error between input and output in the steady state must generate the rate of change of output and not merely the output itself.   Proof of this as a necessary condition is given in Chapter 6.

The integrating property may be provided by replacing the torque amplifier with a device which produces a displacement θ_k proportional to the time integral of the error signal from the summing device.   In other words, the steady-state value of $d\theta_k/dt$ must be proportional to ε_{ss}. The arrangement shown in Figure 7, fulfills the requirement.   All

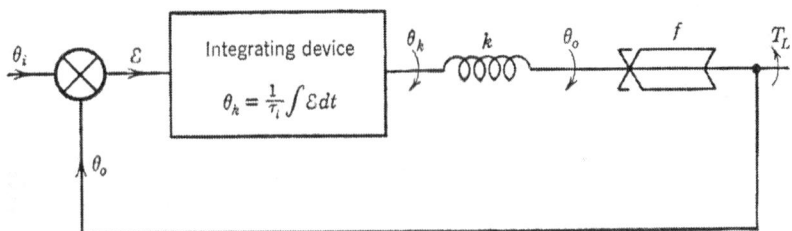

FIGURE 7.   Elementary servomechanism (mechanical).

parameters and quantities other than those for the integrating device are the same as those used in Figure 4.

The equations of motion for Figure 7 may be written as

$$\varepsilon(t) = \theta_i(t) - \theta_o(t) \tag{51}$$

$$\theta_k(t) = \frac{1}{\tau_i} \int \varepsilon(t)\, dt \tag{52}$$

$$k[\theta_k(t) - \theta_o(t)] = f\frac{d\theta_o(t)}{dt} + T_L(t) \tag{53}$$

By differentiating Equations 52 and 53, they may be merged and solved for the output response or the error response.   Thus

$$\frac{d\theta_k(t)}{dt} = \frac{1}{\tau_i}\varepsilon(t) \tag{54}$$

$$k\left[\frac{d\theta_k(t)}{dt} - \frac{d\theta_o(t)}{dt}\right] = f\frac{d^2\theta_o(t)}{dt^2} + \frac{dT_L(t)}{dt} \tag{55}$$

which, when combined with Equation 51, give

$$f\frac{d^2\theta_o(t)}{dt^2} + k\frac{d\theta_o(t)}{dt} + \frac{1}{\tau_i}k\theta_o(t) = \frac{1}{\tau_i}k\theta_i(t) - \frac{dT_L(t)}{dt} \tag{56}$$

or

$$f\frac{d^2\varepsilon(t)}{dt^2} + k\frac{d\varepsilon(t)}{dt} + \frac{1}{\tau_i}k\varepsilon(t) = f\frac{d^2\theta_i(t)}{dt^2} + k\frac{d\theta_i(t)}{dt} + \frac{dT_L(t)}{dt} \tag{57}$$

The introduction of the integrating element in the closed loop has increased the number of energy storage elements in the problem. The resulting system is now defined by a second-order linear differential equation for which the relative adjustment of the parameters f, k, and $1/\tau_i$ can cause the response to be three types of stable motion: (1) damped but oscillatory, (2) aperiodically damped, or (3) overdamped. A note of complexity has been introduced into the physical system in the attempt to provide the unity follow-up property. While this is undesirable, it may not be very serious if the problem is thoroughly understood.

From Equation 56, the relation for the output response, θ_{oss}, in the steady state for any magnitude of θ_i is

$$\theta_{oss} = \left| \theta_i \right| \text{ when } T_L \text{ is zero} \tag{58}$$

The error $\mathcal{E}_{ss}$ is then always zero. Furthermore, for any value of load T_L and any fixed θ_i, the steady-state error is again zero. Thus the system of Figure 7 functions as a servomechanism and as a regulator without steady-state droop.

The use of a spring, damper, and an integrating device to illustrate the properties of an elementary servomechanism has about served its purpose. Little further use can be made of this illustration because it represents a situation not often encountered in practice. It is unusually well suited to the problem at hand, however. It clearly represents a system that could be built with physically available components, and it presents to a student of dynamics the interesting problem of explaining why the so-called damping term of the characteristic equation of the closed loop is a spring instead of a dissipative term. Failure to allow remote location of output and input because of the mechanical feedback feature is its principal weakness.

It will suffice to point out that a system of Figure 7 becomes an ideal servomechanism as the stiffness of the spring increases. If the characteristic equation of the system is written in the form

$$f \frac{d^2}{dt^2} + k \frac{d}{dt} + \frac{1}{\tau_i} k = 0 \tag{59}$$

or

$$\frac{f}{k} \frac{d^2}{dt^2} + \frac{d}{dt} + \frac{1}{\tau_i} = 0 \tag{60}$$

it will be seen that increasing the spring stiffness will, in the limit, reduce the characteristic equation from that of a second-order one to that of a first-order, that is,

$$\tau_i \frac{d}{dt} + 1 = 0 \tag{61}$$

and the integrating constant τ_i becomes the time constant of the system. As the integrator sensitivity $1/\tau_i$ is made larger, the speed of response of the system is increased.

7 Elementary Remote Control Positional Servomechanism

The foregoing mechanical closed-loop systems show certain advantages over their open-loop counterpart, but they do not represent good solutions to the remote control feature postulated as desirable. For the purpose of illustrating a remote control technique as well as additional closed-loop dynamical properties, the system shown in Figure 8

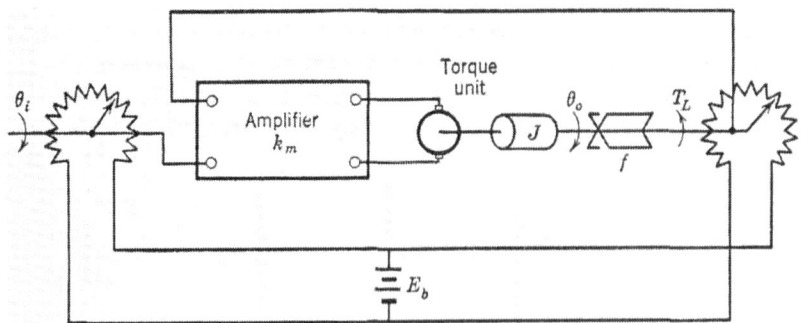

FIGURE 8.   Elementary remote control positional servomechanism.

is studied. This system is similar to that treated in Section 5, with the exception that here the error ε will, in the steady state, establish a rate of change of the controlled position θ_o, whereas, in Section 5, the error ε_ω, being a velocity, established merely the controlled velocity ω_o. In other words, in this positional servomechanism, the output θ_o is proportional to the time integral of the positional error. The so-called integration property is in the loop of this system but not in the loop of the rate system of Figure 6.

Figure 8 illustrates the problem of maintaining the position of an output shaft θ_o in correspondence with that of an input shaft θ_i, when the shafts θ_i and θ_o are located remotely from one another. This property was not a feature of the system shown in Figure 7. Figure 8 is a remote control positional servomechanism. Attached to the shaft θ_i is a rotary potentiometer across whose terminals is connected a battery of voltage E_b. A similar potentiometer is connected to the output shaft θ_o. Its terminals are also connected to the battery of voltage E_b. The connection to the movable arm of each potentiometer is made to one input terminal of a vacuum tube amplifier; the amplifier in turn furnishes excitation to a motor. The internal torque of the motor is assumed to be proportional to the voltage applied at the amplifier input. The moving parts of the motor are defined by inertia, J, and viscous friction, f. The load torque is $T_L(t)$.

Since the connection between the shaft θ_i and θ_o comprises only electric circuits, considerable flexibility exists for the remote location of the input or the output. Furthermore, the only mechanical power expended at the input is that dissipated by wiping friction in the potentiometer. The only electrical power expended at the input is the heating loss in the resistors. Thus a remotely located command of low energy level may control the motion of an electric motor of unspecified power rating.

The procedure for the analysis of a problem of this kind is first to evaluate the properties of the potentiometers and input and output shaft arrangements, since these comprise the error-measuring means. If the diagram of the potentiometer system, Figure 8, is redrawn, as shown in Figure 9, it is seen that the potentiometers are connected in the manner

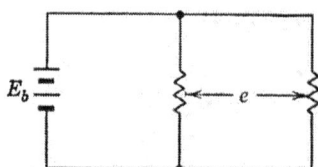

FIGURE 9.   Error-measuring means of Figure 8.

of a bridge. For an applied battery voltage E_b, the potential per unit angle along each potentiometer, for both input and output motion, from the reference point equals $E_b/\theta_{\max}$. The voltage e appearing between the two sliders of the potentiometers is

$$e(t) = \frac{E_b}{\theta_{\max}} [\theta_i(t) - \theta_o(t)] \tag{62}$$

$$e(t) = \frac{E_b}{\theta_{\max}} \varepsilon(t) \tag{63}$$

The equation of motion of the motor is

$$J \frac{d^2\theta_o(t)}{dt^2} + f \frac{d\theta_o(t)}{dt} = k_m e(t) - T_L(t) \tag{64}$$

where k_m is the torque per unit error voltage.   Substituting Equation 63 into 64 gives

$$J \frac{d^2\theta_o(t)}{dt^2} + f \frac{d\theta_o(t)}{dt} = k\varepsilon(t) - T_L(t) \tag{65}$$

where

$$k = \frac{k_m E_b}{\theta_{max}} = \frac{\text{torque}}{\text{angle}} \tag{66}$$

The solution of Equation 65 for output $\theta_o(t)$ and error $\varepsilon(t)$ gives

$$J \frac{d^2\theta_o(t)}{dt^2} + f \frac{d\theta_o(t)}{dt} + k\theta_o(t) = k\theta_i(t) - T_L(t) \tag{67}$$

$$J \frac{d^2\varepsilon(t)}{dt^2} + f \frac{d\varepsilon(t)}{dt} + k\varepsilon(t) = J \frac{d^2\theta_i(t)}{dt^2} + f \frac{d\theta_i(t)}{dt} + T_L(t) \tag{68}$$

Rewriting these equations in fractional form gives

$$\theta_o(t) = \frac{k\theta_i(t) - T_L(t)}{\left(J \dfrac{d^2}{dt^2} + f \dfrac{d}{dt} + k \right)} \tag{69}$$

$$\varepsilon(t) = \frac{\left(J \dfrac{d^2}{dt^2} + f \dfrac{d}{dt} \right)\theta_i(t) + T_L(t)}{\left(J \dfrac{d^2}{dt^2} + f \dfrac{d}{dt} + k \right)} \tag{70}$$

That the system of Figure 8 is a servomechanism is demonstrated by Equation 70, which gives the steady-state error ε_{ss} equal to zero for all constant values of θ_i in the absence of load torques.   The system acts in the steady state as a follow up with respect to input disturbances. However, when a steady load is applied to its output, the error ε_{ss} is proportional to this load.   This latter property is characteristic of all servomechanisms whose control torque is proportional only to error.

A comparison of Equations 56 and 57 with Equations 67 and 68 shows that the systems of Figures 7 and 8 are dynamically similar with respect to the error performance following a suddenly applied input disturbance, but they are not similar with respect to the error following a suddenly applied load torque.   There is a subtle reason for this, but its discussion is reserved until Chapter 9.

The transient behavior of these servomechanisms is treated in the following section.

8 Transient Behavior of Elementary Servomechanism [29]

Consider the transient response of the closed-loop system of Figure 8 for a sudden displacement of the input θ_i. The characteristic equation is now a second-order one of the form

$$J\frac{d^2}{dt^2} + f\frac{d}{dt} + k = 0 \tag{71}$$

It has the two roots r_1 and r_2:

$$r_1, r_2 = \frac{-f \pm \sqrt{f^2 - 4Jk}}{2J} \tag{72}$$

For all stable systems, that is, those whose oscillations always attenuate to zero, the roots r_1 and r_2 may be (1) conjugate complex with negative real parts, (2) equal negative real, or (3) unequal negative real, depending upon the numerical values of J, f, and k.

Two parameters, namely, the undamped natural angular frequency, ω_n, and the damping ratio, ζ, may be chosen so that the roots r_1 and r_2 may be expressed in terms of two quantities instead of three, as in Equation 72. One of these quantities, ω_n, has the dimensions of time; the other one, ζ, is dimensionless. A study of system behavior in dimensionless form can then be made.

The quantity ω_n is given by the characteristic Equation 71 when the damping is zero, that is,

$$J\frac{d^2}{dt^2} + k = 0 \tag{73}$$

giving roots

$$r_1 \text{ and } r_2 = \pm j\sqrt{\frac{k}{J}} = \pm j\omega_n \tag{74}$$

that is, $\omega_n \doteq \sqrt{k/J}$. The parameter ζ or damping ratio is the ratio of actual damping to critical damping. Critical damping occurs when the radical of Equation 72 is zero or when the two roots r_1 and r_2 are equal. The critical value of damping, f_c, which can cause this condition is

$$f_c = 2\sqrt{kJ} \tag{75}$$

The damping ratio is then

$$\zeta = \frac{\text{actual damping}}{f_c} = \frac{f}{2\sqrt{kJ}} \tag{76}$$

If ω_n and ζ as parameters are used to replace appropriate combinations of J, f, and k, the entire set of equations thus far derived may be rewritten in a new form which provides not only greater facility to our work but also more clarity to our thinking. Specifically, if Equations 67 and 68 are divided through by J, the output response and the error response become

$$\frac{d^2\theta_o(t)}{dt^2} + 2\zeta\omega_n \frac{d\theta_o(t)}{dt} + \omega_n^2\theta_o(t) = \omega_n^2\theta_i(t) - \frac{T_L(t)}{J} \qquad (77)$$

and

$$\frac{d^2\varepsilon(t)}{dt^2} + 2\zeta\omega_n \frac{d\varepsilon(t)}{dt} + \omega_n^2\varepsilon(t) = \frac{d^2\theta_i(t)}{dt^2} + 2\zeta\omega_n \frac{d\theta_i(t)}{dt} + \frac{T_L(t)}{J} \qquad (78)$$

The new characteristic equation becomes

$$\frac{d^2}{dt^2} + 2\zeta\omega_n \frac{d}{dt} + \omega_n^2 = 0 \qquad (79)$$

and the roots become

$$r_1 \text{ and } r_2 = -\zeta\omega_n \pm j\omega_n\sqrt{1 - \zeta^2} \qquad (80)$$

where $\omega_n\sqrt{1 - \zeta^2}$ is the actual frequency of damped oscillation.

The solution to Equations 77 or 78 for suddenly applied disturbances have the general form

$$\theta_o(t) = A_1 e^{r_1 t} + B_1 e^{r_2 t} + \theta_{oss} \qquad (81)$$

or

$$\varepsilon(t) = A_2 e^{r_1 t} + B_2 e^{r_2 t} + \varepsilon_{ss} \qquad (82)$$

The roots r_1 and r_2 of the characteristic Equation 79 may be of three possible forms for a stable system, depending upon the magnitude of the damping ratio ζ. When $\zeta < 1.0$, the roots are conjugate complex with negative real parts and *the system is underdamped;* when $\zeta = 1.0$, the roots are negative real and equal *and the system is critically damped;* and when $\zeta > 1.0$, the roots are negative real and unequal *and the system is overdamped.* Each form of roots gives a different form to the time solution. For practical purposes, the solutions representative of the underdamped case, $\zeta < 1$, are of most interest, first because many systems may *with advantage* be made slightly oscillatory, $0.4 < \zeta < 1.0$, and, second, because the form of solution for $\zeta < 1$ is readily converted into forms for $\zeta = 1$ or $\zeta > 1$. The substitution of roots r_1 and r_2 from Equation 80 into Equation 81 and the expansion of the exponentials having complex exponents into their equivalent sine and cosine form, and assuming a suddenly applied angle $|\theta_i|$ but zero load torque $T_L(t)$, gives

$$\theta_o(t) = e^{-\zeta\omega_n t}[A_3 \cos \omega_n\sqrt{1 - \zeta^2}\, t + A_4 \sin \omega_n\sqrt{1 - \zeta^2}\, t] + |\theta_i| \qquad (83)$$

where the coefficients A_3 and A_4 must be evaluated in conformance with the initial conditions. The quantity θ_{oss} of Equation 81 has been written as $|\theta_i|$ in Equation 83 because the system is a servomechanism.

The initial conditions at the *time t equals zero approached from positive time*, symbolically $t = (0+)$, are peculiar to the problem at hand. For purposes of illustration, consider that at time $t = 0+$ the input has changed from rest by an amount θ_i. The instantaneous torque on the output will then be $k\theta_i$. Despite the fact that the torque $k\theta_i$ will accelerate the output inertia at $t = 0+$, the output cannot attain a finite velocity in the infinitesimal time interval $t = 0-$ to $t = 0+$. Consequently, the output member cannot move in the infinitesimal time interval $t = (0-)$ to $t = (0+)$, during which the change in θ_i occurs.

The initial conditions to be injected into the analysis are, therefore, at $t = 0+$.

$$\left.\begin{array}{c} \theta_o(0+) = 0 \\[2mm] \dfrac{d\theta_o}{dt}(0+) = 0 \end{array}\right\} \qquad (84)$$

Substitution of these conditions gives

$$\left.\begin{array}{c} A_3 = -|\theta_i| \\[2mm] A_4 = -\dfrac{\zeta}{\sqrt{1-\zeta^2}}|\theta_i| \end{array}\right| \qquad (85)$$

The underdamped output transient response following a sudden input displacement θ_i becomes

$$\theta_o(t) = |\theta_i|\left\{1 - e^{-\zeta\omega_n t}\left[\cos\omega_n\sqrt{1-\zeta^2}\,t \right.\right.$$

$$\left.\left. + \frac{\zeta}{\sqrt{1-\zeta^2}}\sin\omega_n\sqrt{1-\zeta^2}\,t\right]\right\} \qquad (86)$$

Equation 86 may be rewritten in a more compact form as

$$\theta_o(t) = |\theta_i|\left\{1 - \frac{e^{-\zeta\omega_n t}}{\sqrt{1-\zeta^2}}\sin(\omega_n\sqrt{1-\zeta^2}\,t + \phi)\right\} \qquad (87)$$

where

$$\phi = \tan^{-1}\frac{\sqrt{1-\zeta^2}}{\zeta} \qquad (88)$$

The transient solution to Equation 82 giving the error $\varepsilon(t)$ following a suddenly applied input may be obtained by writing Equation 87 as

$\theta_o(t)/\theta_i$ and subtracting it from unity. Alternatively, the differential equation 78 may be solved for the condition that the load torque is zero and that at $t = 0+$

$$\left.\begin{array}{l} \mathcal{E}(0+) = \theta_i \\[2mm] \dfrac{d\mathcal{E}}{dt}(0+) = 0 \end{array}\right\} \tag{89}$$

The result is

$$\frac{\mathcal{E}(t)}{\theta_i} = \frac{e^{-\zeta\omega_n t}}{\sqrt{1 - \zeta^2}} \sin\left(\sqrt{1 - \zeta^2}\,\omega_n t + \phi\right) \tag{90}$$

where

$$\phi = \tan^{-1} \frac{\sqrt{1 - \zeta^2}}{\zeta} \tag{91}$$

The steady-state solution of Equation 78 for both a constant input θ_i and load T_L is

$$\mathcal{E}_{ss} = 0 + \frac{T_L}{k} \tag{92}$$

that is, there is no error resulting from θ_i because of the follow-up feature. Another form of input of real interest is the constant velocity ω_i. Since $d\theta_i/dt$ may be replaced by ω_i, Equation 78 may be rewritten as

$$\frac{d^2\mathcal{E}(t)}{dt^2} + 2\zeta\omega_n \frac{d\mathcal{E}(t)}{dt} + \omega_n^2 \mathcal{E}(t) = \frac{d\omega_i(t)}{dt} + 2\zeta\omega_n\omega_i(t) + \frac{T_L(t)}{J} \tag{93}$$

from which the steady-state error, for a constant ω_i and load T_L, is

$$\mathcal{E}_{ss} = \frac{2\zeta\omega_i}{\omega_n} + \frac{T_L}{k} \tag{94}$$

The error is here equal to the algebraic sum of that caused by the input velocity plus that caused by the load.

The various solutions given above show that the dynamic behavior of the closed-loop system has become intimately related to its steady-state behavior. Any change to a single system parameter to improve performance with respect to one requirement may jeopardize the behavior with respect to other requirements. For example, in the system of Figure 8 any attempt to decrease the steady error in the presence of a steady load torque would necessitate an increase in k. But this increase will decrease the damping ratio ζ and increase the frequency of oscillation $\omega_n\sqrt{1 - \zeta^2}$. If the damping ratio gets too low the viscous drag f must be increased or the inertia J decreased. Thus viscous drag becomes an essential in the system in order to establish stability. That

TABLE 1

ERROR RESPONSE EXPRESSIONS FOR AN ELEMENTARY SERVOMECHANISM HAVING CONTROL TORQUE PROPORTIONAL TO ERROR
(See Figure 8.)

Form of Disturbance	$\zeta < 1$	$\zeta = 1$	$\zeta_1 > 1$
Suddenly applied input velocity ω_i	$$\frac{\mathcal{E}(t)}{\varepsilon_{ss}} = 1 - \frac{e^{-\zeta\omega_n t}}{2\zeta\sqrt{1-\zeta^2}}\sin\left(\sqrt{1-\zeta^2}\,\omega_n t + \phi\right)$$ $$\varepsilon_{ss} = \frac{2\zeta\omega_i}{\omega_n}; \quad \phi = \tan^{-1}\frac{2\zeta\sqrt{1-\zeta^2}}{2\zeta^2 - 1}$$	$$\frac{\mathcal{E}(t)}{\varepsilon_{ss}} = 1 - e^{-\omega_n t}\left(1 + \frac{\omega_n t}{2}\right)$$	$$\frac{\mathcal{E}(t)}{\varepsilon_{ss}} = 1 - e^{-\zeta\omega_n t}\left\{\cosh\sqrt{\zeta^2-1}\,\omega_n t + \frac{2\zeta^2-1}{2\zeta\sqrt{\zeta^2-1}}\sinh\sqrt{\zeta^2-1}\,\omega_n t\right\}$$
Suddenly applied input angle θ_i	$$\frac{\mathcal{E}(t)}{\theta_i} = \frac{e^{-\zeta\omega_n t}}{\sqrt{1-\zeta^2}}\sin\left(\sqrt{1-\zeta^2}\,\omega_n t + \phi\right)$$ $$\phi = \tan^{-1}\frac{\sqrt{1-\zeta^2}}{\zeta}$$ Steady-state error = zero	$$\frac{\mathcal{E}(t)}{\theta_i} = (1 + \omega_n t)e^{-\omega_n t}$$	$$\frac{\mathcal{E}(t)}{\theta_i} = e^{-\zeta\omega_n t}\left\{\cosh\sqrt{\zeta^2-1}\,\omega_n t + \frac{\zeta}{\sqrt{\zeta^2-1}}\sinh\sqrt{\zeta^2-1}\,\omega_n t\right\}$$
Suddenly applied shaft torque T_L	$$\frac{\mathcal{E}(t)}{\varepsilon_{ss}} = 1 - \frac{e^{-\zeta\omega_n t}}{\sqrt{1-\zeta^2}}\sin\left(\sqrt{1-\zeta^2}\,\omega_n t + \phi\right)$$ $$\varepsilon_{ss} = \frac{T_L}{J\omega_n^2}; \quad \phi = \tan^{-1}\frac{\sqrt{1-\zeta^2}}{\zeta}$$	$$\frac{\mathcal{E}(t)}{\varepsilon_{ss}} = 1 - (1 + \omega_n t)e^{-\omega_n t}$$	$$\frac{\mathcal{E}(t)}{\varepsilon_{ss}} = 1 - e^{-\zeta\omega_n t}\left\{\cosh\sqrt{\zeta^2-1}\,\omega_n t + \frac{\zeta}{\sqrt{\zeta^2-1}}\sinh\sqrt{\zeta^2-1}\,\omega_n t\right\}$$

$$\omega_n = \sqrt{\frac{k}{J}} \qquad\qquad \zeta = \frac{f}{2\sqrt{Jk}}$$

this is an undesirable feature is discussed in Section 10. No blanket statement can be made as to the proper value of any particular parameter. All aspects of the problem, including steady-state and transient performance for input and load disturbances, must be examined simultaneously as a design progresses. The later chapters of this book aim to show how these matters may be handled. In the following section of this chapter, some of the more salient properties of the transient behavior are discussed.

9   Transient Response Curves

· The differential equations 77 and 78 lead to the generalized tabulation of the response equations shown in Table 1. If external position disturbances θ_i, velocity disturbances ω_i, and load disturbances T_L are computed separately, the theories of linear superposition permit the expression for the response of the closed loop to simultaneous application of more than one external disturbance by the algebraic addition of the component responses.

The dimensionless graphs of Figures 10 and 11 express the entire set of equations in Table 1. For instance, the error $\varepsilon(t)$ in the absence of load for a suddenly applied velocity disturbance ω_i is given by the family of curves in Figures 10a and 10b. The curves of Figure 10a are, strictly speaking, dimensionless, whereas those of 10b are dimensionless only to the extent that angle is dimensionless. Both forms of curves are presented in order to illustrate various ways to present dimensionless data. The error $\varepsilon(t)$ for a suddenly applied angular disturbance θ_i in the absence of load, and for a suddenly applied load disturbance T_L with a fixed input θ_i is given by the single family of curves in Figure 11. Each graph has dimensionless ordinates $\varepsilon(t)/\varepsilon_{ss}$ or $\varepsilon(t)/\theta_i$, dimensionless abscissae $\omega_n t$, and the single parameter ζ. The damping ratio ζ is assigned values 0.4, 0.6, 0.8, 1.0, and 1.5.

Present-day engineering practice establishes a limit to the degree of oscillation that is acceptable. Although the system of Figure 8 is relatively simple, its oscillation is closely representative of the behavior of more complicated systems because, even though their solution may have several oscillating modes, one mode usually predominates. In terms of Figures 10 or 11, the lowest value of ζ giving acceptable performance is about 0.4, although this figure is influenced more by judgment than by mathematical choice.

The choice of the upper limit for ζ is again based upon experience. Most mechanical systems contain coulomb friction, which tends to make the output stick within a zone of uncertainty when the correction torque falls below the static friction level. Therefore a slight tendency for the output to oscillate when it comes into agreement with the input follow-ing any disturbance is desirable.   The upper limit of ζ is therefore placed at $\zeta < 1.0$ consistent with the slight oscillation desired.

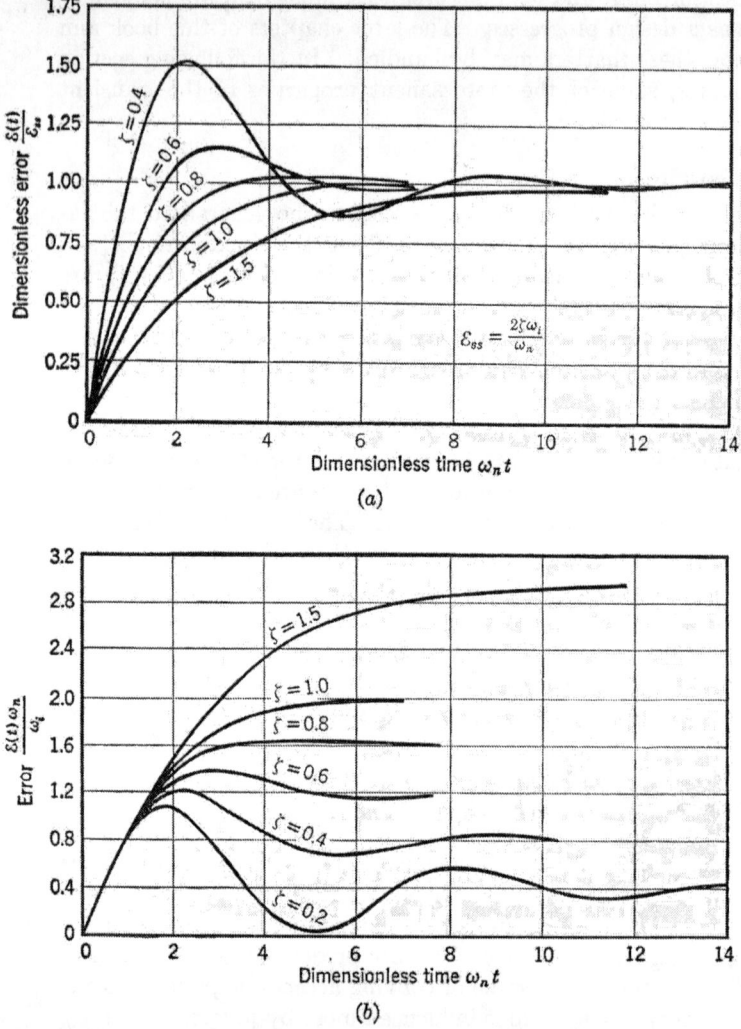

FIGURE 10.   Dimensionless transient error curves of elementary servomechanism of Figure 8 subjected to suddenly applied input ω_i.

The zone of the damping ratio $0.4 \leq \zeta \leq 1.0$ is a good starting point in adjusting the transient response of a system.   Later, when systems of a more complicated nature are discussed, it will be noted that the equivalent of ζ about 0.4 tends to become a rule-of-thumb concept rather than a criterion for closed-loop system adjustment.

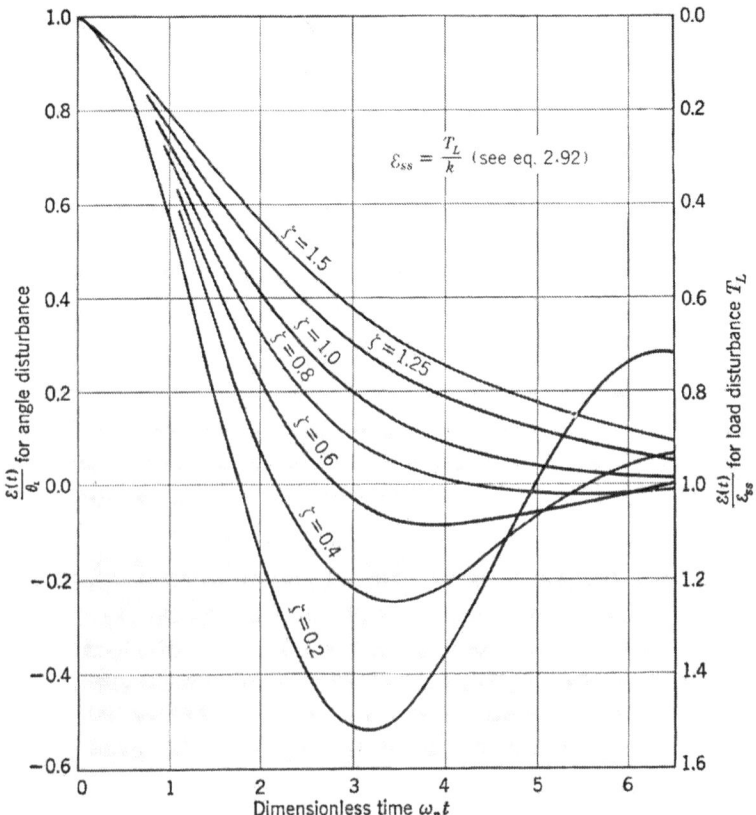

FIGURE 11.   Transient error curves of elementary servomechanism of Figure 8 subjected to suddenly applied input angle θ_i or load torque T_L.

The speed of response can now be established quantitatively for the system under consideration.   The exponential term has the following tabulated values:

$\zeta \omega_n t$	$e^{-\zeta \omega_n t}$	Percentage of Final Value
1	0.367	63.3
2	0.135	86.5
3	0.05	95.0
4	0.018	98.2

Using the rule of thumb concept it follows that all underdamped systems represented by a second-order characteristic equation will have reached 98 per cent of their final state when $\zeta \omega_n t = 4$. The dimensionless response time is then

$$\omega_n t = \frac{4}{\zeta} \tag{95}$$

or the true time in terms of the parameters ω_n and ζ is

$$t = \frac{4}{\zeta \omega_n} \tag{96}$$

10   Review of Illustrative Positional Servomechanism

The example selected for illustration in Section 7 represents a physically realizable system only if certain simplifying assumptions are made. As a rule, the number of energy storage elements in the system exceeds two, thus giving a higher than second-order characteristic equation. The solutions plotted in Figures 10 and 11 are not greatly in error, however, whenever the time constants of the additional energy storage elements in cascade in the loop are small compared with $1/\omega_n$.

The principal objection to the system of Figure 8 is that its stabilization is achieved by the viscous damping in the output member. The damping causes undesirably large errors whenever the input is changing even at a constant rate ω_i and excessive energy dissipation in the output relative to any useful energy output. To illustrate these matters, consider the following problem.

Assume that an output member including a drive motor armature has an inertia of 0.25 in.² lb. Assume that as a positional servomechanism the output $\theta_o(t)$ is to be positioned with an accuracy of $\pi/2$ radians when it is rotated at a velocity ω_i of 120 rpm in the absence·of load torque. Determine the torque per unit error k and the undamped angular frequency ω_n required by these specifications if the damping ratio ζ is unity.

From Equation 94

$$\varepsilon_{ss} = \frac{2\zeta}{\omega_n} \omega_i$$

or

$$\omega_n = \frac{2 \times 4\pi \times 2}{\pi} = 16 \text{ radians per second}$$

From Equation 74

$$\omega_n = \sqrt{\frac{k}{J}}$$

Since

$$J = \frac{0.25}{144} \times \frac{1}{32} = 0.53 \times 10^{-4} \text{ slug ft}^2$$

$$k = 16^2 \times 0.53 \times 10^{-4} = 1.35 \times 10^{-2} \text{ lb-ft per radian}$$

$$= 2.6 \text{ in. oz per radian}$$

The system would have a good dynamic response since from Equation 96 the time t for 98 per cent of a transient to disappear is

$$t = \tfrac{4}{16} = 0.25 \text{ second}$$

The system is far from efficient, however, since all the energy is dissipated as heat in the viscous drag. The system delivers no useful work. From Equation 76

$$\zeta = \frac{f}{2\sqrt{Jk}} = 1.0$$

or

$$f = 2\sqrt{0.53 \times 10^{-4} \times 1.35 \times 10^{-2}}$$

$$= 1.68 \times 10^{-3} \text{ lb-ft per radian per second}$$

Since power dissipated is $f\omega_i^2$, the heat lost is, in practical units,

$$\frac{1.68 \times 10^{-3} \times (4\pi)^2 \times 746}{550} = 0.36 \text{ watt}$$

This value of 0.36 watt is not small when one realizes that an inertia of 0.25 in.^{2} lb is about equivalent to that existing in the rotor of a small synchro or selsyn or in the armature of about a 0.01-horsepower motor. The difficulty, of course, comes when one tries to design simple devices having a viscous property. As is shown in later chapters, certain electric motors have inherently the equivalent of a viscous damper in their back emf. The techniques for computing this effect are treated in Chapter 5.

Because of the presence of the following error $\varepsilon_{ss} = 2\zeta\omega_i/\omega_n$, and the loss of energy needed by damping in proportional-error systems such as that of Figure 8, they are used only in applications calling for powers of a few watts and then only when the following error ε_{ss} need not be small. The error of $\pi/2$ radians allowed at the velocity of 2 rps is large considering good present-day practice. Systems having one tenth of this value are common.

Whenever high-power servomechanisms are needed, methods other than viscous damping in the output must be used for stabilization purposes. So-called kinetic damping is used. It is sometimes called derivative damping [7, 29, 46, 47] and represented mathematically by a controller equation—Torque $= k\varepsilon + \ell(d\varepsilon/dt)$. Unfortunately a device that will yield a true derivative is difficult to obtain. Therefore, in most systems kinetic damping is introduced by the insertion of phase-compensating networks in the error-output chain in order to control the instantaneous energy storage in the system. In some simple systems such as synchros, kinetic damping is accomplished by adding a mass or flywheel to the shaft and coupling it by friction to the shaft.[38] Thus, dissipation of energy occurs only when the relative velocity of flywheel and output differ. This latter technique is briefly considered in Chapter 9. The procedures whereby the more versatile phase-compensating techniques are accomplished are treated in Chapters 7 and 8.

3

Transient Response Using the Laplace Transform

1 General

Analyzing the behavior of closed-loop dynamical systems to any kind of disturbance creates one specific form of engineering problem. *Synthesizing* the physical closed loop to accomplish a given response for a given disturbance presents another problem decidedly more interesting to the modern designer. Increased complexity creates the need for symbolism or a shorthand system of expression similar to the shorthand of stenographic work to reduce the bulkiness of expressing the problem. Here the transform methods of analysis become of inestimable value.

The classical analysis [50] involves the preparation of differential equations to express dynamically the interrelationships of the physical quantities within the system. Any form of classical mathematics may be used to solve these differential equations, though even here operational methods are valuable. When synthesis must be accomplished, the treatment of the problem wholly in terms of differential equations leads to great complexity. Operational calculus is almost always used for manipulating the equations which are written for the control systems. Function theory is used to obtain compactness when defining the equations for groups of elements, or the functional relationships necessitated by the portion of the system that is synthesized to give the desired dynamic properties. As a matter of fact, a function theory approach to the problem appears to be the only effective one for this kind of work.

Operational calculus bears the same relationship to the simplification of the analyses of differential equations today as the use of complex numbers does to the solution of conventional electric circuits under the influence of alternating voltages.[51] It is fortunate that so many users of operational calculus are unwilling to use this form of mathematics as an engineering tool without asking the reasons why, because the clear appreciation of the underlying philosophy is a great aid to the direct application of the methods to synthesis. As the user finds operational calculus a familiar subject, he can treat differential equations algebraically as functions of a complex variable. He then loses the general state of awe which is attached to the name "theory of functions." Function theory is grown-up mathematical reasoning. For example, when differential equation theory is studied in the light of servomechanism synthesis, we first observe that many differential equations relating response and disturbance are completely unspecific. A guess must be established about the possible correct answers before any exact answer can be obtained. Such a guess is not a problem of random thinking. It can be guided by the observation that operators, relating the dependent and independent variables expressing the behavior of linear systems, must have definite algebraic forms. A finite number of physically realizable or practical systems can be obtained for the solution to a problem of synthesis. Upon extending this line of thought into the theory of functions we find that operators, which were formerly expressed as algebraic polynomials in operational calculus, become curved surfaces and zones on complex planes where certain areas or volumes are related to definite forms of dynamical response of systems being studied.

The ultimate objective of using operational calculus and the theory of functions for synthesis work, whether it is in the study of closed-loop systems or in completely unrelated fields, is to permit the user to acquire a mental dexterity of reasoning in a mathematical realm. By the acquisition of such dexterity, he can select suitable combinations of physical elements to arrange or fashion a properly designed machine. A very important property of the philosophy under discussion is that it gives a good picture of the overall characteristics of the system.

In order to illustrate certain matters of parallelism, as well as certain differences between the classical and operational methods, the classical method of solution of a differential equation is first summarized. An operational method using the Laplace Transform is then presented.

2   Solution of a Differential Equation by Classical Methods·

The solution of linear integro-differential equations by classical methods requires: (1) the formulation of the differential equation, (2) the determination of the roots of the characteristic equation, (3) the formulation of the complementary solution, (4) the formulation of the particular solution, (5) the insertion of known boundary or initial conditions to evaluate correctly the undetermined coefficients of the combined complementary and particular solutions.

The steps in the solution of Equation 2·78, which give the error response of the physical system shown in Figure 2·8, will now be restated to illustrate the classical mathematical approach to the solution of linear integro-differential equation.   Then Equation 2·78 becomes

$$\frac{d^2\varepsilon(t)}{dt^2} + 2\zeta\omega_n\frac{d\varepsilon(t)}{dt} + \omega_n{}^2\varepsilon(t) = \frac{d^2\theta_i(t)}{dt^2} + 2\zeta\omega_n\frac{d\theta_i(t)}{dt} + \frac{T_L(t)}{J} \quad (1)$$

where ζ and ω_n are parameters defined in Chapter 2, Section 8.   Assume that the load torque $T_L(t)$ is zero, that the system is initially at rest, and let the variable θ_i experience a sudden rate of change or step disturbance of velocity, frequently called a *unit function of velocity*.   This condition may be written mathematically as

$$\left.\begin{array}{l} t < 0, \quad \omega_i(t) = 0 \\[4pt] t = 0, \quad \omega_i(t) \text{ is indeterminate} \\[4pt] t > 0, \quad \omega_i(t) = |\,\omega_i\,| \end{array}\right\} \quad (2)$$

and represents the time-varying behavior of the input disturbance. Since the controlled member was initially at rest and had no rate of change at the time $t = 0+$ (the symbol $0+$ means an infinitesimally small period of time following the instant zero during which the disturbance occurs), the output quantity may be expressed as

$$\left.\begin{array}{l} \theta_o(0+) = 0 \\[4pt] \dfrac{d\theta_o(0+)}{dt} = 0 \end{array}\right\} \quad (3)$$

Since

$$\left.\begin{array}{l} \varepsilon(t) = \theta_i(t) - \theta_o(t) \\[4pt] \varepsilon(0+) = 0 \\[4pt] \dfrac{d\varepsilon(0+)}{dt} = |\,\omega_i\,| \end{array}\right\} \quad (3a)$$

Equations 3 and 3a comprise the boundary or initial conditions for the problem.   A specific solution can be found for $\varepsilon(t)$ at any time subsequent to the disturbance.

The forced or sustained solution, often called the particular integral in the classical method, may be found by one of several fundamental algebraic methods adequately described in any book on differential equation theory.[50]   However, when a step function disturbance is used, a relatively simple technique is applicable.   Specifically, since the disturbance is not varying with time except during the interval $0- < t < 0+$, all derivatives of $\varepsilon(t)$ may be set equal to zero to yield the desired steady-state solution.   This is permissible because in the steady state, when only the forced solution exists, there will be no time derivatives of output if the transient eventually must die away. The steady-state value of the error, $\mathcal{E}_{ss}$, is then found algebraically from Equation 1, which gives

Thus

$$\left.\begin{array}{c} \omega_n{}^2\mathcal{E}(\infty) = 2\zeta\omega_n\omega_i(\infty) \\[2mm] \mathcal{E}_{ss} = \dfrac{2\zeta\omega_i}{\omega_n} \end{array}\right\} \tag{4}$$

In addition to the steady-state solution, there must be added the unforced or force-free system response, sometimes called the complementary function. This part of the solution is found by setting the left-hand side of Equation 1 equal to zero, that is, making the forcing function zero. Thus

$$\frac{d^2\mathcal{E}(t)}{dt^2} + 2\zeta\omega_n\frac{d\mathcal{E}(t)}{dt} + \omega_n{}^2\mathcal{E}(t) = 0 \tag{5}$$

after which a substitution of the trial solution

$$\mathcal{E}(t) = e^{rt} \tag{6}$$

yields the determinental characteristic equation

$$r^2 + 2\zeta\omega_n r + \omega_n{}^2 = 0 \tag{7}$$

Solving for the roots r_1 and r_2 of Equation 7 makes possible the construction of the complementary function

$$\mathcal{E}(t) \text{ (complementary function)} = K_1 e^{r_1 t} + K_2 e^{r_2 t} \tag{8}$$

The complete solution for the differential equation 1 is then written

or

$$\left.\begin{array}{c} \mathcal{E}(t) = K_1 e^{r_1 t} + K_2 e^{r_2 t} + \mathcal{E}_{ss} \\[2mm] \mathcal{E}(t) = K_1 e^{r_1 t} + K_2 e^{r_2 t} + \dfrac{2\zeta\omega_i}{\omega_n} \end{array}\right\} \tag{9}$$

When the initial conditions of Equation 3a are applied to Equation 9, undetermined coefficients K_1 and K_2 of the complete solution can be found. The final result will have different dynamical modes of behavior, depending upon the nature of the roots r_1 and r_2, namely,

For conjugate complex roots

$$\left.\begin{array}{c} r = -\zeta\omega_n \pm j\omega_n\sqrt{1 - \zeta^2} \\[2mm] = a \pm jb \end{array}\right\} \tag{10}$$

giving

$$\mathcal{E}(t) = e^{at}[K_3 e^{jbt} + K_4 e^{-jbt}] + \mathcal{E}_{ss} \tag{10a}$$

For real but unlike roots

$$r = -\zeta\omega_n \pm \omega_n\sqrt{\zeta^2 - 1}$$
$$r = a \pm b$$
$$\left.\right\} \quad (11)$$

giving

$$\varepsilon(t) = K_5 e^{(a+b)t} + K_6 e^{(a-b)t} + \varepsilon_{ss} \qquad (11a)$$

For real and identical roots

$$r = -\zeta\omega_n \pm jo$$
$$r_1 = r_2 = a$$
$$\left.\right\} \quad (12)$$

giving

$$\varepsilon(t) = K_7 e^{at} + K_8 t e^{at} + \varepsilon_{ss} \qquad (12a)$$

The solution of most general interest is that for $\zeta < 1$ as given by Equation 10a. It is noted that the exponentials in this equation have complex exponents. But the solution $\varepsilon(t)$ is a real quantity; hence, a real equivalent form for Equation 10a must exist.

The equivalent form follows from the expansions of $e^{\pm jbt}$ into the form

$$K_3 e^{jbt} = K_3 \cos bt + K_3 j \sin bt$$
$$K_4 e^{-jbt} = K_4 \cos bt - K_4 j \sin bt$$
$$\left.\right\} \quad (13)$$

which, when substituted in Equation 10a, gives

$$\varepsilon(t) = e^{at}[(K_3 + K_4) \cos bt + j(K_3 - K_4) \sin bt] + \varepsilon_{ss}$$

which, since $(K_3 + K_4)$ and $j(K_3 - K_4)$ must be real quantities and hence K_3 and K_4 are conjugates, may be written

$$\varepsilon(t) = e^{at}[K_9 \cos bt + K_{10} \sin bt] + \varepsilon_{ss} \qquad (13a)$$

where

$$K_9 = K_3 + K_4$$

$$K_{10} = j(K_3 - K_4)$$

The constant K_9 may be evaluated by applying the boundary condition of Equation 3a, namely that at $t = 0+$, $\varepsilon(t) = 0$; thus Equation 13a becomes

$$0 = K_9 + \varepsilon_{ss}$$

or

$$K_9 = -\varepsilon_{ss} = -\frac{2\zeta\omega_i}{\omega_n} \qquad (14)$$

The other constant K_{10} must be evaluated for the second boundary condition of Equation 3a, namely, that at $t = 0+$, $d\varepsilon/dt = \omega_i$.

Differentiating, Equation 13a gives

$$\frac{d\varepsilon}{dt} = ae^{at}[K_9 \cos bt + K_{10} \sin bt] + e^{at}[-K_9 b \sin bt + K_{10} b \cos bt]$$

which, when $t = 0+$, reduces to

$$\omega_i = aK_9 + K_{10}b$$

$$= -a\varepsilon_{ss} + K_{10}b$$

giving

$$K_{10} = \frac{\omega_i + a\varepsilon_{ss}}{b}$$

The substitution of a and b from Equation 10 gives

$$K_{10} = \frac{\omega_i[1 - 2\zeta^2]}{\omega_n\sqrt{1 - \zeta^2}} \tag{14a}$$

The complete solution for Equation 10a is then

$$\varepsilon(t) = \frac{2\zeta\omega_i}{\omega_n} + e^{-\zeta\omega_n t}\left[-\frac{2\zeta\omega_i}{\omega_n} \cos \sqrt{1 - \zeta^2}\,\omega_n t \right.$$

$$\left. + \frac{\omega_i(1 - 2\zeta^2)}{\omega_n\sqrt{1 - \zeta^2}} \sin \sqrt{1 - \zeta^2}\,\omega_n t \right]$$

$$= \frac{2\zeta\omega_i}{\omega_n} - \frac{2\zeta\omega_i}{\omega_n} e^{-\zeta\omega_n t}\left[\cos \sqrt{1 - \zeta^2}\,\omega_n t \right.$$

$$\left. + \frac{2\zeta^2 - 1}{2\zeta\sqrt{1 - \zeta^2}} \sin \sqrt{1 - \zeta^2}\,\omega_n t \right] \tag{15}$$

or, in dimensionless form,

$$\frac{\varepsilon(t)}{\varepsilon_{ss}} = 1 + \frac{e^{-\zeta\omega_n t}}{2\zeta\sqrt{1 - \zeta^2}} \cos (\sqrt{1 - \zeta^2}\,\omega_n t - 90 - \phi) \tag{15a}$$

where

$$\left.\begin{array}{c} \phi = \tan^{-1}\dfrac{2\zeta\sqrt{1 - \zeta^2}}{1 - 2\zeta^2} \\[4mm] \varepsilon_{ss} = \dfrac{2\zeta\omega_i}{\omega_n} \end{array}\right\} \tag{15b}$$

The solution of the differential equation for $\zeta = 1$ follows simply from Equation 15 by noting that, as the angle approaches zero, the cosine approaches unity and the sinc approaches the angle itself. Thus Equation 15 may be written

$$\mathcal{E}(t)_{\zeta \to 1} = \frac{2\omega_i}{\omega_n} - \frac{2\omega_i}{\omega_n} e^{-\omega_n t} \left[1 + \left(\frac{2\zeta^2 - 1}{2\zeta\sqrt{1 - \zeta^2}} \right) \left(\sqrt{1 - \zeta^2}\, \omega_n t \right) \right]$$

$$= \frac{2\omega_i}{\omega_n} - \frac{2\omega_i}{\omega_n} e^{-\omega_n t} \left[1 + \frac{\omega_n t}{2} \right]$$

or for $\zeta = 1$,

$$\frac{\mathcal{E}(t)}{\mathcal{E}_{ss}} = 1 - e^{-\omega_n t} \left[1 + \frac{\omega_n t}{2} \right]$$

and

$$\mathcal{E}_{ss} = \frac{2\omega_i}{\omega_n}$$

(15c)

The solution for $\zeta > 1$ follows from Equation 15 by noting that $-j \sin jx = \sinh x$ and $\cos jx = \cosh x$. Typical solutions for $\zeta > 1$ are given in Table 2·1.

In summarizing, it can be stated that the task of solving a linear differential equation is basically one of meeting boundary values. The complete solution is the sum of the force-free plus the forced solution, which taken together meet the boundary value requirements at $t = 0+$. The number of exponential terms, real or complex, in the force-free solution equals the number of roots of the determinantal equation. This number equals the order of the equation and equals the number of independent energy storage elements in the system under consideration. Clearly, the labor involved increases rapidly as the number of energy storage elements increases.

The general form of Equations 10a, 11a, and 12a indicate that, for dynamical systems having greater than a first-order differential equation, there are certain modes of behavior associated with certain types of roots of the characteristic equation. The three forms listed above indicate respectively the underdamped, overdamped, and critical damped behavior of a system having only two energy storages.

Any linear physical system can be analyzed by the classical, mathematical approach as outlined. However, when *both* the input disturbance $\theta_i(t)$ and the output response $\theta_o(t)$ are specified, the task of finding the functional relation between the numerous elements in the system to satisfy a given physical problem is more complex by a whole order and requires a more advanced approach. In the first place, the only way the two quantities $\theta_i(t)$ and $\theta_o(t)$ can be initially related is by means of an operator because no provision has been set down for writing a general differential equation whose terms are general and unspecified. Although classical mathematics can be altered to accommodate the synthesis problem in some measure, it is more natural to turn to the operational calculus for its solution because of the compactness of the procedure and the greater advantages that result from reasoning in an operational manner.

3   Operational Mathematics—Laplace Transforms

Operational mathematics is a shorthand method for solving differential equations and for reasoning in terms of them.   There are many forms of operational calculus, but the one that appears to be most reliable and that seems to be gaining greatest popularity today is based upon the Laplace transformation.   The Laplace transformation permits a transformation from one domain to another through the use of the Laplace integral.   In the analysis of linear control systems, the Laplace transform brings about a change from the time domain, in which the dynamical behavior of the system is expressed in the differential equation, to a functional domain, in which the differential equation is expressed as an algebraic relationship.   These functional expressions can be manipulated by the laws governing ordinary algebra, even though the variable is really a complex quantity.   After the original transformation, certain manipulations enable us to orthogonalize the mathematical forms and to perform an *inverse transformation* which returns the dynamical problem again to a time domain, but in such a manner that the solution to the original differential equation has been obtained.

The basic mathematics for this so-called operational calculus has been thoroughly developed and can be found in a number of mathematics textbooks dealing with functions of a complex variable.[52]   In the electrical engineering field, especially, the transform method is widely applied.   This is true to a much greater degree than is usually realized.   Steady-state alternating current circuit theory can be readily derived using the transform integral.   Fourier series analysis relates to a similar form of integral.   This is also true of Heaviside operational calculus. All three of these techniques were developed for engineering usage without always conforming to rigorous mathematics and at times without even knowledge of the existence of the transform integral.   Consequently, each is subject to conditions which limit its field of application. This is the price paid for engineering simplification.

The Heaviside operational calculus was developed to facilitate the study of transient problems.   It has, however, grown to be one of the most widely used tools for all problems involving transient conditions following an initial state of equilibrium.   It would seem that this technique would be most admirably suited to the study of servomechanisms. It is not, however, altogether the case. That the disturbance should be of one kind only and that the system should be initially at equilibrium are conditions which are often confining. It is, however, possible for one thoroughly versed in the method to avoid pitfalls associated with an attempt to overcome one or the other of the conditions. In general this is a situation which places an unfair burden on the engineering student. The unfairness lies in the fact that a more rigorous approach to the study of transient behavior is available in a form more readily assimilated than much of the Heaviside technique. This is the approach derived directly from the application of the Laplace transform integral and usually called the Laplace method.

It should be noted here that, once the Laplace method is mastered, the elementary Heaviside techniques as too often misapplied are immediately apparent. It will also be observed that the two methods can be used interchangeably in many cases. It is well for the student to be aware of this fact since he will undoubtedly be required to talk in terms of both methods after he enters the engineering field.

A firm groundwork in the Laplace method is of great value for a wide understanding of the dynamics of closed-loop control. However, the scope of this book cannot possibly include a complete treatment of the subject. Therefore, only the rudiments needed to develop the operational notation can be presented. The reader is referred to the book *Transients in Linear Systems*,[48] by Gardner and Barnes, for a comprehensive treatment of the subject.

4 Laplace Transform Symbolism

A distinction is made between a function of time and a function of the transform variable by the following definition or symbolism:

$$F(s) \triangleq \mathcal{L}f(t) \tag{16}$$

in which

$$\left.\begin{array}{l} F(s) \text{ is a function of the transform variable } s \\ s \text{ is a complex variable of the form } \sigma + j\omega \\ \triangleq \text{ denotes equality by definition} \\ \mathcal{L} \text{ denotes application of transform integral} \\ f(t) \text{ is a function of time} \end{array}\right\} \tag{17}$$

For example, suppose a length x varies as a function of time and is denoted as $x(t)$. When this function is transformed it is written $X(s)$. The equation defining the relationship is

$$X(s) \triangleq \mathcal{L}x(t) \tag{18}$$

The transform integral, which is simply denoted above by the symbol $\mathcal{L}$, in its complete form is

$$F(s) \triangleq \int_0^\infty f(t)e^{-st}\, dt \tag{19}$$

This relationship is the basis for all operational transforms used herein for the study of linear closed-loop systems. It should be understood that there are limitations on the application of Equation 19 when considered in terms of generalized mathematics. If, however, $f(t)$ is always a linear differential equation with a finite number of terms, the integral equation 19 may be applied without qualification. That is to say, for lumped parameter linear systems the identities derived from Equation 19 are applicable.

5 Illustrative Transforms

The subsequent illustrations apply the direct transform integral to typical time functions found in servomechanism studies. They follow the pattern given by Gardner and Barnes.[48]

1. *Unit step function* $u(t)$

$$\text{Symbolically } \mathcal{L}[u(t)] = U(s) \tag{20}$$

A graph of this function is shown in Figure 1. The transform of this function is given as

$$U(s) = \int_0^\infty 1 \cdot e^{-st}\, dt = \left[-\frac{1}{s} e^{-st} \right]_0^\infty \tag{21}$$

$$= \frac{1}{s}(-e^{-s\infty} + e^0) = \frac{1}{s} \tag{22}$$

Thus

$$\mathcal{L}[u(t)] = U(s) = \frac{1}{s} \tag{23}$$

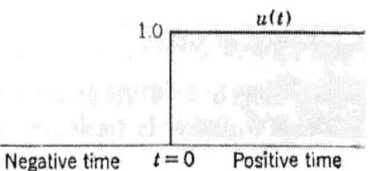

FIGURE 1. Unit function.

2. *Exponential decay* $f(t) = e^{-\alpha t}$

Where α is real or complex,

$$F(s) = \int_0^\infty e^{-\alpha t} e^{-st}\, dt = \int_0^\infty e^{-(s+\alpha)t}\, dt = \frac{1}{s + \alpha} \qquad (24)$$

Thus

$$\mathcal{L}[e^{-\alpha t}] = \frac{1}{s + \alpha} \qquad (25)$$

3. *Sinusoid* $f(t) = \sin \beta t$

$$F(s) = \int_0^\infty \sin \beta t\, e^{-st}\, dt$$

$$= \frac{1}{2j} \int_0^\infty (e^{j\beta t} - e^{-j\beta t}) e^{-st}\, dt \qquad (26)$$

$$= \frac{1}{2j} \int_0^\infty [e^{-(s-j\beta)t} - e^{-(s+j\beta)t}]\, dt \qquad (27)$$

$$= \frac{1}{2j}\left(\frac{1}{s - j\beta} - \frac{1}{s + j\beta}\right) = \frac{\beta}{s^2 + \beta^2} \qquad (28)$$

Thus

$$\mathcal{L}[\sin \beta t] = \frac{\beta}{s^2 + \beta^2} \qquad (29)$$

These three examples serve to illustrate the method by which transform pairs are derived. For convenience, transform pairs frequently used in closed-loop system studies are given in Table 1. For a more complete listing of transform pairs, the reader is referred to Gardner and Barnes.[48] It is possible, using the methods outlined in the above examples, to derive any of the pairs listed in the tables.

6   Commonly Used Transform Theorems

In addition to the transform integral, there are several theorems relating to the use of transforms that are much used in this work.

Linearity Theorem.

(1) If $Af(t)$ is a transformable function in which A is a constant, then

$$\mathcal{L}[Af(t)] = A\mathcal{L}[f(t)] = AF(s) \qquad (30)$$

(2) If $f_1(t)$ and $f_2(t)$ are transformable time functions, then

$$\mathcal{L}[f_1(t) + f_2(t)] = F_1(s) + F_2(s) \qquad (31)$$

TABLE 1—DIMENSIONLESS $\mathcal{L}$ TRANSFORM PAIRS

No.	$F(s)$	$f(t)$ $0 \leq t$	Comment
1	$1/s$	1 or $u(t)$	Unit function or step function
2	$\dfrac{1}{\tau s + 1}$	$\dfrac{1}{\tau}e^{(-t/\tau)}$	Exponential lag
3	$\dfrac{\omega}{s^2 + \omega^2}$	$\sin \omega t$	
4	$\dfrac{s}{s^2 + \omega^2}$	$\cos \omega t$	
5	$\dfrac{1}{s^2 + 2\zeta\omega_n s + \omega_n^2}$	$\zeta < 1,\ \dfrac{1}{\omega_n \sqrt{1-\zeta^2}} e^{-\zeta\omega_n t} \sin \omega_n \sqrt{1-\zeta^2}\, t$	Underdamped quadratic factor
		$\zeta = 1,\ te^{-\omega_n t}$	Critically damped quadratic factor
		$\zeta > 1,\ \dfrac{1}{\omega_n \sqrt{\zeta^2-1}} e^{-\zeta\omega_n t} \sinh \omega_n \sqrt{\zeta^2-1}\, t$	Overdamped quadratic factor
6	$1/s^2$	t	
7	$1/s^n$	$\dfrac{1}{(n-1)!} t^{(n-1)}$	
8	$\dfrac{1}{(\tau s + 1)^n}$	$\dfrac{1}{(n-1)!} \dfrac{t^{(n-1)}}{\tau^n} e^{(-t/\tau)}$	nth order exponential lag
9	$\dfrac{1}{s} e^{-as}$	$u(t-a)$	Delayed unit function, step function lag
10	$\dfrac{1}{s}(1 - e^{-bs})$	$u(t) - u(t-b) \quad b > o$	Impulse of b time units in duration beginning at time $t = 0$
11	$\dfrac{1}{s}(e^{-as} - e^{-bs})$	$u(t-a) - u(t-b) \quad b > a$	Impulse of $b - a$ time units in duration delayed by the time $t = a$

Example. The terms of a linear differential equation with constant coefficients may be transformed separately and the transformed terms added. The constant coefficients are carried over to the transformed equation unaltered.

Real Differentiation Theorem. If $f(t)$ is a transformable time function, then

$$\mathcal{L}\left[\frac{d}{dt}f(t)\right] = sF(s) - f(0+) \tag{32}$$

The term "real" in this case refers to the *real domain* or untransformed state, that is, $f(t)$ is not a vector function. The transformed state is denoted as the *complex domain*. The way this theorem may be derived from the transform integral, following the treatment given in Gardner and Barnes, is to write the integral

$$\int_0^\infty f(t)e^{-st}\,dt = F(s) \tag{33}$$

Then using the method of integration by parts, let $u = f(t)$ and $dv = e^{-st}\,dt$ in

$$\int u\,dv = uv - \int v\,du \tag{34}$$

This gives

$$\int_0^\infty f(t)e^{-st}\,dt = -\frac{1}{s}f(t)e^{-st}\Big|_0^\infty + \frac{1}{s}\int_0^\infty\left[\frac{df(t)}{dt}\right]e^{-st}\,dt \tag{35}$$

$$= \frac{f(0+)}{s} + \frac{1}{s}\int_0^\infty\left[\frac{df(t)}{dt}\right]e^{-st}\,dt \tag{36}$$

Rearranging terms and multiplying by s give

$$\int_0^\infty\left[\frac{df(t)}{dt}\right]e^{-st}\,dt = s\int_0^\infty f(t)e^{-st}\,dt - f(0+) \tag{37}$$

Thus

$$\mathcal{L}\left[\frac{d}{dt}f(t)\right] = sF(s) - f(0+) \tag{38}$$

Example.

$$\mathcal{L}\left[k\frac{dy}{dt}\right] = k[sY(s) - y(0+)] \tag{39}$$

in which $y(0+)$ is the value of y when time is zero as approached by diminishing positive time, that is, as the origin is approached from the right in a y versus t plot.

Second derivatives may be treated as two first derivatives taken successively, namely,

$$\mathcal{L}\left[\frac{df(t)}{dt}\right] = sF(s) - f(0+) \tag{40}$$

hence,

$$\mathcal{L}\left[\frac{d^2f(t)}{dt^2}\right] = \mathcal{L}\left[\frac{d}{dt}\left(\frac{d}{dt}f(t)\right)\right] = s^2F(s) - sf(0+) - \frac{df}{dt}(0+) \tag{41}$$

in which $df(0+)/dt$ denotes the first derivative of the function evaluated at $t = (0+)$.

Similarly the third derivative becomes

$$\mathcal{L}\left[\frac{d^3f(t)}{dt^3}\right] = s^3F(s) - s^2f(0+) - s\frac{df(0+)}{dt} - \frac{d^2f(0+)}{dt^2} \tag{41a}$$

Real Integration Theorem.　If $f(t)$ is a transformable time function, its time integral is also transformable and has the following form:

$$\mathcal{L}\left[\int f(t)\,dt\right] = \frac{F(s)}{s} + \frac{1}{s}\left[\int f(t)\,dt\right]\Bigg|_{t=0+} \tag{42}$$

in which

$$\left[\int f(t)\,dt\right]\Bigg|_{t=0+}$$

means the value of the integral at $t = 0+$ and is sometimes denoted by $f^{-1}(0+)$. The proof of the above theorem will be omitted with the statement that it can be proved in a manner similar to that used for the real differentiation theorem.

Final Value Theorem.　A definite relation exists between the value of $f(t)$ when t approaches infinity and the value of the transform $F(s)$ when s approaches zero. The so-called final value theorem, which specifically states this relation, enables us to determine the steady-state or static sensitivities of various dynamic elements. It also provides a quick means for checking the validity of response given by the transform equations. For example, a network containing resistance, capacitance and inductance may have differential equations too complicated to solve in a short time for the exact transient behavior. The steady-state currents flowing at any place in the physical network can be quickly predicted by the use of the final value theorem, except when $f(t)$ is sinusoidal or increasing with time.

The theorem as generally stated is

$$\operatorname*{limit}_{s \to 0} sF(s) = \operatorname*{limit}_{t \to \infty} f(t) \tag{43}$$

where $f(t)$ is the time function following a sudden constant disturbance.

As an example, consider that a physical system is defined by the differential equation

$$\tau \frac{d\omega(t)}{dt} + \omega(t) = e(t)$$

When subjected to a sudden change of the disturbing function $|e|u(t)$ it has the transform

$$\Omega(s) = \frac{1}{\tau s + 1} |e| \frac{1}{s}$$

from which the time solution is

$$\omega(t) = |e|[1 - e^{-(t/\tau)}]$$

The application of the final value theorem shows that

$$\left.\begin{array}{l}
\operatorname*{limit}_{s \to 0} [s\Omega(s)] = \operatorname*{limit}_{s \to 0} s \left[\frac{1}{\tau s + 1} |e| \frac{1}{s} \right] = |e| \\[2mm]
\text{and} \\[1mm]
\operatorname*{limit}_{t \to \infty} [\omega(t)] = \operatorname*{limit}_{t \to \infty} |e|[1 - e^{-(t/\tau)}] = |e|
\end{array}\right\} \tag{44}$$

Notice that the transform $1/(\tau s + 1)$ is for the undisturbed physical system. The transform $|e|(1/s)$ relates to the disturbance. Unless the disturbance is specifically known and included in $F(s)$ the relation of Equation 43 should be modified.

The Initial Value Theorem. The initial value theorem gives useful information about the behavior of a system at $t = 0+$ in a manner similar to that in which the final value theorem gives information at $t = \infty$. This theorem makes it possible to recognize initial conditions applied to the physical system. It permits the determination of the values of the time function at the instant $t = 0+$ when only the transform is known.

The theorem states that the behavior of $sF(s)$ in the neighborhood of the point $s = \infty$ in the s domain corresponds to the behavior of $f(t)$ in the neighborhood of $t = 0+$ in the time domain. That is,

$$\operatorname*{limit}_{s \to \infty} sF(s) = \operatorname*{limit}_{t \to 0} f(t) \tag{45}$$

where t is allowed to approach zero from positive value of time and $f(t)$ is the time solution following a sudden constant disturbance.

The use of the initial value theorem can be shown by considering the same problem used to illustrate the final value theorem.

Thus the initial speed $\omega(0+)$ is found from the time solution as

or

$$
\left.
\begin{array}{c}
\underset{t \to 0}{\text{limit}} \ [|\ e\ | (1 - e^{-t/\tau})] = 0 \\[2ex]
\underset{s \to \infty}{\text{limit}}\ s \left[\dfrac{1}{\tau s + 1} |\ e\ | \cdot \dfrac{1}{s} \right] = 0
\end{array}
\right\}
\tag{46}
$$

The same general precautions relative to the insertion of the system transform and the disturbance transform must be observed here as in the final value theorem.

7   Inverse Transformation

The inverse transformation, symbolized as $\mathcal{L}^{-1}$, is the operation for converting functions of s from the complex domain back into the time domain. Except for a few special cases where the inverse transformation is not unique, the inverse transform is the time function from which the particular transform was derived. Thus,

$$
\mathcal{L}^{-1}\left(\frac{1}{s}\right) = u(t) \text{ or } 1 = \text{unit step or constant} \tag{47}
$$

$$
\mathcal{L}^{-1}\left(\frac{1}{s + \alpha}\right) = e^{-\alpha t} \tag{48}
$$

$$
\mathcal{L}^{-1}\left(\frac{\beta}{s^2 + \beta^2}\right) = \sin \beta t \tag{49}
$$

As will be seen later, much use is made of the simple relation that $\mathcal{L}^{-1}\left(\dfrac{1}{s + \alpha}\right) = e^{-\alpha t}$. Even at this stage in the treatment of the subject, it is probably apparent to the student that when any problem in the transformed state may be represented as terms of the form $A/(s + \alpha)$, the solution in the time domain is given immediately as exponentials of the form, $Ae^{-\alpha t}$.

8   Transform of a Differential Equation

A rudimentary theory of Laplace transformations has been presented. It is now appropriate to apply the transform technique to the solution of a physical problem. The same problem formerly solved without detail in Chapter 2, relating to the system of Figure 2·8, will again be considered. The fundamental time relationship for this physical system, originally prepared in Equation 2·78, when the load is omitted, becomes

$$\left[\frac{d^2}{dt^2} + 2\zeta\omega_n\frac{d}{dt} + \omega_n^2\right]\varepsilon = \left[\frac{d^2}{dt^2} + 2\zeta\omega_n\frac{d}{dt}\right]\theta_i \tag{50}$$

Each term of Equation 50 is first transformed according to the previously stated theorems of Sections 5 and 6. These transformations * are tabulated term by term below:

$$\left.\begin{aligned}
\mathcal{L}\left[\frac{d^2\varepsilon}{dt^2}\right] &= s^2E(s) - s\varepsilon(0+) - \frac{d\varepsilon}{dt}(0+) \\[4pt]
\mathcal{L}\left[2\zeta\omega_n\frac{d\varepsilon}{dt}\right] &= 2\zeta\omega_n[sE(s) - \varepsilon(0+)] \\[4pt]
\mathcal{L}\left[\omega_n^2\varepsilon\right] &= \omega_n^2E(s) \\[4pt]
\mathcal{L}\left[\frac{d^2\theta_i}{dt^2}\right] &= s^2\theta_i(s) - s\theta_i(0+) - \frac{d\theta_i}{dt}(0+) \\[4pt]
\mathcal{L}\left[2\zeta\omega_n\frac{d\theta_i}{dt}\right] &= 2\zeta\omega_n[s\theta_i(s) - \theta_i(0+)]
\end{aligned}\right\} \tag{51}$$

Two undefined types of terms appear in the tabulation of the above equations. They are the external disturbance $\theta_i(s)$ and the initial values of $\theta_i(0+)$ and $d\theta_i(0+)/dt$. The appearance of the disturbance transform $\theta_i(s)$ and the initial conditions as an inherent part of the procedure is a departure from the other forms of operational calculus which should be noted and especially kept in mind because of the benefit it gives. Ordinarily the next step in the procedure for solving any problem of differential equations would be to define the nature of the disturbance applied to the physical system and to define the initial or terminal conditions expressing the state of behavior of the physical system at the instant the disturbance is applied. Holding these two problems momentarily, let us gather the terms in the tabulated transforms to write the transformed equation. Symbolically, we have taken the Laplace transform of each side of the differential equation

$$\mathcal{L}\left[\frac{d^2\varepsilon(t)}{dt^2} + \cdots\cdots\right] = \mathcal{L}\left[\frac{d^2\theta_i(t)}{dt^2} + \cdots\cdots\right] \tag{52}$$

* The reader will note that, in general, the symbols $x(t)$, $f(t)$, $e(t)$ become $X(s)$, $F(s)$, and $E(s)$ when transformed. Because it often becomes unnecessarily cumbersome to follow this convention, instances will be noted where $\mathcal{L}\varepsilon(t)$ is written as $E(s)$ or $\varepsilon(s)$, and $\mathcal{L}\theta_i(t)$ is written $\theta_i(s)$.

and have obtained

$$[s^2 + 2\zeta\omega_n s + \omega_n{}^2]E(s) = [s^2 + 2\zeta\omega_n s]\theta_i(s)$$

$$+\left[\frac{d\mathcal{E}}{dt}(0+) + 2\zeta\omega_n\mathcal{E}(0+) + s\mathcal{E}(0+)\right.$$

$$\left. - s\theta_i(0+) - \frac{d\theta_i}{dt}(0+) - 2\zeta\omega_n\theta_i(0+)\right] \quad (53)$$

When all the terms containing s related to the error $E(s)$ are collected on the left-hand side and when all the terms containing s related to $\theta_i(s)$ are collected on the right-hand side, it is noted that there are additional terms left over. These are purely numerical values which must be evaluated in terms of the initial conditions. One way of considering these additional terms is to place them on the right-hand side of the equal sign where they appear as a separate forcing function or as a separate disturbance which may be added to the primary or external disturbance by virtue of the theory of linear superposition. As will be seen later, use is made of this condition in deriving what are called the *system transform* and the *initial condition transform*. The former is used extensively in the functional analysis and synthesis for it characterizes wholly the nature of the physical system.

Assume that unit velocity $|\omega_i|$ is suddenly applied to the physical system shown in Figure $2\cdot8$. Then the input position can be expressed by

$$\theta_i(t) = |\omega_i|t \qquad (54)$$

and the relations

$$\mathcal{E}(t) = \theta_i(t) - \theta_o(t) \left.\vphantom{\frac{d\mathcal{E}(t)}{dt}}\right]$$
$$\frac{d\mathcal{E}(t)}{dt} = \frac{d\theta_i(t)}{dt} - \frac{d\theta_o(t)}{dt} \left.\vphantom{\frac{d\mathcal{E}(t)}{dt}}\right\} \qquad (55)$$

are available. If the physical system was initially at rest when the step function of velocity was applied, the initial conditions of Equation 53 are

$$\text{at } t = 0+\left\{\begin{array}{l}\theta_i(0+) = 0 \\[1mm] \theta_o(0+) = 0 \\[1mm] \dfrac{d\theta_i}{dt}(0+) = |\omega_i| \\[1mm] \dfrac{d\theta_o}{dt}(0+) = 0\end{array}\right\} \qquad (56)$$

where it must be noted that the state of the output at time $t = (0+)$ involves knowledge of the physical system.

From Equation 56, the initial conditions pertaining specifically to the error can be obtained using the difference equation expressed in Equation 55, such that

$$\left.\begin{aligned} \varepsilon(0+) &= \theta_i(0+) - \theta_o(0+) = 0 \\ \frac{d\varepsilon}{dt}(0+) &= \frac{d\theta_i}{dt}(0+) - \frac{d\theta_o}{dt}(0+) = \left|\,\omega_i\,\right| \end{aligned}\right\} \qquad (57)$$

The transform for $\theta_i(s)$ may now be obtained by applying the transform integral or referring to Table 1. Thus

$$\theta_i(s) = \mathcal{L}\left[\theta_i(t)\right] = \mathcal{L}\left[\left|\,\omega_i\,\right|t\right] = \frac{\left|\,\omega_i\,\right|}{s^2} \qquad (58)$$

When the results of Equations 56, 57, and 58 are placed in Equation 53, the completely defined algebraic relation for the error of the system is

$$[s^2 + 2\zeta\omega_n s + \omega_n{}^2]E(s) = +s^2\frac{\left|\,\omega_i\,\right|}{s^2} + 2\zeta\omega_n s\frac{\left|\,\omega_i\,\right|}{s^2} + \left|\,\omega_i\,\right| - \left|\,\omega_i\,\right| \qquad (59)$$

which gives

$$E(s) = \frac{(s + 2\zeta\omega_n)\,\omega_i}{s(s^2 + 2\zeta\omega_n s + \omega_n{}^2)} \qquad (60)$$

The reader should recognize the importance of retaining all the terms when performing the transformation of a differential equation. While experience may enable him to establish short cuts, the authors feel it is inadvisable to use the short form of writing the transformations by inspection and inserting initial conditions subsequently. Terms will inevitably be omitted from the solution. This omission may very well change the entire nature of the answer. Perhaps the greatest factor in support of the use of Laplace transform methods in the operational calculus, over all other existing methods, is the high degree of mathematical organization which can be obtained by this method. This organization is obtained with little effort once the user adopts a consistent plan of attack and a consistent method of manipulating the transform.

Equation 60 is an algebraic expression. It can be manipulated according to the ordinary laws of algebra. The objective of any manipulation is to obtain a recognizable function which can be inversely transformed by inspection. As stated in Section 6, the simple operational form $K/(s + \alpha)$ has the simple time function $Ke^{-\alpha t}$ as its inverse transform. This fact and the ease with which exponential time functions may be manipulated naturally lead us to seek means for expressing Equation 60 in a form that makes possible an easy return to the time domain.   One such approach to the objective is to change Equation 60 by means of a partial fraction expansion into terms of the form $K/(s+\alpha)$. Each term of the expansion is then inversely transformable by inspection.

To illustrate the inverse transformation, consider the right-hand side of Equation 60 to be made up of a fraction which is the ratio of two polynomials $A(s)$ and $B(s)$.   If these polynomials contain large numbers of terms arranged in descending order of the powers of the variable s, a general treatment can be made for the fraction.   For example, let $\phi(s) = A(s)/B(s)$, where $A(s)$ and $B(s)$ are mth and nth order polynomials in s respectively.

$$\phi(s) = \frac{A(s)}{B(s)} = \frac{a_m s^m + a_{m-1} s^{m-1} + a_{m-2} s^{m-2} + \cdots a_1 s + a_0}{b_n s^n + b_{n-1} s^{n-1} + b_{n-2} s^{n-2} + \cdots b_1 s + b_0} \quad (61)$$

If $A(s)/B(s)$ is improper, it can be reduced to

$$\frac{A(s)}{B(s)} = c_{m-n} s^{m-n} + c_{m-n-1} s^{m-n-1} + \cdots + \frac{A_1(s)}{B_1(s)} \quad (62)$$

where $A_1(s)/B_1(s)$ is now proper.

For ease of manipulation, assume that $A(s)/B(s)$ is proper.   Then $B(s)$ can be factored as

$$B(s) = (s - s_1)(s - s_2)(s - s_3) \cdots (s - s_{n-1})(s - s_n) \quad (63)$$

where all the roots of the polynomial $B(s)$ are unlike.   When the roots are obtained, the ratio $A(s)/B(s)$ is broken up into a sequence of terms where a general coefficient K appears in the numerator and the denominator is an individual factor in the expansion of $B(s)$ in Equation 63.   Thus

$$\frac{A(s)}{B(s)} = \frac{K_1}{s - s_1} + \frac{K_2}{s - s_2} + \cdots \frac{K_{n-1}}{s - s_{n-1}} + \frac{K_n}{s - s_n} \quad (64)$$

It is now necessary to obtain values for K_1, K_2, and K_3, for the partial fraction expansion, with known values of the roots s_1, s_2, s_3.   This is a problem of arithmetic.   There are easy and difficult ways to accomplish it.   Instead of attempting to solve for the coefficients in Equation 64 simultaneously, each side of the equation can be multiplied first by $(s - s_1)$, then by $(s - s_2)$, and so forth, and the method of limits can be used to give the constant.   The value of s is allowed to approach s_1 for the case involving multiplication by $(s - s_1)$.   It is then allowed to approach s_2 for the case involving $(s - s_2)$, and so on.   When the limit is taken, every term of the expansion will be zero except that having the form $(s - s_j)K_j/(s - s_j)$, which equals K_j.   Thus the coefficient of each term of the expansion is given by evaluating the general expression

$$K_j = \lim_{s \to s_j} \left[\frac{A(s)(s - s_j)}{B(s)} \right] \tag{65}$$

from which the specific coefficients K_1 and K_2 are

$$K_1 = \frac{A(s)(s - s_1)}{B(s)} \bigg|_{s=s_1} \tag{66}$$

$$K_2 = \frac{A(s)(s - s_2)}{B(s)} \bigg|_{s=s_2} \tag{67}$$

The form of Equation 65 is correct only for *nonrepeating roots*. When $B(s)$ has a repeating root, say the qth, that repeats n times, the partial fraction expansion becomes

$$\frac{A(s)}{B(s)} = \frac{K_{q1}}{(s - s_q)^n} + \frac{K_{q2}}{(s - s_q)^{n-1}} \cdots + \cdots$$

$$+ \frac{K_{qn}}{(s - s_q)} + \frac{K_1}{(s - s_1)} + \frac{K_m}{(s - s_m)} \tag{68}$$

The coefficient for the repeated root terms are found from

$$K_{q1} = \left\{ \frac{A(s)(s - s_q)^n}{B(s)} \right\} \bigg|_{s=s_q} \tag{69}$$

$$K_{q2} = \left\{ \frac{d}{ds} \frac{A(s)(s - s_q)^n}{B(s)} \right\} \bigg|_{s=s_q} \tag{70}$$

$$K_{qj} = \left\{ \frac{1}{(j-1)!} \frac{d^{j-1}}{ds^{j-1}} \left[\frac{A(s)(s - s_q)^n}{B(s)} \right] \right\} \bigg|_{s=s_q} \tag{71}$$

The coefficients for the regular terms K_1, K_2 are found as before in Equation 65.

9   Inverse Transformation of a Differential Equation

The inverse transformation of Equation 60 may now be performed to give the time solution to the differential equation. A numerical problem in which $\zeta = 0.6$ and $\omega_n = 20$ is treated simultaneously with the general problem to assist the reader in following the individual steps. The characteristic equation has the form

$$s(s^2 + 2\zeta\omega_n s + \omega_n^2) = 0 \tag{72}$$

$$s(s^2 + 24s + 400) = 0 \tag{72a}$$

for which the form

$$(s - s_0)(s - s_1)(s - s_2) \tag{73}$$

is specifically

$$(s + 0)(s + \zeta\omega_n + j\omega_n\sqrt{1 - \zeta^2})(s + \zeta\omega_n - j\omega_n\sqrt{1 - \zeta^2}) = 0 \tag{74}$$

$$(s + 0)(s + 12 + j20\sqrt{1 - 0.36})(s + 12 - j20\sqrt{1 - 0.36}) = 0 \tag{74a}$$

giving

$$E(s) = \frac{A(s)}{B(s)}$$

$$= \frac{(s + 2\zeta\omega_n)\omega_i}{(s + 0)(s + \zeta\omega_n + j\omega_n\sqrt{1 - \zeta^2})(s + \zeta\omega_n - j\omega_n\sqrt{1 - \zeta^2})} \tag{75}$$

$$= \frac{(s + 2\zeta\omega_n)\omega_i}{(s + 0)(s + \zeta\omega_n + j\omega)(s + \zeta\omega_n - j\omega)} \tag{76}$$

$$= \frac{(s + 24)\omega_i}{(s + 0)(s + 12 + j16)(s + 12 - j16)} \tag{76a}$$

where

$$\omega = \omega_n\sqrt{1 - \zeta^2} \tag{77}$$

$$16 = 20\sqrt{1 - 0.36} \tag{77a}$$

Plotting the three roots for the denominator of Equation 76 on the s plane gives three first-order poles. The one for $s = 0$ is located at the origin. The other two being conjugates are symmetrically located in the left-hand half plane. The plot is shown in Figure 2. Note that the position of the roots on the s plane are geometrically related to the damping ratio and the damped natural frequency of the closed loop. The meaning of the plots of complex functions of the algebraic polynomials is discussed in a general way in Chapter 6. Nevertheless, it is a well-recognized theorem that no roots for the denominator of Equation 76 may lie in the right-hand half plane of Figure 2. If they do, the physical system will be unstable and will exhibit oscillatory behavior

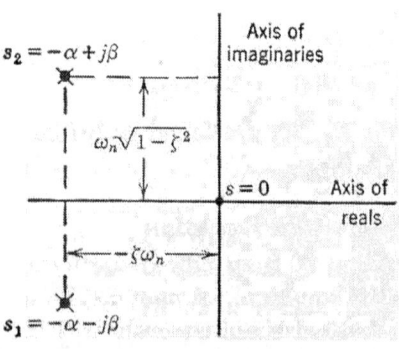

FIGURE 2.   Roots plotted on the s plane.

that is destructive in nature. No conjugate roots may lie on the imaginary axis, and no multiple-order zero roots at the origin.

The coefficients K_0, K_1, and K_2 of the partial fraction expansion of Equation 76 should now be determined. For the root at $s = 0$, the coefficient K_0 is given by

$$K_0 = \frac{(s + 2\zeta\omega_n)\omega_i}{(s^2 + 2\zeta\omega_n s + \omega_n{}^2)}\bigg|_{s=0}$$

$$= \frac{2\zeta\omega_i}{\omega_n} \tag{78}$$

$$= \frac{(s + 24)\omega_i}{s^2 + 24s + 400}\bigg|_{s=0}$$

$$= 0.06\omega_i \tag{78a}$$

For the root at $s = -\zeta\omega_n - j\omega$,

$$K_1 = \frac{(s + \zeta\omega_n + j\omega)(s + 2\zeta\omega_n)\omega_i}{(s + \zeta\omega_n + j\omega)(s + \zeta\omega_n - j\omega)s}\bigg|_{s=-\zeta\omega_n-j\omega} \tag{79}$$

$$= \frac{(-\zeta\omega_n - j\omega + 2\zeta\omega_n)\omega_i}{(-\zeta\omega_n - j\omega + \zeta\omega_n - j\omega)(-\zeta\omega_n - j\omega)} \tag{80}$$

$$= \frac{(\zeta - j\sqrt{1 - \zeta^2})\omega_i}{-2j\omega[-\zeta - j\sqrt{1 - \zeta^2}]} \tag{81}$$

$$= \frac{s + 24}{s(s + 12 - j16)}\bigg|_{s=-12-j16} \tag{79a}$$

$$= \frac{(12 - j16)\omega_i}{-2j16(-12 - j16)} \tag{80a}$$

$$= \frac{(0.6 - j0.8)\omega_i}{-2j16(-0.6 - j0.8)} \tag{81a}$$

Since the roots of the quadratic factor are a conjugate complex pair, it can be proved that the coefficients K_1 and K_2 of the partial fraction expansion resulting from these roots will likewise be a conjugate complex pair. In order to see this, it is best to rationalize the coefficient K_1 given in Equation 81 by multiplying the numerator and denominator by $-\zeta + j\sqrt{1 - \zeta^2}$ and then changing K_1 from a vector in Cartesian coordinates to a vector in polar coordinates. The details of this algebraic step are left for the reader to complete, but the result is

$$K_1 = \frac{e^{+j(\phi+90)}}{2\omega_n\sqrt{1-\zeta^2}}\,\omega_i \tag{82}$$

$$= \frac{e^{j163.74°}}{32}\,\omega_i \tag{82a}$$

where

$$\phi = \tan^{-1}\frac{2\zeta\sqrt{1-\zeta^2}}{1-2\zeta^2} \tag{83}$$

$$= \tan^{-1}\frac{0.96}{0.28} = 73.74° \tag{83a}$$

The value for K_2, equal to the conjugate of K_1, is obtained by using the conjugate root

$$s_2 = -\zeta\omega_n + j\omega \tag{84}$$

$$= -12 + j16 \tag{84a}$$

which then gives a value for K_2 using identical algebraic steps as for K_1. Thus

$$K_2 = \frac{e^{-j(\phi+90)}}{2\omega_n\sqrt{1-\zeta^2}}\,\omega_i \tag{85}$$

$$= \frac{e^{-j163.74°}}{32}\,\omega_i \tag{85a}$$

It is now possible to perform inverse transformation using the results obtained thus far. By using Equations 78, 82, and 85, the transformed Equation 60 becomes

$$E(s) = \frac{K_0}{s-s_0} + \frac{K_1}{s-s_1} + \frac{K_2}{s-s_2} \tag{86}$$

$$\mathcal{L}^{-1}E(s) = \mathcal{L}^{-1}\left[\frac{K_0}{s-s_0} + \frac{K_1}{s-s_1} + \frac{K_2}{s-s_2}\right] \tag{87}$$

$$\mathcal{L}^{-1}E(s) = \mathcal{L}^{-1}\left[\frac{K_0}{s-s_0}\right] + \mathcal{L}^{-1}\left[\frac{K_1}{s-s_1}\right] + \mathcal{L}^{-1}\left[\frac{K_2}{s-s_2}\right] \tag{88}$$

$$\mathcal{E}(t) = K_0 e^{s_0 t} + K_1 e^{s_1 t} + K_2 e^{s_2 t} \tag{89}$$

For the particular values of K and s, Equation 89 becomes

$$\mathcal{E}(t) = \frac{2\zeta\omega_i}{\omega_n}e^{-0t} + \frac{\omega_i e^{j(\phi+90)}}{2\omega_n\sqrt{1-\zeta^2}} \cdot e^{[-\zeta\omega_n - j\omega]t}$$

$$+ \frac{\omega_i e^{-j(\phi+90)}}{2\omega_n\sqrt{1-\zeta^2}} \cdot e^{[-\zeta\omega_n + j\omega]t} \tag{90}$$

$$= 0.06\omega_i + \frac{\omega_i}{32}e^{j163.74°} \cdot e^{(-12-j16)t} + \frac{\omega_i}{32}e^{-j163.74°} \cdot e^{(-12+j16)t} \tag{90a}$$

Since the vector sum of a pair of conjugate complex vectors is twice the real part of either, Equation 90 may be written as

$$\mathcal{E}(t) = \frac{2\zeta\omega_i}{\omega_n} + \frac{\omega_i e^{-\zeta\omega_n t}}{2\omega_n\sqrt{1-\zeta^2}}[2 \text{ Real part of } e^{j[\omega t - \phi - 90]}] \tag{91}$$

$$= 0.06\omega_i + \frac{\omega_i}{32}e^{-12t}[2 \text{ Real part of } e^{j(16t - 163.74°)}] \tag{91a}$$

$$\mathcal{E}(t) = \frac{2\zeta\omega_i}{\omega_n}\left\{1 + \frac{e^{-\zeta\omega_n t}}{2\zeta\sqrt{1-\zeta^2}}\cos[\omega_n t\sqrt{1-\zeta^2} - 90 - \phi]\right\} \tag{92}$$

where

$$\phi = \tan^{-1}\frac{2\zeta\sqrt{1-\zeta^2}}{1-2\zeta^2} \tag{93}$$

$$\mathcal{E}(t) = 0.06\omega_i\left\{1 + \frac{e^{-12t}}{0.96}\cos(16t - 163.74°)\right\} \tag{94}$$

The result shown by Equation 92 is identical with that given by Equation 15a and in Table 2·1 for a velocity input disturbance ω_i and $\zeta < 1$. The solution is plotted in Figure 2·10 with dimensionless ordinate $\mathcal{E}(t)/\mathcal{E}_{ss}$, abscissa $\omega_n t$, and ζ as a parameter.

It may appear from a hasty comparison of the work involved in Sections 2 and 8 that the effort required to reach the result shown in Equation 15a by classical methods is less than that required to reach the same result as shown in Equation 92 by transform methods. While there may be little to choose between the methods when only second-order differential equations are involved, the score is greatly in favor of the transform method when higher order problems are involved. One reason, of course, for the apparent lengthiness of the transform method as here illustrated is the inclusion of rules for partial fraction expansion and its application to the inverse transform operation.

10   Derivation of Transfer Function

Reference to the work of Section 8 indicates that the transform of the basic differential equation leads to the concept of a system function as well as an initial condition function. This fact will now be developed to show the significance of a *system transfer function*.

During the analysis of the elementary servomechanism in Chapter 2, the differential equation relating error $\mathcal{E}(t)$ and the output $\theta_o(t)$ was shown to be

$$J\frac{d^2\theta_o(t)}{dt^2} + f\frac{d\theta_o(t)}{dt} = k\mathcal{E}(t) \tag{95}$$

or in dimensionless form using closed-loop parameters

$$\frac{d^2\theta_o(t)}{dt^2} + 2\zeta\omega_n\frac{d\theta_o(t)}{dt} = \omega_n{}^2\mathcal{E}(t) \tag{96}$$

If the procedure of Section 8 is now followed and the transform of Equation 96 is taken, each term is

$$\mathcal{L}\left[\frac{d^2\theta_o}{dt^2}\right] = s^2\theta_o(s) - s\theta_o(0+) - \frac{d\theta_o}{dt}(0+) \tag{97}$$

$$\mathcal{L}\left[2\zeta\omega_n\frac{d\theta_o}{dt}\right] = 2\zeta\omega_n[s\theta_o(s) - \theta_o(0+)] \tag{98}$$

$$\mathcal{L}[\omega_n{}^2\mathcal{E}(t)] = \omega_n{}^2E(s) \tag{99}$$

which, when substituted into Equation 96, gives

$$\omega_n{}^2E(s) = s^2\theta_o(s) - s\theta_o(0+) - \frac{d\theta_o}{dt}(0+) + 2\zeta\omega_n[s\theta_o(s) - \theta_o(0+)] \tag{100}$$

or

$$\frac{1}{\omega_n{}^2}[s^2\theta_o(s) + 2\zeta\omega_n s\theta_o(s)]$$
$$= E(s) + \frac{1}{\omega_n{}^2}[s\theta_o(0+) + \frac{d\theta_o}{dt}(0+) + 2\zeta\omega_n\theta_o(0+)] \tag{101}$$

which gives

$$\theta_o(s) = \underbrace{\frac{1}{s\left[\dfrac{s}{\omega_n{}^2} + \dfrac{2\zeta}{\omega_n}\right]}E(s)}_{\substack{\text{Transfer function} \\ \text{or operator}}} + \underbrace{\frac{\dfrac{1}{\omega_n{}^2}\left[s\theta_o(0+) + \dfrac{d\theta_o}{dt}(0+) + 2\zeta\omega_n\theta_o(0+)\right]}{s\left[\dfrac{s}{\omega_n{}^2} + \dfrac{2\zeta}{\omega_n}\right]}}_{\text{Initial condition operator}} \tag{102}$$

Much significance attaches to the term

$$\frac{1}{s\left[\dfrac{s}{\omega_n{}^2} + \dfrac{2\zeta}{\omega_n}\right]} \text{ of Equation 102}$$

When it can be assumed that all the initial conditions are zero, Equation 102 reduces to

$$\frac{\theta_o(s)}{E(s)} = \frac{1}{s\left[\dfrac{s}{\omega_n{}^2} + \dfrac{2\zeta}{\omega_n}\right]} \tag{103}$$

giving

$$\frac{\theta_o(s)}{E(s)} = \frac{\dfrac{\omega_n}{2\zeta}}{s\left[\dfrac{s}{2\zeta\omega_n} + 1\right]} \tag{104}$$

$$= \frac{K_v}{s[\tau_m s + 1]} \tag{105}$$

The term K_v of Equation 105 has the dimensions of 1/seconds. In a positional servomechanism it is called the *velocity constant* because actually its dimensions come from the fact that the basic integration inside the loop of an elementary servomechanism necessitates that a steady error generate a rate of change of output, and not merely the output. The term $1/2\zeta\omega_n$ of Equation 104, having the dimensions of time, is a mechanism time constant τ_m. The matter of great importance, however, is that the system of Figure 2·8 is now defined in terms of the function of Equation 105, which relates the output $\theta_o(s)$ to the error $E(s)$. As written, the function has one part that is merely a constant, namely $\omega_n/2\zeta = K_v$. The other part is a function of s, namely, $1/s(\tau_m s + 1)$.

Right here is the key to much of the synthesis procedure given in Chapters 6 and 7, because the function of s in Equation 105 is uniquely related both to theory-of-functions approach in terms of the variable ω as treated in Chapters 4 and 6 and to the time domain approach using transient solutions. It is convenient to symbolize the function, such as $K_v/s(\tau_m s + 1)$, and to name it. In what follows it is called a *transfer function*. It is defined by the symbol $KG(s)$, where

$$\left.\begin{array}{l} K = \text{the constant, or frequency invariant, portion of the} \\ \quad \text{function,} \\ G(s) = \text{the frequency variant portion, or the portion depend-} \\ \quad \text{ent on time derivatives.} \end{array}\right\} \tag{106}$$

Thus for the system of Figure 2·8, or its equivalent,

$$\frac{\theta_o(s)}{E(s)} = KG(s) = \frac{K_v}{s[T_m s + 1]} \tag{107}$$

which states that, subject to the limitations imposed above on the boundary or initial conditions, the mechanism in any system defined mathematically by the differential equation

$$\left[a_1 \frac{d^n \theta_o}{dt^n} + b_1 \frac{d^{n-1} \theta_o}{dt^{n-1}} \right] = \left[a_2 \frac{d^m \varepsilon}{dt^m} + b_2 \frac{d^{m-1} \varepsilon}{dt^{m-1}} \right] \tag{108}$$

has as its symbolic equivalent

$$\frac{\theta_o(s)}{E(s)} = KG(s) \tag{109}$$

which may be conveniently represented by the symbolic block diagram of Figure 3.

By the rules of Laplace transformation given in Sections 5 and 6, elements of a physical system may be treated by the simple process of

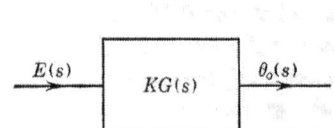

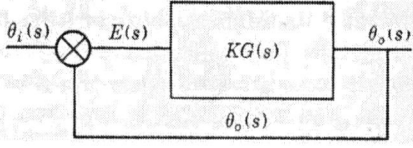

FIGURE 3. Block diagram of a   FIGURE 4. Block diagram of a closed
        mechanism.   loop.

multiplying their transfer functions to get the overall operator. This matter is given extensive treatment in Chapter 5.

For the closed-loop system shown in Figure 4, the following algebraic manipulations are possible

$$E(s) = \theta_i(s) - \theta_o(s) \tag{110}$$

$$\frac{\theta_o(s)}{E(s)} = KG(s) \tag{111}$$

$$\frac{\theta_o(s)}{\theta_i(s)} = \frac{KG(s)}{1 + KG(s)} \tag{112}$$

$$\frac{E(s)}{\theta_i(s)} = \frac{1}{1 + KG(s)} \tag{113}$$

Equations 112 and 113 show that for the closed loop having unity feed-
back defined by the relation $\varepsilon = \theta_i - \theta_o$, the characteristic equation
for the closed-loop system is always

$$1 + KG(s) = 0 \qquad (114)$$

It is now possible to define sections of a physical system or the entire
system in terms of symbolic functions $KG(s)$. A new method for
formulating the problem may be considered. By means of the procedure
treated in Chapter 10, certain measurements performed on elements or
groups of elements in the open loop may be interpreted as functions
$KG(s)$. Thus a technique for knowing the functional behavior of *actual*
parts of a system as they operate subject to environment, wear, and the
like can replace idealizations otherwise necessary in order to formulate
their differential equation. These matters are amplified in later chapters.

11   Transient Analysis of Systems Involving High-Order Characteristic Equations

The examples of closed-loop systems considered thus far have involved
mathematical simplifications rarely justified in practice. The characteristic equations of these examples have involved only quadratics in
s. In the systems encountered in practice, the characteristic equations
invariably involve high powers of s. This occurs even though in the
formulation of the problem in terms of differential equations, only the
most dominant characteristics of the system can be described. It is
difficult and sometimes impossible to determine all the parameters of
all elements such as inertia, elastance, inductance, damping, amplification, and torque gradient. The transient analysis using equations which
give even this approximation to the problem then becomes complicated
because of the labor of getting the roots and the time solutions. Although the analysis may be classified as tedious, the synthesis by the
transient methods is almost impossible because the coefficients of the
powers of s in the characteristic equation are a heterogeneous arrangement of many of the parameters of the system. Even when the work of
obtaining the transient solution has been completed, it is difficult to
identify any particular element in the system that must be changed to
cause any preselected modification in system behavior.

A qualitative knowledge of the transient behavior that is useful for
many purposes, however, may be obtained by recognizing that the characteristic equation can be factored into the product of quadratic factors
as follows:

$$s^n + bs^{n-1} + cs^{n-2} + \cdots$$
$$= (s^2 + 2\zeta_a\omega_{na}s + \omega_{na}{}^2)(s^2 + 2\zeta_b\omega_{nb}s + \omega_{nb}{}^2) \cdots (s + \alpha) \qquad (115)$$

Each quadratic factor contributes to a mode of oscillation in the solution having damping ratios $\zeta_a, \zeta_b, \zeta_c, \cdots$ respectively, and undamped natural frequencies $\omega_{na}, \omega_{nb}, \omega_{nc}, \cdots$ respectively. By the principle of linear superposition, the servomechanism response is the sum of the responses attributed to the specific modes $a, b, c, \cdots$. Thus for each component of error response, the duration of the transient is given qualitatively by reference to the types of solutions given in this and the preceding chapter for simple quadratics, and the relative magnitudes of the transients can often be approximated from the observation that the higher the magnitude of the root, the smaller the coefficient of the time solution involving that root. It should be remembered that the parameters of the several elements in a system are not always known to high degrees of accuracy. Therefore approximate or graphical methods of calculation that give the roots to a few significant figures are justifiable and time saving. This matter is discussed in Section 13.

Because of the difficulties mentioned, the transient method of analysis of complicated systems becomes most valuable as an aid to the *visualization* of the performance of a system or a final verification of the suitability of performance, rather than an aid in its design. If a designer has carried out the analysis of the dynamic performance based upon transient studies he can correlate the information with the actual performance. He only need give any physical system a transient disturbance by any one of several means readily available and then observe or measure the response. Even though this is about all the transient analysis offers, the method is nevertheless important.

12   Stability Criteria or Conditions for Stability

Much work has been published relative to the matter of stability of dynamical systems. The early work of Routh [48, 53] showed among other things a method of examining the characteristic equation to determine the number of roots present having a positive real part. This information is obtainable without undertaking the work of actually finding the roots. Later investigators [16, 55] in the field developed nomograph charts, some of which show merely the boundaries between stable or unstable operation, or boundaries giving oscillatory behavior or nonoscillatory behavior. Other charts give the roots of the characteristic equation. It is now the opinion of the authors that design studies of servomechanisms, and particularly the designs that lean heavily upon the more recent synthesis techniques, are but partially aided by the results of the above-mentioned work. Not many years ago these works presented the only effective aid to the synthesis problems.

The criteria for stability of a system as represented by its characteristic equation may be summarized rather simply.   The dominant criteria are that (1) all powers of s in descending order in the characteristic equation must exist, (2) the coefficients of all the powers of s must have the same algebraic sign, and (3) the coefficients must bear a definite algebraic relation to each other.[54]   A design which fulfills these conditions may or may not oscillate indefinitely.   Mere fulfillment of these conditions tells the designer nothing about how suitable the dynamics of the system will be for a particular application.   In other words, these criteria serve to distinguish between stability and instability, but they say nothing about the question of relative stability.   At best they show that the roots when plotted in the complex plane appear in certain zones.   They indicate nothing which will actually locate the roots in the complex plane as shown by Figure 2.

Continued contact with the problem of design and synthesis shows that the designer is constantly battling the problem of relative stability. Unfortunately, many desirable short cuts for optimizing the system performance with respect to one or another particular operating characteristic often involve design practices that decrease the relative stability but may not involve actual instability.

The design problem becomes essentially that of knowing the absolute stability of the system, or, more specifically, knowing the exact location of the roots in the complex plane.[54]   While the synthesis or design work is in progress it is generally necessary to determine the roots of polynomials.   Sometimes these roots relate to the closed-loop behavior; at other times they relate to the transfer function $KG(s)$.   Of real interest to the design, therefore, is the knowledge of useful methods for determining arithmetically the roots of any particular polynomial.

13   Determination of Roots of High-Order Characteristic Equations

Many methods exist in the literature for obtaining arithmetically the roots of high-order polynomials.[56, 57]   The authors consider many of these methods too complex, considering the needs of the problem. Although they may give highly accurate values for the roots, the approximations usually necessitated in a solution by differential equations make it appear unreasonable to compute the roots to a high order of numerical accuracy.

In the opinion of the authors, a quick, approximate method is useful if it is so simple that it can be memorized.   The method originally developed by Lin [56] appears to be of this kind.   Furthermore, it can be made as accurate as occasion demands.   It is basically one of synthetic division. Subject to the general requirement that any two frequencies in the normal modes are a few octaves apart, the results usually converge rapidly and are quite accurate for most problems. The method is illustrated as follows.

Consider the polynomial

$$x^n + bx^{n-1} + cx^{n-2} \cdots + gx^2 + hx + k = 0 \qquad (116)$$

As a first approximation to representing this system by a second-order equation, form the quadratic factor

$$x^2 + \frac{h}{g}x + \frac{k}{g}$$

by dividing the last three terms of the polynomial by the coefficient of the third last term. Then, long division using this quadratic as a divisor gives

$$
x^2 + \frac{h}{g}x + \frac{k}{g} \overline{\smash{\big)}\ x^n + bx^{n-1} + cx^{n-2} \cdots gx^2 + hx + k}
$$

$$x^{n-2} + \cdots$$

$$g_1 x^2 + h_1 x + k$$

$$g_1 x^2 + h_2 x + k_2$$

Remainder

If the remainder from this division is not negligible, the procedure is repeated using as the second divisor or second approximation

$$x^2 + \frac{h_1}{g_1}x + \frac{k}{g_1}$$

and repeating the division process. The operation is continued until the remainder terms are negligible. The quotient now is a polynomial of $n - 2$ order. Another quadratic factor is obtained in a similar manner by again dividing the last three terms of this quotient by the coefficient of the third last term and using the result as the first approximation.

Where the highest value of n of the exponent in the original polynomial is odd, a useful procedure is first to solve for a single factor $(x + z)$ by using as a first approximation

$$(x + z) = x + \frac{k}{h}$$

The quotient now has an even number for its highest order of exponent and can be factored into quadratic factors.

As an illustrative numerical example, consider the polynomial

$$s^4 + 10.65s^3 + 89s^2 + 15.5s + 27 = 0 \qquad (117)$$

The first trial divisor is

$$s^2 + \frac{15.5}{89}s + \frac{27}{89} \quad \text{or} \quad s^2 + 0.174s + 0.304$$

The long division process can be conducted in synthetic form. The actual steps for the first trial are

$$
\begin{array}{r}
s^2 + 10.48s \quad + 86.9 \\
s^2 + 0.174s + 0.304 \overline{\smash{\big)}\ s^4 + 10.65s^3 \quad + 89s^2 \quad\quad + 15.5s \quad + 27} \\
s^4 + \quad .174s^3 + \quad .304s^2 \\
\hline
10.48s^3 + 88.7s^2 \quad + 15.5s \\
10.48s^3 + \quad 1.8s^2 \quad + 3.18s \\
\hline
86.9s^2 \quad + 12.3s \quad + 27 \\
86.9s^2 \quad + 15.1s \quad + 26.4 \\
\hline
\end{array}
$$

The second trial divisor is

$$s^2 + \frac{12.3}{86.9}s + \frac{27}{86.9}$$

or

$$s^2 + 0.142s + 0.311$$

The third trial divisor is

$$s^2 + \frac{12.23}{87.2}s + \frac{27}{87.2}$$

or

$$s^2 + 0.14s + 0.31$$

which gives substantially no remainder term after the long division process. Therefore the factors for the original polynomial in Equation 117 are,

$$(s^2 + 0.14s + 0.31)(s^2 + 10.51s + 87.2) = 0 \qquad (118)$$

The roots for each individual quadratic factor can be found by inspection.

14 Conclusion

The next chapters of this book treat a method of analysis that is particularly useful in the synthesis of complicated systems. The method is based upon the frequency response characteristic of the transfer function. It is frequently referred to as the frequency response method, transfer-loci method, or steady-state method. It draws heavily on much of the work developed decades ago by communications engineers working on network synthesis and feedback amplifier design.

4

Sinusoidal Response of Closed-Loop Systems

1 Introduction

The difficulties of synthesizing closed-loop systems by the transient method of analysis become apparent as soon as systems involving three or more energy storage elements are encountered. Much notable work has been done to increase the power of the transient method by systematizing the procedure [16,45] or by preparing nomograph charts [55,58] for the roots of the characteristic equations. These results, however, were not sufficient in themselves to solve the synthesis problem. Other ways to attack it, therefore, have been developed.

Looking back on the situation in the control engineering field as it was during its infancy, we note that the engineering problems were treated with a predominantly steady-state concept. This situation was forced upon the engineers because of the relative dearth of analysis in a form that would assist them with their dynamic problems. There were, of course, many persons thoroughly conscious of the full scope of dynamic analyses, but they represented such a minority with respect to the whole that their knowledge could be disseminated only slowly. The quantitative aspects of the mathematics that related to vibrations, oscillations, or hunting were accessible to only a mere handful of the total personnel associated with control engineering.

History seems to show that the communications field had assembled by about 1920 a large engineering organization and a relatively large group of mathematical physicists whose problems were predominantly those of oscillations, sinusoidal varying phenomena, or vibrations in electrical equipment. This latter group * had, as one of its major problems, the synthesis of electrical networks to yield prescribed frequency functions. It had devoted much effort to the interpretation of mathe-

* It is not possible to give acknowledgment to all the persons who have contributed to this work. Among those whose contributions are well known are Black,[59] Nyquist,[60] Bode,[61] Guillemin,[62] Wiener,[71] to cite merely a few.

matical theorems that related sinusoidal to transient or steady-state behavior. Its effort on these fronts proved highly effective, probably because (1) a new field attracted the leading theoretical people in the profession, (2) electrical systems may be assembled in model form with ease and low cost, (3) highly refined measuring instruments existed or could be developed for experiment and study, and (4) the systems operated linearly over a wide range. Few of these conditions existed during the early days in the field of automatic control engineering.

The early experiences of the communications group were often supported by a research laboratory or university program, while those of the control group were spread from shop to factory to field. The technical language of the electrical group became specialized. There was a marked difference between the elements or instruments used in the communications field and those used in the industrial control or regulator field. It was natural, therefore, that persons working in the control field were not conversant with developments in the communications field. In other words, there was only slight appreciation by one group of the problems and technical resources of the other.

Fortunately, technical people have always had a tendency to intermingle gradually at the fringes of each profession. Professional society activity and university research and teaching serve to stimulate this condition. It now appears that these technical people have been very effective in bringing to the attention of persons familiar with the problems of control synthesis, and vice versa, the methods employed for the analysis and synthesis of electrical networks and amplifiers.

One of the early results of the work of the communications engineers was the integration of circuit theory and network synthesis which, when coupled with techniques developed by Bell Telephone Laboratory personnel for the determination of the stability of feedback amplifiers, gave a powerful analytical tool to be used in control studies. When the similarity between feedback amplifier phenomena and closed-loop automatic control phenomena was publicized, many accomplishments in electric circuit analysis were recognized as common to both fields. Only a unification of language was necessary to bridge the gap between the developments in communications and the needs of control. With the advent of the war, the unification moved rapidly. Many wartime publications * gave comprehensive treatments of servomechanism analysis

* Much of this work appeared originally in restricted documents. Some of it has since been published; some has not. Unfortunately, the original work of many persons may never appear under their own name. Those whose work is known to the authors and may be cited are Bombarger-Weber,[63] MacColl,[4] Hall,[6] Harris,[32] Marcy,[33] Ferrell,[34] Graham,[35] Herr-Gerst,[64] Nichols,[65] Wiener.[71]

and synthesis by frequency response methods. Largely as a result of these early publications, the frequency response approach has been developed into a powerful tool in the analysis and synthesis of servomechanisms and regulators.

The following sections of this chapter illustrate the general properties of closed-loop systems subjected to disturbances which vary sinusoidally with time. No attempt is made in this chapter to exploit these properties in the synthesis of systems. Certain general relations between transient and frequency behavior, however, are pointed out. In Chapter 5, the preparation of system data into a form convenient for synthesis using frequency response techniques is treated extensively. Chapters 6, 7, snd 8 show how the synthesis is actually applied.

2   Frequency Characteristic

The term *frequency characteristic*, when applied to a mechanism, refers to the magnitude and phase relationship between the input, or forcing function, and the output, or response function, when the time variation of the input is sinusoidal. If $\theta_i(t)$ is the input and $\theta_o(t)$ is the output, and if

$$\theta_i(t) = A \sin \omega t \tag{1}$$

it is always true that

$$\theta_o(t) = B \sin (\omega t + \phi) \tag{2}$$

provided that A is sufficiently small to hold the system excursion within the linear range. In these equations, A is the amplitude of the input variation, B is the amplitude of the output response, ω is the angular frequency of the forcing function of $\theta_i(t)$ (equals $2\pi f$, where f is in cycles per second), and ϕ is the relative phase angle between $\theta_i(t)$ and $\theta_o(t)$. Furthermore, for a closed-loop system, the time variation of error $\mathcal{E}(t) = \theta_i(t) - \theta_o(t)$ will be of the form

$$\mathcal{E}(t) = C \sin (\omega t + \gamma) \tag{3}$$

An ideal or perfect follow-up system would function so that for all angular frequencies ω within the range $0 < \omega < \infty$, the output response would correspond to the input so that

$$\left.\begin{array}{l} B = A \\ \phi = \text{zero} \\ C = \text{zero} \end{array}\right\} \tag{4}$$

The condition expressed by Equation 4 is equivalent to the statement that the system response would be constant over the frequency range

$0 < \omega < \infty$, and the phase shift would be zero within the same frequency range. No physical system can achieve this condition on account of the energy storage and dissipation conditions encountered within it. All practical systems fulfill the condition only to a partial extent as shown by the curves of Figure 1, which are the frequency response characteristic expressed as the ratio of B/A and the phase ϕ, each plotted as functions of ω. In Figure 1, curve a represents an ideal system, whereas curves b and c represent physically realizable systems.

The ability of any system to respond uniformly to all frequencies, as shown by curve a of Figure 1, would be the perfection needed in a servomechanism that could reproduce the sharp corners and infinite

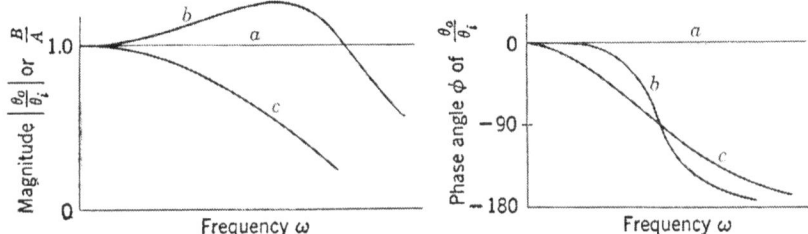

FIGURE 1.   Frequency response characteristic.

rates of change found in the step disturbances $\theta_i(t) = u(t)$. Fortunately, such performance is neither possible nor desirable as we realize when a system must do a good job of reproducing at the output a signal $\theta_i(t)$ which carries with it spurious signals, termed roughness or noise. The frequency of the roughness or noise usually occurs in the frequency spectrum somewhat above the upper frequency of the true signal so that, to respond to the true and not to the false, the servo system is made to have definite cutoff characteristics above a limiting frequency.

Physically realizable systems will operate over a finite frequency band $0 \rightarrow \omega_{max}$, and it is within this band that the frequency response studies have great value. At the low-frequency end of the spectrum, the output to input ratio B/A approaches unity and the phase angle ϕ approaches zero as ω approaches zero. Otherwise the closed-loop would not meet the definition of a servomechanism. However, as ω tends to ∞, the impossibility of instantaneous transfer of energy from one place in the system to another causes the ratio B/A to approach zero as a limit. Furthermore, as the frequency ω approaches infinity, the angle ϕ approaches $n\pi/2$ radians. The quantity n is an integer equal to the number of energy storage elements in the system or the order of the characteristic equation for the closed loop.

A matter of great significance illustrated by the frequency response characteristic concerns the magnitude of the ratio B/A in the intermediate-frequency range. As shown by curve b in Figure 1, the ratio B/A may be greater than unity. The importance of this fact is discussed in detail in later sections of the chapter.

3 Laplace Transform for Sinusoidal System Operation

It is well known to engineers already familiar with the conventional methods of electric circuit analysis that the expression relating two sinusoidally varying quantities functionally defined by the transform $KG(s)$, as derived in Chapter 3, is given by $KG(j\omega)$ where $j\omega$ merely replaces s. A brief proof of this statement follows.

Consider an open-loop array of dynamic apparatus defined by the relation

$$R(s) = KG(s)F(s) \tag{5}$$

where

$$R(s) = \mathcal{L}[R(t)] = \text{response function and} \left. \right\} \tag{6}$$
$$F(s) = \mathcal{L}[f(t)] = \text{forcing function}$$

Assume that

$$f(t) = P \sin \omega t$$

Then

$$\mathcal{L}[f(t)] = \frac{P\omega}{s^2 + \omega^2} \tag{7}$$

The substitution of Equation 7 in Equation 5 gives

$$R(s) = PKG(s)\frac{\omega}{s^2 + \omega^2} \tag{8}$$

In any general problem, the transform $KG(s)$ will be of the form $A(s)/B(s)$. Therefore, the roots or zeros of the characteristic equation $B(s)[s^2 + \omega^2] = 0$ are of the form

$$(s - s_1)(s - s_2)(s - s_3) \cdots (s - j\omega)(s + j\omega) = 0$$

The general solution to Equation 8 is then

$$R(t) = K_1 e^{s_1 t} + K_2 e^{s_2 t} \cdots K_{j\omega} e^{+j\omega t} + K_{-j\omega} e^{-j\omega t} \tag{9}$$

following the treatment in Section 9 of Chapter 3.

If, after any disturbance, time is permitted to elapse until all the quantities $e^{s_1 t}$, $e^{s_2 t}$, $e^{s_3 t}$, $\cdots$, etc., of the response have decayed to zero, the only response remaining is the so-called steady-state portion $R_{ss}(t)$

as given wholly by that part of the result coming from $K_{j\omega}$ and $K_{-j\omega}$ of Equation 9. Thus

$$R_{ss}(t) = K_{j\omega}e^{+j\omega t} + K_{-j\omega}e^{-j\omega t} \tag{10}$$

But from Section 8 of Chapter 3,

$$K_{j\omega} = (s - j\omega)\frac{A(s)}{B(s)}\frac{P\omega}{(s^2 + \omega^2)}\bigg|_{s = +j\omega} \tag{11}$$

$$= \frac{PKG(j\omega)}{2j} \tag{12}$$

Likewise,

$$K_{-j\omega} = \frac{PKG(-j\omega)}{-2j} \tag{12a}$$

The substitution of Equation 12 and Equation 12a in Equation 10 gives

$$R_{ss}(t) = PK\frac{G(j\omega)e^{j(\omega t)} - G(-j\omega)e^{-j(\omega t)}}{2j} \tag{13}$$

but

$$\left.\begin{array}{l} G(j\omega) = (a + jb) = |G(j\omega)|e^{j\psi} \\ G(-j\omega) = (a - jb) = |G(j\omega)|e^{-j\psi} \end{array}\right\} \tag{14}$$

where

$$\psi = \tan^{-1}\frac{b}{a} \tag{15}$$

giving

$$R_{ss}(t) = PK|G(j\omega)|\left[\frac{e^{j(\omega t + \psi)} - e^{-j(\omega t + \psi)}}{2j}\right]$$

$$= PK|G(j\omega)|\sin(\omega t + \psi) \tag{16}$$

where

$$\psi = \tan^{-1}\frac{\text{imaginary part of } G(j\omega)}{\text{Real part of } G(j\omega)} \tag{17}$$

Equation 16 shows that when any system defined by the transfer function $KG(s)$ is excited by a sinusoidal time-varying disturbance, its steady-state behavior $R_{ss}(t)$ is equally well expressed by the complex quantity $R(j\omega)$ whose magnitude is $KG(j\omega)$ multiplied by the magnitude P of the forcing function. The quantity $R(j\omega)$ is a vector with an amplitude $PK|G(j\omega)|$ and a phase $\psi(j\omega)$, both of which vary with frequency. The term K is that part of the transfer function which is invariant with frequency. It is frequently called the *gain* or the *sensi-*

tivity factor, and in physical systems it is a function of amplifier gain, gear ratios, lengths of levers, speeds of generators, and the like. The second part of the transfer function denoted by $G(j\omega)$ represents that portion which changes with frequency and is a function of energy storage within the system.

The frequency response of the servomechanism as a closed loop is related to the transfer function by the vector equation

$$\frac{\theta_o}{\theta_i}(j\omega) = \frac{KG(j\omega)}{1 + KG(j\omega)} \tag{18}$$

The transfer function may be calculated by straightforward circuit analysis techniques or by determining the differential equation relating the output to the error, transforming to the s-plane, and replacing s by $j\omega$, or more directly by replacing d/dt by $j\omega$.

4   Frequency Response of a Typical Closed-Loop System

$\dfrac{\theta_o}{\theta_i}(j\omega)$ **Characteristic.**   As an illustration of sinusoidal system analysis, consider the system of Figure 2·8, for which the differential equation expressing $\theta_o(t)$ and $\theta_i(t)$ is

$$\frac{d^2\theta_o(t)}{dt^2} + 2\zeta\omega_n\frac{d\theta_o(t)}{dt} + \omega_n{}^2\theta_o(t) = \omega_n{}^2\theta_i(t) \tag{19}$$

The $\mathcal{L}$ transform of this equation may now be written for $\theta_i(t) = \theta_i \sin \omega t$ and for the initial conditions equal to zero. If the procedure of Equation 16 for $R(j\omega)$ is followed, the frequency characteristic is

$$\theta_o(j\omega) = \left[\frac{\omega_n{}^2}{(\omega_n{}^2 - \omega^2) + j(2\zeta\omega_n\omega)}\right]\theta_i \tag{20}$$

which, in vector form, may be written as

$$\frac{\theta_o}{\theta_i}(j\omega) = \left|\frac{\theta_o}{\theta_i}(j\omega)\right| e^{j\phi(j\omega)} \tag{21}$$

where

$$\left|\frac{\theta_o}{\theta_i}(j\omega)\right| = \frac{\omega_n{}^2}{\sqrt{(\omega_n{}^2 - \omega^2)^2 + (2\zeta\omega_n\omega)^2}} \tag{22}$$

and

$$\phi(j\omega) = -\tan^{-1}\frac{2\zeta\omega_n\omega}{\omega_n{}^2 - \omega^2} \tag{23}$$

If a new frequency variable u is defined as

$$u = \frac{\omega}{\omega_n} \tag{24}$$

a change in variable may be made in Equations 22 and 23 to reduce these two equations to a dimensionless frequency base expressed by the relation

$$\left| \frac{\theta_o}{\theta_i}(ju) \right| = \frac{1}{\sqrt{(1-u^2)^2 + (2\zeta u)^2}} \tag{25}$$

and

$$\phi(ju) = -\tan^{-1} \frac{2\zeta u}{1-u^2} \tag{26}$$

Examination of Equation 25 shows that the magnitude of the vector ratio $\frac{\theta_o}{\theta_i}(ju)$ becomes equivalent to the former ratio B/A.

An examination of Equations 25 and 26 at high and low values of frequency u is of interest. The magnitude relation is defined for low frequencies as

$$\lim_{u \to 0} \left| \frac{\theta_o}{\theta_i}(ju) \right| = \lim_{u \to 0} \frac{1}{\sqrt{(1-u^2)^2 + (2\zeta u)^2}} = 1 \tag{27}$$

and for high frequencies as

$$\lim_{u \to \infty} \left| \frac{\theta_o}{\theta_i}(ju) \right| = \lim_{u \to \infty} \frac{1}{\sqrt{(1-u^2)^2 + (2\zeta u)^2}} = 0 \tag{28}$$

The phase relation at low frequencies is

$$\lim_{u \to 0} \phi(ju) = \lim_{u \to 0} \left[-\tan^{-1} \frac{2\zeta u}{1-u^2} \right] = 0 \tag{29}$$

and at high frequencies by the

$$\lim_{u \to \infty} \phi(ju) = \lim_{u \to \infty} \left[-\tan^{-1} \frac{2\zeta u}{1-u^2} \right] = -\pi \tag{30}$$

The results of Equations 27 through 30 verify the statements made concerning the general response of servomechanisms at high and low frequencies.

When the damping ratio ζ is small, the resonant frequency for the system becomes nearly equal to ω_n, the undamped natural angular frequency, making $u \cong 1$. In the absence of all damping, that is, $\zeta = 0$,

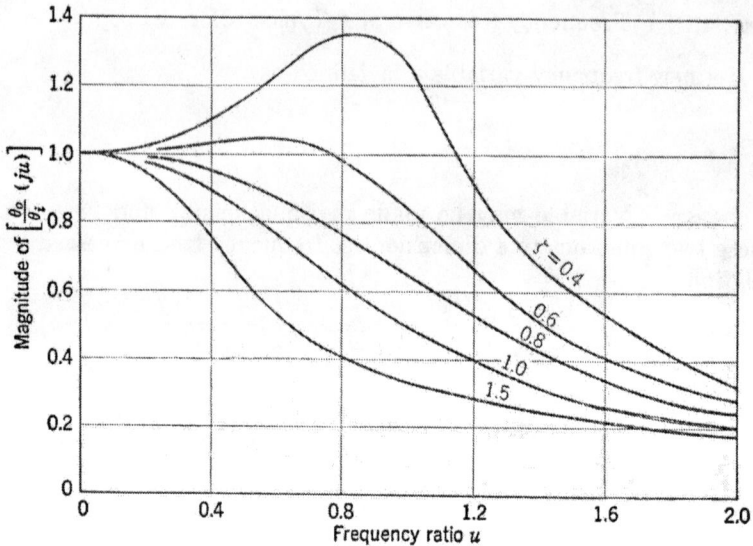

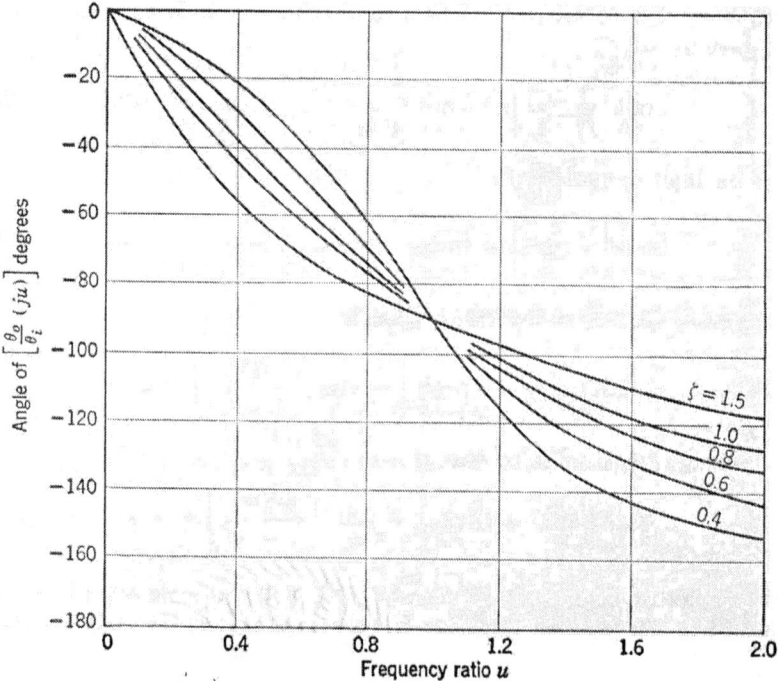

FIGURE 2. Magnitude and phase characteristics $\frac{\theta_o}{\theta_i}(ju)$ for servomechanism of

Figure 2·8.

the resonant frequency $\omega_R = \omega_n$. Thus, as shown by Equation 25, an unrestrained resonance will occur. That is,

$$\lim_{\substack{u \to 1 \\ \zeta \to 0}} \left| \frac{\theta_o}{\theta_i}(ju) \right| = \frac{1}{0} = \infty \tag{31}$$

and

$$\lim_{\substack{u \to 1 \\ \zeta \to 0}} \phi(ju) = \tan^{-1} -\infty = -\frac{\pi}{2} \tag{32}$$

For other values of damping ratio ζ, Equation 25 can be written as

$$\lim_{u \to 1} \left| \frac{\theta_o}{\theta_i}(ju) \right| = \frac{1}{2\zeta} \tag{33}$$

but the value of the phase angle $\phi(ju)$ remains unchanged at $-\pi/2$ degrees.

Figure 2 shows a plot of the magnitude and phase of the vector ratio $\frac{\theta_o}{\theta_i}(ju)$ to coordinates for the system defined by the differential equation 19. The data are presented in separate charts having a common abscissa scale of dimensionless angular frequency u. Figure 3 shows a plot of the same function to polar coordinates.

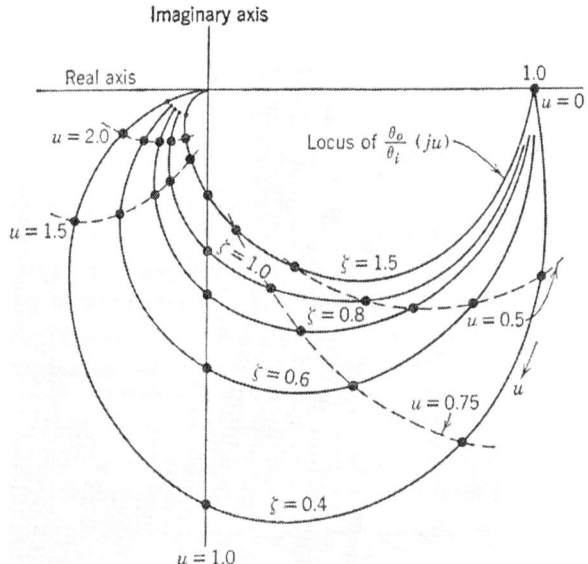

FIGURE 3. Polar plot of magnitude and phase characteristics $\frac{\theta_o}{\theta_i}(ju)$ for servo mechanism of Figure 2·8.

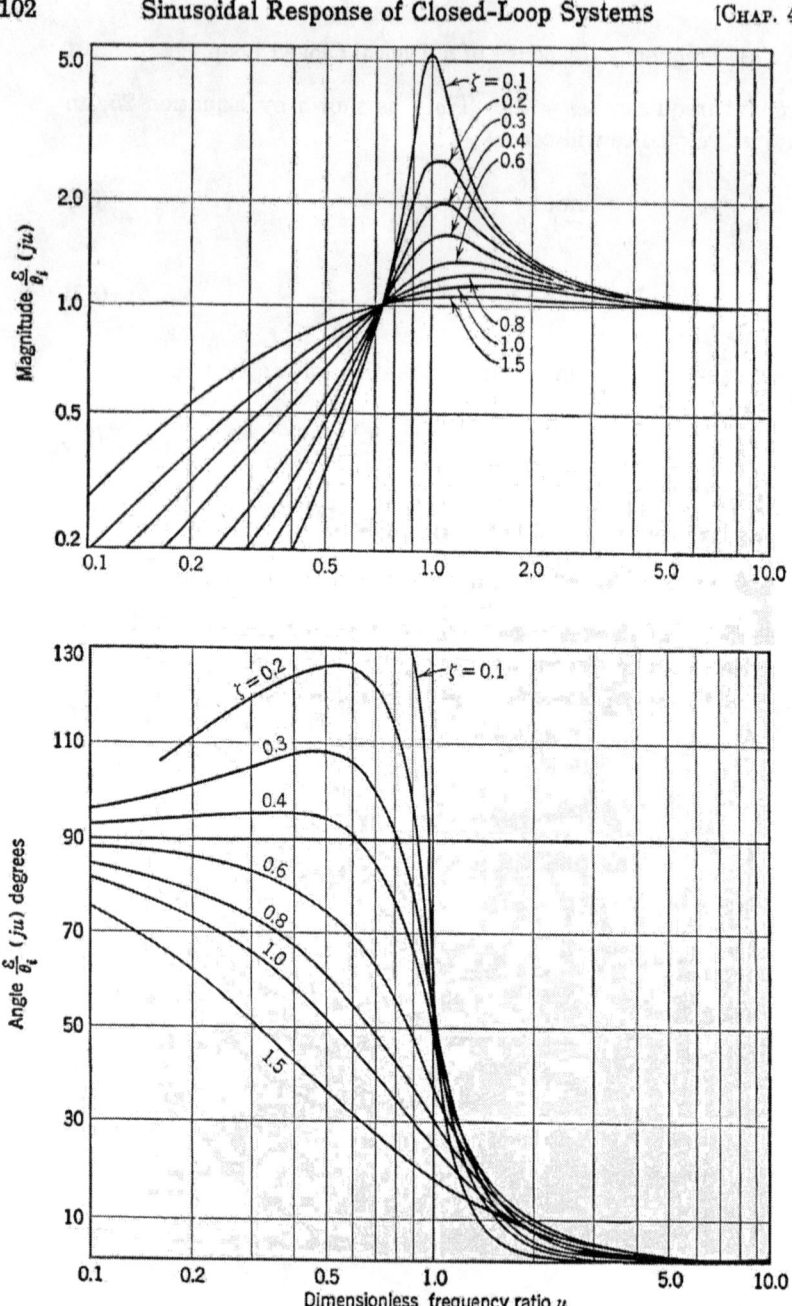

Figure 4. Magnitude and phase characteristics of $\frac{\mathcal{E}}{\theta_i}$ (ju) for servomechanism of

Figure 2·8.

$\dfrac{\mathcal{E}}{\theta_i}$ $(j\omega)$ Characteristic. The differential equation for error $\mathcal{E}(t)$ of the system of Figure 2·8 is

$$\frac{d^2\mathcal{E}(t)}{dt^2} + 2\zeta\omega_n \frac{d\mathcal{E}(t)}{dt} + \omega_n{}^2\mathcal{E}(t) = \frac{d^2\theta_i(t)}{dt^2} + 2\zeta\omega_n \frac{d\theta_i(t)}{dt} \quad (34)$$

Transforming this equation and putting $s = j\omega$, or directly replacing d/dt by $j\omega$, gives

$$\mathcal{E}(j\omega) = \left[\frac{-\omega^2 + j2\zeta\omega_n\omega}{\omega_n{}^2 - \omega^2 + j2\zeta\omega_n\omega}\right]\theta_i \quad (35)$$

By introducing the dimensionless frequency ratio,

$$u = \frac{\omega}{\omega_n} \quad (36)$$

The dimensionless vector ratio is

$$\frac{\mathcal{E}}{\theta_i}(ju) = \frac{-u^2 + j2\zeta u}{(1 - u^2) + j2\zeta u} \quad (37)$$

The magnitude for Equation 37 becomes

$$\left|\frac{\mathcal{E}}{\theta_i}(ju)\right| = \frac{u\sqrt{u^2 + (2\zeta)^2}}{\sqrt{(1 - u^2)^2 + (2\zeta u)^2}} \quad (38)$$

The phase angle for Equation 37 becomes

$$\phi(ju) = \tan^{-1}\frac{2\zeta u}{-u^2} - \tan^{-1}\frac{2\zeta u}{1 - u^2} \quad (39)$$

By following the procedure used with $\dfrac{\theta_o}{\theta_i}(ju)$, curves for Equations 38 and 39 may be prepared in terms of the variable parameter ζ, as shown in Figure 4. The critical dependence of the magnitude of $|\mathcal{E}(ju)|$ on the damping ratio ζ and the abrupt change in phase of $\mathcal{E}(ju)$ occurring near resonance for low values of ζ are clearly evident.

5   Closed-Loop Vector Diagram

The treatment of Sections 3 and 4 makes it possible to write the error equation of 2·13 as a vector relation instead of a time relation; that is,

$$\mathcal{E}(j\omega) = \theta_i(j\omega) - \theta_o(j\omega) \quad (40)$$

or, on a dimensionless basis,

$$\mathcal{E}(ju) = \theta_i(ju) - \theta_o(ju) \quad (41)$$

Equations 40 and 41 define a vector relation between the input, the output, and the error of a servomechanism such that the three vector quantities form a closed vector triangle. If $\theta_i(ju)$ is chosen as a unit vector of zero phase angle, the three vector quantities $\mathcal{E}(ju)$, $\theta_i(ju)$, and $\theta_o(ju)$ will be related as Figure 5.

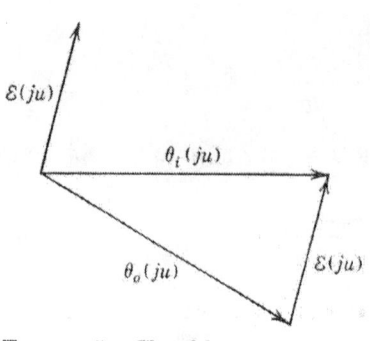

FIGURE 5.   Closed-loop vector diagram.

By choosing a specific value of ζ and allowing the frequency parameter to have values $0 < u < \infty$, the locus of the tip of $\theta_o(ju)$ may be found. The locus of the tip of $\mathcal{E}(ju)$ may also be found. These loci are shown in Figure 3 for several values of the damping ratio ζ. The superposition of Figure 5 on Figure 3 is left to the reader.

6   Correlation of Sinusoidal and Transient Behavior

Many persons examining this subject casually have assumed that the information given by the transform integral [62] and its inverse fully meets the needs of the problem. Admittedly, if we know the behavior of a system in the frequency domain, that is, if its frequency response $F(j\omega)$ is given, the behavior $f(t)$ in the time domain can be found. Conversely, if the time response $f(t)$ to an impulse disturbance is given, the behavior $F(j\omega)$ in the frequency domain can be found. The relations are:

$$f(t) = \frac{1}{2\pi} \int_{-\infty}^{\infty} F(j\omega)e^{jt\omega}\, d\omega$$

$$F(j\omega) = \int_{-\infty}^{\infty} f(t)e^{-j\omega t}\, dt \qquad (42)$$

Mere knowledge of the fact that an array of dynamic elements would have a frequency characteristic such as that shown in Figure 1 would not prove of much benefit to the synthesis of closed-loop systems. Admittedly the curves for any specific system have particular shapes. The tendency to peak at resonance is in a sense an indication of the extent to which the system is stable. While in actual practice much use is made of the magnitude and phase functions in the neighborhood of resonance, the fact that such use can be made of these functions ties back to their relation to the corresponding transient behavior of the particular system. It is only because correlation [6, 32, 35] of a kind exists between the transient response following a step disturbance and the magnitude of the sinusoidal response, as given by the frequency function, that the frequency response methods or loci studies of closed-loop synthesis have assumed such importance. The dominant problem at the desk of the engineer synthesizing a system is to know for his particular application, the frequency function required of specific elements in order that (1) the degree of stability for the complete system following a pulse or step disturbance shall be acceptable, (2) the dynamic error $\varepsilon(t)$ for prescribed time variations of input $\theta_i(t)$ or load $T_L(t)$ shall not exceed certain limits, and (3) the phase shift ϕ between $\theta_i(t)$ and $\theta_o(t)$ shall not exceed an upper limit at a specified frequency. This latter condition is frequently the most important and often the one that is least recognized. It is important whenever a particular closed-loop array of mechanism becomes an element in another closed loop. It is not very satisfying to know that the degree of transient stability can be calculated when once the frequency response is known. The calculation is generally a tedious one in its exact form. The designer really needs to know ahead of time what variations of frequency function would be permissible assuming he can establish a design to give them. He would like to design for a particular frequency function.

This problem is being attacked on many fronts. Attempts to establish criteria of frequency performance that will be criteria of relative transient stability have had notable success in a qualitative way. The two are related by correlation of certain properties as discussed below. An analytical approach to the transition problem was recently evolved by George F. Floyd, a graduate student in servomechanisms at the Massachusetts Institute of Technology. His work has materially reduced the labor of computing transient response from a known frequency response of the transfer function $KG(j\omega)$. The essentials of Floyd's results are given in Chapter 11. It is hoped that future efforts will bring further accomplishments along these lines.

Present-day synthesis techniques lean heavily on two properties shown by the plots of solutions $\dfrac{\theta_o}{\theta_i}(j\omega)$ and $\dfrac{\theta_o(t)}{|\theta_i|}$ for a system such as that used herein for illustrative purposes (Figure 2·8). In particular, a comparison of the $\dfrac{\theta_o}{\theta_i}(j\omega)$ versus ω characteristic shown by Figure 2, with the $\theta_o(t)/\theta_i(t)$ versus time characteristic of Figure 6 for different values of damping ratio ζ, shows a definite correlation between the magnification of $\left|\dfrac{\theta_o}{\theta_i}(j\omega)\right|$ and the peak overshoot in $\theta_o(t)$. Specifically, as ζ decreases, the maximum value of $\left|\dfrac{\theta_o}{\theta_i}(j\omega)\right|_{\text{max}}$ increases, and the overshoot in $\theta_o(t)$ increases. This maximum value is defined as M_p, since it is in a sense a magnification of the input. The generalization is then made that in *any* system a design that holds $\left|\dfrac{\theta_o}{\theta_i}(j\omega)\right|$ less than a value given by a particular ζ in Figure 2, will have a transient performance not differing appreciably from that of Figure 6 for the same

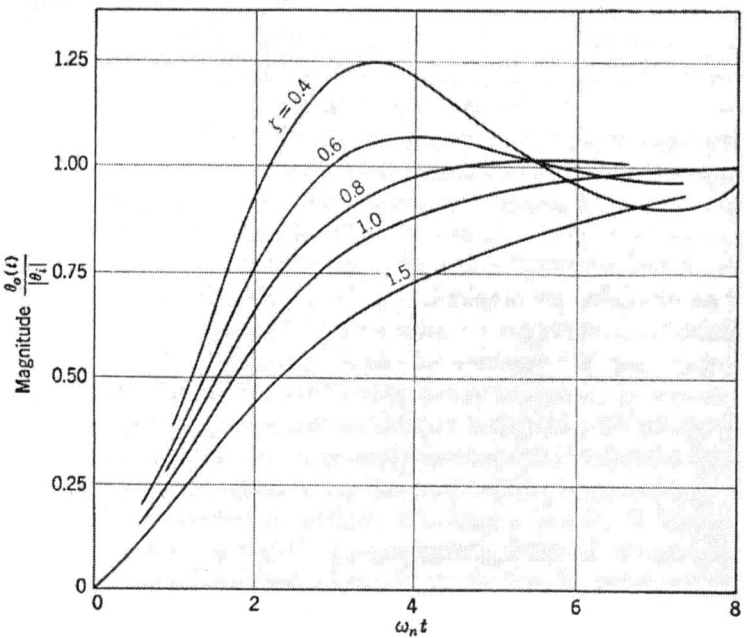

FIGURE 6. Typical transient response characteristic of elementary servomechanism.

value of ζ. There are, of course, exceptions to this generalization, but in many problems important natural frequencies in the transient response are indicated by peaks in the amplitude response. The magnitudes of the peaks of the amplitude response are then measures of the relative damping of the natural modes of oscillation of the transient response. Furthermore, the frequency band over which the amplitude response has a substantially constant magnitude is a measure of the speed of response to transients, since a high natural frequency, and therefore a high speed of response, is linked with a high resonant frequency in the amplitude or sinusoidal response.

For a system characterized by a second-order differential equation, an exact relationship for $\left| \dfrac{\theta_o}{\theta_i}(j\omega) \right|_{\text{max}}$ as a function of the single parameter ζ can be computed. From Equation 25,

$$\frac{\theta_o}{\theta_i}(ju) = \frac{1}{-u^2 + 1 + j2\zeta u} \tag{43}$$

from which

$$\left| \frac{\theta_o}{\theta_i}(ju) \right| = M = \frac{1}{[(-u^2 + 1)^2 + (2\zeta u)^2]^{\frac{1}{2}}} \tag{44}$$

but

$$\frac{dM}{du} = -\frac{1}{2}[u^4 + 1 - 2u^2 + 4\zeta^2 u^2]^{-\frac{3}{2}}(4u^3 - 4u + 8\zeta^2 u) \tag{45}$$

For values of $M > 1$, the frequency u at which M is a maximum, defined as M_p, is given by $dM/du = 0$. That is, M_p occurs when

$$4u^3 - 4u + 8\zeta^2 u = 0 \tag{46}$$

or when

$$u = \sqrt{1 - 2\zeta^2} \tag{47}$$

Since $u = \omega/\omega_n$, Equation 47 says that the peak magnification in the response occurs at a frequency $\omega = \omega_n\sqrt{1 - 2\zeta^2}$. Note that M is greater than unity only for $\zeta < 0.707$ for the system defined by Equation 43. The substitution of the value of u given by Equation 47 in Equation 44 gives

$$M_p = \frac{1}{2\zeta\sqrt{1 - \zeta^2}} \tag{48}$$

A plot of M_p versus ζ from Equation 48 is given in Figure 7. It is noted that M_p increases rapidly for values of damping ratio $\zeta < 0.4$. An examination of the various transient solutions of servomechanisms defined by the second-order differential equation shows that the overshoot of the first swing tends to get excessive for values of $\zeta < 0.4$. As a result of this observation, it has become widespread practice in servomechanisms synthesis to establish, among other specifications, a value for M_p such that

$$1.2 < M_p = \left| \frac{\theta_o}{\theta_i}(j\omega) \right|_{\text{max}} < 1.6 \tag{49}$$

Unfortunately a design based wholly on an M_p of Equation 49 occasionally exhibits the undesirable property of having a long tail to its transient response. This means that the characteristic equation has real roots of small magnitude. The coefficients of the solution that go

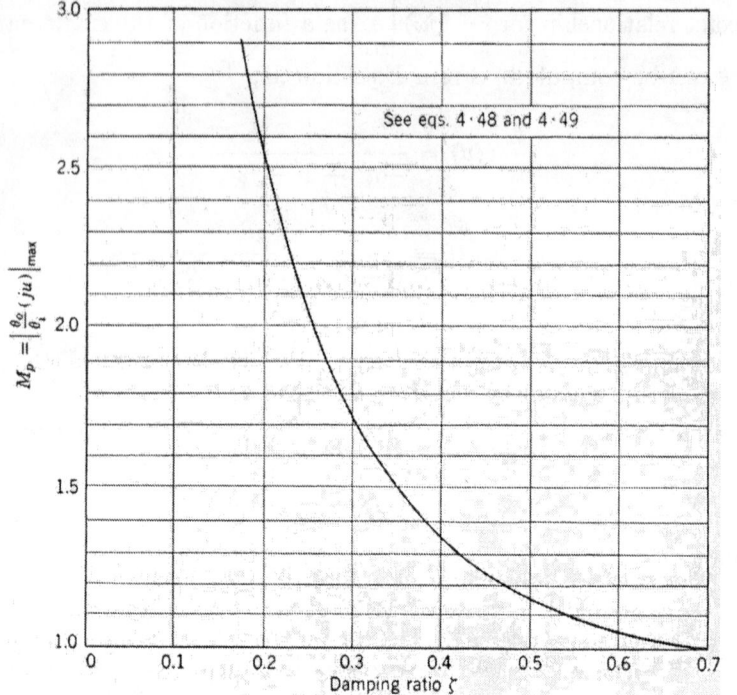

FIGURE 7.   Magnification M versus damping ratio ζ for elementary servomechanism of Figure 2·8.

with the exponential having these roots may often be quite large. The precise reason for this condition is not too well understood, but experience has shown that whereas frequency response characteristics of the

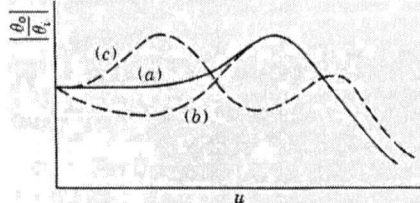

FIGURE 8.   Contrast of frequency response characteristics of servomechanisms.

kind shown by curve a of Figure 8 give acceptable transient behavior, those given by curves b or c do not. Thus, in addition to knowing the

magnitude of the sinusoidal response, it is necessary to know something
about the phase relations of the response. At this stage in the treatment
of the subject, the background for discussing the phase condition does
not exist. Chapter 6 discusses certain effects on system performance of
magnitude and phase properties of $KG(ju)$ in the frequency region
$0.6 < u < 1.2$. Also in Chapters 6 and 8, such terms as "phase margin" and "gain margin," as used extensively by communications' engineers in feedback amplifier design, are explained. It will suffice here to
point out that these terms serve to specify certain magnitude and phase
requirements of the function $KG(ju)$ in the region $0.6 < u < 1.2$, which
in the light of design experience with several kinds of problems will yield
acceptable designs.

7 Conclusion

At this stage in the presentation of synthesis, it is sufficient to state
that any system design for which $\left| \dfrac{\theta_o}{\theta_i} (ju) \right| = M_p$ does not exceed about
1.4 probably will have a transient performance acceptable for most
applications. It must be remembered, however, that this specification
of M_p bounds the design only at a region in the frequency spectrum
near the principal resonance, that is, where $0.7 < u < 1.0$. Other performance criteria are necessary to guide the design to give acceptable
performance at the zero frequency end of the spectrum and at frequencies greater than $u = 1.0$. These matters are treated in Chapters
6 and 7.

5

System Diagrams, Equivalent Circuits, and Block Diagrams

1 Need for Simplified Diagrams

System diagrams or *engineering drawings* of closed-loop systems are frequently too congested with detail to be usable. The *equivalent circuit* or *schematic diagram* may also contain so much detail that to make reference to it involves much tedious work. The so-called *block diagram* expresses the needed data in a compact form. It bears the same relation to the nuts, bolts, vacuum tubes, gears, wires, bearings, coils, and so forth of which a system is built as the architect's plan of a house, room by room, bears to the bricks, nails, beams, and so forth of which a house is built.

The closed-loop systems considered thus far are greatly simplified versions of systems likely to occur in practice. The differential equations representing them are not particularly complicated. When the systems are of a complicated nature, however, it is valuable to use a clean-cut method of simplification and organization. Otherwise the study will carry along with it a lot of excess detail that will be an unnecessary burden on the worker and will distract his attention from the main objective of his effort, namely, dynamic synthesis.

A system diagram, as shown in Figure 1, is in effect an artistic or pictoral presentation of a physical system. The components are represented with the conventional engineering symbols. Their interconnection corresponds to that of the actual servomechanism. Figure 1 gives an engineer a complete picture of the overall nature of the closed loop and also an insight into the exact location and kind of physical elements which are used. However, to work only with such a diagram may unnecessarily complicate the analytical treatment of the problem. A simplification process as shown by the diagrams of Figure 2 may often be adopted and will aid us to see the woods for the trees.

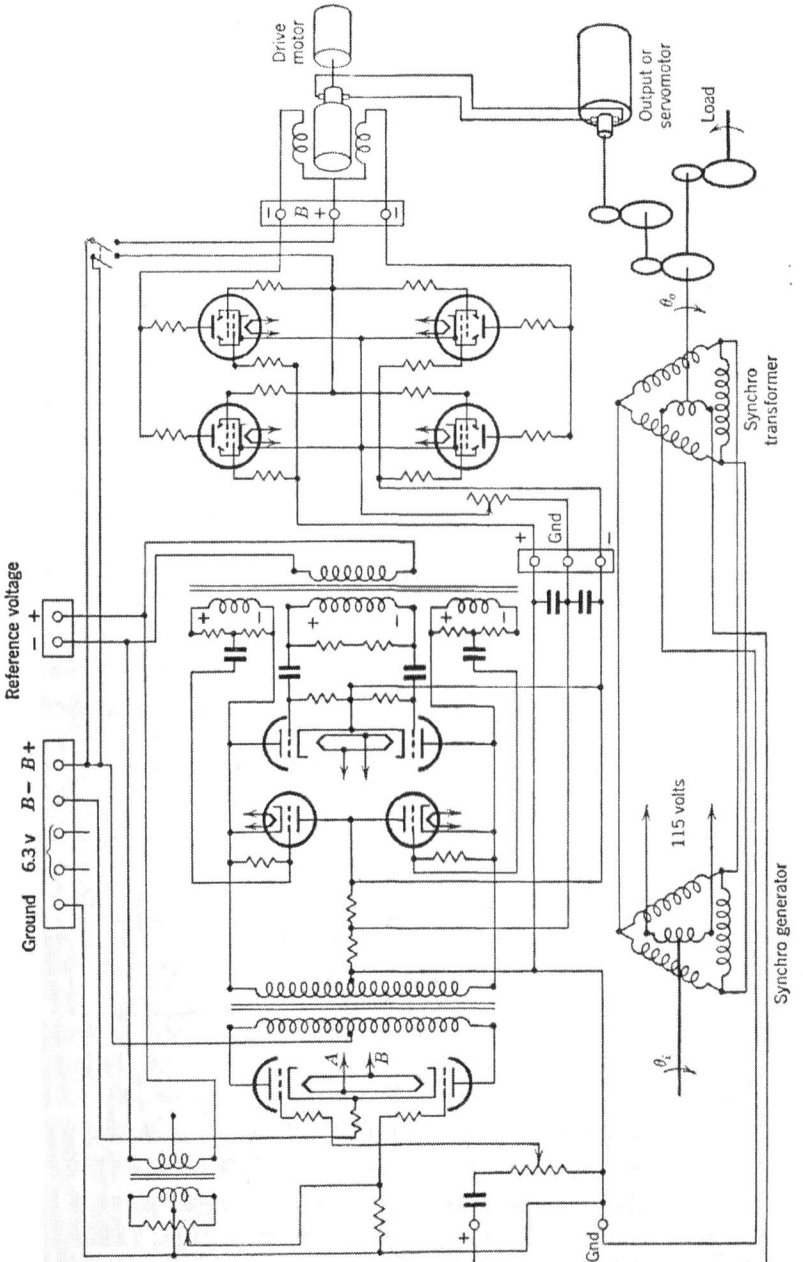

Figure 1.   Illustrating the complexity of a system wiring diagram.

Many devices, such as electronic amplifiers, are made up of components of one general kind. Control systems rarely comprise components of one kind. Frequently we find combinations of electronic,

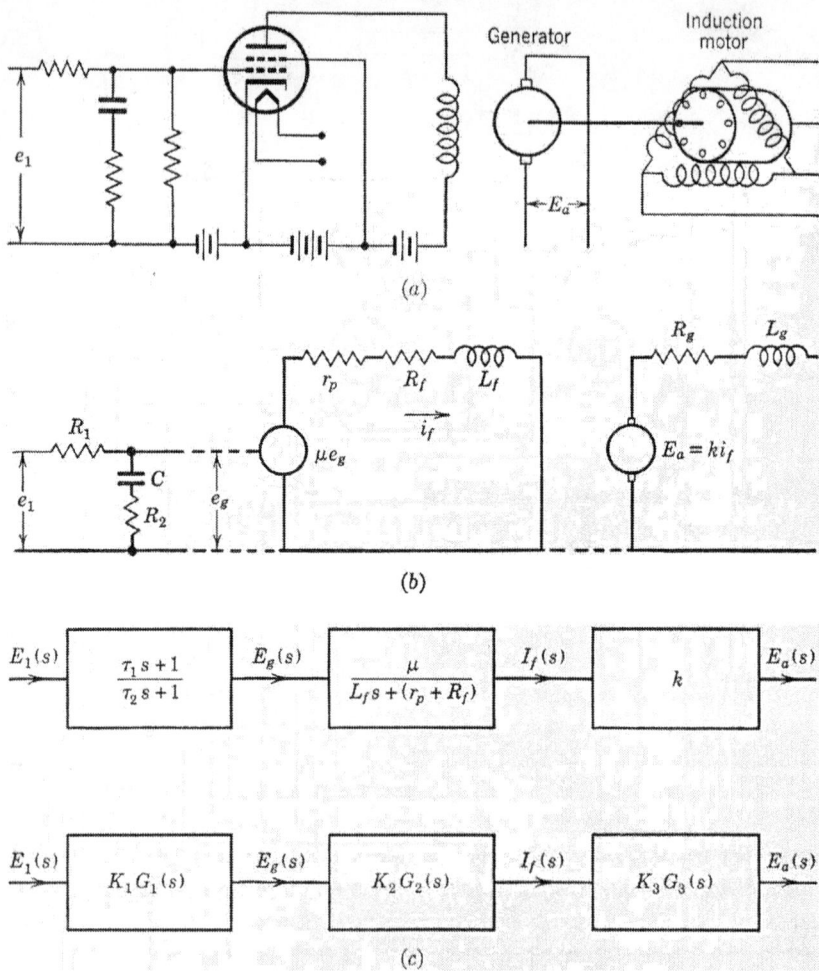

FIGURE 2. (a) System diagram, (b) equivalent circuit, and (c) block diagrams.

hydraulic, pneumatic, electric-magnetic, thermometric, optical, and many other conceivable physical gadgets scrambled into one composite whole. The electric components may serve to energize the field coils of magnetic devices, which in turn may produce torques. These may cause motion of flywheels, and sometimes the flywheels in motion give rise to optical signals in a manner that provides the final closure of the loop. These components, having different physical shapes, sizes, functions, and certainly different symbols in modern engineering practice, make difficult the preparation of the more complicated system diagrams, such as Figure 1.

Often the preparation of the equivalent circuit can be made too difficult and unwieldy by the inclusion of many unnecessary components. On the other hand, no dynamical element may be ignored in the system diagram if subsequent mathematical analysis is to be indicative of actual system behavior over a wide band of frequencies.

A convenient procedure for preparing the equivalent circuit and block diagram is first to establish the principal components or groups of components that exist in the closed loop; second, to determine how these components are connected together in order to establish the closed path or paths; and third, to make a detailed study of the individual components to establish their importance in the dynamic behavior of the system. It is generally unwise to oversimplify the representation until we are certain that the diagram truly represents the dynamical problem. Then, as qualitative understanding of the components becomes quantitative, simplification may become justifiable. Instances occur time and again where the omission of a capacitor in a circuit, or a length of pipe carrying hydraulic fluid, will lead to completely erroneous results.

Consider the system diagram for the rather complicated arrangement of components indicated in Figure 1. The system comprises (1) an error-measuring system using a control transformer connected to the input terminals of an electronic amplifier; (2) an amplifier consisting of tubes, resistors, capacitors, terminals, and so forth, used to energize a pair of field coils of a direct current generator; (3) a generator which energizes the armature of the motor; (4) shafts, gears, and load. The stator of the synchro attached to the motor shaft is energized by the transmitting synchro, and its rotor winding is used to give the input signal to the electronic amplifier. The system diagram in Figure 1 is similar to the blueprint that an engineer would furnish his shop for the construction of the system rather than a diagram to be used by a mathematician for analysis purposes. However, the person who is conducting the analysis must be able to utilize data in such a form as Figure 1 and must be able to transmit information to the engineer that will guide the preparation of a figure such as Figure 1. Actually, these operations are conducted simultaneously as analysis guides design.

2 Formulation of the Equivalent Circuit of an Electrical System

Assume that the analysis is to start from data furnished in the form of Figure 1. The first problem is to find the dynamical components and the nondynamical components which are pertinent to the particular study.

A good starting point is to consider the mechanical portion of the system. It is easy to see how this part of the system is constructed and to visualize how it operates. The motor armature is connected to a

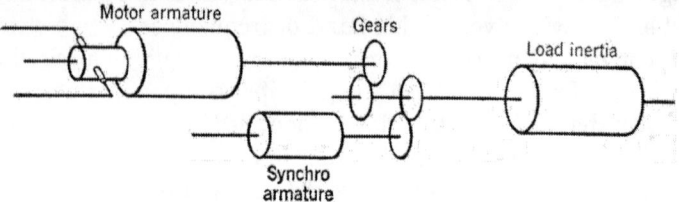

FIGURE 3. Mechanical portion of Figure 1.

flywheel and to the synchro by means of gears and shafts. The mechanical part of the system can be represented as one component of the whole as in Figure 3.

Next consider the data transmission and error-measuring system. Simple wiring diagrams of these systems, especially when synchros are used, would ignore the inertia of the synchro rotors. Persons skilled in the formulation of closed-loop system studies will have acquired the ability to identify the inertias that can be neglected and those that cannot. In the latter case they are sometimes included by lumping them with other rotating members. At the early stage of a study,

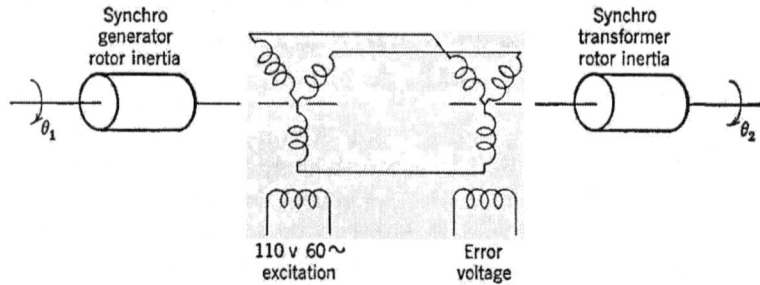

FIGURE 4. Error-measuring system of Figure 1.

however, the form of diagram shown in Figure 4 is useful where both the mechanical and the electrical properties are indicated.

The electronic part of the system may next be studied. Transformers, tubes, resistors, capacitors, all appear in the circuit. The problem is to decide which ones should be considered and which ones are unnecessary to the analysis. It is assumed that the tubes are operating in the linear regions of their characteristics and the transformers do not saturate. The voltage signal furnished by the synchro can be traced, first, through a gain or sensitivity control; second, through a triode voltage amplifier stage; third, through a coupling transformer; fourth, through a phase-sensitive rectifier detector in the output circuit of which appears an R-C filter; and finally into a power amplifier that energizes fields of the generator. The quiescent operating point of the vacuum tubes has no particular part in the dynamical study. The electronic circuits are practically instantaneous in response by comparison with the response time of motors. The amplifier may then be replaced by a box labeled "amplification" or "voltage amplifier," as shown in Figure 5.

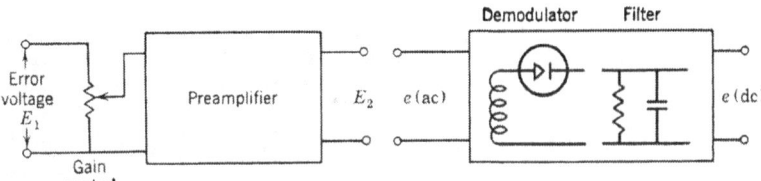

FIGURE 5. Gain control and preampli-   FIGURE 6. Phase-sensitive demodula-
fier of Figure 1.   tor and filter of Figure 1.

The portion of the circuit comprising the phase-sensitive rectifier system produces a direct voltage whose magnitude is proportional to the magnitude of the error signal and whose polarity, positive or negative, pairs with the positive or negative sign of the error signal. The filter used in this detector smoothes the ripples in the direct voltage which result from the rectification. Transformers may be replaced by a turns ratio whenever their leakage reactance is negligible. The filter circuit must be included because, if it is effective, its elements comprise sufficient energy storage to contribute to the dynamical behavior of the closed loop. Also, in the rectifier circuit, the dynamical effect is not simply the resistance and capacitance combination used in the filter. The rectifier delay [40] caused by the finite carrier frequency on the demodulator is a finite effect. However, the scope of the treatment presented herein is not sufficient to warrant a full discussion of the properties of demodulator dynamics. Thus we shall choose a diagram of the form shown in Figure 6, with the realization that equivalent time constants must be used to facilitate this simplification.

The power stage of the amplifier may next be considered. It may function as a voltage source or as a current source, depending upon the types of tubes used. By the use of pentodes, it is permissible to show the diagram as a conventional current source even though the field in-

ductance of the generator may be several henries.   However, if triodes
are used or if the field inductance is great, it may be necessary to represent the dynamical effects in the plate circuit by a diagram, such as

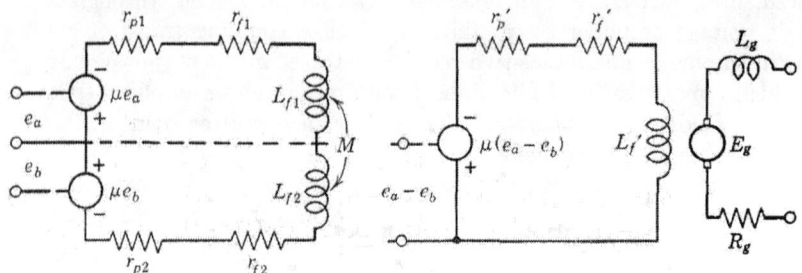

FIGURE 7.   Power amplifier equivalent circuit of Figure 1.

FIGURE 8.   Power amplifier equivalent
circuit of Figure 7 showing excitation of
the generator of Figure 1.

Figure 7.   Only the upper half or the lower half of the circuit need be
used, as in Figure 8.   Notice that the tube plus its load is treated as an
integral assembly that furnishes excitation current to the generator field.
The generator voltage is then expressed as a function of field current.
The generator output, in turn, energizes the motor.

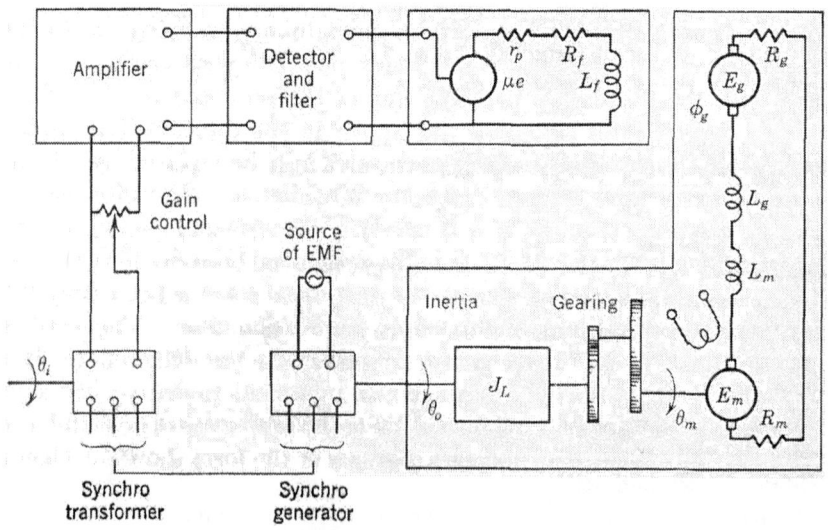

FIGURE 9.   Composite equivalent circuit of Figure 1.

The entire system has now been considered.   Merging of all the individual parts gives the overall equivalent circuit diagram shown in Figure 9.

Two basic types of dynamical element exist in the overall system, namely, electrical components with corrective networks, and mechanical components such as inertia and friction at the rotating shafts of the output members. They have no influence upon the manner used subsequently to set up equations for system response. Naturally, there are exceptions to the suggestions made here. In more complicated circuits it may not be possible even to approach some of the simplified methods of presentation used for this system. The objective here is to indicate a *method of thinking* that can guide the formulation of rules for reducing such electrical, electronic, mechanical systems to schematic diagrams and equivalent circuits rather than prescribe a specific rule.

3 Formulation of the Equivalent Circuit of an Hydraulic System

In contrast to the electric system, consider the system diagram for the hydraulic servomechanism shown in Figure 10. The assembly comprises a synchro data transmission system, an hydraulic valve, an hydraulic amplifier of both force and motion, an adjustable stroke pump powered by an electric motor and stroked by the hydraulic amplifier, an hydraulic motor operated by the flow of oil from the hydraulic pump, and the feedback to the synchro data system. The combination of electric-magnetic-hydraulic parts forms a closed-loop system.

The data transmission system comprises three members, namely, a synchro generator, a synchro differential, and another synchro generator, as shown in Figure 11. This device measures the difference between desired and actual output position and sends the error signal to the pilot valve which causes the operation of the hydraulic amplifier. One synchro generator acts to measure input position, the other to measure output position, and each energizes a set of windings of the synchro differential. The torque or rotor position of the differential is a function of the difference between the input and output positions. In the former study of the electrical-electronic system the inertia of the output synchro was lumped with the drive-motor inertia. Here the problem of including the synchro inertia effect occurs again. Inertia of the output synchro generators may be lumped with the hydraulic motor. The differential synchro presents a more difficult problem for it must be represented not merely as an inertia but also as an electromagnetic device that experiences a torque on its rotor when the rotor position deviates from the neutral position. Viscous drag is also present at the shaft of this rotor partly because of its own eddy-current-drag effects and partly because it is often submerged in an hydraulic fluid. The equivalent picture of the data transmission error-measuring system is given in

Figure 11, where θ_3 represents the actual angular position of the rotor of the synchro differential.

The motion of the synchro differential causes a lever system, indicated in Figure 10, to move the pilot valve of the hydraulic amplifier. This

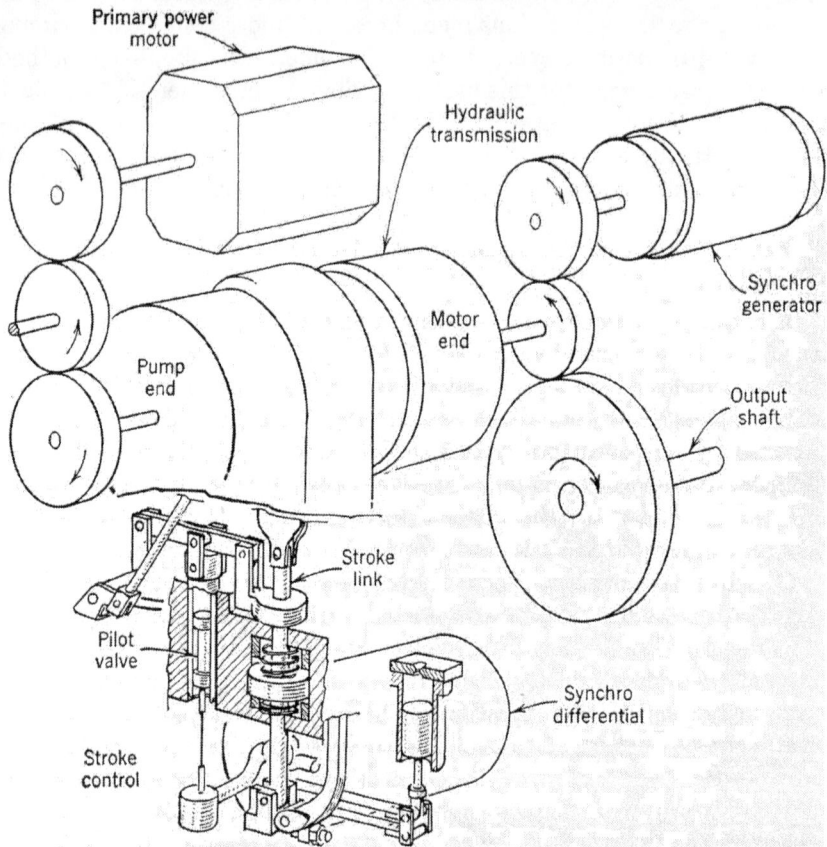

FIGURE 10. Diagram of an hydraulic servomechanism.

hydraulic amplifier is actually a closed loop in itself. By an arrangement indicated in Figure 10, the output or power piston motion is fed back to a sleeve which surrounds the pilot valve and regulates the flow of oil to the power piston as the pilot valve gets ahead of the sleeve. This, in effect, makes the unit a position follow-up. The power piston which strokes the pump tends to follow the motion of the pilot valve attached to an arm on the synchro differential shaft. The springs and the dashpot shown in the diagram, Figure 10, establish a restraint on the synchro differential rotor for sensitivity control and furnish regenerative feed-

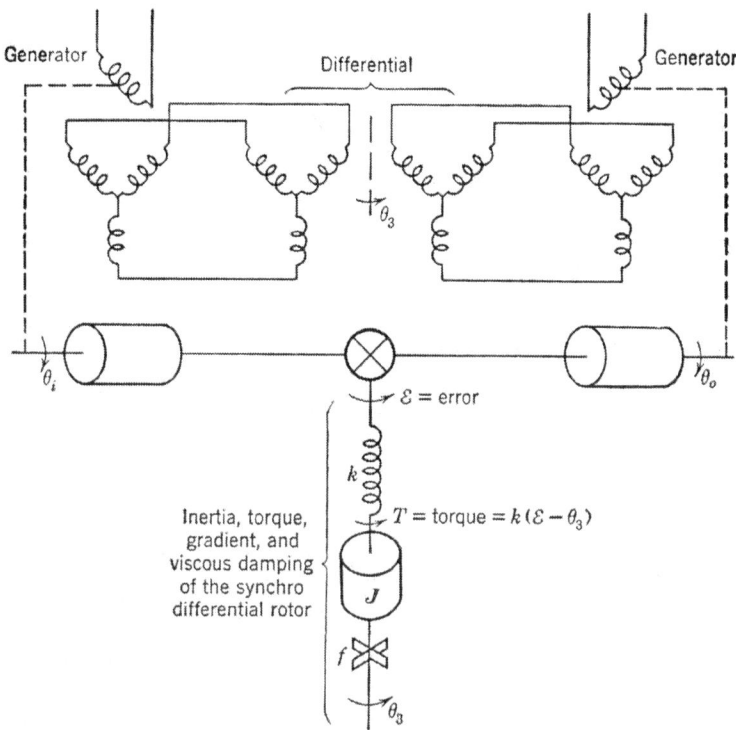

FIGURE 11. Equivalent circuit of synchro differential combination as error
measuring means.

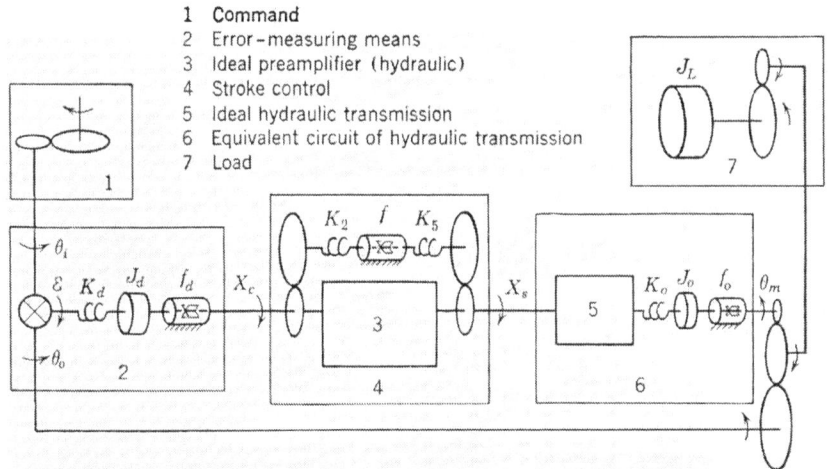

1 Command
2 Error-measuring means
3 Ideal preamplifier (hydraulic)
4 Stroke control
5 Ideal hydraulic transmission
6 Equivalent circuit of hydraulic transmission
7 Load

FIGURE 12. Equivalent circuit of hydraulic servomechanism of Figure 10.

back [44] to this restraint in order to remove all zero frequency or steady velocity errors from the system. The reader will note from the treatment in Chapter 7 that such action injects integral control or memory into the system. The pump stroke established by the power piston controls the direction of flow of oil to the hydraulic motor, which in turn moves the load member and establishes the system follow-up.

The equivalent circuit of the complete assembly is shown in Figure 12.

4 Block Diagrams and Transfer Functions

This section treats the step-by-step procedure for deriving a block diagram and transfer function from a wiring diagram or engineering drawing for a variety of components.

An Elementary Electrical Network. The four-terminal network in Figure 13 can be analyzed, using a system diagram to form the mathematical relationships of the circuit. The transfer function for the voltage

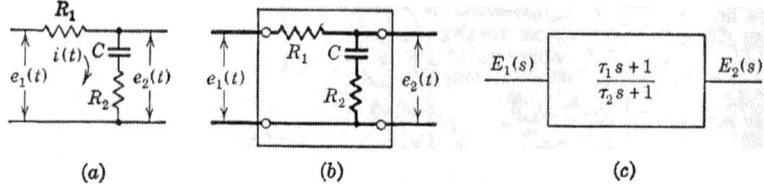

(a) (b) (c)

FIGURE 13. Symbolic treatment for a simple network.

transfer across the network can be written and finally a block diagram can be drawn to represent the mathematical behavior of the system. The system diagram, the equivalent circuit, and the block diagram are shown as a, b, and c, respectively, of Figure 13.

The loop equations for the network, assuming the output terminals are open-circuited, are

$$e_1(t) = R_1 i(t) + \frac{1}{C} \int i(t)\, dt + R_2 i(t) \tag{1}$$

$$e_2(t) = \frac{1}{C} \int i(t)\, dt + R_2 i(t) \tag{2}$$

The Laplace transforms for these equations are then formed:

$$E_1(s) = R_1 I(s) + \frac{1}{Cs} I(s) + \frac{1}{Cs} i^{-1}(0+) + R_2 I(s) \tag{3}$$

$$E_2(s) = \frac{1}{Cs} I(s) + \frac{1}{Cs} i^{-1}(0+) + R_2 I(s) \tag{4}$$

If the capacitor of the network is initially uncharged, the relation between the applied voltage and the response voltage, that is, the transfer function for this network, is

$$\frac{E_2(s)}{E_1(s)} = \frac{1 + R_2 Cs}{1 + (R_1 + R_2) Cs} \tag{5}$$

The transfer function is best expressed in a dimensionless form. The following algebraic changes are made so that

$$\frac{E_2(s)}{E_1(s)} = \frac{\tau_1 s + 1}{\tau_2 s + 1} = KG(s) \tag{6}$$

where

$$\left. \begin{array}{l} K = 1 \\ G(s) = \dfrac{\tau_1 s + 1}{\tau_2 s + 1} \end{array} \right\} \tag{7}$$

and

$$\left. \begin{array}{l} \tau_1 = CR_2 \\ \tau_2 = (R_2 + R_1)C \end{array} \right\} \tag{8}$$

The mathematical form of the voltage ratio for the network of Figure 13 may now be represented as a box or block diagram, as shown in Figure 13c, when any applied voltage enters at the left. The transfer function $KG(s)$ indicates the nature of the output or responding voltage. Note that the transfer function is a mathematical definition for the internal structure of the physical network. In no sense does it define the nature of the applied voltage. This is important, for the input voltage must be transformed if we are to predict the exact response of the network for any known time variation of input.

A Vacuum Tube Amplifier. Consider now the behavior of a simple electronic voltage amplifier. Figure 14a shows the circuit in which a

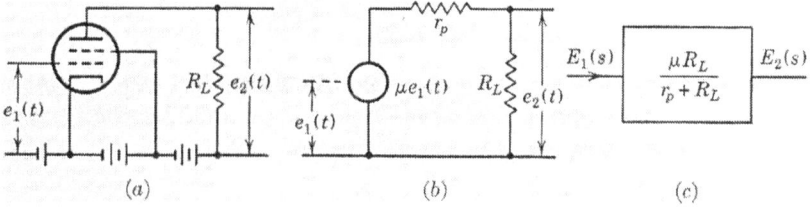

(a)   (b)   (c)

FIGURE 14. Symbolic treatment of a vacuum tube amplifier.

voltage $e_1(t)$, applied to the grid of the tube, causes a voltage to appear across the load resistor, R_L. The conventional equivalent circuit may be drawn as in Figure 14b. The loop equations may be written for the current in the plate circuit:

$$\mu e_1(t) = (r_p + R_L)i(t) \tag{9}$$

$$e_2(t) = R_L i(t) \tag{10}$$

The transforms of the circuit equations give

$$\mu E_1(s) = (r_p + R_L)I(s) \tag{11}$$

$$E_2(s) = R_L I(s) \tag{12}$$

and the transfer function may be written

$$\frac{E_2(s)}{E_1(s)} = \frac{\mu R_L}{R_L + r_p} = KG(s) \tag{13}$$

where

$$\left. \begin{array}{c} K = \dfrac{\mu R_L}{R_L + r_p} \\[2mm] G(s) = 1 \end{array} \right\} \tag{14}$$

The block diagram is now formed as in Figure 14c.

A Network with a Vacuum Tube Amplifier. Figure 15 shows the connection of the two circuits of Figures 13 and 14. *If the input impedance to the amplifier is large, the burden of the amplifier on the network is negligible.* The equations formerly written for the network are, therefore, again applicable. The equations for the amplifier are also unaltered. The transformed voltage relations along the cascade connection are

$$\frac{E_2(s)}{E_1(s)} = \frac{\tau_1 s + 1}{\tau_2 s + 1} = K_1 G_1(s) \tag{15}$$

$$E_3(s) = E_2(s) \tag{16}$$

$$\frac{E_4(s)}{E_3(s)} = \frac{\mu R_L}{r_p + R_L} = K_2 G_2(s) \tag{17}$$

By preparing an expression for the ratio of voltage $e_4(t)$ across the load resistance of the amplifier, to an applied voltage $e_1(t)$ across the input terminals of the network, the overall transfer relation for the cascade may be written:

$$\frac{E_4(s)}{E_1(s)} = \left(\frac{\tau_1 s + 1}{\tau_2 s + 1} \right) \left(\frac{\mu R_L}{r_p + R_L} \right) \tag{18}$$

Note that this function is the product of the transfer functions for the individual network and for the amplifier. This product condition exists only because the burden of the amplifier has no effect on the function $K_1G_1(s)$ as defined. The condition would not exist if the grid leak resistance of the amplifier were comparable with the impedance $R_2 + 1/Cs$ of the network. Thus .

$$\frac{E_4(s)}{E_1(s)} = K_1G_1(s) \cdot K_2G_2(s) \tag{19}$$

The frequency invariant terms or static sensitivities of the individual functions may be grouped together, forming a single sensitivity K. The

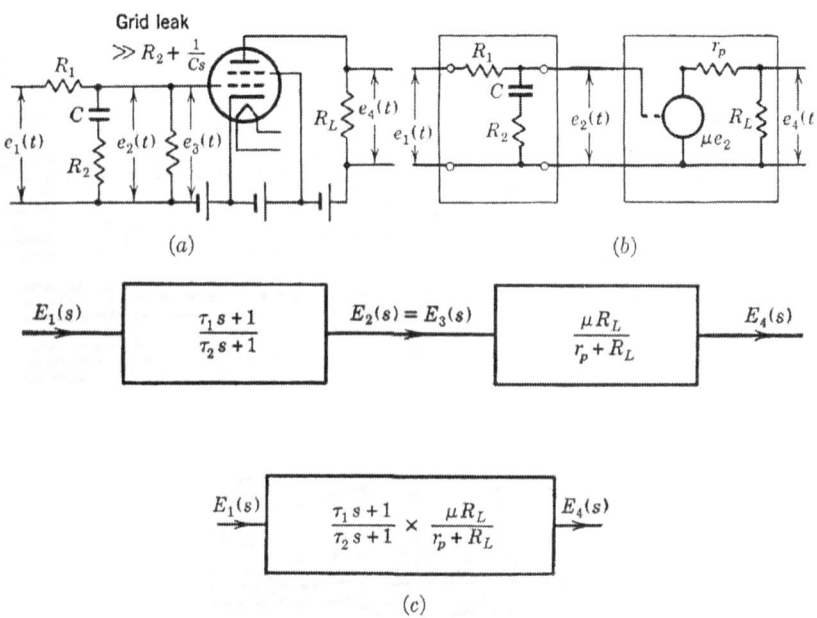

(a)   (b)

(c)

FIGURE 15.   Network with isolating amplifier.

dynamic or frequency-dependent portions of the functions likewise may be grouped together, forming a single $G(s)$, thus

$$\frac{E_4(s)}{E_1(s)} = K_1K_2G_1(s)G_2(s) \tag{20}$$

$$= KG(s) \tag{21}$$

where

$$K = K_1K_2 = \frac{\mu R_L}{r_p + R_L}$$

$$G(s) = G_1(s)G_2(s) = \frac{\tau_1 s + 1}{\tau_2 s + 1} \tag{22}$$

The diagram now consists of two blocks arranged in cascade, each defined by a transfer function. When the overall transfer function is defined it is possible to use a single block to represent the overall system for which the overall transfer function defines the single block, as shown in Figure 15c.

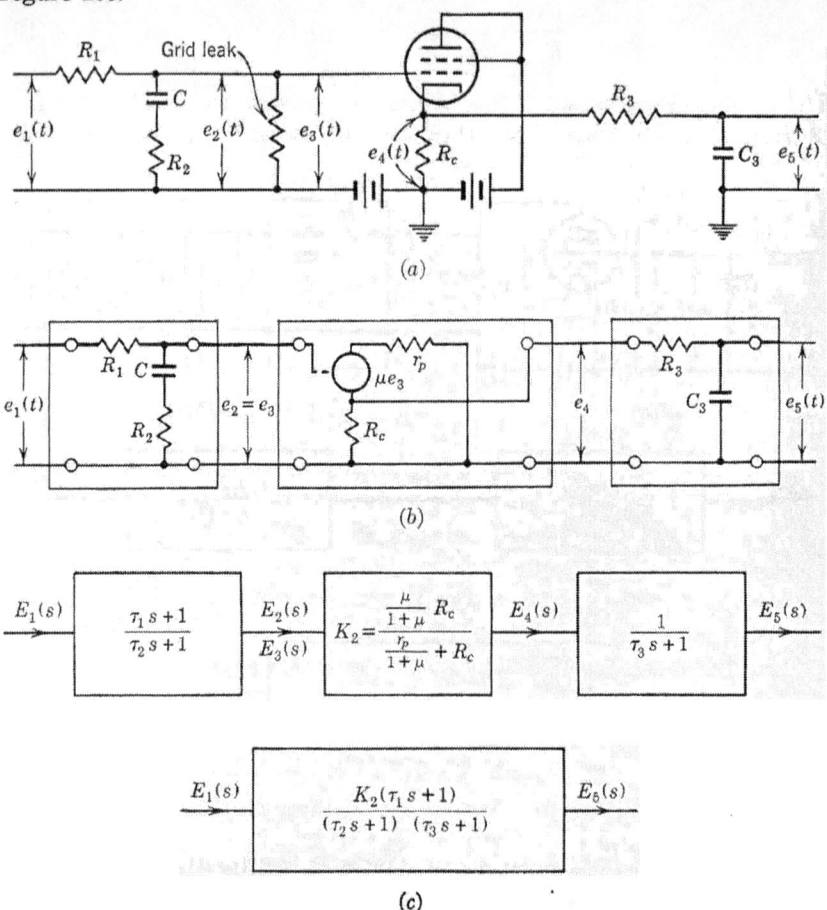

FIGURE 16.   Two networks separated by isolating amplifier.

The presence of additional circuits on the output of an amplifier, as in Figure 16, may permit a simple extension of the above multiplication of functions to give the overall transfer function. In Figure 16a, let the network comprising R_3 and C_3 be connected across the cathode * resistor R_c of the amplifier. If the burden of this network does not

* Cathode follower stages are frequently used as isolating elements in electronic circuits giving a net gain slightly less than unity.[69]

alter the voltage $e_4(t)$ across R_c within the frequency band considered in the study, the procedure is a simple one.   The transformed relations for the voltages along the cascade, under the assumption that the R_3C_3 loop is a negligible load on the amplifier, are

$$\frac{E_2(s)}{E_1(s)} = \frac{\tau_1 s + 1}{\tau_2 s + 1} = K_1 G_1(s) \tag{23}$$

$$E_3(s) = E_2(s) \tag{24}$$

$$\frac{E_4(s)}{E_2(s)} = \frac{\dfrac{\mu}{1+\mu} R_c}{\dfrac{r_p}{1+\mu} + R_c} = K_2 G_2(s) = K_2 \tag{25}$$

$$\frac{E_5(s)}{E_4(s)} = \frac{1}{C_3 R_3 s + 1} = \frac{1}{\tau_3 s + 1} = K_3 G_3(s) \tag{26}$$

The overall transfer relation is given by the product of the individual transfer functions, that is,

$$\frac{E_5(s)}{E_1(s)} = K_1 G_1(s) K_2 G_2(s) K_3 G_3(s) \tag{27}$$

$$= \left(\frac{\tau_1 s + 1}{\tau_2 s + 1}\right) K_2 \left(\frac{1}{\tau_3 s + 1}\right) \tag{28}$$

$$= KG(s) \tag{29}$$

where

$$\left.\begin{aligned} K &= K_1 K_2 K_3 = K_2 \\ G(s) &= G_1(s) G_2(s) G_3(s) \\ &= \frac{\tau_1 s + 1}{\tau_2 s + 1} \cdot \frac{1}{\tau_3 s + 1} \end{aligned}\right\} \tag{30}$$

The diagram again is a combination of the three original blocks in cascade, as shown in Figure 16c.   The equivalent block for the entire structure is a single block containing the overall transfer function.   However, the condition given above relative to the effect of the loop R_3, C_3 on the amplifier output voltage cannot be overemphasized.   It is the characteristic of most vacuum tube amplifiers to permit a change in impedance level that has made possible the cascading of individual frequency variant functions $G_1(s)$ and $G_3(s)$.   The simple connection of R_3C_3 across the voltage $e_3(t)$ would not have given the feature of individuality.   It is this isolating characteristic of the vacuum tube that makes this simple treatment permissible. The amplifier and each network can here be represented as an isolated two-terminal pair, but only because they are *noninteracting*.

Interacting Networks. When coupling or interaction exists between sections of the cascade network, only a single unique function gives the output-input relation. This means that it is not permissible to represent the sections of the cascade as isolated two-terminal pairs. The network must be analyzed in a manner that gives the overall ratio of output to input as a unique transfer function.

To illustrate this situation, consider the direct connection of two networks of the previous section, as shown in Figure 17a. Because it is

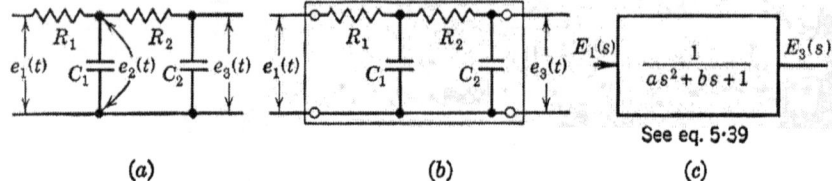

See eq. 5·39

(a)   (b)   (c)

FIGURE 17.   Symbolic treatment of interacting networks.

probable that R_1, C_1 and R_2, C_2 are circuits having comparable impedance, Figure 17b represents the only correct equivalent circuit as a two-terminal pair. Loop equations for the currents and voltages are

$$e_1(t) = R_1 i_1(t) + \frac{1}{C_1}\int [i_1(t) - i_2(t)]\, dt \tag{31}$$

$$0 = \frac{1}{C_1}\int [i_2(t) - i_1(t)]\, dt + R_2 i_2(t) + \frac{1}{C_2}\int i_2(t)\, dt \tag{32}$$

$$e_3(t) = \frac{1}{C_2}\int i_2(t)\, dt \tag{33}$$

The transforms are

$$E_1(s) = R_1 I_1(s) + \frac{1}{C_1 s}[I_1(s) - I_2(s)] + \frac{1}{C_1 s}[i_1{}^{-1}(0+) - i_2{}^{-1}(0+)] \tag{34}$$

$$0 = \frac{1}{C_1 s}[I_2(s) - I_1(s)] + \frac{1}{C_1 s}[i_2{}^{-1}(0+) - i_1{}^{-1}(0+)] + R_2 I_2(s)$$

$$+ \frac{1}{C_2 s} I_2(s) + \frac{1}{C_2 s} i_2{}^{-1}(0+) \tag{35}$$

$$E_3(s) = \frac{1}{C_2 s} I_2(s) + \frac{1}{C_2 s} i_2{}^{-1}(0+) \tag{36}$$

Assuming that the charge on the capacitors is zero at $t = 0+$, the simultaneous solution of Equations 34, 35, and 36 for the output-input voltage gives

$$I_2(s) = \frac{E_1(s)\,\dfrac{1}{C_1 s}}{\left[R_1 + \dfrac{1}{C_1 s}\right]\left[R_2 + \dfrac{1}{C_1 s} + \dfrac{1}{C_2 s}\right] - \left[\dfrac{1}{C_1 s}\right]^2} \tag{37}$$

$$\frac{E_3(s)}{E_1(s)} = \frac{\left[\dfrac{1}{C_1 s}\right]\left[\dfrac{1}{C_2 s}\right]}{\left[R_1 + \dfrac{1}{C_1 s}\right]\left[R_2 + \dfrac{1}{C_1 s} + \dfrac{1}{C_2 s}\right] - \left[\dfrac{1}{C_1 s}\right]^2} \tag{38}$$

$$\frac{E_3(s)}{E_1(s)} = \frac{1}{C_1 C_2 R_1 R_2 s^2 + (C_2 R_1 + C_2 R_2 + C_1 R_1)s + 1} \tag{39}$$

$$= KG(s) = \frac{1}{as^2 + bs + 1} \tag{40}$$

The function $KG(s)$ now is of quadratic form. It may be factored into two first-order terms with time constants τ_1 and τ_2, as follows:

$$\frac{1}{as^2 + bs + 1} = \frac{1}{(\tau_1 s + 1)(\tau_2 s + 1)} \tag{41}$$

This factorizing procedure should not be interpreted as implying the existence of two blocks in cascade to represent $KG(s)$. In the first place $\tau_1 \neq R_1 C_1$ and $\tau_2 \neq R_2 C_2$. Neither τ_1 nor τ_2 is directly associated with particular resistors or capacitors. Furthermore, the voltage mathematically expressible at the midpoint cascade of the two fictitious blocks has no real significance. Thus the representation of the circuit of Figure 17a by the transform $KG(s) = 1/(as^2 + bs + 1)$ is the only reliable one.

Rotating Electrical Machinery. Subject to the validity of certain simplifying assumptions, transfer functions for electromagnetic machinery used in control systems are readily prepared. A direct current motor, having constant armature current and controlled by a voltage $e(t)$ applied to its field may be represented as in Figure 18a. The motor has a rotor inertia J and a friction denoted by the viscous coefficient f. It may be assumed (1) that air gap flux, ϕ, is proportional to field current

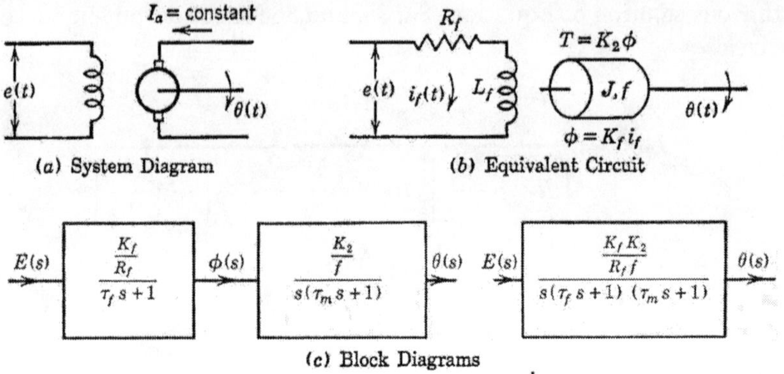

(a) System Diagram   (b) Equivalent Circuit

(c) Block Diagrams

FIGURE 18.   Direct-current motor with field control and constant armature current.

i_f, and (2) that rotor torque, T, is proportional to the air gap flux.   The equations for the system are

$$e(t) = R_f i_f(t) + L_f \frac{di_f(t)}{dt} \tag{42}$$

$$\phi(t) = K_f i_f(t) \tag{43}$$

$$T(t) = K_2 \phi(t) \tag{44}$$

$$T(t) = J \frac{d^2\theta(t)}{dt^2} + f \frac{d\theta(t)}{dt} \tag{45}$$

These equations are transformable to

$$E(s) = R_f I_f(s) + L_f s I_f(s) - L_f i_f(0+) \tag{46}$$

$$\phi(s) = K_f I_f(s) \tag{47}$$

$$T(s) = K_2 \phi(s) \tag{48}$$

$$T(s) = Js^2\theta(s) + fs\theta(s) - J\left[s\theta(0+) + \frac{d\theta}{dt}(0+)\right] - f[\theta(0+)] \tag{49}$$

If it is assumed that $i_f(0+)$, $\theta(0+)$, and $d\theta(0+)/dt$ are zero, that is, the motor was at rest at $t = 0+$, the transfer function for the field structure is

$$\frac{\phi(s)}{E(s)} = \frac{K_f}{L_f s + R_f} \tag{50}$$

and for the rotor structure is

$$\frac{\theta(s)}{\phi(s)} = \frac{K_2}{(Js^2 + fs)} \tag{51}$$

Since

$$\frac{\theta(s)}{E(s)} = \frac{\phi(s)}{E(s)} \frac{\theta(s)}{\phi(s)} \tag{52}$$

giving

$$KG(s) = \frac{K_f K_2}{(Js^2 + fs)(L_f s + R_f)} \tag{53}$$

Equation 53 is a transfer function which relates the position θ of the armature to the voltage e applied to the field. Further simplification of this expression can be obtained by nondimensionalizing it. Thus, as shown in Figure 18c,

$$\frac{\theta(s)}{E(s)} = \frac{\left(\dfrac{K_f}{R_f}\right)\left(\dfrac{K_2}{f}\right)}{s(\tau_m s + 1)(\tau_f s + 1)} = KG(s) \tag{54}$$

where

$$\left.\begin{aligned} K &= \frac{K_f K_2}{R_f f} \\[2mm] \tau_m &= \frac{J}{f} \\[2mm] \tau_f &= \frac{L_f}{R_f} \end{aligned}\right\} \tag{55}$$

As a matter of contrast, consider that the field excitation of the motor is constant and that a control voltage $e(t)$ is applied to the armature. Also consider that the brush and bearing friction are negligible. This is permissible here because the equations for the system now contain a term for the back emf $e_b(t)$. The diagram representing this system is given in Figure 19a. The torque which accelerates the armature is now influenced by the reaction of the back emf of the armature which contributes considerable damping to the system. The differential equations are

$$e(t) = R_a i_a(t) + L_a \frac{di_a(t)}{dt} + e_b(t) \tag{56}$$

$$e_b(t) = K_1 \omega(t) = K_1 \frac{d\theta(t)}{dt} \tag{57}$$

$$T(t) = K_2 i_a(t) \tag{58}$$

$$T(t) = J \frac{d^2\theta(t)}{dt^2} \tag{59}$$

These equations may be transformed as

$$E(s) = R_a I_a(s) + L_a s I_a(s) + E_b(s) - L_a i_a(0+) \qquad (60)$$

$$E_b(s) = K_1 \omega(s) = K_1 s \theta(s) - K_1 \theta(0+) \qquad (61)$$

$$T(s) = K_2 I_a(s) \qquad (62)$$

$$T(s) = J s^2 \theta(s) - J s \theta(0+) - J \frac{d\theta}{dt}(0+) \qquad (63)$$

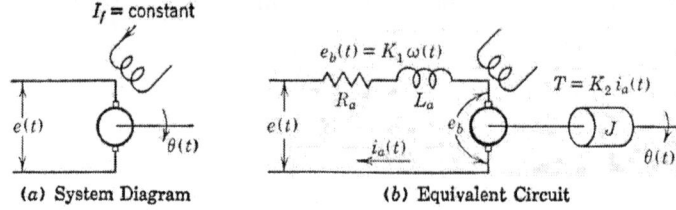

(a) System Diagram   (b) Equivalent Circuit

$$\boxed{E(s) \xrightarrow{\quad} \frac{K_2}{s(JL_a s^2 + JR_a s + K_1 K_2)} \xrightarrow{\quad} \theta(s)}$$

(c) Block Diagram

FIGURE 19. Direct-current motor with armature-voltage control and constant field flux.

If the armature current and armature speed are zero at $t = 0+$, the simultaneous solution of Equations 60 to 63 give

$$\frac{\theta(s)}{E(s)} = \frac{K_2 \dfrac{1}{R_a + sL_a}}{Js^2 + \dfrac{K_1 K_2}{R_a + sL_a} s} \qquad (64)$$

$$= \frac{K_2}{s[L_a J s^2 + J R_a s + K_1 K_2]} = KG(s) \qquad (65)$$

The back emf is a quantity that is related to the motion of the armature, and to the armature current. Thus there is interaction between the electrical and mechanical portions of the machine. The opportunity to separate the transfer function for this motor into factors characterized by mechanical and electrical time constants τ_m and τ_f in the analysis of

Figure 18 no longer exists.   The transfer function is now a unique single quantity as shown in Figure 19c.

Often the armature inductance of the motor is small enough to have negligible effect upon the system operation.   When L_a is set equal to zero, a new transfer function is

$$\frac{\theta(s)}{E(s)} = \frac{K_2}{JR_a s^2 + K_1 K_2 s} = \frac{K_v}{s(\tau_m' s + 1)} = KG(s) \tag{66}$$

Since the time constant τ_m' of Equation 66 is a function of both electrical and mechanical parameters, the block diagram for $KG(s)$ of Equation 66 is still not factorable into two blocks, namely, $1/s$ and $K_v/(\tau_m' s + 1)$, where each block would relate to a definite part of the machine.

That there is no single rule for the formulation of these block diagrams may be further demonstrated.   Consider a situation wherein the properties of the motor, Figure 20a, are given only in the form of a speed torque characteristic [7] as in Figure 20b.   For rapid time variations of

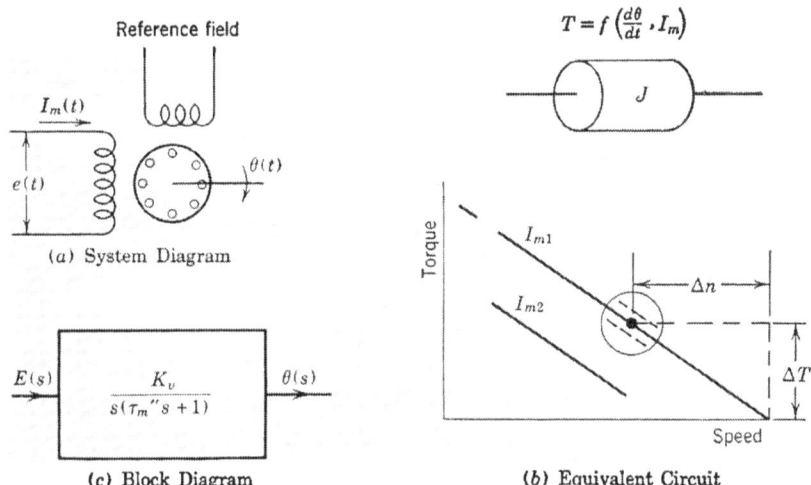

(a) System Diagram

(c) Block Diagram

(b) Equivalent Circuit

FIGURE 20.   Treatment of electric motor described by torque-speed characteristic.

the control signal and the motor speed, the data of Figure 20b are not a good representation of the behavior, as a careful study of electric machinery will show.   However, since the frequencies of the time variation of control signal or speed are only of the order of a few cycles per second in most servomechanisms, the conditions of Figure 20b are often assumed applicable.   This is equivalent to saying that the instantaneous behavior in the dynamic state does not appreciably differ from the steady state as represented by the characteristics, Figure 20b.

From this speed torque characteristic * it follows that

$$\text{Motor speed } n = \frac{d\theta}{dt} = \left(\frac{\text{speed}}{\text{unit current}}\right) I_m + \left(\frac{\text{speed}}{\text{unit torque}}\right) T$$

$$= \left(\frac{\partial n}{\partial I_m}\right) I_m + \left(\frac{\partial n}{\partial T}\right) T \tag{67}$$

If the motor is energized from a power source that makes motor current I_m proportional to a positional error signal ε, the motor current I_m is given by $I_m = (\partial I_m / \partial \varepsilon)\varepsilon$. The substitution for I_m in Equation 67 gives

$$\frac{d\theta}{dt} = \left(\frac{\partial n}{\partial I_m}\right)\left(\frac{\partial I_m}{\partial \varepsilon}\right) \varepsilon + \left(\frac{\partial n}{\partial T}\right) T \tag{68}$$

The portion of Equation 68 comprising $(\partial n / \partial I_m)(\partial I_m / \partial \varepsilon)$ has the dimensions of speed n divided by angle, that is, degrees per second per degree. It equals second^{-1}. Furthermore, it defines the steady-state relation between the positional signal that establishes motor current and the motor speed as connected in the system. In terms of the controlled quantity θ, it represents a so-called velocity constant defined by the symbol

$$K_v = \frac{\text{degrees per second}}{\text{degree}} = \frac{1}{\text{second}} \tag{69}$$

Since, in the absence of load, the instantaneous torque shown by the motor characteristic is expended wholly in accelerating the output,

$$T = J \frac{d^2\theta}{dt^2} \tag{70}$$

Therefore $\dfrac{\partial n}{\partial T} T$ of Equation 68 has the form

$$\frac{\partial n}{\partial T} T = -J \left| \frac{\partial n}{\partial T} \right| \frac{d^2\theta}{dt^2} \tag{71}$$

---

* The reader will note that a starting point for this analysis could have postulated the motor as a torque device. The analysis would then start from the relation

$$\text{Motor torque } T = \frac{\partial T}{\partial n} n + \frac{\partial T}{\partial I_m} I_m$$

The pattern of analysis then followed would lead to the writing of a torque identity

$$J \frac{d^2\theta}{dt^2} = \frac{\partial T}{\partial n} \frac{d\theta}{dt} + \frac{\partial T}{\partial I_m} \frac{\partial I_m}{\partial \varepsilon} \varepsilon$$

The partial coefficients in this relation would be determined as above and would lead to the result of Equation 76, where the negative sign results from the negative slope of the curve of Figure 20b, but

$$J \frac{\partial n}{\partial T} = \frac{\partial n}{\partial T/J} = \frac{\text{speed}}{\text{acceleration}} = \frac{\text{degrees per second}}{\text{degrees per second}^2} = \text{seconds} \quad (72)$$

Therefore $\left| J \dfrac{\partial n}{\partial T} \right|$ is a motor time constant τ_m'' and, in terms of Equations 69 and 72, the output velocity $d\theta/dt$ equals

$$\frac{d\theta}{dt} = K_v \mathcal{E} - \tau_m'' \frac{d^2\theta}{dt^2} \quad (73)$$

or

$$\tau_m'' \frac{d^2\theta}{dt^2} + \frac{d\theta}{dt} = K_v \mathcal{E} \quad (74)$$

The terms in Equation 74 transform to give

$$\tau_m'' s^2 \theta(s) - \tau_m'' s\theta(0+) - \tau_m'' \frac{d\theta}{dt}(0+) + s\theta(s) - \theta(0+) = K_v \mathcal{E}(s) \quad (75)$$

Assuming $\theta(0+)$ and $d\theta(0+)/dt$ as zero, the transfer relation between θ and signal $\mathcal{E}$ is

$$\frac{\theta(s)}{\mathcal{E}(s)} = \frac{K_v}{s(\tau_m'' s + 1)} = KG(s) \quad (76)$$

Equation 76 has the same general form as Equation 66, but the time constant τ_m'' is related uniquely to the partial derivative $\partial n/\partial T$ of the speed torque characteristic of Figure 20b corresponding to a small region, such as (a) on the characteristic. If the operation changes to another region on the characteristic where $\partial n/\partial T$ changes, the time constant τ_m'' changes. As in Equation 66, the time constant here is not directly associated with any single physical part of the machine.

Gear Trains and Inertias. Mechanical systems having inertia and friction are frequently coupled together through gear trains or levers. Transfer functions must then be prepared for these dynamical systems. Consider the system illustrated in Figure 21a. The rotating bodies have inertias J_1 and J_2 and viscous frictions f_1 and f_2. The gear ratio is $1:n$. When the inertia of the gears and the elastance of the shafts can be neglected, the differential equations for the torques on the two separate bodies are related to each other by the torque $T(t)$ which appears at the gear mesh. Let a torque $T_1(t)$ be applied to shaft θ_1; then

$$J_1 \frac{d^2\theta_1(t)}{dt^2} + f_1 \frac{d\theta_1(t)}{dt} = T_1(t) - T(t) \tag{77}$$

$$J_2 \frac{d^2\theta_2(t)}{dt^2} + f_2 \frac{d\theta_2(t)}{dt} = nT(t) \tag{78}$$

$$n\theta_2(t) = \theta_1(t) \tag{79}$$

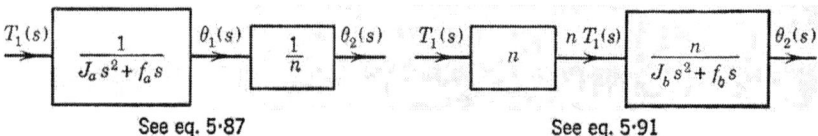

(a) System Diagram

| $T_1(s)$ | $\dfrac{1}{J_a s^2 + f_a s}$ | $\theta_1(s)$ | $\dfrac{1}{n}$ | $\theta_2(s)$ | $T_1(s)$ | n | $n\,T_1(s)$ | $\dfrac{n}{J_b s^2 + f_b s}$ | $\theta_2(s)$ |

See eq. 5·87   See eq. 5·91

(b) Block Diagrams

FIGURE 21.   Gear trains and inertias.

These equations may be transformed and then solved simultaneously for a relation giving the motion of the second mass with respect to the torque applied to the first, namely,

$$J_1 s^2 \theta_1(s) + f_1 s \theta_1(s) = T_1(s) - T(s) + \text{(initial conditions)} \tag{80}$$

$$J_2 s^2 \theta_2(s) + f_2 s \theta_2(s) = nT(s) + \text{(initial conditions)} \tag{81}$$

$$n\theta_2(s) = \theta_1(s) \tag{82}$$

Two methods for performing the simultaneous solution are possible. One method is to find the motion of the first body and then refer it to the second body through the gear train. Thus with the initial conditions equal to zero, the elimination of $\theta_2(s)$ and the substitution for $T(s)$ in Equation 80 gives

$$[J_1 s^2 + f_1 s]\theta_1(s) = T_1(s) - \frac{1}{n^2}[J_2 s^2 + f_2 s]\theta_1(s)$$

$$\left[\left(J_1 + \frac{J_2}{n^2}\right)s^2 + \left(f_1 + \frac{f_2}{n^2}\right)s\right]\theta_1(s) = T_1(s) \tag{83}$$

which may be written as

$$\frac{\theta_1(s)}{T_1(s)} = \frac{1}{\left(J_1 + \dfrac{J_2}{n^2}\right)s^2 + \left(f_1 + \dfrac{f_2}{n^2}\right)s} \tag{84}$$

$$= \frac{1}{J_a s^2 + f_a s} \tag{85}$$

$$= KG(s) = \frac{K_a}{s(\tau_a s + 1)} \tag{86}$$

where

$$\left. \begin{aligned} J_a &= J_1 + \frac{J_2}{n^2} \\[2mm] f_a &= f_1 + \frac{f_2}{n^2} \\[2mm] \tau_a &= \frac{J_a}{f_a} \\[2mm] K_a &= \frac{1}{f_a} \end{aligned} \right\} \tag{87}$$

The quantities J_a and f_a represent the total inertia and total friction referred to the first shaft. Thus a block diagram may be established for the system as in Figure 21b, where the torque is applied to a member that contains all the lumped inertia and the lumped friction. The motion of this lumped member is referred to another block which contains a function representing only the gear ratio as a number, and the output of the second block is the output motion θ_2.

The second method for preparing the response equation is to refer the inertia and the friction of the first member to the shaft of the second. Thus the equations become

$$[J_2 s^2 + f_2 s]\theta_2(s) = nT_1(s) - n^2[J_1 s^2 + f_1 s]\theta_2(s) \tag{88}$$

$$[(J_2 + n^2 J_1)s^2 + (f_2 + n^2 f_1)s]\theta_2(s) = nT_1(s) \tag{89}$$

and the transfer function for the system is now written as

$$\frac{\theta_2(s)}{T_1(s)} = \frac{n}{J_b s^2 + f_b s} = KG(s) = \frac{K_b}{s(\tau_b s + 1)} \tag{90}$$

where the inertia and friction referred to the second shaft is

$$
\left.\begin{aligned}
J_b &= J_2 + n^2 J_1 \\
f_b &= f_2 + n^2 f_1 \\
\tau_b &= \frac{J_b}{f_b} = \tau_a \\
K_b &= \frac{n}{f_b}
\end{aligned}\right\}
\tag{91}
$$

Another block diagram may be drawn wherein the torque applied to the first member is referred through a perfect gear train to a second shaft leading into a box where all the parameters of the system are lumped. The output motion is the output of the second box. Figure 21b shows the block diagram for this condition.

Complicated gear trains frequently introduce additional inertia because of the gear masses, backlash at the meshes due to tolerances in manufacture and working clearances, and elastance in the shafting and the gears, depending on the stresses in the materials established by the loads. These factors introduce problems of design. The extent to which they enter into the dynamics must be evaluated for each particular instance.[65]

Hydraulic Transmissions. A device often used as a servomotor has been variously known as *hydraulic transmission, speed gear, oil gear,* and *positive displacement transmission.* The steady-state characteristics of the device are such that the hydraulic motor shaft rotates at a speed proportional to the *pump stroke.* This speed-stroke relationship is maintained nearly independent of load torques. In order to maintain the pump on-stroke when the motor is delivering torque, considerable force is required. This usually means that considerable amplification of an error signal is required before it is applied to the stroking mechanism of the pump. Both hydraulic and electrical amplifiers have been used for this purpose.[27, 44]

The dynamic behavior of a transmission is dependent upon many factors, most of which are nonlinear. However, if the three most important factors are considered and assumptions are made which permit linear analysis, an acceptable mathematical representation [27] of the device may be made. These three factors are output inertia, pump and motor leakage, and oil compressibility.

Pictures of an hydraulic transmission and of its equivalent circuit are shown in Figures 22a and 22b, respectively. The closed hydraulic circuit is kept full by means of an oil-replenishing system not shown.

The torque output T_m of the hydraulic motor is proportional to the pressure, P. The output speed of the motor is proportional to the volumetric flow rate Q_m through the motor. The volumetric delivery

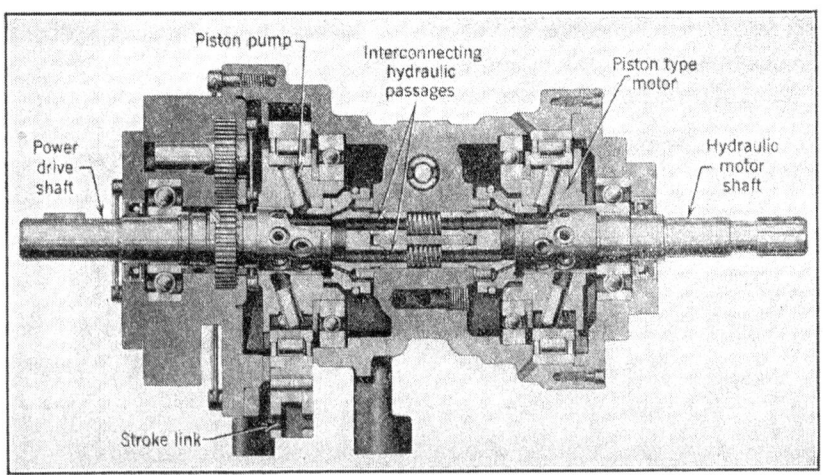

(a) Internal structure of Hydraulic transmission. (Courtesy Oilgear Co., Milwaukee, Wis.)

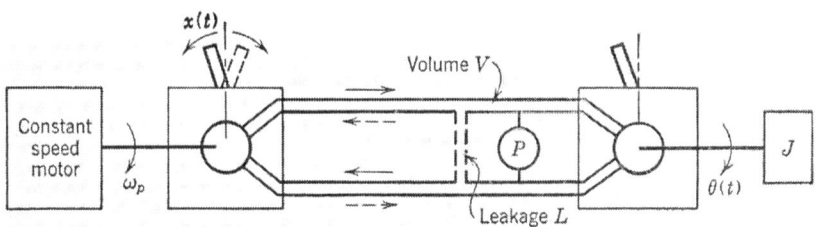

(b) Equivalent circuit.

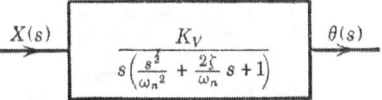

$$\frac{K_V}{s\left(\frac{s^2}{\omega_n{}^2} + \frac{2\zeta}{\omega_n}s + 1\right)}$$

(c) Block diagram.

FIGURE 22.   Hydraulic transmission.

Q_p of the pump is proportional to the pump stroke x and is independent of the back pressure, P. The leakage L of both the pump and motor may be taken into account by assuming an equivalent external leakage path. The volumetric flow Q_L through this path is assumed proportional to the pressure, P. Oil compressibility is given by the relation

$$P = B \frac{\Delta V}{V} \tag{92}$$

where ΔV is the decrease in volume for positive pressure; that is, the oil changes volume in proportion to the pressure, P.

The following symbols are used in the analysis:

$$\left.\begin{array}{l} n = \text{pump shaft speed} \\ d_p = \text{pump displacement for maximum stroke} \\ x = \text{per unit stroke of pump} \\ d_m = \text{motor displacement} \\ J_m = \text{motor and output inertia} \\ L = \text{leakage coefficient} \\ B = \text{bulk modulus of oil } (0.27 \times 10^6 \text{ psi}) \\ V = \text{total volume of oil under compression in system} \end{array}\right\} \tag{93}$$

The flow relations, considering the above assumptions, are

$$\text{Pump flow} = \text{motor flow} + \text{leakage flow} + \text{compressibility flow}$$

or

where

$$Q_p = Q_m + Q_L + Q_c \tag{94}$$

$$Q_p = d_p n x \tag{95}$$

$$Q_m = d_m \frac{d\theta}{dt} \tag{96}$$

$$Q_L = LP \tag{97}$$

$$Q_c = \frac{dV}{dt} = \frac{V}{B} \frac{dP}{dt} \tag{98}$$

For an ideal hydraulic motor, the theoretical torque T_m is given by the product of displacement times pressure since mechanical work equals hydraulic work. That is,

$$T_m{}' = d_m P \tag{99}$$

If the only load on the hydraulic motor is assumed to be inertia,

$$T_m = J_m \frac{d^2\theta}{dt^2} \tag{100}$$

Substituting in Equation 94 the individual expression for flow gives

$$d_p nx = d_m \frac{d\theta}{dt} + LP + \frac{V}{B}\frac{dP}{dt} \tag{101}$$

but

$$d_m P = J_m \frac{d^2\theta}{dt^2} \tag{102}$$

giving

$$P = \frac{J_m}{d_m}\frac{d^2\theta}{dt^2} \tag{103}$$

or

$$\frac{dP}{dt} = \frac{J_m}{d_m}\frac{d^3\theta}{dt^3} \tag{104}$$

Substituting Equation 103 and Equation 104 in Equation 101 gives

$$d_p nx = d_m \frac{d\theta}{dt} + \frac{LJ_m}{d_m}\frac{d^2\theta}{dt^2} + \frac{VJ_m}{Bd_m}\frac{d^3\theta}{dt^3} \tag{105}$$

The transform of Equation 105 for all initial conditions equal to zero is

$$\frac{\theta(s)}{X(s)} = \frac{d_p n}{s\left(\dfrac{VJ_m}{Bd_m}s^2 + \dfrac{LJ_m}{d_m}s + d_m\right)} = KG(s) \tag{106}$$

or

$$KG(s) = \frac{\theta(s)}{X(s)} = \frac{K_v}{s\left(\dfrac{s^2}{\omega_n{}^2} + \dfrac{2\zeta s}{\omega_n} + 1\right)} \tag{107}$$

where

$$\left.\begin{array}{c} \dfrac{1}{\omega_n{}^2} = \dfrac{VJ_m}{Bd_m{}^2} \\[2mm] \dfrac{2\zeta}{\omega_n} = \dfrac{LJ_m}{d_m{}^2} \\[2mm] K_v = n\dfrac{d_p}{d_m} \end{array}\right\} \tag{108}$$

The relation of Equation 107 leads to the block diagram of Figure 22c.
It is interesting to note from the transfer function $KG(s)$ that (1) the system tends to be oscillatory, (2) the speed of the pump has nothing

to do with the natural frequency or damping, (3) the volume of oil in either side of the closed system and the motor inertia establish, to a large degree, the upper value of resonant frequency ω_n since $1/\omega_n^2$ is proportional to VJ_m, and (4) the leakage L determines the degree of damping in the system. These factors have considerable bearing on the economics of design and on the precision of the fits of piston, valves, and seals that are justifiable in any application.

5 Algebra of Block Diagrams in Closed Loops

Cascade Connections. The transfer function for the individual components of a system can be formed into a closed-loop function by elementary rules of algebra. It is immaterial whether these components are specified by equations, graphs, or tabulated data. Furthermore, certain components may be unspecified as to mathematical form until a study has established the behavior desired of the closed loop.

The transfer function and the system block diagram permit the formulation of generalized theorems from which the overall response functions may be written in terms of the transfer functions of series or parallel arrangements, or even minor closed-loop arrangements of elements within larger loops. The portions of the loop that are not initially specified are representable by undefined functions. Once the mathematical nature of these functions is defined, their physical form can usually be established. In fact, there may often be a wide choice of physical unit that will fulfill the requirements.

Perhaps the simplest use of the algebraic manipulation is in the simplification of an array of blocks in the diagram. The series connection of blocks is the most common. Since individual transfer functions pertain only to noninteracting sections of the system, the overall transfer function is the product of the individual functions. Thus for the connections shown in Figure 23,

$$\left.\begin{aligned}
\frac{F(s)}{E(s)} &= K_1 G_1(s) \\[2mm]
\frac{H(s)}{F(s)} &= K_2 G_2(s) \\[2mm]
\frac{K(s)}{H(s)} &= K_3 G_3(s) \\[2mm]
\frac{\theta_o(s)}{K(s)} &= K_4 G_4(s)
\end{aligned}\right\} \tag{109}$$

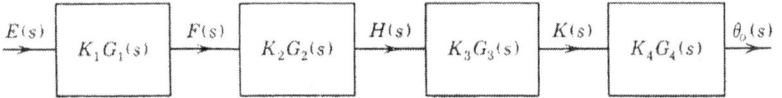

FIGURE 23.   Cascade connection of blocks.

The overall function is given by

$$\frac{\theta_o(s)}{E(s)} = K_1 K_2 K_3 K_4 G_1(s) G_2(s) G_3(s) G_4(s)$$

$$= KG(s) \tag{110}$$

where

$$\left. \begin{aligned} K &= K_1 K_2 K_3 K_4 \\ G(s) &= G_1(s) G_2(s) G_3(s) G_4(s) \end{aligned} \right\} \tag{111}$$

The usefulness of this condensation of the series connection of blocks is evident when the single block of Figure 24 resulting from the application of Equation 110 is made into a closed loop as shown in Figure 25.

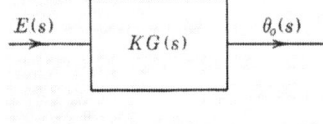 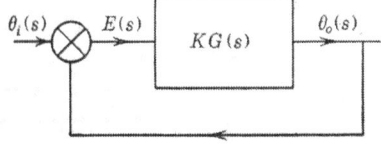

FIGURE 24.   Equivalent of Figure 23.   FIGURE 25.   Block diagram of a closed loop.

The response of the series connection of elements in Figure 25 is the system response $\theta_o(s)$. The driving function is the error signal $E(s)$. If it is assumed for purposes of simplification that no external load disturbance is applied to this system, the equations representing the loop response are

$$\left. \begin{aligned} \frac{\theta_o(s)}{E(s)} &= KG(s) \\ E(s) &= \theta_i(s) - \theta_o(s) \end{aligned} \right\} \tag{112}$$

$$\left. \begin{aligned} \frac{E(s)}{\theta_i(s)} &= \frac{1}{1 + KG(s)} \\ \frac{\theta_o(s)}{\theta_i(s)} &= \frac{KG(s)}{1 + KG(s)} \end{aligned} \right\} \tag{113}$$

where $KG(s)$ is defined by Equation 110.

By appropriate manipulation of Equations 113, a frequency response or a transient response study can be carried out. The transient study will require consideration of the initial conditions of the various energy storage components in the system. Hence, it is desirable to keep in mind the form of the initial condition transform mentioned in Chapter 3. Furthermore, if impulsive circuits are used in closed-loop systems for special compensation purposes, their manner of operation during suddenly changing signals must be recognized. The student is especially cautioned to make certain that the form of transfer function used in his study is correct for the physical behavior of the closed loop when transients are being studied. One of the more frequent errors committed during these studies is to assume that the control has a response proportional to the error and its derivative, that is, to represent the controller response $R(t)$ as

$$R(t) = k\varepsilon(t) + \ell\frac{d\varepsilon}{dt} \qquad (114)$$

A control response of this kind is physically unlikely, if not impossible. If test functions involving a step or a pulse of error are applied, the derivative term involves an infinity. While the mathematical treatment of this infinity may not introduce any complexity, the system generally ignores the infinity. This follows from the fact that no physical system can establish an infinite torque, and in a mechanism involving mass, the presence of even a near infinite torque applied for zero time as in a pulse would produce no displacement of the mass. In any physical system the displacement at $t = 0+$ would be zero. In any mathematical study it can be made zero by appropriate selection of the boundary conditions applied when making the solution by the classical method, or by the use of the initial condition transform as it appears in the operational method.

It is the opinion of the authors that the transfer function representation of a system is more helpful in the performance of frequency response studies than in transient response studies. The greatest value resulting from its use lies in synthesis rather than in analysis. One of the very common instances of its use in synthesis involves a series connection of boxes in which the specific aim of the study is to modify the overall $KG(j\omega)$ by the addition of a series box or compensating element to give a desired system performance. The emphasis is then placed on defining and synthesizing this compensating box. These matters are the principal subjects of Chapters 6 through 9.

Parallel Connections. Generalizations of closed-loop phenomena can be extended to such systems as the one found in Figure 26. The distinguishing feature of this system is the appearance of the dynamic element in the feedback path. This situation often arises in closed-loop studies. Sometimes the feedback element is deliberately introduced to alter the relation between a given excitation and the response. Sometimes the dynamic element is inherent in the error-measuring or data

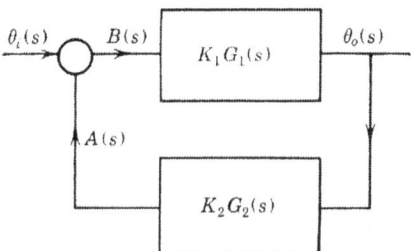

FIGURE 26.   Closed loop with elements in the feedback path.

transmission system. The lag of a thermometer used as a sensing element in temperature regulation is a good example.

The equations relating the quantities shown in the system of Figure 26 are

$$\left.\begin{array}{l} \theta_o(s) = K_1 G_1(s) B(s) \\ A(s) = K_2 G_2(s) \theta_o(s) \\ B(s) = \theta_i(s) - A(s) \\ T_L(s) = 0 \end{array}\right\} \tag{115}$$

The output response is

$$\theta_o(s) = \frac{K_1 G_1(s)}{1 + K_1 G_1(s) K_2 G_2(s)} \theta_i(s) \tag{116}$$

Note that the error $E(s)$ as a physical quantity does not now exist. $B(s)$ is not equal to the error $E(s)$. The substitution of error $E(s)$ for $\theta_i(s) - \theta_o(s)$ gives

$$E(s) = \frac{1 + K_1 G_1(s) K_2 G_2(s) - K_1 G_1(s)}{1 + K_1 G_1(s) K_2 G_2(s)} \theta_i(s) \tag{117}$$

We can notice immediately that the error response for this form of closed loop is a complicated function. The output response also shows a different form of characteristic from that for Figure 25. As the synthesis study is extended by the work that follows in Chapters 6 and 7, the reader will see quickly the requirements that must be imposed on $K_2 G_2(s)$ for certain forms of system behavior in spite of the apparent difficulty of visualizing the effect on the system of the dynamical properties of the feedback path. In fact, the reader will soon see that if certain properties are accidentally introduced into the feedback path, very erratic response in the operation of the closed loop may result. On the other hand, feedback other than unity may be beneficial. It need not always be frequency variant. Specifically, the feedback might involve merely an amplification around an element having a long time constant. For example, consider an element having $K_1G_1(s) = a/(\tau s + 1)$. Let the feedback around this element, represented by $K_2G_2(s)$ in Figure 26, be an amplification μ. Substituting these quantities in Equation 115 gives

$$\frac{\theta_o(s)}{\theta_i(s)} = \frac{a}{1 + \mu a}\left[\frac{1}{\dfrac{\tau}{1 + \mu a}s + 1}\right] \tag{118}$$

which illustrates the important fact that, where gain can be sacrificed, a time constant can be reduced in proportion to the loss of gain by the

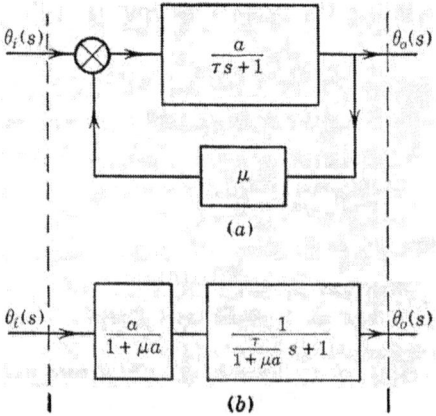

FIGURE 27.   Representation of system equivalents.

feedback process. This condition is illustrated by the diagrams of Figure 27 in which the system of part a within the vertical dotted lines is dynamically equivalent to the two blocks in cascade, shown in part b.

The insertion of internal loops as a means to change the dynamics is effective in performing certain compensations designated for proper adjustment of the main loop. Often an internal loop can be added to a servo with a result that will make the stabilization task simpler or even remove it entirely as a problem. These matters are treated in greater detail in Chapter 7.

6 Conclusion

In the preceding work, the Laplace transform has been used in the preparation of transfer functions. Hence the transfer functions have been functions of the complex variable s. If the Fourier transform method of studying the differential equations had been chosen, the transfer functions would have been functions of the variable $j\omega$. The entire structure of this chapter would have been the same except that all the s-functions would have been $j\omega$-functions. The same result may be obtained by assuming that the driving functions studied in the preparation of the transfer functions were sinusoidally varying time functions whose frequency ω was the independent variable. This makes possible the complex function treatment of synthesis in terms of $KG(j\omega)$ given in Chapter 6.

6

Introduction to Synthesis, Determining the Gain Constant K

1 Introduction

This chapter shows how the frequency invariant term K of the transfer function is determined in studies involving a prescribed form of $G(j\omega)$. The procedure amounts to an elementary form of synthesis. Chapters 7 and 8 treat a more comprehensive aspect of synthesis, namely, the shaping of the frequency variant function $G(j\omega)$ to meet a more extensive system specification.

The point-by-point calculation of families of vector diagrams is dispensed with immediately in favor of loci studies. These loci show the variation of vector quantities over the frequency range $0 < \omega < \infty$ as continuous curves plotted in the complex plane. Continued work of designing and analyzing systems soon establishes an encyclopedia of data for synthesis procedures, which greatly aids a designer by relating the shapes of the vector-loci functions to the shapes of desirable transient responses. As shown in Chapter 11, quantitative graphical-mathematical correlation between the transient and frequency response phenomena can be accomplished using the transfer function. The significance of the shapes of transient curves, frequency response curves, and transfer function loci curves can be integrated and retained in an engineer's mind. For these reasons value of the transfer function as a design tool has probably not been fully exploited.

The transfer function of portions of the closed loop may often be derived from purely theoretical considerations. Equally often, it must be carefully measured by quantitative laboratory or field experiment. Merging the derived values and measured values for different parts of the system leads to the complete specification of a transfer function, $KG(j\omega)$. Whether or not the loop may be closed without readjustment of the physical system depends on a large number of factors, chief of which are stability and dynamic error. Invariably, the function $KG(j\omega)$ as initially obtained must be altered. It may be necessary to insert into the system other elements that will change the gain K or alter the overall system transfer function locus. Each problem, namely, (1) changing and selecting K and (2) shaping $G(j\omega)$, requires rather extensive treatment. For this reason, the two concepts are separately treated in this and the next chapter. The procedures developed in this chapter for indicating changes in gain K are basic in extending the idea of synthesis to the more extensive procedures which follow in Chapter 7.

This alteration of the $G(j\omega)$ function, which is perhaps the most important feature of synthesis, takes cognizance of the fact that when only portions of an overall transfer function are known, direct methods exist for synthesizing the unknown portions for a large number of problems. While there may be unlimited numbers of particular physical circuits which accomplish the desired compensation, they are not individually discussed herein. This is because the keynote to the remainder of this treatment of the subject is method. Synthesis involves essentially creativeness or invention somewhat beyond the scope of this book. The procedures herein given offer a partially organized plan using the transfer function for making a direct approach to the synthesis or creative problem.

2 Synthesis by Analytical Operations with $KG(s)$

Except in the most elementary problems, explicit synthesis by analytical studies using $KG(s)$ is not possible. In order to distinguish between the effectiveness of analytical and graphical methods of synthesis, the analytical procedure is recapitulated. This recapitulation will contrast the use of the function $KG(s)$ with the vector function $KG(j\omega)$.

The transfer $KG(s)$ is given by the ratio of polynomials as

$$\frac{\theta_o(s)}{E(s)} = KG(s) = \frac{a_n s^n + a_{n-1} s^{n-1} + \cdots}{b_m s^m + b_{m-1} s^{m-1} + \cdots} \tag{1}$$

The exact nature of the closed-loop response $\theta_o(s)/\theta_i(s)$ is then expressed in terms of a ratio of two polynomials as

$$\frac{\theta_o(s)}{\theta_i(s)} = \frac{KG(s)}{1 + KG(s)} = \frac{c_n s^n + c_{n-1} s^{n-1} + \cdots}{d_m s^m + d_{m-1} s^{m-1} + \cdots} \tag{2}$$

Initial conditions may be included in Equation 2, as shown in Chapter 3. These initial conditions appear only in the numerator of the response equation, whereas the denominator $1 + KG(s)$ is always a polynomial in the variable s. It is dependent wholly upon the transfer function

$KG(s)$. It is related neither to the initial conditions nor to the external disturbances.

Many rules exist for determining the roots of the characteristic equation [54, 55] and the general nature of the system stability when $1 + KG(s)$ is known. The determination of the roots and the transient response have been discussed in Chapter 3. However, the objective of true synthesis requires a knowledge of the explicit component or components which the desired behavior necessitates. A more useful result than that giving stability criteria or the roots of $1 + KG(s) = 0$ is needed. Consider the transfer function

$$\frac{\theta_o(s)}{E(s)} = \frac{K}{s^2(\tau s + 1)} \tag{3}$$

If a loop is closed around the system described by Equation 3, instability will result as shown by the missing term in the characteristic equation obtained from $1 + KG(s) = 0$.

$$\tau s^3 + s^2 + 0 + K = 0 \tag{4}$$

When $1 + KG(s)$ is a higher order polynomial in s, instability may still result even when all the terms of the polynomial exist, because a particular relationship [53] must exist among the constant coefficients. To illustrate, consider the characteristic equation

$$as^3 + bs^2 + cs + d = 0 \tag{5}$$

In order that the cubic of Equation 5 can be stable, the relation $bc - ad > 0$ must be fulfilled. This is a purely qualitative result and does not tell *how stable* the system is.

Quantitative information about stability requires more than a simple study of $KG(s)$ can provide. The roots $-1/\tau_a, -1/\tau_b, \cdots$ of the characteristic equation shown in Equation 6

$$1 + KG(s) = (\tau_a s + 1)(\tau_b s + 1)(\tau_c^2 s^2 + 2\zeta_c \tau_c s + 1) \cdots \tag{6}$$

should be definitely related to the physical parameters from which $KG(s)$ was formulated. While the roots of $1 + KG(s)$ may be known, $KG(s)$ itself is known only to the extent that

$$KG(s) = \frac{(\tau_3 s + 1) \cdots}{s(\tau_1 s + 1)(\tau_2^2 s^2 + 2\zeta_2 \tau_2 s + 1) \cdots} \tag{7}$$

Clearly an implicit relation exists between $\tau_1, \tau_2, \tau_3, \zeta_2 \cdots$ of the $KG(s)$ and the roots $-1/\tau_a, -1/\tau_b, \cdots$ of $1 + KG(s)$. However, to make this relation explicit is generally a difficult problem of algebra, and even when accomplished has not indicated how τ_1, τ_2, $\cdots$ are related to phys-ical parameters of components.

Therefore, with the exception of being able to treat the most elemen-tary forms of $KG(s)$, the whole structure of *algebraic synthesis* is of very small value. Its strength as a mathematical tool for solving the tasks of dynamic synthesis before us is inadequate and should be looked upon as an implicit assistant rather than an explicit method of attack in synthesis.

3   Introduction to the $KG(j\omega)$ Locus

The procedures treated in the following sections use the transfer func-tion KG expressed in terms of the variable $(j\omega)$. This function is ex-pressed as $KG(j\omega)$. The treatment is basically a graphical one in which the locus of $KG(j\omega)$ contains all the information required.

The locus of a complex vector function is illustrated by the diagrams of Figure 1. In Figure 1a the function $KG(j\omega)$ has first been plotted as

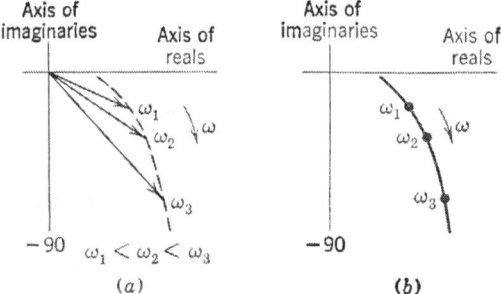

FIGURE 1.   Development of vector locus.

a vector for three values of ω, specifically $\omega_1 < \omega_2 < \omega_3$. The line join-ing the tips of these vectors is shown dotted. This line is the locus.

In graphical studies great confusion would exist if the vectors were plotted. The locus, as shown in Figure 1b, contains all the data of the function it represents if it is supplemented merely by an arrow that shows the direction the vector moves along the locus and if specific values of frequency are indicated by dots or crosses along it.

In the work that follows, the plot of the vector function $KG(j\omega)$ is spoken of as the *transfer function locus on the KG plane*.

4   Introduction to Vector Loci

The loci methods of synthesis used herein are founded upon several factors. The first is that the transfer function $KG(j\omega)$ or its reciprocal $1/KG(j\omega)$, designated herein respectively as KG and KG^{-1}, for a linear

TABLE 1

RELATIONS INVOLVING THE TRANSFER FUNCTION KG

Output-Error Relations

$$\frac{\theta_o}{\varepsilon}(j\omega) = KG(j\omega) \tag{8}$$

$$= |KG(j\omega)| e^{j\phi_1(j\omega)} \tag{9}$$

$$= R_1(\omega) \underline{/\phi_1(\omega)} \tag{10}$$

$$= X_1(\omega) + jY_1(\omega) \tag{11}$$

Output-Input Relations

$$\frac{\theta_o}{\theta_i}(j\omega) = \frac{KG(j\omega)}{1 + KG(j\omega)} \tag{12}$$

$$= \left| \frac{KG(j\omega)}{1 + KG(j\omega)} \right| e^{j\phi_2(j\omega)} \tag{13}$$

$$= R_2(\omega) \underline{/\phi_2(\omega)} \tag{14}$$

$$= X_2(\omega) + jY_2(\omega) \tag{15}$$

RELATIONS INVOLVING THE RECIPROCAL TRANSFER FUNCTION KG^{-1}

Error-Output Relations

$$\frac{\varepsilon}{\theta_o}(j\omega) = \frac{1}{KG(j\omega)} \tag{16}$$

$$= \left| \frac{1}{KG(j\omega)} \right| e^{j\phi_3(j\omega)} \tag{17}$$

$$= R_3(\omega) \underline{/\phi_3(\omega)} \tag{18}$$

$$= X_3(\omega) + jY_3(\omega) \tag{19}$$

Input-Output Relations

$$\frac{\theta_i}{\theta_o}(j\omega) = \frac{1 + KG(j\omega)}{KG(j\omega)} \tag{20}$$

$$= \left| \frac{1 + KG(j\omega)}{KG(j\omega)} \right| e^{j\phi_4(j\omega)} \tag{21}$$

$$= R_4(\omega) \underline{/\phi_4(\omega)} \tag{22}$$

$$= X_4(\omega) + jY_4(\omega) \tag{23}$$

TABLE 1 *(Continued)*

GENERAL RELATIONS

$$\frac{\theta_i}{\theta_o}(j\omega) = \frac{1}{KG(j\omega)} + 1 \tag{24}$$

$$\frac{\theta_i}{\theta_o}(j\omega) = \frac{\varepsilon}{\theta_o}(j\omega) + 1 \tag{25}$$

$$\frac{\theta_i}{\theta_o}(j\omega) - 1 = \frac{\varepsilon}{\theta_o}(j\omega) \tag{26}$$

system can uniquely define the response of the closed loop to external sinusoidally varying disturbances if specified over the frequency range $0 < \omega < \infty$. The second factor is that the same transfer function KG which defines the frequency response of the closed loop can be used to predict the transient response of the physical system subject to impulses or step disturbances by means of the inverse Fourier integral. The third factor is that loci plots of the function KG in the KG plane may be readily obtained. Because of this latter factor, synthesis should draw heavily upon many familiar graphical techniques to facilitate use of the function.

Reference to the literature [6, 32] shows that considerable effort has been expended in the development of general methods of synthesis using the KG function as a polar locus. One method involves an approach similar to the "impedance" or loop basis for study of networks. The alternate one [33] closely parallels the former and emphasizes the "admittance" or node basis. Strictly speaking, neither is used exclusively in any comprehensive study. Therefore, we choose to consider the two approaches basically as one and the same. They differ in detail, not in principle.

A comparison of the vector forms encountered in either method is given in Table 1. A comparison of the loci shapes encountered in either method is given in Sections 5 and 6. Subsequently, when actual problems are solved, the readers will note that certain problems of synthesis are better handled by one method than the other. Some problems may require the merger of both. Thus a person skilled in this work will understand both methods and use them with equal dexterity. For example, if the transfer function KG is known uniquely for all frequencies $0 < \omega < \infty$, all the other relations involving it then can be found. Similarly, when the transfer function KG^{-1} is known for all values of $0 < \omega < \infty$, the values of all other vector relations can be calculated for each value of frequency.

Although arithmetical manipulations of the tabulated equations are frequently necessary to carry out synthesis problems, it is rare that they play the primary role in the actual task. Usually, mere vector solutions are inadequate because they tend to place emphasis on a single frequency. They are likely to concentrate too much attention on a steady-state behavior at a single frequency. As such, a method dependent wholly on them would fail as did the algebraic manipulations of the polynomials resulting from studies of $KG(s)$ and $1 + KG(s)$ outlined in Section 2. What is needed is a simple entry into a technique which inherently focuses attention on the behavior throughout a spectrum. The properties of the parametric families of loci that can be plotted from the relations in Table 1 become the real thing sought in synthesis. Once the designer can recognize the meaning of the vector loci on the KG plane and the meaning of the relative shape and location of these vector loci to other vector loci, the entire closed-loop synthesis comes within reach as a directly solvable engineering problem.

5   Graphical Relations Involving KG

All the relations indicated in Table 1 pertaining to KG can be obtained graphically. While the graphical manipulations which give them do not

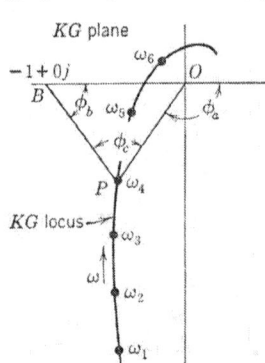

FIGURE 2.   Transfer function locus in the KG plane.

in themselves strictly constitute synthesis, they have a definite value when performing synthesis. For example, consider the function $KG(j\omega)$ as plotted in Figure 2. The radius vector OP from the origin to the locus at point P is $KG(j\omega)$ for $\omega = \omega_4$. The vector BP from the point $-1 + oj$ on the real axis to the point P on the locus is $[1 + KG(j\omega)]$ for $\omega = \omega_4$, but the vector is plotted with respect to an origin at $-1 + oj$. The value of θ_o/θ_i can thus be obtained from Figure 2 for each discrete value of angular frequency ω_1, ω_2, ω_3, $\cdots$ by means of a protractor and a pair of dividers. The procedure is as follows: (1) Read the magnitude and phase angle of the vector $KG(j\omega)$ as $|OP|$ and ϕ_a, respectively, and (2) read the magnitude and phase angle of the vector $1 + KG(j\omega)$ as $|BP|$ and ϕ_b, respectively. The response θ_o/θ_i is then found for each frequency by the ratio

$$\frac{\theta_o}{\theta_i}(j\omega) = \frac{KG(j\omega)}{1 + KG(j\omega)} = \frac{|OP|e^{j\phi_a}}{|BP|e^{j\phi_b}} = \left|\frac{OP}{BP}\right|e^{j\phi_c} \qquad (27)$$

where $\phi_c = \phi_a - \phi_b$, the angle between the two vectors at the apex P of the triangle.

The data obtained from Equation 27 can be plotted again on the complex plane as shown in Figure 3. Each point on the $KG(j\omega)$ locus establishes a point on the θ_o/θ_i locus. Although this particular curve is not used to any great extent in the preparation of closed-loop designs, it is nevertheless important in understanding specifications that may be established. However, the data plotted in Figure 3 can be converted to the more familiar "magnitude and phase" form of graphs shown in Figure 4. These two curves of Figures 3 and 4, representing the response

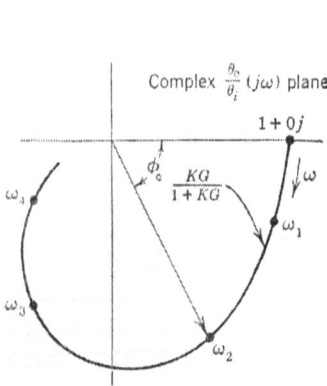

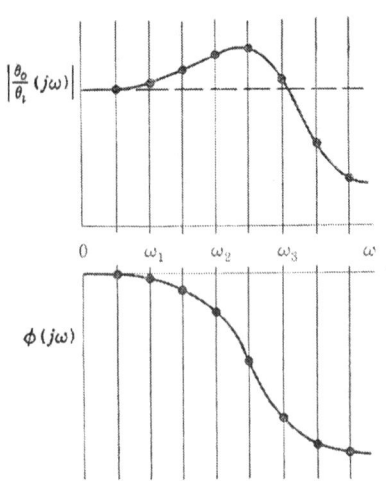

FIGURE 3. Closed-loop response locus from Figure 2.

FIGURE 4. Closed-loop magnitude and phase curves.

of a closed loop, can be discussed simultaneously so far as system specifications are concerned. At present, it should suffice to note that the response θ_o/θ_i was obtained graphically from the complex plane plot of the transfer function $KG(j\omega)$. All combinations of Equations 8 through 15 can be related by similar procedures.

6   Graphical Relations Involving KG^{-1}

In a manner almost identical with that of Section 5, Equations 16 through 23 of Table 1 can be obtained by a graphical study of the inverted transfer function $1/KG(j\omega)$. Furthermore, the values of the inverse vector KG^{-1}, representing the transfer function for $\omega_1, \omega_2, \omega_3, \cdots$ plotted upon the complex plane, can be related point by point to the values of the regular vector KG plotted upon the complex plane.

To demonstrate these facts, consider again several values of frequency $\omega_1, \omega_2, \omega_3, \cdots$ for which the function KG^{-1} is defined. When plotted on the complex plane, the resulting locus is that shown in Figure 5. The vector KG^{-1} for $\omega = \omega_3$ is the radius vector OR from the origin to the point R on the locus. From the point $-1 + oj$ to the locus at the point R, the vector AR is the response θ_i/θ_o for the closed-loop system for the same frequency $\omega = \omega_3$. These values of response can be obtained as before by use of a protractor and a pair of dividers. However, another simplification is achieved if the locus in Figure 5 is shifted one unit toward the positive real axis, such that the origin of a new plot, shown in Figure 6, coincides with the former point A of Figure 5. By making this shift of the locus the result plotted in Figure 6 can be

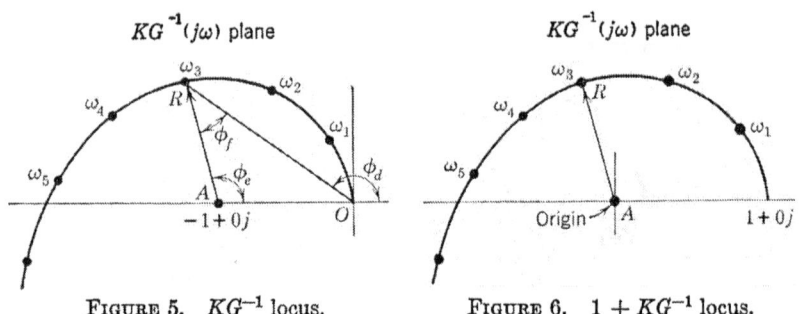

FIGURE 5. KG^{-1} locus.   FIGURE 6. $1 + KG^{-1}$ locus.

readily converted graphically from θ_i/θ_o to θ_o/θ_i. Either the graphical construction or simple visual inspection permits the output-to-input response to be obtained. The result shown in Figure 3 is more often used than the inverted form.

7   Building Blocks of the Overall Transfer Function

Motors, tachometers, hydraulic transmissions, hydromechanical amplifiers, and electric circuits, such as those shown in Chapter 5, are all physical mechanisms characterized by internal energy storages and energy dissipations. Each mechanism can in turn be described by equations readily expressed as functions in which cascaded or even parallel combinations of physical elements lead to a single overall transfer function KG. Regardless of the method of plotting this function, it soon becomes evident that definite loci result on the complex plane for definite groupings of energy storages and dissipations.

One should not assume that analogies are being made to relate these mechanical, electrical, and hydraulic components. The very opposite is true. A completely general treatment of dynamics shows that all single-energy storages, regardless of their physical form, lead to the same functional representation and to the same curves when plotted on the complex plane. Likewise, all double-energy storages result in definite loci shapes and so on, regardless of system complexity. These properties result from the use of a function theory approach to dynamics.

Only three general types of algebraic factors can exist for the factored form of a transfer function representative of a linear lumped parameter system. When expressed as factors in the variable $j\omega$ they are

$$(1) \quad [j\omega]^{\pm 1} \tag{28}$$

$$(2) \quad [j\omega\tau + 1]^{\pm 1} \tag{29}$$

$$(3) \quad [-\tau^2\omega^2 + j2\zeta\tau\omega + 1]^{\pm 1} \tag{30}$$

When these factors appear in $KG(j\omega)$, they represent respectively (1) a pole or a zero at the origin of the s plane; (2) a pole or a zero at some point on the negative real axis of the s plane; (3) a pair of conjugate complex poles or zeros located in the left-hand half of the s plane.

The exponents of the factors in Equations 28, 29 and 30 may be positive or negative and often greater than unity. These factors can be used as building blocks to form transfer functions. The overall transfer function for any dynamical system however complicated is formulated by grouping these blocks or factors. The procedure is the same whether the physical components are electrical, electronic, mechanical, magnetic, or hydraulic, or their combinations. They only need not be interacting. (See Chapter 5, Section 4.)

Since a definite loci shape is associated with each factor of Equations 28, 29, and 30, an overall loci shape can be visually related to the transfer function of any complicated physical system. Pictorial as well as mathematical blocks can therefore be formed. Loci can be drawn for these factors as they appear in both the KG and the KG^{-1} planes. Combinations of these loci as shown in Table 2 can be merged graphically to form the loci for the overall transfer functions.

When studying the mathematical and graphical forms that appear in Table 2, it is worth noting the dimensionless procedures that can be used to advantage in preparing these functions and their graphs. Generally a new choice of frequency variable $j\omega\tau = ju$ is made. This refers the frequency scale to a unit base frequency. When making this simplification we should not commit the error of making too many changes of variable. Such changes of variable result in changing all the numerical parameters of the system to the new base. Thus the transfer function $KG(j\omega)$ becomes $KG(ju)$, and all the related functions become variable in u rather than ω. The now familiar response equations are

$$\frac{\theta_o}{\varepsilon}(ju) = KG(ju) \tag{31}$$

$$\frac{\theta_o}{\theta_i}(ju) = \frac{KG(ju)}{1 + KG(ju)} \tag{32}$$

$$\frac{\varepsilon}{\theta_o}(ju) = \frac{1}{KG(ju)} \tag{33}$$

$$\frac{\theta_i}{\theta_o}(ju) = \frac{1}{KG(ju)} + 1 \tag{34}$$

The resonance frequencies, natural frequencies, velocity constant, and so forth are all related to u, the new frequency variable by the non-dimensionalizing constant.

Table 2 shows that $G(ju)$ alone determines the loci shape. The constant term K is only a scale factor. It changes the size of the polar graph but cannot change the relative shape. Thus, initially, only the frequency variant portion, $G(ju)$, of the transfer function $KG(ju)$ need be considered when attempting synthesis except when multiple loop systems are encountered. When the shape of the overall "G curves" is established, the last step in the procedure is to select the sensitivity parameter K permitted by the M criterion stated in Chapter 4.

Table 3 shows typical system components with their transfer functions. These functions have $G(ju)$ shapes similar to those shown in Table 2. It will be noted that simplifying assumptions have been made in the preparation of the transfer functions given in column 3 of Table 3. The reader can gradually enlarge this list as he gains experience with additional kinds of components.[39] He should not attempt to maintain exactness of symbolism so much as to use this kind of tabulation as a guide to synthesis technique. This is emphasized because there are many physical components whose pictorial representation is not easy to establish.

Thus far, the study of the loci for the transfer functions arranged to form closed-loop systems has been purely qualitative. No specific numerical values have been assigned to the parameters of the physical system. A few simple semi-quantitative examples are now given.

Example 1.   Consider a closed-loop speed control system made up of an error-measuring device which compares speeds and expresses the difference as a voltage; an amplifier (Table 3), item 10; a direct current motor whose shunt field current is controlled (Table 3), item 3; and a

TABLE 2

TABULATED TRANSFER FUNCTIONS AND LOCI SHAPES ON THE COMPLEX PLANE

Item	$G(ju)$	Locus on the Complex Plane
1	$\dfrac{1}{ju}$	
2	$\left(\dfrac{1}{ju}\right)^2$	
3	$\dfrac{1}{ju+1}$	
4	$\dfrac{1}{ju(ju+1)}$	
5	$\dfrac{1}{(ju)^2+j2\zeta u+1}$	
6	$\dfrac{1}{ju[(ju)^2+j2\zeta u+1]}$	
7	ju	
8	$\dfrac{ju+1}{ju\alpha+1}$	$\alpha>1$
9	$ju(ju+1)$	
10	$(ju)^2+j2\zeta u+1$	

TABLE 3

TYPICAL SYSTEM COMPONENTS AND THEIR TRANSFER FUNCTIONS

Component	Diagram	Transfer Function
1. Synchro transformer system		$\dfrac{E(s)}{\mathcal{E}(s)} = K_1$
2. Synchro differential system		$\dfrac{\theta_c(s)}{\mathcal{E}(s)} = \dfrac{K_2}{s^2 + 2\zeta\omega_n s + \omega_n^2}$
3. Direct current motor with shunt field control		$\dfrac{\theta_o(s)}{I_f(s)} = \dfrac{K_3}{s(\tau_m s + 1)}$
4. Two-phase motor		$\dfrac{\theta_o(s)}{E(s)} = \dfrac{K_4}{s^2}$
5. Tachometer		$\dfrac{E_t(s)}{\theta_o(s)} = K_5 s$
6. Hydraulic amplifier		$\dfrac{X_s(s)}{\theta_c(s)} = \dfrac{K_6}{\tau s + 1}$
7. Hydraulic transmission		$\dfrac{\theta_o(s)}{X_s(s)} = \dfrac{K_7}{s(s^2 + 2\zeta\omega_n s + \omega_n^2)}$
8. Lag network		$\dfrac{E_2(s)}{E_1(s)} = \dfrac{K_8}{\tau s + 1}$
9. Lead network		$\dfrac{E_2(s)}{E_1(s)} = \dfrac{\alpha\tau s + 1}{\tau s + 1}\dfrac{1}{\alpha}$
10. Electronic amplifier		$\dfrac{E_2(s)}{E_1(s)} = K_{10}$

tachometer (Table 3), item 5. The components are arranged to form a closed loop as shown in Figure 7.

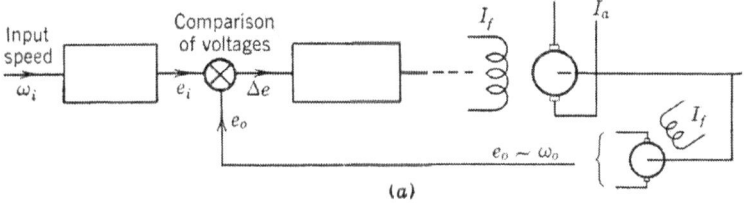

(a)

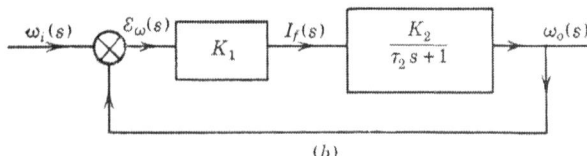

(b)

FIGURE 7.   Closed-loop speed control system.

The object of this study is:

(1) To formulate the overall transfer function.
(2) To draw the locus for the transfer function.
(3) To investigate the possible steady-state performance of this closed-loop speed control system without resorting to elaborate mathematical treatment.
(4) To determine the frequency range over which the output-to-input magnitude and phase response fall within acceptable limits.

This system is the same as the one used in Chapter 2, Figure 2·6. It does not fulfill the criteria for a servomechanism as stated in Chapter 2. It has been idealized so that the diagram of Figure 7b contains only one block in which energy-storing and dissipating elements appear. The mechanical portion of the shunt motor contributes this effect. The overall system function ignores any possible energy storages in the error-measuring system and the tachometer attached to the output. Their sensitivities are lumped in the constant term K_1.

Solution.   (1) The transfer function relating output speed to speed error ε_ω is

$$\frac{\omega_o}{\varepsilon_\omega}(j\omega) = \frac{K_1 K_2}{j\omega\tau_2 + 1} \tag{35}$$

where

$$\varepsilon_\omega(j\omega) = \omega_i(j\omega) - \omega_o(j\omega) \tag{36}$$

A change of variable $j\omega\tau_2 = ju$ yields the simplified form

$$\frac{\omega_o}{\mathcal{E}_\omega}(ju) = \frac{K_1 K_2}{ju + 1} \tag{37}$$

The sensitivity constant $K_1 K_2$ may be lumped into the single term K, giving

$$\frac{\omega_o}{\mathcal{E}_\omega}(ju) = \frac{K}{ju + 1} = KG(ju) \tag{38}$$

(2) The shape of the locus is that shown in Table 2, item 3.

(3) The output speed $\omega_o(ju)$ expressed in terms of the input or reference speed $\omega_i(ju)$ is given by Equation 39. That is

$$\frac{\omega_o}{\omega_i}(ju) = \frac{KG(ju)}{1 + KG(ju)} \tag{39}$$

Substituting for $KG(ju)$ from Equation 38 gives

$$\frac{\omega_o}{\omega_i}(ju) = \frac{\dfrac{K}{ju + 1}}{1 + \dfrac{K}{ju + 1}} \tag{40}$$

or

$$\frac{\omega_o}{\omega_i}(ju) = \frac{\dfrac{K}{1 + K}}{\left(\dfrac{1}{1 + K}\right)ju + 1} \tag{41}$$

The locus of $KG(ju)$ terminates at a finite point on the real axis of the complex plane as shown in Figure 8a. Thus

$$\left.\frac{\omega_o}{\omega_i}\right|_{\text{steady state}} \neq 1 \tag{42}$$

In other words, the closed loop cannot maintain zero speed error in the steady state. Thus the device must be calibrated with respect to an input speed or set point.

(4) The extent to which the magnitude and phase of the output $\omega_o(ju)$ can be considered invariant with increasing frequency u can be seen directly from Figure 8. An interesting comparison results if the open-

loop speed control performance is compared with the closed-loop performance; that is, if the graphs of Figures 8a and 8b are compared. Notice that the frequency range over which the magnitude and phase response of the closed loop are identical with those of the open loop is $1 + K$ times that of the open loop. Separate plots of the magnitude and phase function are shown in Figure 8c.

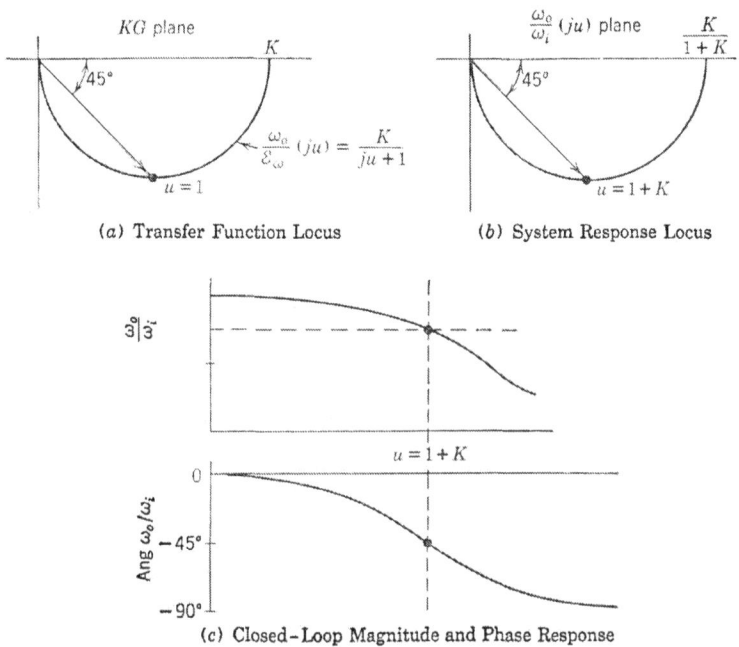

(a) Transfer Function Locus   (b) System Response Locus

(c) Closed-Loop Magnitude and Phase Response

FIGURE 8.   Dimensionless solution to problem of Figure 7.

Note that no value of K exists which can make this closed loop unstable. There is never the possibility of a positive root or a root with a positive real part in $1 + KG(s) = 0$.

Example 2.   Consider a closed-loop position control comprising the same electric motor as used in Example 1; an electronic amplifier (Table 3, item 10); and a synchro transformer system (Table 3, item 1).

Obtain for this closed-loop system:

(1) The overall transfer function.
(2) The locus of the KG function on the complex plane.
(3) An estimate of the closed-loop performance in terms of the frequency range over which magnitude and phase θ_o/θ_i are acceptable.

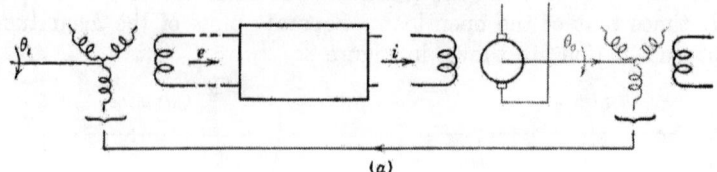

(a)

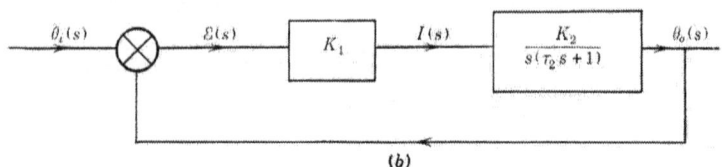

(b)

FIGURE 9.   Closed-loop positional control system.

Solution. (1) Figure 9a shows the physical components arranged in a loop. Figure 9b shows the block diagram for which the transfer function is

$$\frac{\theta_o}{\varepsilon}(j\omega) = \frac{K_1 K_2}{j\omega(j\omega\tau_2 + 1)} \tag{43}$$

A change of variable $j\omega\tau_2 = ju$ gives

$$\frac{\theta_o}{\varepsilon}(ju) = \frac{K_1 K_2 \tau_2}{ju(ju + 1)} \tag{44}$$

$$= \frac{K}{ju(ju + 1)} \tag{45}$$

where

$$K = K_1 K_2 \tau_2 \tag{46}$$

The output response $\theta_o(ju)$ can be formed:

$$\frac{\theta_o}{\theta_i}(ju) = \frac{\dfrac{K}{ju(ju + 1)}}{1 + \dfrac{K}{ju(ju + 1)}} \tag{47}$$

which reduces to the form

$$\frac{\theta_o}{\theta_i}(ju) = \frac{1}{-r^2 u^2 + j2\zeta\tau u + 1} \tag{48}$$

where

$$\left.\begin{array}{c} \tau = \dfrac{1}{\sqrt{K}} \\[2mm] \varsigma = \dfrac{1}{2\sqrt{K}} \end{array}\right\} \tag{49}$$

(2) The locus for $KG(ju)$ of Equation 45 is shown in Figure 10a. The locus for θ_o/θ_i of Equation 48 is shown in Figure 10b, where the frequency parameter is τu.

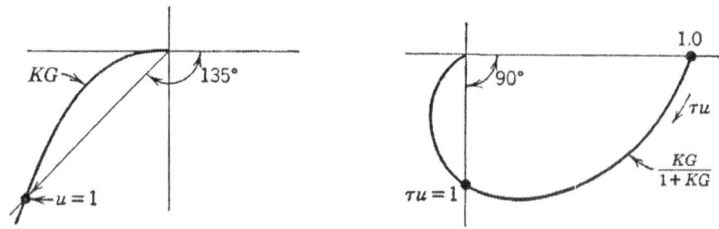

FIGURE 10.   Dimensionless solution to problem of Figure 9.

(3) The θ_o/θ_i plot of Figure 10b represents only one of a family of curves dependent upon the parameter ς. Equations 48 and item 5 of Table 2 show that the frequency range over which θ_o/θ_i is approximately unity is a function of ς. Figure 4·3 also shows a family of these curves. Values indicating the performance of the system for $0.4 < \varsigma < 1.0$ are tabulated in Table 4, where the frequency parameter is again τu.

TABLE 4

ς	Range of τu	Magnitude	Phase
0.4	$0 < \tau u < 0.48$	$0.8 < \dfrac{\theta_o}{\theta_i} < 1.2$	$0 < \phi < -35$ degrees
0.6	$0 < \tau u < 1.0$	$0.8 < \dfrac{\theta_o}{\theta_i} < 1.2$	$0 < \phi < -90$ degrees
0.8	$0 < \tau u < 0.7$	$0.8 < \dfrac{\theta_o}{\theta_i} < 1.2$	$0 < \phi < -70$ degrees
1.0	$0 < \tau u < 0.48$	$0.8 < \dfrac{\theta_o}{\theta_i} < 1.2$	$0 < \phi < -60$ degrees

It should be noted that no value of K can make this simple system unstable. However, this does not imply that instability is not common in positional systems. In fact, the opposite is true. The absence of instability in this example is due wholly to the fact that the problem was simplified to the extent that made the characteristic equation only a quadratic. Substantially all systems involve higher order characteristic equations for which instability will always occur for values of K in excess of a specific maximum.

Example 3. Consider a closed-loop position control system having a much greater order of complexity than that illustrated in Examples 1 and 2. Assume that it comprises an hydraulic transmission as illustrated in Table 3, item 7; an hydraulic amplifier for establishing the stroke of the hydraulic transmission as given in Table 3, item 6; and a synchro differential system used for data transmission and error measurement (Table 3, item 2).

Obtain for this closed-loop system:

(1) The overall transfer function.
(2) The locus of the KG function in the complex plane.
(3) An estimate of the closed-loop performance in terms of the frequency range over which the magnitude and phase of θ_o/θ_i are acceptable.

Solution. (1) Figure 11a shows the physical components arranged in a loop. Figure 11b shows the block diagram for which the transfer function $KG(j\omega)$ is

$$\frac{\theta_o}{\varepsilon}(j\omega) = \frac{K_2 K_7 K_6}{j\omega(-\omega^2 + 2\zeta_1\omega_1 j\omega + \omega_1^2)(j\tau_1\omega + 1)(-\omega^2 + 2\zeta_2\omega_2 j\omega + \omega_2^2)} \tag{50}$$

A change of variable $j(\omega/\omega_2) = ju$, where ω_2 is the natural frequency of the transmission, gives

$$\frac{\theta_o}{\varepsilon}(ju) = \frac{\dfrac{1}{\omega_1^2}\dfrac{1}{\omega_2^3} K_2 K_7 K_6}{ju[-\tau_a^2 u^2 + j2\tau_a\zeta_1 u + 1][ju\tau_b + 1][-u^2 + j2\zeta_2 u + 1]} \tag{51}$$

$$= KG(ju) \tag{52}$$

where

$$\left.\begin{array}{c} \tau_a = \dfrac{\omega_2}{\omega_1} \\[2mm] \tau_b = \omega_2\tau_1 \\[2mm] K = \dfrac{K_2 K_7 K_6}{\omega_1^2\omega_2^3} \end{array}\right\} \tag{53}$$

(2) The locus for each part of the transfer function, as given by Equation 51, is shown as curves *a*, *b*, and *c*, respectively, of Figure 12.

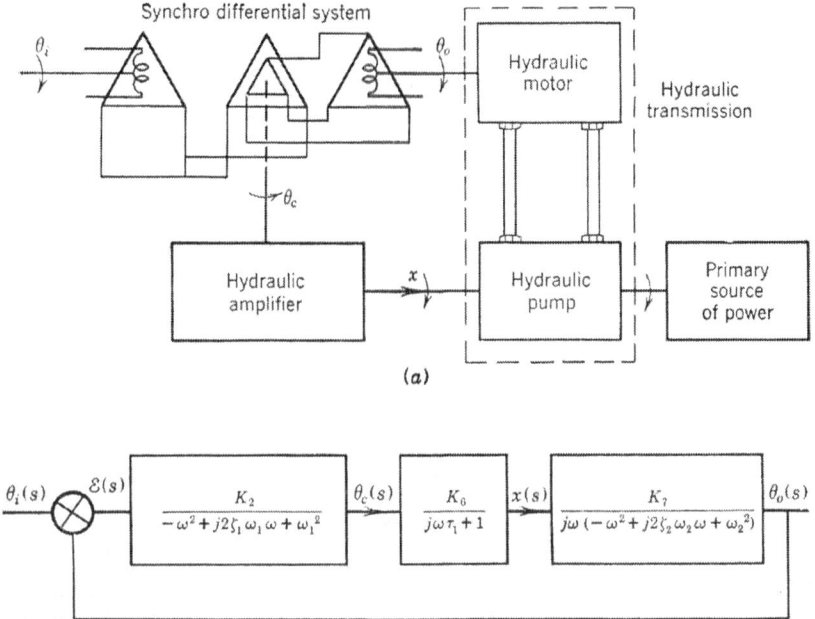

(a)

(b)

FIGURE 11.   Closed-loop position control system (hydraulic).

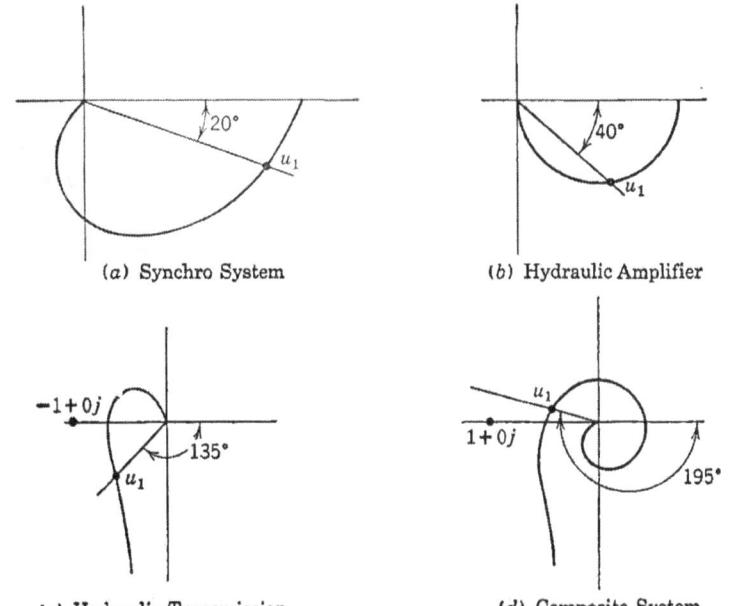

(a) Synchro System

(b) Hydraulic Amplifier

(c) Hydraulic Transmission

(d) Composite System

FIGURE 12.   Plots of individual and composite loci of elements of Figure 11.

Combining these three curves by vector multiplication at corresponding frequencies, following the procedure shown in Chapter 5 for cascade multiplication of functions, gives the overall system locus KG shown in Figure 12d. Notice that the angles add and the magnitudes multiply. The phase shift approaches -540 degrees as u approaches infinity.

(3) No explicit solution for this part of the problem can be stated at this time. Inspection of the locus of Figure 12d shows that if the gain K is large, the locus can be made to coincide with the point $-1 + j0$. For this value of K, the function $KG(ju) = -1$ and

$$\frac{\theta_o}{\theta_i}(ju) = \frac{-1}{1 - 1} = \frac{-1}{0} \tag{54}$$

This corresponds to a condition when the quantity fed back from the output exactly equals the signal fed to the input, thus permitting sustained oscillation. It is apparent, therefore, that criteria of stability must be relevant to the study that will determine the value of K. Discussion of this matter follows in the next section of this chapter.

The value of the building block method for preparing KG functions and their loci is much more extensive in scope than these examples illustrate. The organization of the procedure makes it self-teaching.

8   Interpretation of Loci Shapes

General.   The shape of the locus of the transfer function is a valuable guide to system behavior. Emphasis is placed on the low-frequency region, the high-frequency region, and the region near the point $-1 + 0j$ on the complex plane. The low-frequency region of the locus relates to the steady-state behavior of the system. The high-frequency region relates to the general physical complexity of the closed loop. The region near the point $-1 + 0j$ relates to the stability of the system.

Low Frequency.   To illustrate the meaning of the low-frequency asymptote or the $\omega = 0$ point, of the KG locus, consider Examples 1 and 2 treated in Section 7. The first was a closed-loop speed control having the transfer function

$$\frac{\omega_o}{\varepsilon_\omega}(j\omega) = \frac{K}{j\omega\tau_2 + 1} \tag{55}$$

The second was a closed-loop positional control having the transfer function

$$\frac{\theta_o}{\varepsilon}(j\omega) = \frac{K}{j\omega(j\omega\tau_2 + 1)} \tag{56}$$

For the condition $\omega = 0$, the locus for the speed control terminates on the real axis at the point K, such as shown in Figure 8a, whereas the locus for the position control system approaches infinity along a line parallel to the negative imaginary axis as shown in Figure 10a.

The fact that the locus of Equation 55 terminates on the real axis of the complex plane precludes the possibility of a one-to-one correspondence between the steady-state input ω_i and output ω_o. This lack of correspondence occurs because of the absence of integration within the closed loop. In contrast, the locus of the position control exhibits an integration by reaching infinity along the negative imaginary axis of the KG plane. The integration establishes one-to-one correspondence between input θ_i and output θ_o. Thus a general rule or theorem can be established which relates loci shapes to steady-state system behaviors. By making the study indicated below in Equations 57, 58, and 59, we can establish for any typical closed-loop *position system*: a position constant K_p, a velocity constant K_v, and an acceleration constant K_a, where

$$K_p = \lim_{\omega \to 0} \left[\frac{\theta_o}{\varepsilon} (j\omega) + 1 \right] = \lim_{\omega \to 0} [KG(j\omega) + 1] \tag{57}$$

$$K_v = \lim_{\omega \to 0} (j\omega) \left[\frac{\theta_o}{\varepsilon} (j\omega) \right] = \lim_{\omega \to 0} (j\omega)[KG(j\omega)] \tag{58}$$

$$K_a = \lim_{\omega \to 0} (j\omega)^2 \left[\frac{\theta_o}{\varepsilon} (j\omega) \right] = \lim_{\omega \to 0} (j\omega)^2[KG(j\omega)] \tag{59}$$

The position error ε is zero for a steady angle input θ_i, when $K_p = \infty$. The position error ε is zero for a steady velocity input ω_i, when $K_v = \infty$. The position error ε is zero for a steady acceleration input α_i, when $K_a = \infty$. From these relations, Figure 13 can be drawn indicating the low-frequency asymptotic behavior necessitated for various kinds of steady-state performances of a closed-loop control system. Specifically for $K_p = \infty$ the loci shape corresponds to curve a, for $K_v = \infty$ the shape corresponds to curve b, for $K_a = \infty$ the shape corresponds to curve c. To give these asymptotes to the locus, the transfer function KG must have at least a single order pole at $j\omega = 0$ for $K_p = \infty$, that is,

$$KG(j\omega) = \frac{K}{(j\omega)^1(j\omega + 1)(j\omega a + 1) \cdots} \tag{60}$$

and at least a second order pole at $j\omega = 0$ for $K_v = \infty$, that is,

$$KG(j\omega) = \frac{K}{(j\omega)^2(j\omega + 1)(j\omega a + 1) \cdots} \tag{61}$$

and at least a third order pole at $j\omega = 0$, for $K_a = \infty$, that is,

$$KG(j\omega) = \frac{K}{(j\omega)^3(j\omega + 1)(j\omega a + 1) \cdots} \tag{62}$$

Equations 60, 61, and 62 indicate that the low-frequency region of the locus rotates negatively one quadrant from the positive real axis of the complex plane for each order of pole $j\omega = 0$.

A parallel treatment can be made for the inverse transfer function KG^{-1}. It yields Figure 13b, which gives a result similar in meaning to that shown in Figure 13a. It is merely expressed in the inverse form.

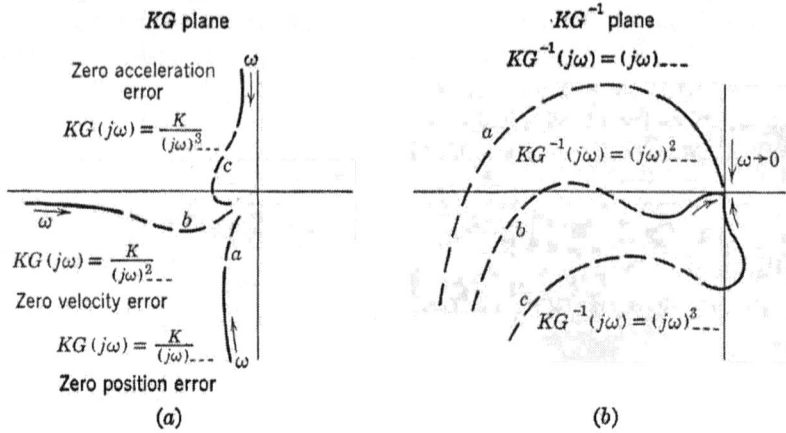

FIGURE 13.   Shapes of typical transfer function loci for small values of ω.

The fact that these asymptotes are required for certain types of system performance is no guarantee that the physical system corresponding to them can be realized. In dissipative systems the loci shapes required by the conditions $K_v = \infty$ and $K_a = \infty$, necessitate regenerative components in the loop, of which the lever, spring, and dashpot system [44] of Figure 5·10 is one example. An interesting performance criterion, however, has been established independent of the possibility of realizing the physical components. The magnitude K_p is a figure of merit for a regulatory system. The magnitude K_v is a figure of merit for a servomechanism whether or not it is a positional one. These two quantities indicate only the static performance of the closed loop. The magnitude assigned to them is a measure of the scale factor K which determines the final location of the $G(j\omega)$ locus throughout the KG plane. Therefore, these numbers are intimately related to the degree of stability and consequently to the overall frequency response obtainable for the closed loop.

High Frequency. The high-frequency asymptote of the KG locus may or may not give information about the overall complexity of the physical system. The order of the characteristic equation resulting from $1 + KG = 0$ is indicated by the highest power of ω appearing in the denominator of KG. The angle swept through by the KG locus from the positive real axis is $(m - n)\pi/2$ degrees as $\omega \to \infty$, where m and n are respectively the highest powers of ω appearing in the numerator and denominator of KG. Typical functions and their characteristic equations given in Equations 63 to 66 illustrate these properties. Specifically, a transfer function

$$KG(j\omega) = \frac{K}{j\omega(j\omega\tau + 1)}$$

has an angle of -180 degrees at $\omega = \infty$. When placed in $1 + KG(j\omega) = 0$, it leads to the quadratic

$$a(j\omega)^2 + b(j\omega) + c = 0 \tag{63}$$

Likewise,

$$KG(j\omega) = \frac{K}{j\omega(j\omega\tau_1 + 1)(j\omega\tau_2 + 1)}$$

has an angle of -270 degrees at $\omega = \infty$. When placed in $1 + KG(j\omega) = 0$, it leads to the cubic

$$a(j\omega)^3 + b(j\omega)^2 + c(j\omega) + d = 0 \tag{64}$$

On the other hand, the function

$$KG(j\omega) = \frac{K(j\omega\tau_2 + 1)}{j\omega(j\omega\tau_1 + 1)(j\omega\tau_3 + 1)} \tag{65}$$

in which $\tau_2 \neq \tau_1$ or $\tau_2 \neq \tau_3$ has an angle of only -180 degrees at $\omega = \infty$, but when placed in $1 + KG(j\omega) = 0$, it leads to the cubic equation

$$e(j\omega)^3 + f(j\omega)^2 + g(j\omega) + h = 0 \tag{66}$$

Thus the order of the characteristic Equations 64 and 66 are equal, but the total angles of each of the KG functions from which the characteristic equations are derived differ by 90 degrees because of the differences in their numerators. In practice, it may often be observed that τ_2 approximately equals τ_1 or τ_3. In some instances, design synthesis attempts to make them equal. For an absolute identity $\tau_2 = \tau_1$ or τ_3, the characteristic equation $1 + KG = 0$ then reduces to a quadratic,

but the total angle of KG is unaltered.   Thus in some instances, it is
not feasible to predict the order of the characteristic equation merely
from an inspection of the shape of the high-frequency end of the KG
locus.

   Region near $-1 + 0j$ (Stability).   The study of closed-loop system
stability is generally given extensive treatment as a separate topic
related to the Nyquist diagram.   However, in *single-loop systems*, that
is, systems having no minor loop within the main loop and hence those
in which $\theta_o(s)/\varepsilon(s) = KG(s)$ has no poles in the right-hand half of the
s plane, an elaborate mathematical treatment is not necessary to obtain
a useful understanding of stability.   For these simple systems, the entire
subject of stability can be subordinated to a phase of interpretation of
loci shapes on the complex plane.   Some relatively simple rules can be
stated which predict the stability.   While the proof of these rules may
not be obvious, the space required to include them is not practical considering that detailed treatments appear in most textbooks on the
theory of functions.[52, 61]   However, most of the general theorems on
stability that involve the theory of functions utilize line integrals or
surface integrals and studies of analytic functions.   They rarely give
the needed information pertaining to stability in a manner readily
usable by the designer.   At the expense of sounding redundant, the
designer needs quantitative information about relative stability.   He is
not greatly aided by qualitative rules which provide only a stable-
unstable test.

   In earlier chapters, it has been shown that the degree of relative stability depends largely upon the numerical value of the roots of the characteristic equation of $\theta_o(s)/\theta_i(s)$ obtained by *clearing the fractions* from
$1 + KG(s) = 0$, where $KG(s)$ may here represent the composite of several internal transfer functions and feedback loops.   The specific location of the roots of the characteristic equation on the s plane is the vital
factor in determining closed-loop performance and stability.   The right-
hand half of the s plane and the imaginary axis must be excluded as
possible locations for roots.   Roots * located here give poles † in the
right-hand plane of $\theta_o(s)/\theta_i(s)$ and hence will always lead to instability

---

   * This condition is often expressed by the statement that there shall be no zeros
of $1 + KG(s)$ in the right-hand half of the s plane.   The term *zeros* comes from the
fact that when $1 + KG(s)$ is equated to zero and written as $(s + a)(s + b)(s + c)$
$\cdots = 0$, the root is obtained by equating each factor of the characteristic equation
to zero.   This gives roots $-a$, $-b$, $-c$.   But for each of these roots, the corresponding factor is zero.   Therefore the root puts a zero in $1 + KG(s) = 0$.

   † A root or zero of the characteristic equation gives a pole to the function θ_o/θ_i.
Whenever the root or zero is located in the right-hand half plane, the system response
is of the form ε^{at} and leads to an infinity.

or sustained oscillation. The roots of $1 + KG(s) = 0$ indicated in Figure 14 which fall in undesirable locations are:

$$\begin{bmatrix} \text{Root 1} & s = +a \\ \text{Root pair 2} & s = +b \pm jc \\ \text{Root 3} & s = 0 \\ \text{Root pair 4} & s = \pm jd \end{bmatrix} \qquad (67)$$

In contrast, the roots plotted in Figure 14 which lead to stable performance are:

$$\begin{Bmatrix} \text{Root 5} & s = -e \\ \text{Root pair 6} & s = -f \pm jg \end{Bmatrix} \qquad (68)$$

Some interesting speculations arise. Since the imaginary axis of the s plane corresponds to $s = \pm j\omega$, the locus $KG(j\omega)$ is related to it as a

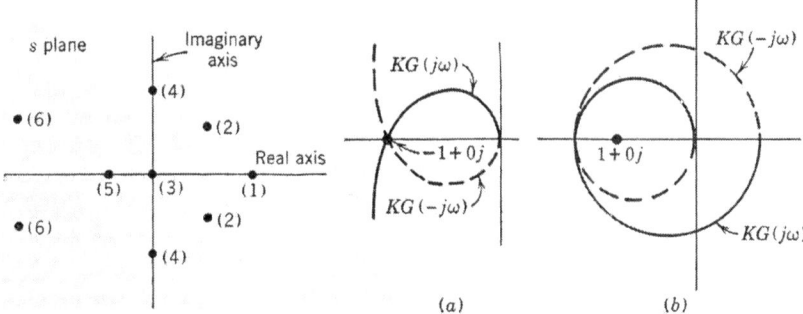

FIGURE 14.   Roots in the s plane.   FIGURE 15.   Instability of closed-loop systems.

boundary line between the zone of absolute stability and absolute instability. Furthermore, once the transfer function locus has been plotted on the complex plane, function mathematics shows that it is possible to scan the right-hand half of the s plane and determine regions or paths for KG on the complex plane which indicate system instability. Performing the study for the single-loop system shows that (1) the point $-1 + 0j$ on the KG plane is directly related to the imaginary axis of the s plane; (2) sustained oscillation is certain when the locus KG passes through this point; (3) destructive instability results when the locus of $KG(j\omega)$ plotted for both positive and negative values of frequency ω encloses the point $-1 + 0j$ (nonlinearities may limit the violence of oscillations). The two conditions of instability are indicated by the diagrams in Figure 15. Sustained or unending oscillation is indicated by the locus of Figure 15a. Destructive oscillation is indicated by the locus of Figure 15b. These simple tests, however, may need modification when the system is composed of multiple loops.

Multiple-loop systems may have composite transfer functions $\theta_o/\mathcal{E}$ with poles in the right-hand half of the s plane. When they do, a condition of instability exists if the main loop is opened. On the other hand, if the loop is closed, the overall system may be stable. The Nyquist criterion, if applied in the manner that is sufficient for the single-loop systems, does not serve as an adequate test for stability in multiple-loop systems. Its extension to the multiple-loop system comes from an application of Cauchy's theorem, which gives the contribution to the integral of a function of s taken over a closed contour in the s plane. This theorem leads to the condition that the net change in phase $2\pi N$ going around the closed contour of the overall function $f(s)$ is equal to 2π times the number of poles P minus the number of zeros Z of the function that lie in the right-half plane. That is,

$$N = P - Z \qquad (69)$$

where N is the number of encirclements in going around the contour. The choice of algebraic sign depends on the direction taken around the contour. The extension * of this theorem to the closed-loop problem leads to a complete stability criterion. *Because the relation for θ_o/θ_i is stable only if there are no zeros Z in the right-hand half plane of $1 + KG(s)$, Equation 69 requires that the open-loop transfer function plotted in the $KG(j\omega)$ plane from $-\infty$ to ∞ must encircle the point $-1 + j0$ as often as there are poles P of the transfer function in the right-hand half plane.* Thus, the Nyquist criterion in its comprehensive form [65] involves the *number* and direction of encirclements of $-1 + j0$ which the plot of $KG(j\omega)$ makes as the frequency is varied from $-j\infty$ to $+j\infty$. Only in the case of the simple single-loop system for which $P = 0$, does zero net encirclement of the point $-1 + j0$ indicate a stable system.

Figure 16 shows a few examples of these stability tests. The enclosures at the value $\omega =$ zero are indicated by the dash-dot line, whereas the conjugate of $KG(j\omega)$ or the portion for negative frequencies $-j\omega$ is dotted. Curves a, b, c, and d are plots of the transfer functions of single-loop systems. Curves e and f are plots typical of some multiple-loop systems. The curves in a and c represent stable systems. Curve b is an unstable system while that of d is a "conditionally" stable one; that is, for a particular range of values of K it is unstable, but it is stable for both larger and smaller values. It is unstable as shown.

---

* The reader who is interested in the proof of this theorem is referred to the book by Bode.[61]

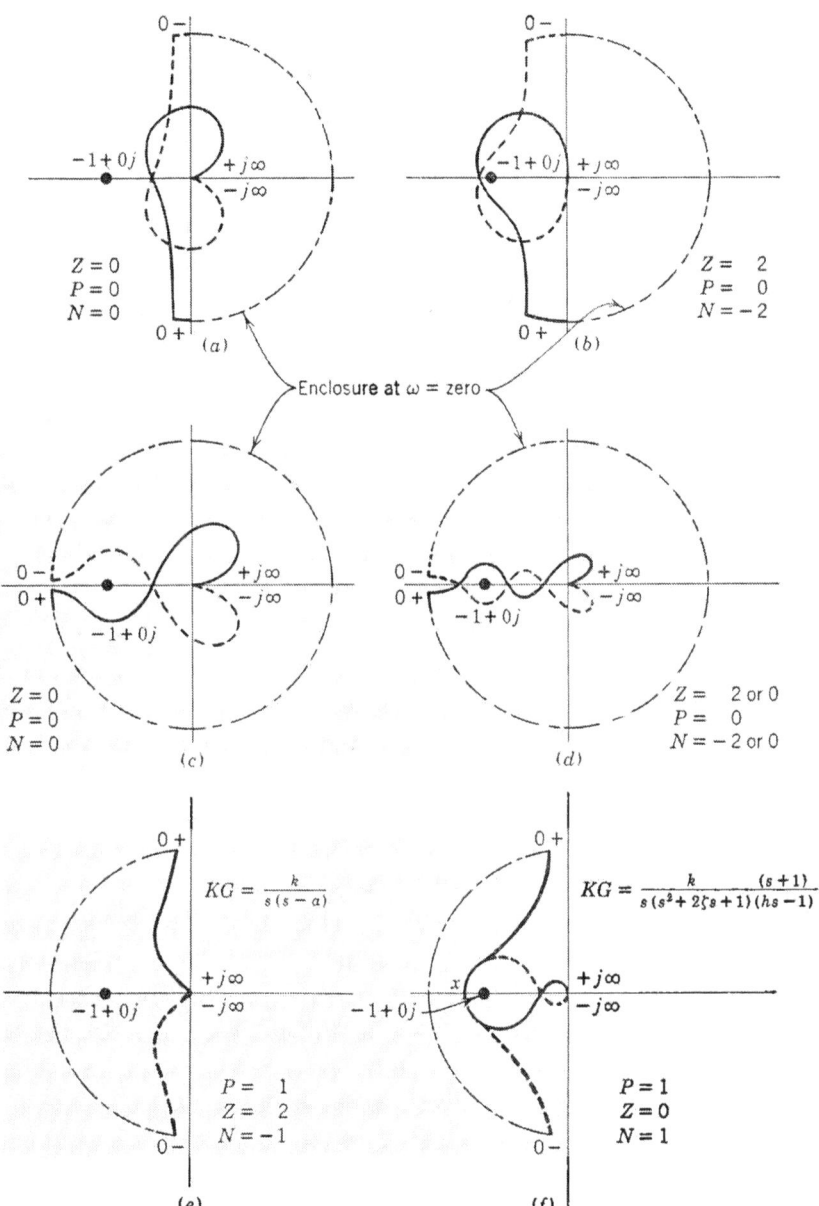

FIGURE 16.   Graphical illustration of stability equation $N = P - Z$.

In the systems of curves e and f, the function $KG(s)$ has a pole on the right-hand half of the s plane. Application of the Nyquist criterion in its comprehensive form here states that the net encirclement N of the point $-1 + j0$ equals the number of poles P of KG minus the numbers of zeros Z of $1 + KG = 0$. That is,

$$N = P - Z$$

If we trace along curve e, we make one encirclement of the point $-1 + j0$ in the negative direction as we go from $-j\infty$ to $+j\infty$, which makes $N = -1$. But $P = 1$ because of the pole in $KG(s)$ at $+a$. The closed-loop system is unstable because Z must be equal to 2 in order to fulfill Equation 69. On the other hand, if we trace along the curve f, we make one encirclement of the point $-1 + 0j$ in the positive direction. Therefore $N = 1$. But again $P = 1$ because of the pole in $KG(s)$ at $1/h$. Hence $Z = 0$ and the system is stable. The closed-loop system of curve f is stable only because the value of k makes the point x fall outside the point $-1 + 0j$. If k were decreased to locate the point x between the point -1 and the origin, the system would be unstable.

For the benefit of the practical man concerned with closed-loop design problems, it is probably sufficient to assume that the system will be stable provided the point $-1 + j0$ is always on the left as we progress along the locus in the direction of increasing frequency merely from zero to infinity. Perhaps the most difficult problem related to stability involves open-ended loci plots on the complex plane, that is, loci that close at infinity when $\omega = 0$ so that the positive and negative frequency portions do not appear to close. When this situation exists, it is not always easy to determine whether the locus closes with or without encircling the $-1 + 0j$ point. A useful method for showing how the locus closes is to study the phase of $KG(j\omega)$. This phase function must be continuous in the frequency variable ω through the range $-\infty < \omega < \infty$. If this procedure fails, a change of variable can sometimes be made and the locus plotted on another plane, for example, the W plane, so that the region at infinity of the KG plane becomes a definite point located on the new plane. Then the closure of the original locus with respect to the point $-1 + 0j$ is shown by the closure of the new locus on the new plane. The use of the G^{-1} plane is frequently helpful when making these studies of stability.

Experience with closed-loop designs shows that when unusual shapes of the KG loci are encountered, the system is likely to be a very special one, necessitating special design practice. The more conventional types of closed-loop system have quite common loci shapes. Consequently their stability is often quickly predicted.

Summary. Table 5 summarizes briefly the general studies which have been presented in this section relative to the low-frequency and

TABLE 5

SUMMARY OF LOW-FREQUENCY, HIGH-FREQUENCY, AND STABILITY CRITERIA

$G(ju)$	Low-Frequency Region	High-Frequency Region	Stability
$\dfrac{1}{ju+1}$			
$\dfrac{1}{ju(ju+1)}$			
$\dfrac{1}{(ju)^2}$			
$\dfrac{1}{ju(-u^2+j2\zeta u+1)}$			
$\dfrac{(ju\tau_1+1)}{(ju)^2(ju\tau_2+1)\cdots}$ $\tau_1>\tau_2$			

the high-frequency properties of the KG locus. This table emphasizes that no quantitative data are obtained from mere loci studies for the degree of stability of a closed-loop system. Despite this review of theorems pertaining to stability, the only criteria yet obtained for predicting the exact *degree of stability* come from the roots of the characteristic equation. By resorting to a different approach to this problem, quantitative results can be obtained. Specifically, the location of the locus of the transfer function $KG(j\omega)$ with respect to lines of constant magnitude and constant phase of θ_o/θ_i is next examined on the KG plane as a method for determining the degree of stability desired and a means for specifying closed-loop system design.

9 Constant Magnitude (M) and Constant Phase (N) Contours

of $\dfrac{\theta_o}{\theta_i}(j\omega)$ on the Complex Plane

For the KG Plane. Contours on the KG plane for constant values of $\left|\,\theta_o/\theta_i\,\right|$ and constant values of tangent of Ang θ_o/θ_i may be plotted as shown in Figures 17 and 18. The value $\left|\,\theta_o/\theta_i\,\right|$ is defined as M and

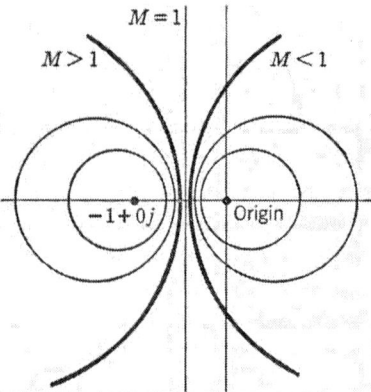

FIGURE 17.　Contours of constant M in the KG plane.

the tangent of Ang θ_o/θ_i is defined as N. By the use of these M-N contours, it is possible to mark off zones on the plot through which the locus of KG or KG^{-1} must pass in order that the magnitude and phase of θ_o/θ_i shall fall within prescribed bounds. Furthermore, the transection of the locus KG with these contours locates for the discrete frequencies on the locus, the corresponding discrete frequencies of the magnitude and phase of the response. The general location of the locus KG can be altered by changing the value K. The relative location of frequency points on the locus can be altered by reshaping the function $G(j\omega)$. This alteration provides a definite method for executing design synthesis and introduces another point of view toward dynamical stability.

The expression for the M loci or the M contours on the complex plane can be found by representing KG in Cartesian coordinates as

$$KG(j\omega) = x(\omega) + jy(\omega) \tag{70}$$

$$M = \left| \frac{\theta_o}{\theta_i}(j\omega) \right|$$

$$= \left| \frac{KG(j\omega)}{1 + KG(j\omega)} \right|$$

$$= \left| \frac{x + jy}{1 + x + jy} \right| \tag{71}$$

Rationalizing Equation 71 and rearranging the terms give the equation for a circle with M as a parameter. Thus

$$y^2 + \left[x + \frac{M^2}{M^2 - 1} \right]^2 = \frac{M^2}{(M^2 - 1)^2} \tag{72}$$

The variables x and y are parametrically related through the variable ω. However, the ω does not appear in the formula for the locus of the M circle. The center of the circle is

$$x_o = -\frac{M^2}{M^2 - 1} \\ y_o = 0 \tag{73}$$

the radius of the circle is

$$r = \left| \frac{M}{M^2 - 1} \right| \tag{74}$$

and the intercept of the circle nearest the origin on the real axis is

$$x_1 = -\frac{M}{M + 1} \tag{75}$$

Thus, for different numerical values of M, for example 0.1, 0.2, $\cdots M$, a set of related circles can be superposed upon the KG plane independent of the frequency variable ω. A family of M circles is shown in Figure 17. They indicate among other things that:

(1) The value $|\theta_o/\theta_i|$ of a closed-loop system having a perfect response, that is, flat over $0 < \omega < \infty$, would follow the straight line for $M = 1$ which passes through the point $-\frac{1}{2} + 0j$ on the KG plane.

(2) In order that $|\theta_o/\theta_i|$ shall never be less than a limiting value, for example, $M = 0.7$, the locus of KG must not enter the contour

specified $M = 0.7$. Notice that contours for all values of $M < 1$ lie to the right of the $M = 1$ contour.

(3) In order that $|\theta_o/\theta_i|$ shall not exceed a given value of M, that is, shall not exhibit a violent resonance condition, the transfer function locus KG must not enter the circle defined by this limiting M value. Note that this M contour is located to the left of the $M = 1$ contour.

From these observations it becomes obvious that definite zones on the KG plane can be related to definite behavior of the closed-loop system.

The family of constant phase contours defined by tan [Ang θ_o/θ_i] can be found following much the same procedure used to determine the M contours. The transfer function KG is again expressed in Cartesian coordinates as in Equation 70, and the angle relation is formed as in Equation 76.

$$\text{Ang} \frac{\theta_o}{\theta_i} (j\omega) = \tan^{-1} \frac{y}{x} - \tan^{-1} \frac{y}{1+x} \tag{76}$$

The individual angles for the numerator and denominator of Ang θ_o/θ_i giving the two inverse tangent terms in Equation 76 can be collected by the sum and difference angle formula giving

$$\text{Ang} \frac{\theta_o}{\theta_i} (j\omega) = \tan^{-1} \left\{ \frac{\dfrac{y}{x} - \dfrac{y}{1+x}}{1 + \left[\dfrac{y}{x}\right]\left[\dfrac{y}{1+x}\right]} \right\} \tag{77}$$

which simplifies to

$$\tan \left[\text{Ang} \frac{\theta_o}{\theta_i} (j\omega) \right] = N = \frac{y}{x^2 + x + y^2} \tag{78}$$

The relation in Equation 78 is a circle with the parameter N defining the parametric set of curves. The equation of the circle is

$$\left(x + \frac{1}{2}\right)^2 + \left(y - \frac{1}{2N}\right)^2 = \frac{1}{4}\left[\frac{N^2 + 1}{N^2}\right] \tag{79}$$

The center is located at

$$\left. \begin{array}{l} x_o = -\frac{1}{2} \\[2mm] y_o = +\dfrac{1}{2N} \end{array} \right\} \tag{80}$$

The radius is

$$r = \frac{1}{2N} \sqrt{N^2 + 1} \tag{81}$$

The constant phase or N contours are plotted on the KG plane in Figure 18. The significance of the family of curves of Figure 18 in bounding the phase of the KG locus which will give desired values for the Ang θ_o/θ_i follows the pattern just discussed in (1), (2), and (3) for the M contours.

Both families of curves can be superposed on the KG plane. Consider a particular KG plane upon which these two families are plotted to be transparent and placed in front of the KG plane upon which the transfer

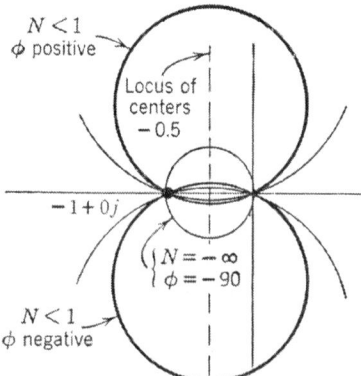

FIGURE 18.   Contours of constant phase ϕ in the KG plane.

function locus is plotted. The problem of design synthesis is now apparent. First, the loop sensitivity K can be altered until the $KG(j\omega)$ locus is tangent to any specified M circle. Second, the shape of the $G(j\omega)$ function can be altered to produce a specific location of the locus relative to the M and N contours. Both these problems continually arise in synthesis, each being a complete topic in itself.

For the KG^{-1} Plane. An identical treatment can be prepared for the inverse locus KG^{-1} following the outline already established in Equations 71 through 81. These results are tabulated in Table 6 along with the principal equations for the M and N contours of the KG plane. The graphical representation of the two new families of contours for the KG^{-1} plane is given by Figure 19. The contours for M are again circles, but the contours for phase N are radial lines. Two families of contours are already superposed in Figure 19. The synthesis problem as outlined in the foregoing paragraph is now possible following a parallel treatment in terms of the locus of the inverse functions. The treatment given in Sec. 6, Chapter 7, will demonstrate the fact that the use of the locus KG^{-1} leading to response functions θ_i/θ_o, often simplifies studies which involve dynamic members in the feedback path.

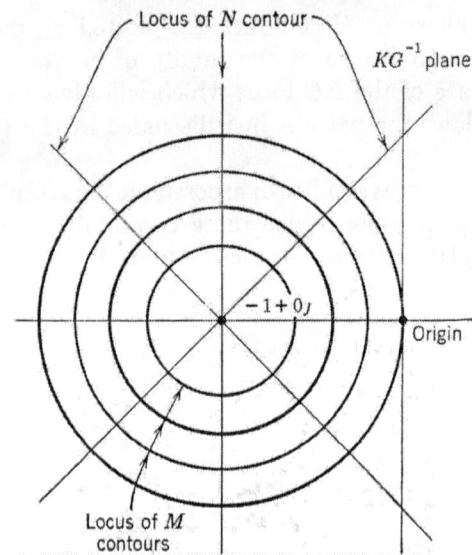

FIGURE 19.　Contours of constant M and constant phase ϕ in the KG^{-1} plane.

TABLE 6

Magnitude M and Phase N Contours for the KG Plane	Magnitude M and Phase N Contours for the KG^{-1} Plane

M Contours

$$y^2 + \left(x + \frac{M^2}{M^2 - 1}\right)^2 = \frac{M^2}{(M^2 - 1)^2} \quad (82)$$

Center at $\left(-\dfrac{M^2}{M^2 - 1},\, 0\right)$　(83)

Radius $\left|\dfrac{M}{M^2 - 1}\right|$　(84)

Intercept nearest origin $-\dfrac{M}{M + 1}$　(85)

N Contours

where $N = \tan\left[\mathrm{Ang}\,\dfrac{\theta_o}{\theta_i}\,(j\omega)\right]$　(86)

$$\left(x + \frac{1}{2}\right)^2 + \left(y - \frac{1}{2N}\right)^2$$

$$= \frac{1}{4}\left(\frac{N^2 + 1}{N^2}\right) \quad (87)$$

Center at $\left(-\dfrac{1}{2},\, \dfrac{1}{2N}\right)$　(88)

Radius $\dfrac{1}{2}\dfrac{\sqrt{N^2 + 1}}{N}$　(89)

M Contours

$$y^2 + (1 + x)^2 = \frac{1}{M^2} \quad (90)$$

Center at $(-1, 0)$　(91)

Radius $\dfrac{1}{M}$　(92)

Intercept nearest origin $\dfrac{1 - M}{M}$　(93)

N Contours

$$N = \tan\left[\mathrm{Ang}\,\frac{\theta_i}{\theta_o}\,(j\omega)\right] \quad (94)$$

$$y + Nx + N = 0 \quad (95)$$

Note. N contours are a family of radial lines emanating from the center of the M circles.

TABLE 7

NUMERICAL DATA RELATED TO MAGNITUDE AND PHASE CONTOURS ON THE
KG PLANE

Magnitude M	Center $\dfrac{M^2}{M^2 - 1}$	Radius $\dfrac{M}{M^2 - 1}$	Intercept $\dfrac{M}{M + 1}$	Angle $\psi = \sin^{-1} \dfrac{1}{M}$
0.3	+0.099	0.33	−0.23	. . . . .
0.4	+0.191	0.48	−0.29	. . . . .
0.5	+0.333	0.67	−0.333	. . . . .
0.6	+0.562	0.94	−0.375	. . . . .
0.7	+0.960	1.37	−0.410	. . . . .
0.8	+1.777	2.22	−0.445	. . . . .
0.9	+4.26	4.74	−0.473	. . . . .
1.0	∞	∞	−0.500	90°
1.1	−5.77	5.24	−0.524	65.2°
1.2	−3.27	2.73	−0.545	56.5°
1.3	−2.45	1.88	−0.566	50.2°
1.4	−2.04	1.46	−0.584	45.6°
1.5	−1.80	1.20	−0.600	41.8°
1.6	−1.64	1.03	−0.615	38.7°
1.7	−1.53	0.90	−0.630	36.0°
1.8	−1.47	0.842	−0.643	33.7°
1.9	−1.38	0.729	−0.655	31.7°
2.0	−1.33	0.666	−0.666	30.0°
2.25	−1.24	0.550	−0.693	26.4°
2.50	−1.19	0.476	−0.714	23.6°
2.75	−1.15	0.416	−0.734	21.3°
3.00	−1.12	0.375	−0.750	19.5°
3.50	−1.10	0.340	−0.779	16.6°
4.00	−1.07	0.266	−0.800	14.5°
5.00	−1.04	0.208	−0.832	11.5°

TABLE 8

Numerical Data Related to Magnitude and Phase Contours on the KG Plane

ϕ	N	N^2	Radius $\dfrac{\sqrt{N^2+1}}{2N}$	Center $-\dfrac{1}{2}$	Center $\dfrac{1}{2N}$
$+0$	$+0.000$	0.000	∞	-0.5	∞
-10	-0.176	0.031	2.88	-0.5	-2.84
-20	-0.364	0.132	1.46	-0.5	-1.37
-30	-0.577	0.334	1.00	-0.5	-0.866
-40	-0.838	0.705	0.775	-0.5	-0.596
-50	-1.19	1.42	0.656	-0.5	-0.42
-60	-1.73	3.02	0.577	-0.5	-0.289
-70	-2.75	7.58	0.531	-0.5	-0.182
-80	-5.77	33.4	0.506	-0.5	-0.087
-90	∞	∞	0.50	-0.5	0

Tabular Summary. For convenience, the principal numerical values needed to draw the various M and N contours on the KG or the KG^{-1} plane are tabulated in Tables 6, 7, and 8.

10 Effect of the Gain Constant K on Closed-Loop Performance

Variation of the parameter K merely adjusts the scale of the polar plot of the locus $G(j\omega)$. Thus if $G(j\omega)$ is plotted on a magnitude and phase grid formed by superposing Figures 17 and 18, the locus will cut across the M and N contour grid on a different path for each value of the constant K yielding different values for $\left|\, \theta_o/\theta_i \,\right|$ and Ang θ_o/θ_i. This situation is illustrated in Figure 20, where a transfer function locus corresponding to values of $K = 0.5$, 1.0, and 2.0 is plotted. Three distinctly different loci appear on the KG plane. However, they have experienced no relative change in shape as a result of the change in K.

The closed-loop frequency response corresponding to these three values of K, that is, the three values of loop gain, have interesting properties that are directly readable from the polar plot. For example, any particular frequency point is moved along the radius vector as the gain K is changed. Hence, the locus crosses into regions of larger and larger M but less and less phase shift N as the gain K is increased. These data are plotted to form separate graphs as in Figure 21 for the magnitude and phase response. It is often helpful to plot this figure even though all the data are shown in the polar plot. It can be dispensed with when the procedure becomes more understandable by virtue of repetition.

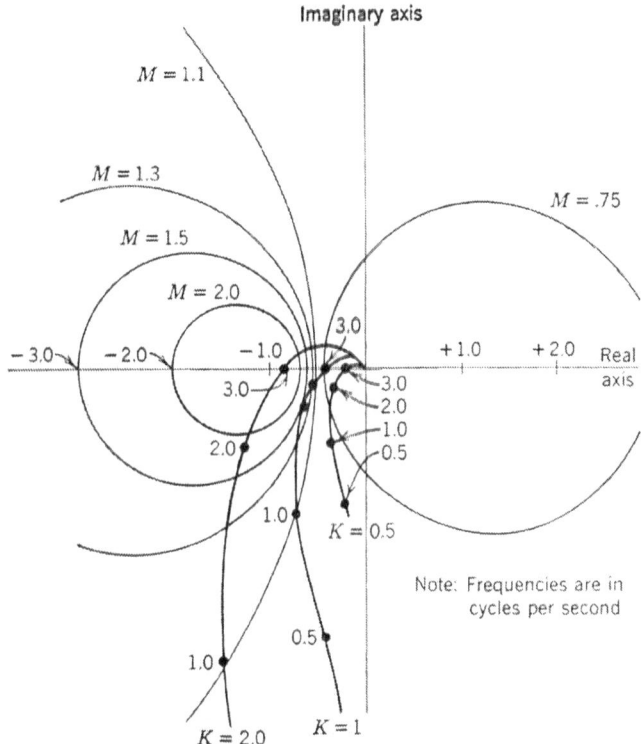

FIGURE 20. M circles superposed on the KG locus.

Figure 21 shows that the $KG(j\omega)$ locus of Figure 20 for $K = 1$ passes through the M-N grid so that:

(1) The maximum magnification of $\theta_o/\theta_i = M_p$ is about 1.4 at a resonant frequency $u = 2.0$.
(2) The phase shift or Ang θ_o/θ_i at this resonant frequency is about -100 degrees.
(3) The frequency band over which the magnitude of θ_o/θ_i does not violate the condition $0.6 < M_p < 1.4$ is about $0 < u < 3.0$.

A decrease in the sensitivity to $K = 0.5$ results in:

(1) The magnitude θ_o/θ_i never being greater than unity. It always diminishes with increasing frequency. The system cannot exhibit resonance phenomena since the KG locus never crosses the $M =$

1.0 contour. (This does not always imply that roots of the characteristic equation of more complicated systems may not have
the form $-a \pm jb$.)

(2) A band width of $0 < u < 2.0$ within which the magnitude of
θ_o/θ_i remains within the range $0.6 < M_p < 1.4$.

(3) A phase shift of -130 degrees at the upper limit of frequency
$u = 2.0$.

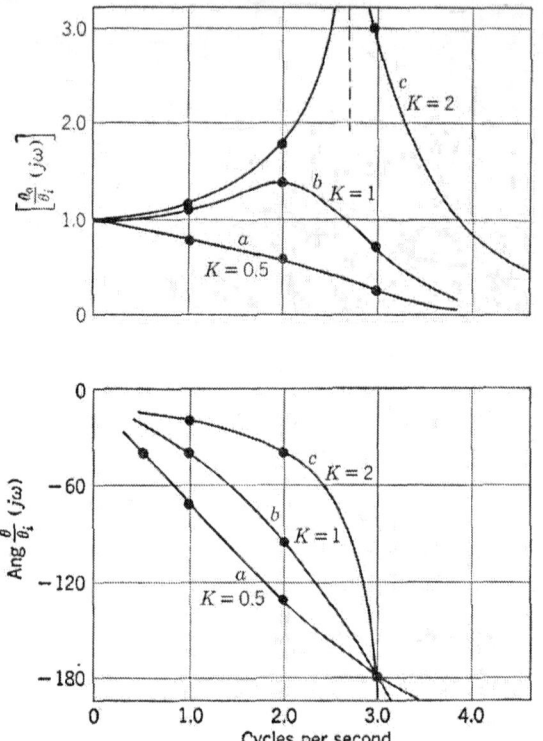

FIGURE 21.   Magnitude and phase characteristics derived from Figure 20.

An increase in the sensitivity to $K = 2.0$ results in:

(1) A violently oscillatory system. The resonant frequency u is about
2.8 and the magnification M_p is far in excess of 5.0.

(2) A band width of $0 < u < 1.4$ within which the magnitude of
θ_o/θ_i remains within the range $0.6 < M_p < 1.4$, because of the
rapid rise of the magnitude curve as it approaches resonance.

(3) A phase shift of only about -20 degrees at $u = 1.4$; the phase
now changes much less rapidly with frequency than when $K =
1.0$ or 0.5.

The above simple study shows that it is possible by mere gain adjustment to obtain substantially uniform magnitude response or substantially uniform phase response over quite a large frequency band. It is not possible to get both together merely by gain adjustment. If absence of peaking in the magnitude response is desired, the phase change is large. With large phase shift (-180 degrees at $u = 3.0$), the error magnitude $| \varepsilon(j\omega) |$ is equal to the sum of the magnitudes of the input $| \theta_i(j\omega) |$ and the output $| \theta_o(j\omega) |$ as shown by the vector diagram of Figure 4·5. Alternatively, if small phase change is desired, the resonance effect is large. Thus the use of only magnitude or phase as a performance specification may result in a poor system.

11   Setting the Gain K for a Specified M Criterion

Using the $G(j\omega)$ Locus.   A compromise must be made if we desire a closed-loop system to have the response simultaneously bounded with respect to magnitude and phase. That is, if for example,

$$0.7 < \left| \frac{\theta_o}{\theta_i} (j\omega) \right|_{\max} < 1.3$$

and

$$\text{Ang} \frac{\theta_o}{\theta_i} (j\omega) < -30° \tag{96}$$

The three zones, shown on the KG plane in Figure 22, may be considered regions from which the KG locus is to be excluded throughout a given frequency band. Anywhere outside these circles, for example, one for $M = 1.3$, one for $M = 0.7$, and one for phase angle $\phi = -30$ degrees or $N = -0.577$, the locus can be adjusted to satisfy the requirements of Equation 96 by variation of the loop sensitivity K. Since the KG locus must not loop the point $-1 + 0j$ and since the shaded circle for the phase exclusion zone and the $M = 0.7$ zone engulf the origin of the KG plane, there is no KG locus which can possibly avoid entering these circles at some upper value of frequency. In view of this, the place where the locus KG should enter the shaded area is probably at the intersection of the two contours $M = 1.3$ and $\phi = -30$ degrees. This gives the maximum frequency range over which the conditions of Equation 96 are satisfied.

While the use of the grid of M and N contours is valuable in the determination of the output response $\theta_o(j\omega)$ of the system, it leads to unnecessary trial-and-error techniques when selecting a proper loop gain, or sensitivity K, consistent with a given M criterion. A relatively simple geometric technique exists for locating the circle corresponding to a particular M at a place on the plot where it will have a tangency with the $G(j\omega)$ locus plotted on the G plane. Once an appropriate circle is located on the plot, the scale of the plot is given by the equations of Table 6, which has the effect of expanding or contracting the $G(j\omega)$

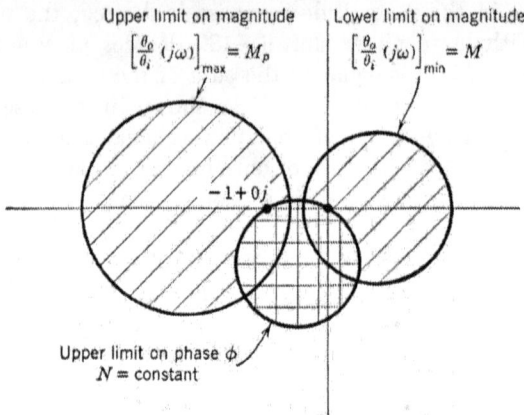

Upper limit on magnitude   Lower limit on magnitude

$$\left[\frac{\theta_o}{\theta_i}(j\omega)\right]_{max} = M_p \qquad \left[\frac{\theta_o}{\theta_i}(j\omega)\right]_{min} = M$$

$-1+0j$

Upper limit on phase ϕ
$N = $ constant

FIGURE 22.   Contours for bounding magnitude and phase performance.

locus to convert it into a KG locus by a mere change of scale of the plot. The procedure is shown on Figure 23. It eliminates any necessity for plotting a new locus for each value of K.

The derivation for the construction of Figure 23 can be established as follows. Consider a circle for any arbitrary M drawn with its center

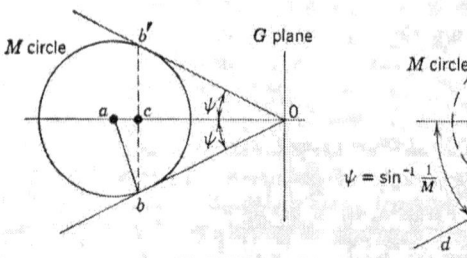

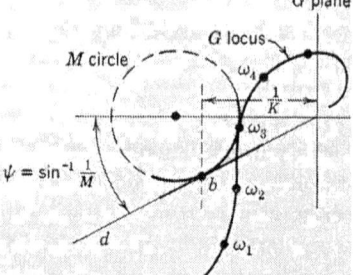

FIGURE 23.   The geometry of an M circle in the G plane.

FIGURE 24.   Calibration of the KG plane from the G plane using $\sin^{-1}\dfrac{1}{M}$ criterion.

as at a of the figure. Draw lines ob and ob' from the origin tangent to the circle. Now assume that the diagram carries an unknown scale factor such that the distance from the origin to the center of the circle,

which for unit scale would be $\dfrac{M^2}{M^2 - 1}$, is assumed to be $\dfrac{1}{K}\left(\dfrac{M^2}{M^2 - 1}\right)$.
Similarly the radius ab, which for a unit scale would be equal to $\dfrac{M}{M^2 - 1}$, now has the magnitude $\dfrac{1}{K}\left(\dfrac{M}{M^2 - 1}\right)$. Then from the geometry of the figure we can write that

$$oa = \frac{1}{K}\frac{M^2}{M^2 - 1} \tag{97a}$$

and

$$ab = \frac{1}{K}\frac{M}{M^2 - 1} \tag{97b}$$

Also that

$$\cos \psi = \frac{oc}{ob} = \frac{ob}{oa} = \frac{ob}{\dfrac{1}{K}\dfrac{M^2}{M^2 - 1}} \tag{98a}$$

and

$$\sin \psi = \frac{ab}{oa} = \frac{1}{M} \tag{98b}$$

Since

$$\sin^2 \psi + \cos^2 \psi = 1$$

it follows that

$$\frac{(ob)^2}{\left[\dfrac{1}{K}\dfrac{M^2}{M^2 - 1}\right]^2} = 1 - \frac{1}{M^2}$$

giving

$$(ob)^2 = \left(1 - \frac{1}{M^2}\right)\left[\frac{1}{K^2}\right]\left[\frac{M^2}{M^2 - 1}\right]^2 \tag{99a}$$

but, from Equation 98a,

$$(ob)^2 = oc\left[\frac{1}{K}\frac{M^2}{M^2 - 1}\right] \tag{99b}$$

Eliminating $(ob)^2$ from Equations 99a and 99b, and solving for oc, gives

$$oc = \frac{1}{K} \tag{100}$$

where oc is the projection on the real axis of the tangent line ob.

The significance of the above analysis is demonstrated by Figure 24, which shows the function $G(j\omega)$ initially plotted to its own scale on the complex plane. A radius ob is shown such that the angle ψ is equal to $\sin^{-1} 1/M$. A circle then drawn with its center on the real axis and tangent to the line ob and the $G(j\omega)$ locus will automatically rescale the plot such that the radius of the circle equals $\dfrac{1}{K}\left(\dfrac{M}{M^2-1}\right)$, and the distance from the origin to the point c is $1/K$.

Thus, to adjust the loop sensitivity K for any $G(j\omega)$ function, the procedure is as follows:

(1) Draw the locus of the $G(j\omega)$ function on the complex plane as in Figure 24.
(2) Select the value of M in accordance with the closed-loop performance. Say $M = 1.3$.
(3) Select the angle ψ and draw the line od of Figure 24. For $M = 1.3$, $\psi = 50.2$ degrees.
(4) Draw a circle that is tangent to both the $G(j\omega)$ locus and the line od as in Figure 24.
(5) Draw a perpendicular bc from the point of tangency b between the circle and the $\sin^{-1}(1/M)$ line. Read the reciprocal $1/K$ of the loop gain directly as the value of the point c.

To prepare the overall frequency characteristic as was done in Figure 21 for the locus of Figure 20, it is necessary to make the resulting G plane scale agree with the scale of the M and N contour grid. A few minutes' work with a pair of dividers will make the change, from which $\left|\theta_o/\theta_i\right|$ and Ang θ_o/θ_i can be read by inspection.

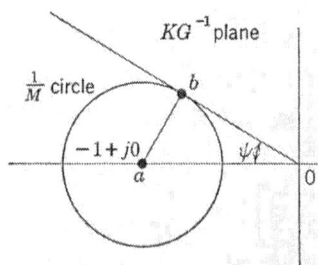

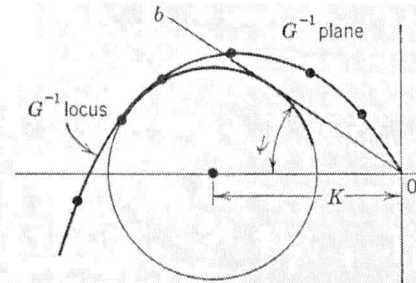

FIGURE 25. The geometry of an M circle in the G^{-1} plane.

FIGURE 26. Calibrating the KG^{-1} plane from the G^{-1} plane using $\sin^{-1}\dfrac{1}{M}$ criterion.

Using the $G^{-1}(j\omega)$ Locus. A treatment paralleling that given for functions plotted in the G plane follows for functions plotted in the G^{-1} plane. Consider the geometric construction of Figure 25 for the KG^{-1} plane. If the center a of a circle is located at the point $-1 + j0$

and the radius ab of the circle is equal to $1/M$, it follows that

$$\sin \psi = \frac{ab}{oa} = \frac{\dfrac{1}{M}}{1} = \frac{1}{M} \tag{101}$$

The significance of Equation 101 is illustrated by the construction shown in Figure 26 for the G^{-1} plane. The line ob is drawn so that $\sin \psi$ is equal to $1/M$, where ψ is the angle boa. The G^{-1} locus is then drawn to its own scale on the G plane. A circle located with its center on the real axis and tangent simultaneously to the line ob and to the G^{-1} locus will have its center at the point $-1 + j0$ of the KG^{-1} plane. Thus the distance from the origin of coordinates to the center of the circle equals the quantity K. It is the factor which converts a G^{-1} plane into a KG^{-1} plane.

12   Gain Margin and Phase Margin

The factors considered in Sections 8 and 9 have been expressed to some degree by other writers [34] on this subject in terms of a *gain margin* and a *phase margin* as design criteria. These terms appear usually in literature on the subject of servomechanisms synthesis in which the problem is treated in terms of plots of the log magnitude and the phase of the transfer function versus the logarithm of frequency. Section 9 of Chapter 8 defines these terms as commonly used. It seems appropriate, however, to inject them into the discussion at this part of the treatment with only a brief explanation. The phase margin is the angle between the negative real axis and the KG vector for the frequency at which $|KG(j\omega)|$ is unity. The gain margin is the reciprocal of $|KG(j\omega)|$ for the frequency at which its phase is -180 degrees. These criteria bound the transfer function in the region of the principal resonance of the overall function. Typical values for phase and gain margins are 30 to 60 degrees and 2.5 to 10, respectively.

13   Problem to Illustrate Setting the Gain K

Using the $G(j\omega)$ Locus. As an illustration of the procedure given in Section 11 for determining K, consider an open-loop system defined by inertia J and viscous function coefficient f such that

$$
\left.
\begin{aligned}
J &= 10.0 \text{ in.}^2 \text{ lb} = 0.026 \text{ in. lb sec}^2 \\
f &= 0.5 \text{ in. lb sec} \\
\frac{J}{f} &= \tau_m = 0.052 \text{ sec}
\end{aligned}
\right\} \tag{102}
$$

Assume that the system is to be made into a closed-loop positional servomechanism defined only by the relation that $\left| \dfrac{\theta_o}{\theta_i}(j\omega) \right|_{max} = M_p = 1.3$. Determine the gain constant K, the velocity constant K_v, the damping ratio ζ, and the natural frequency ω_n.

The transfer function for this system as derived in Chapter 4 is of the form

$$\frac{\theta_o}{\varepsilon}(j\omega) = KG(j\omega) = \frac{K_v}{j\omega(j\omega\tau_m + 1)} \tag{103}$$

By a change of variable $u = \tau_m\omega$, Equation 103 takes the form

$$\frac{\theta_o}{\varepsilon}(ju) = KG(ju) = \frac{K_u}{ju(ju + 1)} \tag{104}$$

where

$$K_u = K_v\tau_m \tag{105}$$

and is the velocity constant expressed in units of dimensionless time t/τ_m.

The values tabulated in Table 9 facilitate the plot of the $G(ju)$ locus from Equation 104. The plot of $G(ju)$ is shown in Figure 27 with the $\sin^{-1} 1/M$ line and the M circle.

TABLE 9

Transfer Function $\dfrac{1}{ju(ju + 1)}$

u	$\left\lvert \dfrac{1}{ju + 1} \right\rvert$	$-\tan^{-1} u$	$\left\lvert \dfrac{1}{ju(ju + 1)} \right\rvert$	$-(\tan^{-1} u) - 90°$
0.2	0.980	−12.0	4.90	−102
0.4	0.925	−22.5	2.31	−112.5
0.6	0.855	−32.0	1.42	−122.0
0.8	0.770	−39.5	0.95	−129.5
1.0	0.707	−45.0	0.71	−135.0
1.2	0.640	−50.5	0.53	−140.5
1.4	0.580	−55.0	0.41	−145.0
1.6	0.530	−58.0	0.33	−148.0
1.8	0.490	−61.0	0.27	−151.0
2.0	0.440	−63.0	0.22	−153.0
2.5	0.380	−68.0	0.15	−158.0
3.0	0.310	−72.0	0.10	−162.0
3.5	0.270	−74.0	0.077	−164.0
4.0	0.240	−76.0	0.066	−166.0

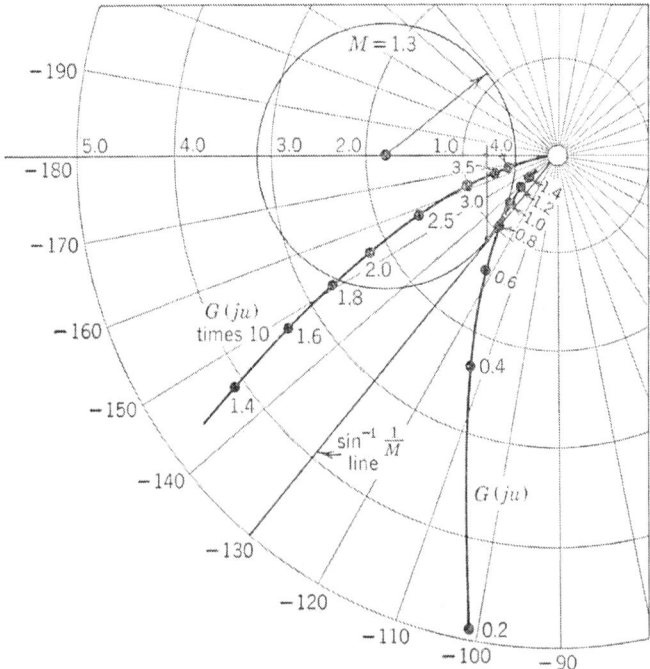

FIGURE 27.   The transfer function $\dfrac{1}{ju(ju + 1)}$ in the $G(ju)$ plane.

The projection on the real axis of the point of tangency between the line and the M circle is at -0.74. This gives

$$K_u = \frac{1}{0.74} = 1.36$$

The velocity constant K_v can now be found from Equation 105, thus

$$K_v = \frac{1.36}{\tau_m} = \frac{1.36}{0.052} = 26.2 \text{ seconds}^{-1}$$

The dimensionless resonant frequency u_R has the value 0.92, being the frequency at which the M circle is tangent to the $G(ju)$ locus. When the frequency is converted to the true time scale, the actual resonant frequency ω_R is

$$\omega_R = \frac{u_R}{\tau_m} = \frac{0.92}{0.052} = 17.6 \; \frac{\text{radians}}{\text{seconds}}$$

giving the resonant frequency as $\dfrac{17.6}{6.28}$ or 2.82 cycles per second.

The damping ratio ζ and the undamped angular frequency ω_n can be obtained by manipulating the dimensionless equation

$$1 + K_u G(ju) = 0 \tag{106}$$

to form

$$(ju)^2 + ju + K_u = 0 \tag{107}$$

which may be written as

$$\tau_m{}^2 (j\omega)^2 + \tau_m(j\omega) + K_v \tau_m = 0 \tag{108}$$

giving

$$\left.\begin{aligned} \omega_n = \sqrt{\frac{K_v}{\tau_m}} \\[2mm] u_n = \sqrt{K_u} \end{aligned}\right\} \tag{109}$$

$$\left.\begin{aligned} \zeta &= \frac{1}{2\sqrt{K_v \tau_m}} \\[3mm] &= \frac{1}{2\sqrt{K_u}} \end{aligned}\right\} \tag{110}$$

For the particular values of K_v and τ_m, the values of ζ and ω_n are 0.43 and 22.3 radians per second, respectively.

For a constant velocity input $|\omega_i|$ of, for example, 60 degrees per second, the steady-state error can be computed from Equation 103 as

$$\mathcal{E}_{ss} = \frac{1}{K_v} \omega_i = \frac{60}{26.2} = 2.3 \text{ degrees} \tag{111}$$

TABLE 10

M	$\psi = \sin^{-1}\dfrac{1}{M}$	Distance from Origin to Center of M Circle on G Plane	u_R	Distance from Origin to Center of M Circle on KG Plane	Dimensionless Velocity Constant, K_u	Damping Ratio, ζ
1.1	65°	7.25	0.55	5.76	0.8	0.56
1.2	56.5	3.00	0.75	3.28	1.09	0.48
1.3	50.4	1.80	0.92	2.46	1.36	0.43
1.5	41.9	1.0	1.2	1.80	1.80	0.37
1.7	36.0	0.6	1.4	1.53	2.55	0.31
2.0	30.0	0.36	1.8	1.33	3.70	0.26
2.5	23.5	0.21	2.4	1.19	5.77	0.21

If the closed loop is subjected to a sudden input disturbance $\left|\theta_i\right|$, the maximum transient error can be found from Figure 2·11. For a damping ratio ζ of 0.43, this figure shows that, on a dimensionless basis, the peak overshoot on the first swing of the oscillation is about 0.2. Thus if the step function of angle θ_i is 10 degrees, for example, the first overshoot is 2 degrees. Table 10 summarizes the results of this graphical study by presenting the values of K_u and ζ for the system of Equation 103.

It is important to realize that the dimensionless undamped angular frequency u_n may be greater than unity in this example even though the system has a quadratic for its characteristic equation. This follows of course from the fact that u is related to ω by an arbitrary time constant. The application of the relation derived in Chapter 4, Equation 4·47, leads to the condition that

$$u_R = u_n\sqrt{1 - 2\zeta^2}$$

giving

$$u_n = \frac{0.92}{\sqrt{1 - 2(0.43)^2}} = 1.16$$

But from Equation 109, u_n is also equal to $\sqrt{K_u}$. The values of u_n obtained from Equation 109 or from Equation 4·47 agree within the limits of error for a graphical solution.

Using the $G^{-1}(ju)$ Locus. The numerical data presented in Table 10 could have been obtained with equal ease using the inverse function $G^{-1}(ju)$. To illustrate this technique consider a sample calculation where the gain K is to be consistent with the value for $M = 1.3$. The inverse transfer function has the form

$$\frac{1}{KG(ju)} = \frac{1}{K_u}[ju(ju + 1)] \tag{112}$$

An interesting graphical construction sometimes used to obtain the curve of $G(ju)^{-1}$ is shown in Figure 28. The function $(ju + 1)$ is readily plotted by inspection as a straight line erected perpendicular to the real axis at the point $(1 + 0j)$ and marked off to a linear scale in u. The vector $ju(ju + 1)$ is then easily found by rotating each vector $(ju + 1)$ by $+90$ degrees and by multiplying it by the value of the frequency u. In other words, there need be very little tabulation of numbers to create the graph Figure 28.

The line corresponding to $\psi = \sin^{-1} 1/M \cong 50$ degrees is drawn on the graph. The $1/M$ circle of appropriate radius and tangent to both the line and the locus is also drawn. From this construction, the center of the circle is found to be at about 1.4 units from the origin. This value equals K_u. The point of tangency with the locus gives the resonant frequency $u_R \cong 0.9$.

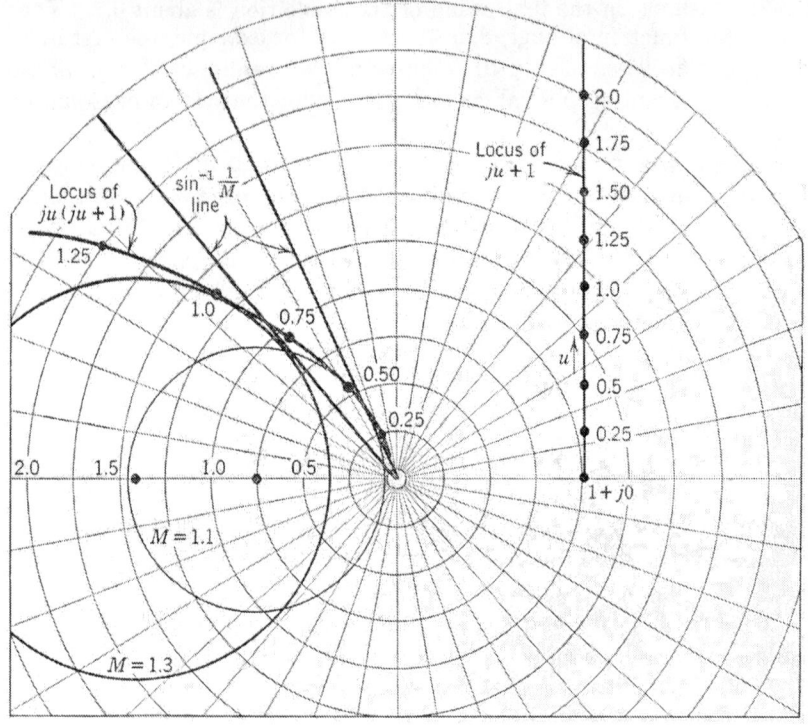

FIGURE 28.   The transfer function $\dfrac{1}{ju(ju + 1)}$ in the G^{-1} plane.

14   Conclusion

The reader is now acquainted with the procedure of adjusting the gain K of a closed loop as a first step toward synthesis. The method has been illustrated by several simple examples, and certain limitations in the procedure have been noted. The completeness with which the data of these examples are tabulated is not intended to imply great importance to a transfer function of the simple form $K_v/s(\tau_m s + 1)$. The completeness has been introduced in the interest of clarity of presentation of the method. The next phase of the synthesis problem is expressed by the question, "What can be done to $G(j\omega)$ to permit better performance of the system for the M_p and other criteria as specified?" An answer to this question involves an alteration to the shape of the G function. It is the subject of the next chapter.

7

Methods of G Function Synthesis — Linear Coordinates

1 Introduction

Some general methods for obtaining the proper transfer function for a closed-loop system were set down in Chapter 6. In particular, it was shown that the low-frequency asymptote of the KG locus determined the nature of the steady-state performance for the closed loop. Thus the order of the pole in $G(j\omega)$ for $\omega = 0$ was the ultimate factor in shaping the low-frequency portion of the G locus. The criterion for selection of $|\theta_o/\theta_i|_{max}$ was given; zones of M_{max} and ϕ_{max} could be drawn on the complex plane to aid in the adjustment of the dynamic performance. However, the frequency range over which the condition $0.7 < M < 1.3$ was met depended almost entirely upon the physical equipment that could be incorporated into a closed loop.

The problem of synthesis as presented in Chapter 6 terminated with the selection of the overall gain constant K consistent with the M_p criterion. This factor alone is not a true yardstick by which the G function for a closed loop should be selected. Specifically, it does not follow that the best closed-loop performance obtainable for a given selection of components is found by choosing the gain K according only to the M_p criterion. Furthermore, no consideration has yet been given the fact that the physical equipment necessary for actual construction of the closed loop may not permit a plausible design when K is the only variable.

Almost every closed-loop design requires that special auxiliary equipment be used in conjunction with the primary physical components. Such equipment is required because few loops permit closure with proper stability simultaneously with a large value of velocity constant K_v, to cite merely one of the many constants of merit. Therefore, control designers find it imperative to be intimately familiar with methods for selecting the proper G locus shape, or for reshaping G loci, in addition to knowing the method for finding K. When G loci must be reshaped, two courses are open: (1) the primary components of the loop may be specifically designed to have certain G functions, or (2) the performance of the existing primary components may be abetted by auxiliary equipment so that the overall G function will have the desired locus. Often valuable new properties are obtained for both the component and the system while seeking to improve the overall performance by reshaping the G locus.

Frequently the method of using auxiliary blocks to shape the G locus is spoken of as *compensating the system*. The specific auxiliary networks and mechanisms are assigned particular mathematical functions and named differentiating, integrating, phase lead, phase lag, low-pass networks, and so forth. Their performance may approximate these mathematical functions to a high degree of perfection, but good engineering taste should prevent narrow and perhaps erroneous names being assigned to any particular network or class of networks. The term compensation is not strictly correct, for it implies the patching up or the offsetting of some defect. The philosophy of design that the word *compensate* implies is dangerous because it does not necessarily lead to optimum solutions. Closed-loop systems exhibit optimum performance in terms of available equipment only when the overall transfer function $KG(j\omega)$ has the best possible combination of magnitude and phase characteristics. Thus the blocks of equipment considered as compensating devices can be elevated in importance relative to the other components of the system. This broader viewpoint may be extremely economical in many designs. The proper design of a field winding of a rotating machine may, for example, prevent an impossible electronics design problem from arising or a properly chosen tube may eliminate the need for complex mechanical devices.

The treatment of the auxiliary equipment, whether networks, levers, dashpots, or entire dynamical systems, is subject to the linearity condition cited during the initial treatment of the closed loop. The mathematical nature of the G functions for the components, whether auxiliary or not, must be such that the magnitude and phase functions $G(j\omega)$ can be represented by rational algebraic functions. As such, this restriction on $G(j\omega)$ precludes the use of nonminimum phase shift devices in the closed loop and further insures that the G functions being treated in this particular book are uniquely confined to physical systems representable by lumped parameter techniques. It is hoped, however, that as interest in this subject continues, the analytical techniques will be extended to distributed parameter systems, or, in general, those that lead to transcendental transforms.

2 Reshaping ,G Loci—General Remarks

If the values for the maximum magnitude and the maximum phase shift of system response are selected along with a suitable band width of frequency of operation, an infinite number of possible solutions to the synthesis problem may still exist. Why then is synthesis considered so difficult? The answer to this question relates to the difficulty of obtaining an optimum solution to the dynamics problem simultaneously with

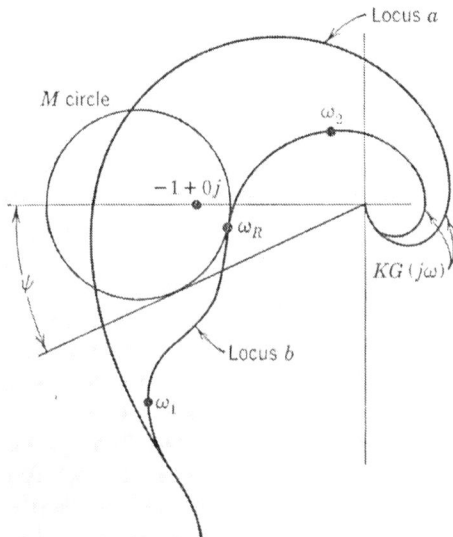

FIGURE 1. Reshaping locus to provide stability.

an optimum solution to the more nebulous problem of engineering economy. Good engineering compromises arrived at mainly through design experience are often the only possible solution to seemingly impossible synthesis problems. For example, a large alternator already constructed obviously cannot be redesigned to accommodate its voltage regulator. Yet the design of a regulator to fulfill certain operating specifications may be rendered impractical by an inept alternator design.

To demonstrate the reasoning which might be necessary in problems concerning reshaping of functions or originally selecting the appropriate functions, consider the loci shown in Figures 1 and 2. A system having the locus a in Figure 1 is unstable for the gain K selected. If this particular value of K is required, the physical system must be redesigned or altered to have the locus shown as b. The proper value K could be obtained along with proper stability if the locus a in the region of frequency $\omega_1 < \omega < \omega_2$ were changed to the shape of the locus b. Clearly this change has modified the performance of the system in the upper frequency region with the result that the performance may not be satisfactory even though the value of K has been obtained.

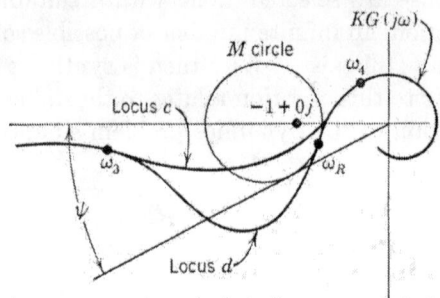

FIGURE 2.   Reshaping locus to increase stability.

Another situation is shown in Figure 2.   A system having the locus c, while stable, is not sufficiently stable to prevent small perturbations in the input command from setting up violent but damped oscillations in the closed loop.   The value of M is too large.   Decreasing the gain K will not improve the system stability appreciably.   However, if a positive phase shift could be established by system redesign or the addition of auxiliary members in the frequency range $\omega_3 < \omega < \omega_4$, the locus d would result.   This new system could have a gain K and loop stability consistent with a reasonable M_p criterion.

The broad general procedure for reshaping G loci was indicated in Chapter 5.   The generalized algebraic equations were developed for closed loops comprising cascaded and parallel arrangements of the blocks.   Thus, as shown in Figure 3, the required auxiliary equipment needed to produce definite shapes of the G locus when used in conjunction

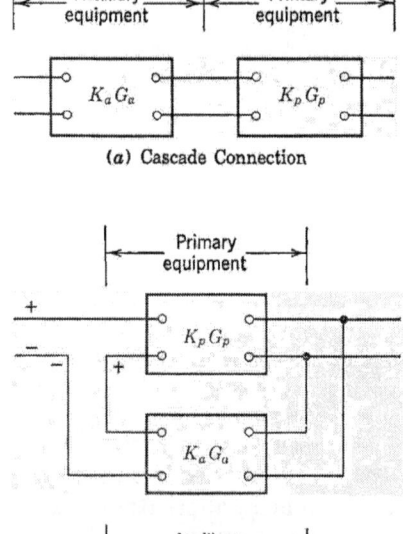

(a) Cascade Connection

(b) Feedback Connection

FIGURE 3.   Use of auxiliary equipment to reshape the G function.

with primary equipment can be connected either in cascade or as feed-back around. For the cascade connection (Figure 3*a*), the overall *G* locus is plotted for the equivalent *G* function arising from the product relation

$$G_o(j\omega) = G_a(j\omega)G_p(j\omega) \tag{1}$$

where $G_o(j\omega)$, $G_a(j\omega)$, and $G_p(j\omega)$ represent, respectively, the overall, auxiliary, and primary *G* functions. Both the primary and the auxiliary components of the equivalent *G* function can retain their identity in the complex plane. Furthermore, if the $G_o(j\omega)$ is known and $G_a(j\omega)$ or $G_p(j\omega)$ is not known, a few minutes of freehand sketching and estimating will yield at least a trial design for the unspecified component $G_a(j\omega)$ or $G_p(j\omega)$ as this chapter will show.

Auxiliary equipment as shown in Figure 3*b* is located in a feedback path around the primary equipment so that the overall system transfer function becomes

$$K_o G_o(j\omega) = \frac{K_p G_p(j\omega)}{1 + K_a G_a(j\omega) K_p G_p(j\omega)} \tag{2}$$

Equation 2 shows that the gain constants K_p and K_a, related respectively to the primary and the auxiliary equipment, cannot be omitted to permit the formation of an equivalent overall *G* function. While the adjustment of system sensitivity in the feedback connection may not appear obvious, the method of feedback connection nevertheless exhibits important advantages, and should in no way be discounted.

Usually the inverse method for representing the system transfer function $K_o G_o$ $(j\omega)$ is used, when feedback arrangements of auxiliary equipment are encountered. Thus Equation 2 converts to the form

$$\frac{1}{K_o G_o(j\omega)} = \frac{1}{K_p G_p(j\omega)} + K_a G_a(j\omega) \tag{3}$$

Aside from the method of treating specific combinations of auxiliary and primary equipment, the procedure for manipulating the *G* or G^{-1} functions relates directly to engineering expediency. The inappropriate closure of loops often causes *G* loci shapes which are readily recognized. The auxiliary equipment that is required in order to remedy for the apparent poorness of system response must be estimated from the *G* locus.

The functions of curves *a* in Figures 4, 5, and 6 represent poor designs. In the particular system of Figure 4, the *KG* locus crosses the line $M = 1$ at a value of frequency ω_a. For all frequencies $0 < \omega < \omega_a$, this locus, designated by curve *a*, remains to the right of the line for $M = 1$.

Therefore the magnitude response $|\theta_o/\theta_i|$ is undesirably attenuated prior to reaching the peak value. Auxiliary equipment can be selected which will eliminate the shaded portion between curves a and b of Figure 4. The overall performance of the system will be better when the KG locus has the shape shown in b.

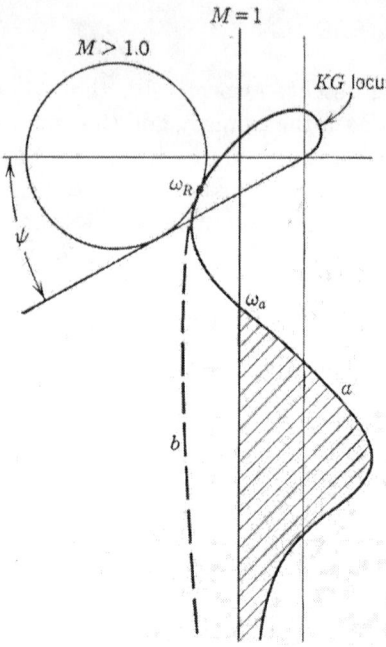

FIGURE 4.   Reshaping locus to improve low-frequency and transient performance.

Another example of poor system operation is shown by the KG locus shape in Figure 5, curve a. The locus tends to follow a radius vector that is very close to the envelope line defined by the angle $\psi = \sin^{-1}(1/M)$. No variation in the gain K of the closed loop can appreciably change the degree of stability below the frequency ω_R. Furthermore, the magnitude function $|\theta_o/\theta_i|$ has a flat-topped effect near the resonant frequency. Ordinarily, this type of system is improved by the insertion of auxiliary equipment which can bend the KG locus away from the radius vector into a shape similar to curve b.

A somewhat different but nevertheless related problem is illustrated by the loci shown in Figure 6. Curve a shows the original system for which the velocity constant K_v was too small. A network placed in

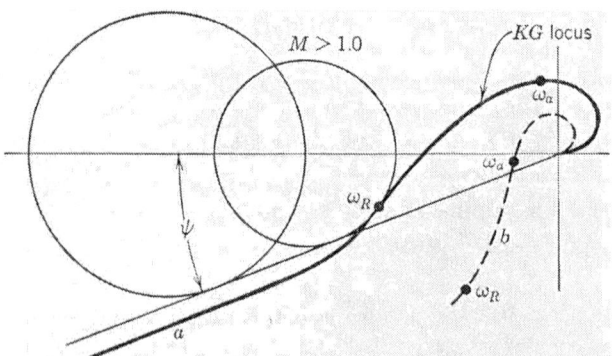

FIGURE 5.   Reshaping locus to improve transient response.

series with the original equipment giving a second-order pole in the system transfer function establishes a zero velocity error system. However, the newly adjusted system exhibits instability as shown by curve b. Additional cascaded equipment can produce the locus shape

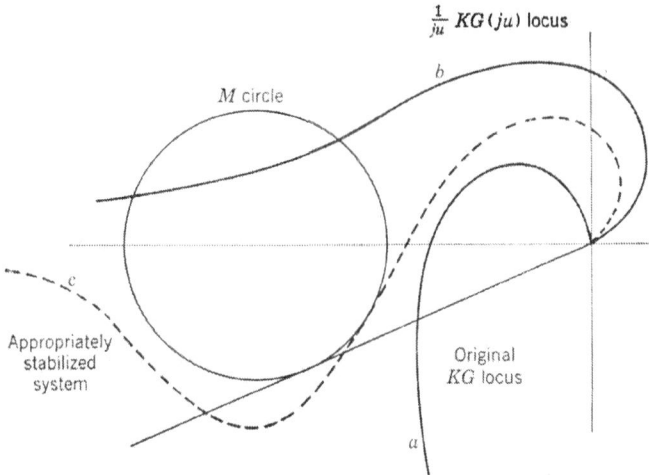

FIGURE 6. Reshaping locus to give infinite velocity constant with stable operation.

shown in curve c. Thus the magnitude function $\left|\, \theta_o/\theta_i \,\right|$ can be made consistent with a reasonable M_p criterion, so that the new locus indicates an improved and satisfactorily stabilized closed loop.

3 Loci of Auxiliary Equipment to Reshape the G Function

General. Definite physical equipment has definite loci. Definite loci shapes cannot always be related to specific auxiliary equipment needed to mold or reshape the loci for a closed-loop system. Unlimited possible numbers of physically different components may have similar or even identical loci shapes.[6] Thus for a general treatment of the synthesis problem we may profit by first considering the most elementary components as fundamental building blocks. Certain fundamental physical devices have their loci in the first and fourth quadrants of the complex plane. The group of devices associated within the first quadrant is therefore predominantly positive phase shifting; the other, associated with the fourth quadrant, predominantly negative phase shifting. Appropriate use of even extremely simple devices or circuits having loci which are merely straight lines or parts of circles is valuable in the construction of closed-loop systems.

Straight Line Locus for Phase Lag. The locus for

$$G(ju) = 1 + \frac{1}{ju} \tag{4}$$

appears in Figure 7a as a straight line perpendicular to the positive real axis at the point $1 + 0j$. For all values of $u < 1.0$, this locus obviously has a phase lag greater than -45 degrees. Thus, this locus represents a device which can introduce an extra pole at $u = 0$ in a system transfer function if it is placed in cascade with the existing equipment.

Straight Line Locus for Phase Lead. The locus for

$$G(ju) = 1 + ju \tag{5}$$

is a straight line as shown in Figure 7b. Again the straight line is perpendicular to the real axis at the point $1 + 0j$, but the locus lies in the first quadrant. Thus, for $u > 1$, a positive phase shift of greater than $+45$ degrees is present. Such a locus can swing a transfer function locus away from the point $-1 + 0j$. It thus represents a stabilizing device.

Circular Loci for Phase Lag. The locus for

$$G(ju) = \frac{ju + 1}{jua + 1} \tag{6}$$

where a is greater than unity is a semicircle lying in the fourth quadrant, as shown in Figure 7c. The diameter of the circular locus is $(a - 1)/a$. There is maximum phase shift ϕ_m corresponding to a frequency u_m. Since a is the only parameter which can be varied to produce different circles, ϕ_m and u_m must be uniquely related to the quantity a. The exact relations are easily found and prove quite useful in elementary synthesis. To illustrate, let

$$\phi = \tan^{-1} u - \tan^{-1} au \tag{7}$$

Then by performing a maximum-minimum study and by setting $d\phi/du = 0$, the value of u_m which gives ϕ_m is

$$u_m = \frac{1}{\sqrt{a}} \tag{8}$$

and

$$\phi_m = \tan^{-1} \frac{1 - a}{2\sqrt{a}} \tag{9}$$

A simpler expression for calculating ϕ_m is

$$\phi_m = \sin^{-1} \frac{1 - a}{1 + a} \tag{10}$$

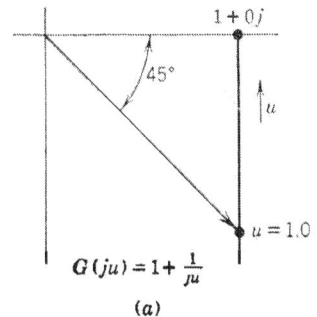

$$G(ju) = 1 + \frac{1}{ju}$$

(a)

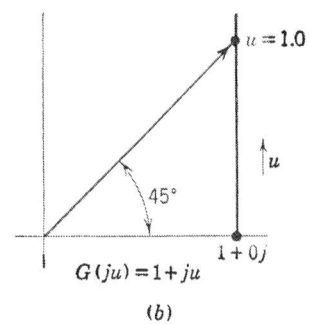

$$G(ju) = 1 + ju$$

(b)

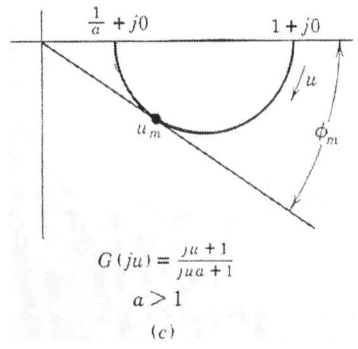

$$G(ju) = \frac{ju + 1}{jua + 1}$$

$$a > 1$$

(c)

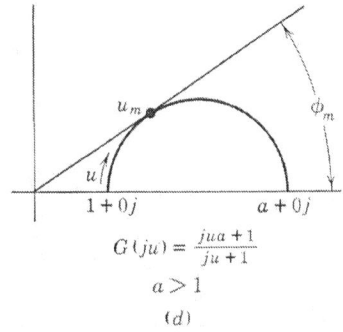

$$G(ju) = \frac{jua + 1}{ju + 1}$$

$$a > 1$$

(d)

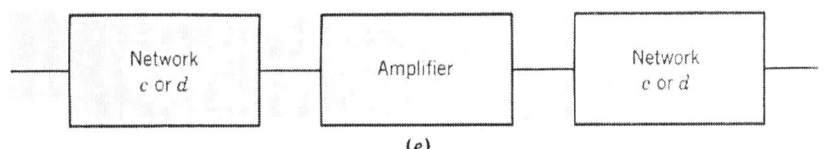

(e)

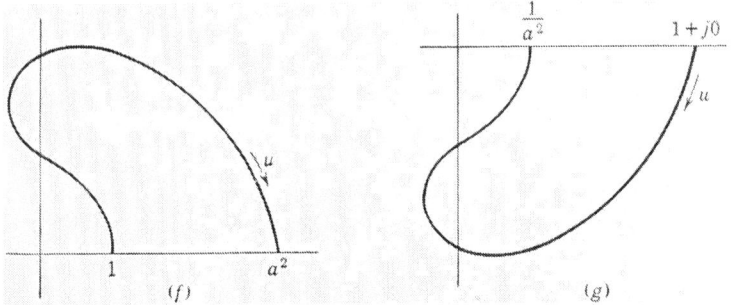

(f)   (g)

FIGURE 7.   Loci of auxiliary equipment to reshape the *G* function.

Since $a > 1$, ϕ_m will always be negative, having negative phase values for all values of ω. For $a = 10$, $\phi_m = -55$ degrees at $u_m = 0.316$, showing that the maximum negative phase shift for the particular locus defined by Equation 6 occurs at the geometric mean frequency defined by the reciprocals of the numerator and denominator time constants, 1 and $1/a$, respectively.

Circular Loci for Phase Lead. The locus for

$$G(ju) = \frac{jua + 1}{ju + 1} \tag{11}$$

where a is greater than unity, is a semicircle lying in the first quadrant of the complex plane as shown in Figure 7d. The locus has geometric properties identical with those derived for the locus of Equation 6. Thus for $a = 10$, the value for $u_m = 1/\sqrt{a}$ and the value

$$\phi_m = \sin^{-1}\frac{a - 1}{a + 1}. \tag{11a}$$

Since $a > 1$, ϕ_m will be positive. The locus of Equation 11 is a lead or positive phase shift type having a maximum value of phase shift ϕ_m. That u_m and ϕ_m may be chosen makes this locus valuable in elementary synthesis problems involving stabilization of the closed loop.

Loci for Greater than 90-Degree Phase Shift. The loci group of Figure 7a to 7d could be extended to include quadratic factors.[6] They would resemble the cardiods and their inverse forms. However, such loci, while classified as simple, represent entire families for each quadratic factor, depending upon two variables, a time constant τ, and a damping ratio ζ. The value, τ, may be eliminated by a dimensionless study, but ζ remains a quantity which must be selected in terms of the purpose to which the particular mechanism will be put. Simpler forms of loci comprise series connections of devices having the loci of Figures 7c or 7d with an isolation amplifier as shown in Figure 7e. If the networks gave typical circular phase-lead loci, the locus would have the shape characterized by Figure 7f. If the networks gave circular phase-lag loci, the locus of the overall locus would be shaped like that in Figure 7g.

4 Improving the Low-Frequency Response of a Closed Loop

General. Many of the imperfections of operation of closed-loop systems can be eliminated by properly shaping the low-frequency portion of the $G(j\omega)$ locus. For example, in positional servomechanisms, the steady-state errors caused by applied loads on the output member can be eliminated, thereby reducing the uncertainty of positioning the output members.   The steady-state errors caused by constant velocity input operation can likewise be reduced or eliminated. Frequently, this technique is also used to improve the performance of systems subjected to sinusoidal disturbances of long periods such as in shipboard stabilization.   Although such shaping of the low-frequency portion of the G locus does not cure all the faults of poor steady-state operation of closed loops, the results obtained from relatively simple design measures are very satisfactory.

A large increase in the velocity constant K_v can be accomplished by appropriate reshaping of the G locus.   Alterations to the G locus to make possible the inclusion of a second-order pole would give the system an infinite velocity constant.   Even when a second-order pole cannot be introduced, a large increase in K_v can be obtained by jointly increasing the frequency invariant portion K of the transfer function, and reshaping of the G locus.   This reshaping of the locus is essential if the degree of stability is not to diminish rapidly to unacceptably low values.   Thus another compromise looms.   The value K_v must be increased to reduce the uncertainties and errors of operation due to loads and internal energy dissipations, and yet a reasonable M_p criterion for stability must be maintained.

Since the presence of a second-order pole in the transfer function has been shown to eliminate the steady-state position errors for loads and rate inputs, the designer naturally seeks mechanisms which will yield such mathematical functions.   Mechanisms are readily found having loci approximately like those required to establish changes in the system locus.   However, the degree of perfection with which these loci represent the required mathematical loci must be carefully evaluated because a poor approximation to the mathematical form may be quite adequate for some applications and quite inadequate for others.

Design problems as encountered in practice often allow a wide choice of the mechanisms or networks to help reshape the G locus.   Sometimes relatively simple passive arrangements of mechanical or electrical elements suffice.   At other times carefully designed closed-loop feedback systems may be needed to make the locus of the auxiliary or compensating equipment fulfill its requirements.

Although the design of any auxiliary equipment is largely dependent upon the particular application for which it is intended, the general method for accomplishing some elementary designs can be shown.   The reader is cautioned, however, that the examples which follow have been extremely simplified to permit emphasis on method.   Therefore, generalizations made of the results obtained from these examples should be used with discretion.

Regenerative Feedback Methods * **for Providing Low-Frequency** *G* **Function Alteration.** A device often suggested for making possible high gain at low frequencies in closed loops is shown by the block diagram of Figure 8. The element represented by K_1G_1 is usually an amplifier, that represented by K_2G_2 is a network or linkage of passive elements. If the particular mechanism of Figure 8 is considered a feedback electrical

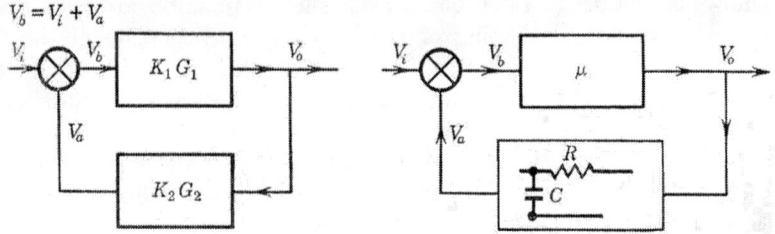

$$V_b = V_i + V_a$$

FIGURE 8. Regenerative feedback   FIGURE 9. Regenerative feedback sys-
system.   tem to perform as ideal integrator.

system, the voltage quantities shown in the figure can be defined as follows:

$$V_b = V_i + V_a \tag{12}$$

that is, the system involves *regenerative feedback* in contrast with the *degenerative feedback* of the servomechanism or regulator. Also let

$$V_o = K_1G_1V_b \tag{13}$$

$$V_a = K_2G_2V_o \tag{14}$$

Then

$$\frac{V_o}{V_i} = \frac{K_1G_1}{1 - K_1G_1K_2G_2} \tag{15}$$

Now if

$$K_1G_1 = \mu \tag{16}$$

and K_2G_2 corresponds to the network shown in Figure 9, that is

$$K_2G_2(j\omega) = \frac{k}{CRj\omega + 1} = \frac{k}{j\omega\tau_i + 1} \tag{17}$$

where

$$\tau_i = RC \tag{18}$$

---

* This section and Section 5 refer only to one of several methods for using amplifiers as energy sources arranged with passive elements to give specified transfer functions. During the last five years, the development of electronic amplifiers as regenerative devices in computers has been extensive. The reader is referred to the publications given as reference 36 for a treatment of this subject.

Equation 15 becomes

$$\frac{V_o}{V_i}(j\omega) = \mu \frac{j\omega\tau_i + 1}{j\omega\tau_i + 1 - \mu k} \tag{19}$$

If the gain μ and the feedback constant k are adjusted so that $\mu k = 1$, the relation for (V_o/V_i) from Equation 19 becomes

$$\frac{V_o}{V_i}(j\omega) = \mu\left[1 + \frac{1}{j\omega\tau_i}\right] \tag{20}$$

and defines a proportional plus *ideal integrating mechanism*. The plot of the voltage-ratio magnitude $|V_o/V_i|$ of Equation 20 as a frequency function is shown in Figure 10, where it has infinite value at $\omega = 0$. As ω increases, note that the magnitude falls rapidly in the low-frequency region until it is constant at the higher frequencies. The locus plot of Equation 20 is shown in Figure 11. It is identical with Figure 7a.

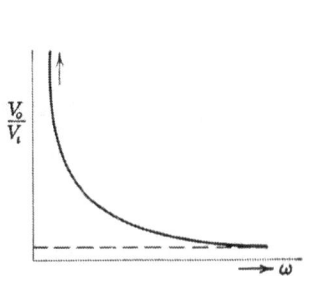

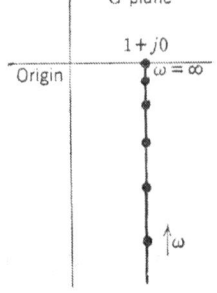

FIGURE 10.   Magnitude-frequency   FIGURE 11.   Locus of
characteristic of ideal integrator of   ideal integrator in the
              Figure 9.   G plane.

The adjustment of the feedback amplifier system of Figure 9 to obtain the integral form of response necessitates a critical adjustment of the loop parameters to maintain the condition equivalent to $\mu k = 1$. When the adjustment is not maintained, a different form of behavior may result as is seen by investigating Equation 19 as a function of the magnitude of the quantity μk. For purposes of analysis, rewrite Equation 19 as

$$\frac{V_o}{V_i}(j\omega) = \frac{\mu}{1 - \mu k} \cdot \frac{j\omega\tau_i + 1}{j\omega \dfrac{\tau_i}{1 - \mu k} + 1} \tag{21}$$

giving

$$\frac{V_o}{V_i}(j\omega) = K_i G_i(j\omega) \tag{22}$$

where

$$K_i = \frac{\mu}{1 - \mu k} \qquad (23)$$

$$G_i(j\omega) = \frac{j\omega\tau_i + 1}{j\omega\alpha_i\tau_i + 1} \qquad (24)$$

and

$$\alpha_i = \frac{1}{1 - \mu k} \qquad (25)$$

Assume that k is held at unity and consider the effect of small variations in the amplifier gain μ when μ is nearly unity. Let $1 - \mu = \Delta\mu$. Then

$$K_i = \frac{\mu}{\Delta\mu} \simeq \frac{1}{\Delta\mu} = \alpha_i \qquad (26)$$

If μ is less than unity, α_i is positive. Then

$$\frac{V_o}{V_i}(j\omega) = \alpha_i \frac{j\omega\tau_i + 1}{j\omega\tau_i\alpha_i + 1} \qquad (27)$$

and the locus of V_o/V_i becomes a circle in the fourth quadrant as shown in Figure 12 instead of the line as in Figure 11. At zero fre-

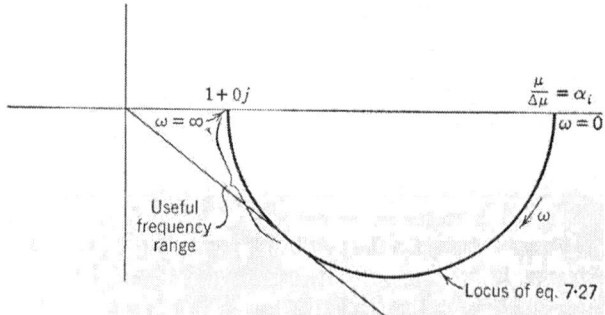

FIGURE 12. Locus $\dfrac{V_o}{V_i}(j\omega)$ of Figure 9, $\mu < 1$.

quency, the ratio V_o/V_i at $\omega = 0$ is α_i, and at infinite frequency V_o/V_i at $\omega = \infty$ is 1.0. Thus the property of the system giving infinite gain at zero frequency has disappeared. The system now has only finite gain α_i, and is commonly referred to as an undercompensated integral. It is equivalent, for all practical purposes except for gain, to the passive network shown in Chapter 5 as Figure 5·13 which has as its transfer function

$$\frac{E_2}{E_1} = \frac{\tau_1 s + 1}{\tau_2 s + 1} = \frac{\tau_1 s + 1}{\alpha_i \tau_1 s + 1} \qquad (28)$$

since

$$\frac{\tau_2}{\tau_1} = \alpha_i = \frac{R_1 + R_2}{R_2} \qquad (29)$$

The absence of the coefficient α_i from Equation 28 is merely equivalent to a change in scale of the polar plot and is cared for by increased gain in the series connection of elements in the loop. The phase shift and the relative magnitude of the vector given by Equation 27 as a function of frequency are the same as those given by Equation 28.

When $1 - \mu = \Delta\mu$ is negative, a slightly different form of locus for Figure 15 results. Equation 21 now has the form

$$\frac{V_o}{V_i}(j\omega) = \alpha_i \frac{j\omega\tau_i + 1}{j\omega\alpha_i\tau_i - 1} \qquad (30)$$

The locus is again a circle, but the phase shift in going from $\omega = \infty$ to $\omega =$ zero is now -180 degrees, as shown by Figure 13. The phase

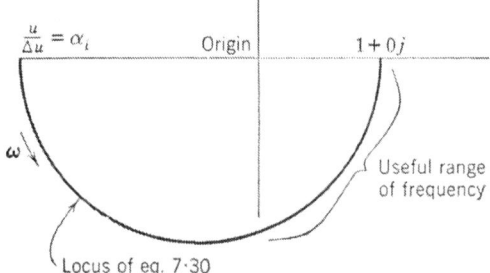

FIGURE 13.   Locus $\dfrac{V_o}{V_i}(j\omega)$ of Figure 9, $\mu > 1$.

shift of 180 degrees and a magnitude amplification of α_i at zero frequency may introduce stability problems in certain types of closed loops because of the introduction of a pole in the right-hand half of the s plane. See Chapter 6, Section 8.

The undercompensated regenerative feedback system of Figure 9 is much more complicated than its equivalent, the passive network of Figure 5·13. Such regenerative feedback systems are not, of course, intended to serve in such a simple manner. For the simple problem it is not surprising that the system shown in Figure 14, comprising the passive R-C network and an amplifier is frequently used. A design in which $(R_1 + R_2)/R_2 = 10$ is quite common.

The foregoing example has been a mere introduction to the more general subject of the design of auxiliary components having large magnitude change and appropriate phase shift throughout the frequency band. Many such devices exist. Not all are electric, as shown by the system [44] of springs, lever, and dashpot of Figures 5·10 and 5·12. Their general interpretation and a discussion of their specific forms cannot be included here. The reader

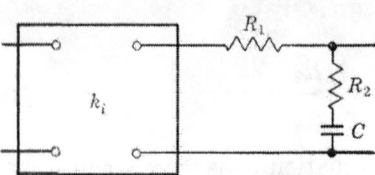

FIGURE 14. Passive network approximating system of Figure 9.

is referred to the extensive treatment of this topic given by Chestnut.[73]

Example of Ideal Integral Control to Improve the Low-Frequency Response of a Closed-Loop System. Consider the closed-loop system shown in Figure 15 to comprise a motor and amplifier such that the overall transfer function becomes

$$\frac{\theta_o}{\varepsilon}(j\omega) = KK_m \frac{1}{j\omega(j\omega\tau_m + 1)} \tag{31}$$

The constant K is the sensitivity of the amplifier, the constant K_m the motor sensitivity. The complete feedback amplifier system shown in

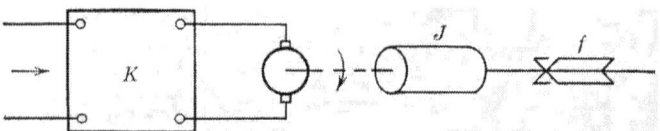

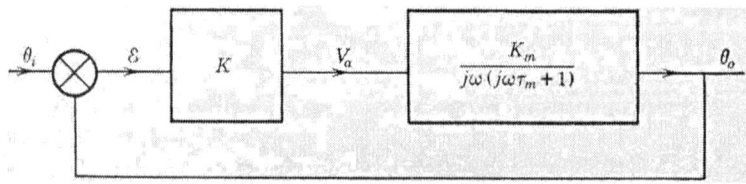

FIGURE 15. System having finite velocity constant.

Figure 9 with additional amplification K_i can replace the simple amplifier in Figure 15, so that

$$\frac{V_a}{\varepsilon}(j\omega) = K_i\left(1 + \frac{1}{j\omega\tau_i}\right) \tag{32}$$

The overall transfer function resulting from a combination of Equations 31 and 32 is

$$\frac{\theta_o}{\varepsilon}(j\omega) = K_i\left(1 + \frac{1}{j\omega\tau_i}\right)\left[\frac{K_m}{j\omega(j\omega\tau_m + 1)}\right] \tag{33}$$

or rearranged Equation 33 becomes

$$\frac{\theta_o}{\varepsilon}(j\omega) = \left[\frac{K_iK_m}{\tau_i}\right]\left[\frac{(j\omega\tau_i + 1)}{(j\omega)^2(j\omega\tau_m + 1)}\right] \tag{34}$$

The overall gain of the two component parts are collected into a single constant, and the overall G function similarly is established by merging the individual G functions. Equation 34 can be converted to dimensionless form by choosing the change of variable

$$\omega\tau_m = u \tag{35}$$

by means of which the dimensionless transfer function for the system is

$$\frac{\theta_o}{\varepsilon}(ju) = K_u\left[\frac{ju\alpha_i + 1}{(ju)^2(ju + 1)}\right] \tag{36}$$

where

$$K_u = \tau_m{}^2 K_m K_i \tau_i{}^{-1}$$

$$\alpha_i = \frac{\tau_i}{\tau_m} \tag{37}$$

The graph for the $G(ju)$ function in Equation 36 is shown in Figure 16 for the block diagram of Figure 17. The second-order pole for $u = 0$ causes the locus to be asymptotic to the negative real axis of the complex plane. Even with such assurance of zero steady-state velocity errors and load errors, the locus shown in Figure 16 must nevertheless have the cor-

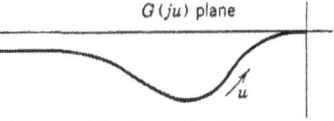

FIGURE 16. Locus for $K_v = \infty$.

rect positive phase margin to permit the selection of a reasonable gain magnitude K_u consistent with $M_p = 1.3$. Furthermore, a method for selecting the magnitude of the time constant τ_i must be adopted.

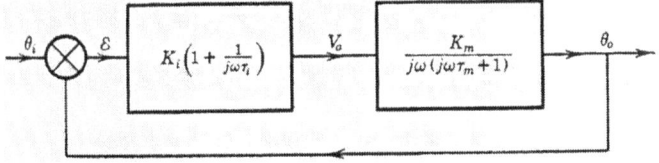

FIGURE 17. System of Figure 15 modified to give $K_v = \infty$.

One method for selecting the value of α_i, and subsequently the time constant τ_i, is first to close the loop without the integral control. That is, close the loop containing only the motor and amplifier of gain K. For the value $M_p = 1.3$, the resonant frequency u_R is 0.9. The auxiliary equipment or networks needed to produce the second-order pole

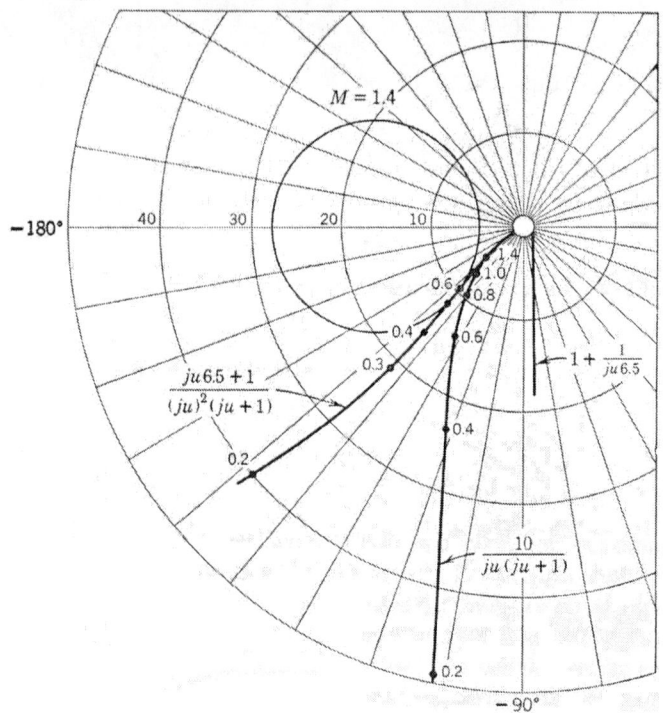

FIGURE 18. Procedure for calculating the effect of ideal integral control.

at $u = 0$ are chosen so that they cause only a small negative phase shift in the original $G(ju)$ locus in the region of the resonant frequency. This requirement of small phase shift is a criterion based on experience. The proper selection of integral time constant will become more apparent as the reader becomes more acquainted with synthesis procedures. In particular, if the value of the phase shift is chosen -10 degrees at the value $u = 0.9$, the constant α_i is found to be 6.5, and the value τ_i will depend upon the magnitude of the constant τ_m. That is, for $u = 0.9$,

$$\text{Ang } G_i(ju) = \tan^{-1} \frac{1}{-\alpha_i u} = -10 \text{ degrees} \qquad (38)$$

from which

$$\left.\begin{array}{c} \dfrac{1}{0.9\alpha_i} = 0.17 \\[2mm] \alpha_i = 6.5 \end{array}\right\} \tag{39}$$

From Equations 36 and 39 the new G function for the system having integral control is

$$\frac{\theta_o}{\varepsilon}(ju) = K_u \frac{(ju6.5 + 1)}{(ju)^2(ju + 1)} \tag{40}$$

The graph for $G(ju)$ in Equation 40 is prepared in Figure 18.

The locus of Equation 40 shows that the value $M_p = 1.3$ can never be obtained for the system having integral control with the value of τ_i selected. The value for $\psi = \sin^{-1}(1/1.3) = 50.2$ degrees from Table 6·7. The maximum margin of phase between the negative real axis and the locus is about 47 to 48 degrees. An observation can be made immediately pertaining to the influence of the negative phase shift introduced in the motor locus by the integral control. The term

$$G_i(ju) = \frac{ju6.5 + 1}{ju} \tag{41}$$

has narrowed the frequency range over which the closed-loop motor system of Figure 15 could perform for a specific value of M_p. A comparison for the two systems is then made by choosing $M_p = 1.4$ for the system having integral control. The data summarizing the performance of the compensated and uncompensated system are given in Table 1.

TABLE 1

Item	Original System	System with Integral
M_p	1.3	1.4
τ_m	0.1 second	0.1 second
τ_i	. . . .	0.65 second
K_u	1.36	0.13
u_R	0.9	0.6
ω_R	9 seconds^{-1}	6 seconds^{-1}
$K_m K$	13.6 seconds^{-1}	. . . .
$K_m K_i$	. . . .	8.5 seconds^{-1}
K_p	∞	∞
K_v	13.6 seconds^{-1}	∞
K_a	zero	13 seconds^{-2}

Clearly the value of τ_i selected for this example was too small to fulfill the $M_p = 1.3$ criterion.

For convenience, the principal relations needed to produce the numerical values of Table 1 are given in Equation 42.

$$
\left.
\begin{aligned}
KK_m &= \frac{K_u}{\tau_m} \text{ (uncompensated system)} \\[2ex]
K_mK_i &= \frac{K_u\tau_i}{\tau_m^2} \text{ (compensated system)} \\[2ex]
\omega_R &= \frac{u_R}{\tau_m} \text{ (both systems)}
\end{aligned}
\right\} \tag{42}
$$

By referring the curves of Figure 18 to the M and N contour families, a direct comparison of the two systems can be made. The comparison provides, in addition to the data formed in the table, a specific evaluation of the magnitude and phase characteristics of the original system and the system compensated by perfect integral control.

Much discussion could be given to the problem of maladjustments that can occur in the feedback amplifier-network system used to produce the integral control. Instead of continuing this particular discussion it seems more worth while to consider now the use of passive networks or mechanisms to accomplish a good approximation to integral control. The primary motivation of the design will be to obtain a maximum value of velocity constant without necessarily seeking to establish the second-order pole in $G(j\omega)$.

Example of Passive Networks for Procuring Integral Effects. To demonstrate the use of passive integral networks comprising R-C elements for altering the low-frequency response, consider altering the $G(ju)$ locus for a motor generator system like the one shown in Figure 5·9. The $G(ju)$ function for a specific set of numerical constants of this motor generator servo system gives

$$
\frac{\theta_o}{\varepsilon}(ju) = K_uG(ju) \tag{43}
$$

$$
= \frac{K_u}{ju(0.086ju + 1)(-u^2 + 2.24ju + 1)} \tag{44}
$$

The control system can have an amplifier and passive network similar to that shown in Figure 14 which has the transfer function

$$
K_iG_i(ju) = K_i\frac{ju\tau_i + 1}{ju\alpha_i\tau_i + 1} \tag{45}
$$

The value α_i may be chosen in the range $0 < \alpha_i < 15$, where the limitations on α_i are determined primarily by the physical equipment. However, τ_i must be chosen in relation to the value M_p which is to be

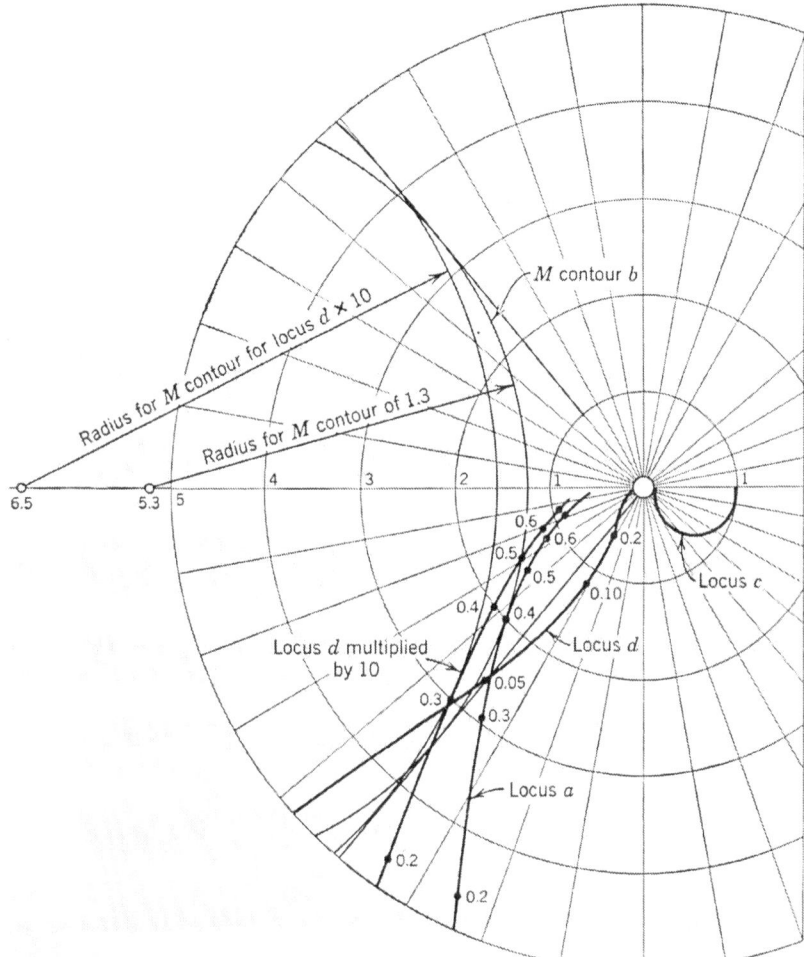

FIGURE 19.   Procedure for calculating the effect of passive network to give integral control.

maintained for the closed loop while seeking to increase the velocity constant K_v. The locus a of Figure 19 shows that the uncompensated system can be adjusted for $M_p = 1.3$ and gives $K_u = 0.45$. The corresponding resonant frequency is $u_R \simeq 0.4$, shown by the tangency of locus a and M contour b, which established K_u.

Experience shows that no more than about -5 degrees of phase shift should be introduced into locus a of Figure 19 by the passive network at the resonant frequency $u_R = 0.4$. Thus for $\alpha_i = 10$, a value τ_i can be found. From Equation 45 the angle is

$$\phi = \tan^{-1} u\tau_i - \tan^{-1} u\alpha_i\tau_i$$

$$= \tan^{-1} \frac{u\tau_i - u\tau_i\alpha_i}{1 + u^2\tau_i^2\alpha_i} \tag{46}$$

which for $\phi = -5$ degrees and $u = 0.4$ gives

$$\tau_i^2 - 25.9\tau_i + 0.624 = 0 \tag{47}$$

providing a trial value of τ_i in the integral network. The specific value for the dimensionless integral time constant τ_i from Equation 47 is 26. Because the values of -5 degrees and 0.4 used for ϕ and u respectively in Equation 47 represent only a first approximation and because a number of other performance criteria must eventually be considered, the value 25 for τ_i giving arithmetical expediency seemed to be a good round number. Locus c is the plot of Equation 45 with unity gain.

The overall locus d of Figure 19 is prepared from the equation

$$G(ju) = \frac{(25ju + 1)}{(ju)(0.086ju + 1)(-u^2 + 2.24ju + 1)(250ju + 1)} \tag{48}$$

The construction of an M circle corresponding to $M_p = 1.3$ gives the new velocity constant $K_u \simeq 3.8$ and a new resonant frequency $u_R \simeq 0.3$.

TABLE 2

Item	Uncompensated System	Compensated System
u_R	0.4	0.3
K_u	0.45	3.8

The ratio of loop gain for compensated and uncompensated system performance consistent with $M_p = 1.3$ is $(3.8/0.45) = 8.5$, showing that the value $\alpha_i = 10$ could not establish the value of the new velocity constant ten times greater than the value for the uncompensated system without making other changes in the system.

Other values of α_i and τ_i could be chosen to extend the scope of the study. Although such exhaustive studies are valuable in presenting to the designer tables or charts specifically related to integral control designs, the problem at hand seems to have been completed. The *method* for studying integral compensation of a closed-loop system has been demonstrated.

5 Improving the High-Frequency Response of the Closed Loop

General. The frequency range throughout which the magnitude response of a closed loop is essentially constant can be extended by placing auxiliary equipment in the loop. This auxiliary equipment may be cascaded with the principal equipment or it may be placed in parallel with it. The essential characteristic of the auxiliary equipment is that it have pronounced positive phase shift over specific portions of, or over the entire frequency band, $0 < \omega < \infty$. Alternatively, it shall have pronounced magnitude and phase modification at certain frequencies.* Auxiliary networks or devices having these characteristics are often called *lead networks* or *differentiating networks*. The design problem is much broader than these two names imply, for not only may their techniques be used to maintain essentially constant magnitude response of the system but they also may be used to maintain small phase shift between output and input over a wide frequency band.

Techniques that will provide circuits or devices having predominantly positive phase shift over a wide frequency band and the methods for their use in closed-loop systems are discussed in the following sections.

Regenerative Feedback to Give G Function Alteration at High Frequency. A regenerative feedback system similar to that of Figure 9 may be used to provide high gain and large phase lead at high frequency. The system differs from Figure 9 only by a change in the function K_2G_2, as shown in the diagram of Figure 20. Such a system is sometimes

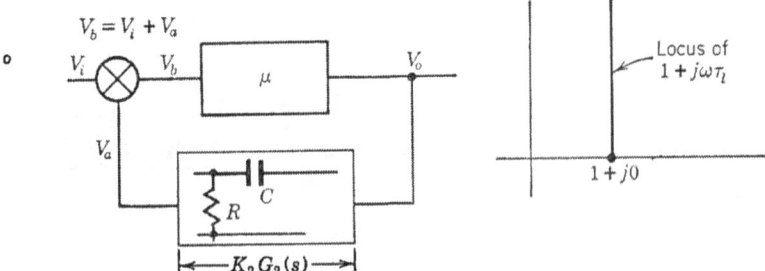

FIGURE 20. Regenerative feedback system to give ideal derivative response.   FIGURE 21. Locus of ideal derivative response.

---

* The work given in Sections 3, 4, and 5 treats networks which are used in connection with direct current amplification. No treatment of compensation networks would be complete without a consideration of error-modulated carriers and the networks which give magnitude and phase corrections to the intelligence signal and not to the carrier. This subject lies in the category of network synthesis. One of the elementary forms of lead network used when a carrier is present is the parallel T or the bridged T network.[66] This is one of many forms which can be derived from a more general network treatment.[61, 62, 65]

called an *ideal lead controller*, because the phase lead of the output with respect to the input increases as the frequency increases. In a manner similar to that developed in Section 4b, the relation V_o/V_i is

$$\frac{V_o}{V_i} = \frac{K_1 G_1}{1 - K_1 G_1 K_2 G_2} \tag{49}$$

If $K_1 G_1 = \mu$, and $K_2 G_2$ corresponds to the network shown in Figure 20, that is,

$$K_2 G_2 = \frac{k \tau_\ell j\omega}{1 + \tau_\ell j\omega} \tag{50}$$

where

$$\tau_\ell = RC \tag{51}$$

Equation 49 then becomes

$$\frac{V_o}{V_i}(j\omega) = \mu \frac{1 + j\omega\tau_\ell}{1 + j\omega\tau_\ell - \mu k j\omega\tau_\ell} \tag{52}$$

If $\mu = k = 1$, Equation 52 reduces to

$$\frac{V_o}{V_i}(j\omega) = 1 + j\omega\tau_\ell \tag{53}$$

The locus of Equation 53 is a straight line as shown in Figure 21. It thus represents an *ideal differentiating system* or *ideal lead controller*. The system of Figure 20 behaves with respect to variations in μ, in a manner similar to the integrating network. Equation 52 may be written as

$$\frac{V_o}{V_i}(j\omega) = \mu \frac{1 + j\omega\tau_\ell}{1 + (1 - \mu k)j\omega\tau_\ell} \tag{54}$$

Assume that k is unity. Then investigate the behavior of V_o/V_i as μ differs from unity. Let $1 - \mu = \Delta\mu$; then

$$\frac{V_o}{V_i}(j\omega) = \mu \frac{(1 + j\omega\tau_\ell)}{1 + \Delta\mu j\omega\tau_\ell}\bigg|_{\text{for } \mu < 1} \tag{55}$$

and

$$\frac{V_o}{V_i}(j\omega) = \mu \frac{(1 + j\omega\tau_\ell)}{1 - \Delta\mu j\omega\tau_\ell}\bigg|_{\text{for } \mu > 1} \tag{56}$$

The loci of Equations 55 and 56 are semicircles as shown in Figure 22. For $\mu > 1$, a 180-degree phase shift at infinite frequency occurs. Whenever μ does not equal unity, the system fails to give infinite gain at infinite frequency, and even for a 10 per cent deviation from this $\mu = 1$ value the gain has only the maximum value of 10.

Whenever the system of Figure 20 is not operating with the critical setting $\mu = k = 1$, it may be replaced for all practical purposes by the

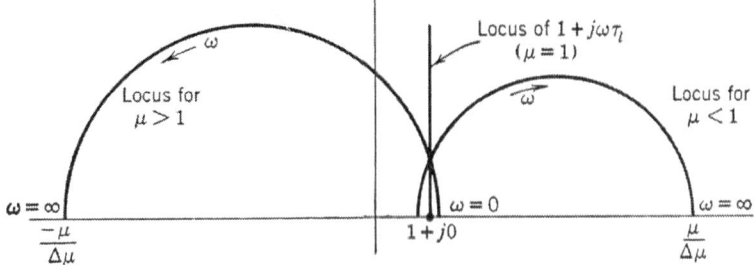

FIGURE 22.   Locus of $\dfrac{V_o}{V_i}$ $(j\omega)$ for $\mu = 1$ and $\mu \neq 1$.

passive network of Figure 23.   The transfer function of this network is readily found to be

$$\frac{V_o}{V_i}(j\omega) = \frac{1}{\alpha_\ell}\frac{1 + \alpha_\ell \tau_\ell j\omega}{1 + \tau_\ell j\omega} \tag{57}$$

where

$$\alpha_\ell = \frac{R_1 + R_2}{R_2} \tag{58}$$

$$\tau_\ell = \frac{R_1 R_2 C_2}{R_1 + R_2} \tag{59}$$

Its locus is a circle as shown in Figure 24.   Passive networks of this kind are frequently used for phase lead compensation either in cascade

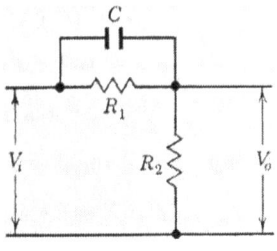

FIGURE 23.   Passive lead network.

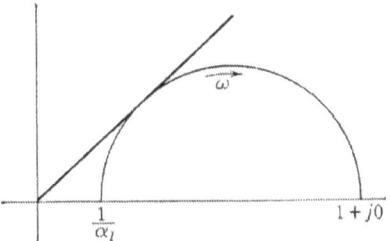

FIGURE 24.   Locus of lead network.

with elements in the loop or designed to be a part of the principal equipment.

Example of a Passive Network Used to Give Improved High-Frequency Performance.   Devices having the property of an ideal lead or differentiating system shown by the characteristic of Figure 21 are very difficult to provide. It is also probable that many systems are not materially aided by the use of the ideal lead systems, or even near ideal systems, because the derivative property of the device magnifies the noise or spurious intelligence that might be in the error signal. Electronic amplifiers frequently saturate because of such noise amplification. For these reasons, discussions of ideal lead control systems having the characteristics of Equation 53 are somewhat academic. On the other hand, passive networks for establishing phase lead are frequently encountered and used effectively. To illustrate the method for synthesizing a system which can be improved by including a passive lead network as a compensating element, the same motor studied in the illustration of integral compensation will be used as an example. The motor transfer function is

$$K_m G_m(j\omega) = \frac{K_m}{j\omega(j\omega\tau_m + 1)} \tag{60}$$

For the illustration the lead network of Figure 23 is to be defined by the function

$$K_\ell G_\ell(j\omega) = \frac{1}{\alpha_\ell} \frac{(j\omega\alpha_\ell\tau_\ell + 1)}{(j\omega\tau_\ell + 1)} \tag{61}$$

where

$$\alpha_\ell > 1$$

When the motor, network and appropriate isolating amplifiers are placed in cascade, the overall transfer function becomes

$$\frac{\theta_o}{\varepsilon}(j\omega) = \left[\frac{K_m}{\alpha_\ell}\mu\right]\left[\frac{(j\omega\alpha_\ell\tau_\ell + 1)}{j\omega(j\omega\tau_m + 1)(j\omega\tau_\ell + 1)}\right] \tag{62}$$

Equation 62 can be reduced to dimensionless form by the change in variable $\omega\tau_m = u$ so that

$$\frac{\theta_o}{\varepsilon}(ju) = K_u G(ju) \tag{63}$$

$$= K_u \frac{ju\alpha_\ell\tau_a + 1}{ju(ju + 1)(ju\tau_a + 1)} \tag{64}$$

where

$$K_u = \frac{K_m\tau_m\mu}{\alpha_\ell} \tag{65}$$

$$\tau_a = \frac{\tau_\ell}{\tau_m} \tag{66}$$

The gain K_u of Equation 64 can be adjusted consistent with an $M_p = 1.3$. To extend the band width over which θ_o/θ_i of the uncompensated system is $0.7 < M_p < 1.3$ requires a particular choice of α_ℓ, τ_ℓ, and K_u. While many loci shapes may be obtained by selecting the various values of R and C in the network of Figure 23, one very simple choice of the parameters can be made. Thus, if

$$\alpha_\ell \tau_a = 1.0 \tag{67}$$

the overall transfer function becomes

$$\left. \begin{aligned} \frac{\theta_o}{\varepsilon}(ju) &= K_u G(ju) \\[2ex] &= \frac{K_u}{ju(ju\tau_a + 1)} \end{aligned} \right] \tag{68}$$

A further change of variable $u\tau_a = \lambda$ gives

$$\left. \begin{aligned} \frac{\theta_o}{\varepsilon}(j\lambda) &= K_\lambda G(j\lambda) \\[2ex] &= \frac{K_\lambda}{j\lambda(j\lambda + 1)} \end{aligned} \right] \tag{69}$$

where

$$K_\lambda = K_u \tau_a = \frac{\tau_m K_m \mu}{(\alpha_\ell)^2} \tag{70}$$

Equation 69 is recognized immediately as the same G function plotted in Figure 6·27 or inverted and plotted in Figure 6·28

From Table 6·10 for $M_p = 1.3$, the values of resonant frequency u_R and the loop gain K_u are 0.9 and 1.36, respectively. Table 3 compares the compensated and uncompensated systems with respect to a lead network of the form described by Equation 61 for $\alpha_\ell = 5$.

In the simplified system studied in Equation 64, the band width over which θ_o/θ_i is such that $0.7 < M < 1.3$ is given by

$$\frac{\omega_{max} \text{ (compensated)}}{\omega_{max} \text{ (uncompensated)}} = \alpha_\ell \tag{71}$$

Equation 71 shows that the band-widening property is here directly proportional to the constant α_ℓ. The manner of achieving this property in this simple example was to give the lead controller a time constant so that $\alpha_\ell \tau_a =$ unity. This merely canceled the lag of the motor and replaced it, so far as system behavior is concerned, by the denominator portion of $K_\ell G_\ell(ju)$, which was explicitly a function having a band width α_ℓ times that of the numerator. As a caution, it is necessary to point out that this process of neutralizing lags in the principal portion of the system by the insertion of phase lead elements cannot be carried on indefinitely, principally because of the noise problem.

TABLE 3

COMPARISON OF COMPENSATED AND UNCOMPENSATED SYSTEM SHOWN IN
EQUATION 62

	Original System	System with Lead
M_p	1.3	1.3
τ_m	0.1	0.1
τ_ℓ	...	0.02
α_ℓ	...	5.0
K_λ	...	1.36
λ_R	...	0.9
K_u	1.36	6.80
u_R	0.9	4.5
τ_a	...	0.2
K_v	13.6	68.0
ω_R	9.0	45.0
For $M = 0.7$		
u_{max}	1.4	
ω_{max}	14	...
For $M = 0.7$		
λ_{max}		1.4
ω_{max}		70

Obviously, Equation 71 has no quantitative value for systems other than the simple one specifically chosen. However, this simple illustration of lead circuit synthesis serves to demonstrate *method and techniques*, as was the objective of the simple integral compensation problem.

Specific Study of Lead Network for Motor Generator System. As another example, a lead network, defined by Equation 61, is applied to the motor generator system used for the illustration in Section 4. The results are summarized by the loci studies of Figure 25. The transfer function of the principal portion of the system is

$$K_u G(ju) = \frac{K_u}{ju(0.086ju + 1)(-u^2 + 2.24ju + 1)} \tag{72}$$

The locus of Equation 72 is shown by curve a. Closure of the loop around only the principal portion of the system shows a resonant frequency $u_R = 0.4$.

The locus for the compensating network is shown as curve b. It has a maximum phase angle ϕ_{max} of $+43$ degrees for a value of $\alpha_\ell = 5$. The criterion for determining the time constant of the lead network

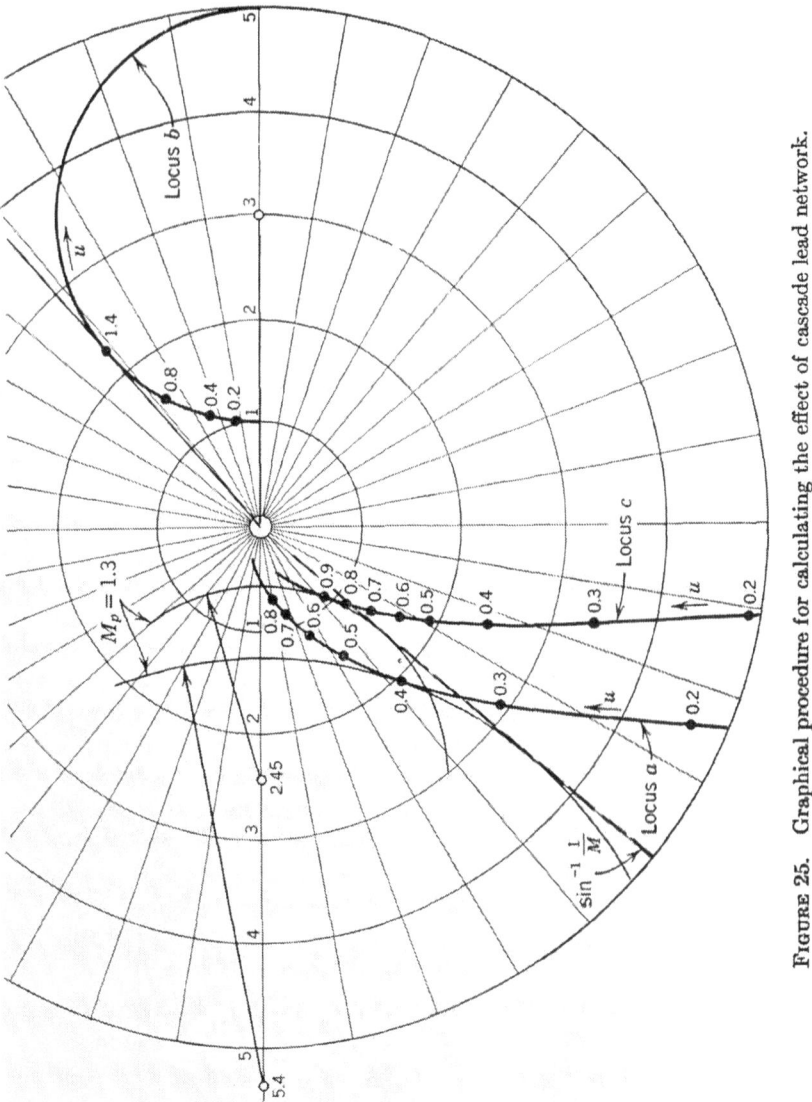

FIGURE 25. Graphical procedure for calculating the effect of cascade lead network.

is now not so apparent as it was for the previous illustration. For one reason, there is a conflict between selecting time constants to give maximum increase in frequency band wherein $0.7 < M < 1.3$ and selecting time constants to give a maximum value to K_v. As a compromise, the value of τ_ℓ for Figure 25 was selected to make ϕ_{max} occur at a frequency $u = 1.4$. The value of $u = 1.4$ was decided upon by first noting that the phase lag of $G(ju)$ at $u_R = 0.4$ was 137 degrees. It was then assumed that the lead network is to introduce its principal effect at $u > u_R$. It is customary to make ϕ_{max} occur at a frequency which corresponds to a phase lag of $G(ju)$ in the neighborhood of 137 degrees $+\phi_{max}$, or about 180 degrees. As an experience compromise, a value somewhat greater than 180 degrees was selected giving ϕ_{max} at $u = 1.4$. The treatment of phase lead compensation given in the next chapter, using loci plots to logarithmic coordinates, will give a more direct approach to this problem. Equation 11a may then be used to give τ_ℓ.

The overall G function including the lead network is

$$G(ju) = \frac{(1.60ju + 1)}{ju(0.32ju + 1)(0.086ju + 1)(-u^2 + 2.24ju + 1)} \qquad (73)$$

The overall system locus for Equation 73 is shown as locus c, Figure 25. Table 4 summarizes the results.

TABLE 4

	Original System	Compensated System
M_p	1.3	1.3
u_R	0.4	0.9
K_u	0.45	1

Considerable improvement of the low-frequency performance of this system has been obtained simultaneously with an increase in the band width of a reasonably constant θ_o/θ_i. The velocity constant K_v was approximately doubled. It can never become infinite by application of these techniques. The value K_a remains undefined. A phase shift of -45 degrees in θ_o/θ_i occurs for the compensated system at a frequency about one octave above that for the uncompensated system.

6 Altering the G Function by the Addition of Networks in Parallel with the Principal Equipment [33, 63]

General. The treatment of parallel connections in Section 5, Chapter 5, indicated that the presence of dynamic elements in the feedback, from the output to the error-measuring device, offers a technique for modifying the overall system performance. It was there shown that the simple technique of placing amplification in the feedback can serve the useful function of decreasing the time constant of the equipment in the through portion of the loop. Feedback through dynamic elements can have many other desirable properties. Unfortunately it may also have many undesirable properties.

Certain properties of these feedback networks, or so-called parallel circuit arrangements, can make them accomplish the same overall result as was accomplished by the cascade insertions of networks treated in the two previous sections. In fact, it should be apparent that, by appropriate selection of the element in the feedback path, the property of infinite gain at zero frequency or infinite gain at high frequency can be provided for the entire system just as readily as they can be provided for a small so-called compensating system. Thus the use of dynamic feedback as a technique for reshaping the overall G function is merely an extension of the techniques given in Sections 4 and 5.

It is important to mention that the use of a feedback around the principal components of a system in order to extend the frequency band of operation can, in practice, prove much more attractive than the technique of putting a lead controller in cascade. This feature is advantageous in systems where the error signal may contain appreciable noise. A lead network that receives error plus noise as its input signal is very likely to saturate if the noise magnitudes for the higher frequencies are appreciable. On the other hand, if the error signal is initially applied to the principal part of the system, it becomes the input to a system that tends to serve as a low-pass filter by virtue of the sharp cutoff of the principal part slightly above its resonant frequency. Thus the principal part of the system tends to filter the noise. Relatively little noise is then fed back from the output, with the result that the overall system is much less noise sensitive than a cascade lead controller system.

Dynamic elements in the feedback path store energy. This energy storage may occur in spite of the desire of a designer to eliminate it. The classic example is the time lag of a thermometer used to measure temperature in temperature control. The energy storage in the thermometer bulb introduces a lag in its indication and thereby a negative phase shift in the feedback path. At other times, carefully selected energy storages can introduce specific G functions in the feedback path. Sometimes positive and sometimes negative phase shift is deliberately introduced.

The next portion of this section introduces certain algebraic manipulations of transfer functions and block diagrams that facilitate the generalized investigations of the effects of elements in the feedback. The subsequent portions of this section treat certain techniques sometimes specifically introduced to give properties to an overall $G(j\omega)$ locus.

Algebra of Parallel Connections of Block Diagrams and Transfer Functions. The block diagram of a simple system having a dynamic

element in the feedback path is shown in Figure 26. Many generalizations of useful closed-loop phenomena can be made from a study involving mere algebraic manipulations of the functions of this figure. The

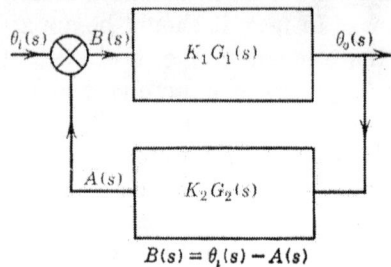

$$B(s) = \theta_i(s) - A(s)$$

FIGURE 26. Block diagram of system with energy storage in feedback path.

general equations for the system of Figure 26 when the load disturbance
is absent are

$$\left.\begin{aligned}
\theta_o(s) &= K_1 G_1(s) B(s) \\
A(s) &= K_2 G_2(s) \theta_o(s) \\
B(s) &= \theta_i(s) - A(s)
\end{aligned}\right\}. \tag{74}$$

Thus for

$$T_L(s) = 0 \tag{75}$$

the output response becomes

$$\theta_o(s) = \frac{K_1 G_1(s)}{1 + K_1 G_1(s) K_2 G_2(s)} \theta_i(s) \tag{76}$$

Note that the error $E(s)$ as a quantity specifically indicated does not now
exist. $B(s)$ is not equal to the error $E(s)$. The substitution of error
$E(s) = \theta_i(s) - \theta_o(s)$ gives

$$E(s) = \frac{1 + K_1 G_1(s) K_2 G_2(s) - K_1 G_1(s)}{1 + K_1 G_1(s) K_2 G_2(s)} \theta_i(s) \tag{77}$$

We notice immediately that the error response for this form of closed
loop is a complicated function. The output response also shows a different form of characteristic from that for Figure 5·25. From the
synthesis studies heretofore mentioned, the reader will see the requirements that must be imposed on $K_2 G_2(s)$ for certain forms of $A(s)/B(s)$,
although it is not always easy to visualize the effect on the system of
the dynamical elements in the feedback path.
    When $K_2 G_2(s) = 1$, Equation 77 reduces to the form found in Equa-
tion 5·112. Also if $K_2 G_2(s)$ should happen to be of the form $1 + K_3 G_3(s)$,

that is, should consist of a unity feedback path in parallel with a dynamic element, Equation 77 would become

$$E(s) = \frac{1 + K_1 G_1(s) + K_1 G_1(s) K_3 G_3(s) - K_1 G_1(s)}{1 + K_1 G_1(s) K_2 G_2(s)} \theta_i(s) \qquad (78)$$

Parallel Circuit Equivalents

General Equivalents. A system that is equivalent to one defined by Equation 78 is shown in Figure 27. It is interesting to note that we can synthesize block diagrams by examining the symbolic expressions that result from these algebraic manipulations. This is an interesting example of synthesis. In other words, this treatment permits the building of systems from the blocks prior to having established the differential equations by the use of information found in Chapter 6, Table 3.

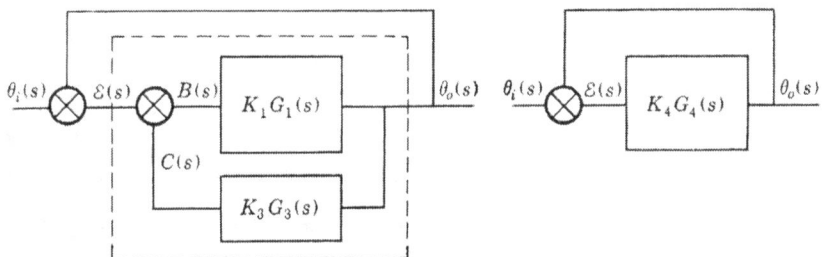

FIGURE 27.   Subdivisions of block diagram.   FIGURE 28.   System equivalent to Equation 79.

Figure 27 shows an internal loop within a main closed loop. The internal loop is found within the dotted lines of the figure. It is possible to write a transfer function for the internal loop by inspection. It has the same form as Equation 76, namely,

$$\frac{\theta_o(s)}{E(s)} = \frac{K_1 G_1(s)}{1 + K_1 G_1(s) K_3 G_3(s)} = K_4 G_4(s) \qquad (79)$$

where $K_4 G_4(s)$ now permits formation of the diagram of Figure 28 as equivalent to that of Figure 27. The characteristics of instability may exist for the internal loop defined by the equivalent transfer function.

Simple generalizations of the problem are evident by manipulating the inverse form of the overall system function, that is, by considering $\theta_i(s)/\theta_o(s)$ instead of $\theta_o(s)/\theta_i(s)$. The system of Figure 26 may then be expressed as

$$\frac{\theta_i(s)}{\theta_o(s)} = K_2 G_2(s) + K_1 G_1(s)^{-1} \qquad (80)$$

If $K_2G_2(s)$ should be of the form $1 + K_3G_3(s)$, the overall response is

$$\frac{\theta_i(s)}{\theta_o(s)} = 1 + K_3G_3(s) + K_1G_1(s)^{-1} \tag{81}$$

From Equation 81 it is apparent that Figure 28 is equivalent to Figure 27 because the portion of Equation 81 comprising $K_3G_3(s) + K_1G_1(s)^{-1}$ is by Equation 80 equivalent to a system of the form of Figure 26 which has a function in the feedback path.

Zero Frequency Equivalents. The ideas implied in these manipulative operations are useful in comparing certain general properties of the various forms of loops. For example, since no specific element exists in Figure 26 that represents error, the quick identification of a quantity such as velocity constant is not immediately apparent. However, for the system of Figure 28 with simple unity feedback,

$$\frac{\theta_i(s)}{\theta_o(s)} = K_4G_4(s)^{-1} + 1 \tag{82}$$

Likewise, from Equation 80 and Figure 26,

$$\frac{\theta_i(s)}{\theta_o(s)} = [K_2G_2(s) + K_1G_1(s)^{-1} - 1] + 1 \tag{83}$$

If the performance of the systems of Figures 28 and 26 are identical, Equations 82 and 83 are identities. It therefore follows that

$$K_4G_4(s)^{-1} = K_2G_2(s) + K_1G_1(s)^{-1} - 1 \tag{84}$$

which by reducing to a common denominator and inverting gives

$$K_4G_4(s)\bigg|_{\text{of Figure 28}} = \frac{K_1G_1(s)}{K_2G_2(s)K_1G_1(s) - K_1G_1(s) + 1}\bigg|_{\text{of Figure 26}} \tag{85}$$

Equation 85 is an identity for all values of frequency. The right-hand side is equivalent to the single transfer function K_4G_4 of a system with unity feedback. If a velocity constant K_v exists for Figure 28, one exists for the system of Figure 26. Since in Chapter 6, Section 8, the velocity constant for a positional servo is given by

$$K_v = \underset{s \to 0}{\text{limit }} s[KG(s)] \tag{86}$$

the velocity constant of the system of Figure 26 is given by

$$K_v = \underset{s \to 0}{\text{limit }} s\left[\frac{K_1G_1(s)}{K_2G_2(s)K_1G_1(s) - K_1G_1(s) + 1}\right] \tag{87}$$

To illustrate the analysis applicable to the parallel circuit problem, consider the system shown in the block diagram of Figure 29a. The lag of a measuring element, such as a thermometer in temperature control, or a rate gyroscope in a stabilization problem, is introduced in the feedback path as $(as + 1)^{-1}$. As mentioned in Chapter 6, the use of the inverse locus KG^{-1} to give θ_i/θ_o is often the more direct

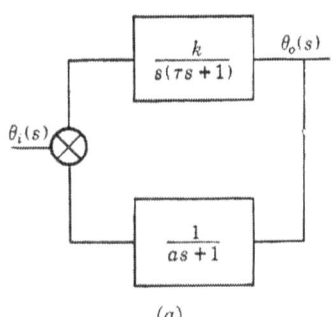

(a)

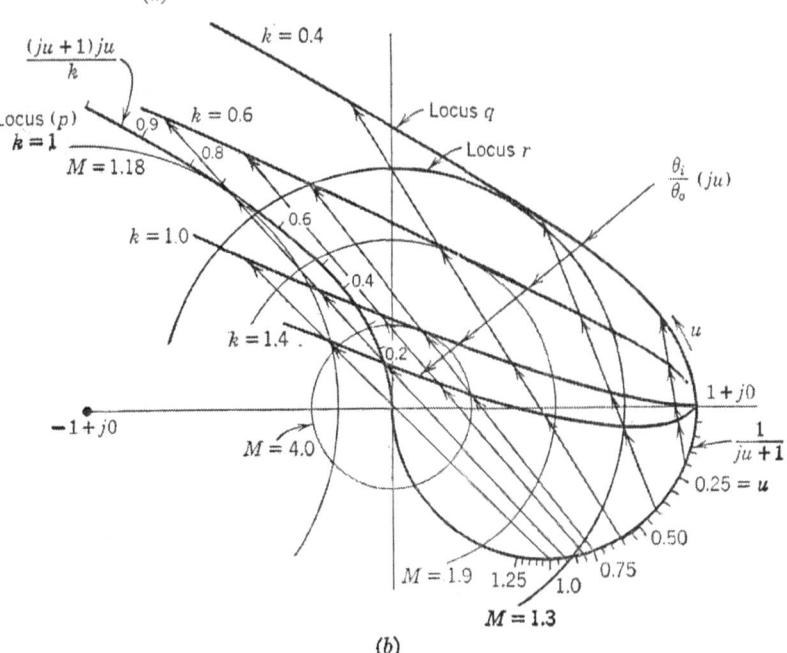

(b)

FIGURE 29.   Example of a problem with energy storage in the feedback path.

approach to analysis of these parallel circuit problems. For this system, assume that

$$K_1G_1(s) = \frac{k}{s(\tau s + 1)}$$
$$K_2G_2(s) = \frac{1}{as + 1}$$

(88)

The substitution of these values in Equation 85 gives the equivalent transfer function

$$KG(s) = \frac{k[s(\tau s + 1)]^{-1}}{k[s(\tau s + 1)(as + 1)]^{-1} - k[s(\tau s + 1)]^{-1} + 1} \tag{89}$$

$$= \frac{kas + k}{a\tau s^3 + (a + \tau)s^2 + s - aks} \tag{90}$$

but K_v for the system from Equation 85 is

$$K_v = \lim_{s \to 0} \left[\frac{s(aks + k)}{a\tau s^3 + (a + \tau)s^2 + s - aks} \right] \tag{91}$$

$$= \frac{k}{1 - ak} \tag{92}$$

The result in Equation 92 may indicate at first glance that a lag in the feedback path is useful since it increased K_v. Such is not the case because the presence of the lag has made the system more unstable, as is seen by an examination of the loci plots in the KG^{-1} plane of Figure 29b which are drawn for $\tau = 1$ and $a = 1$. Clearly, a system that has no lag in the feedback path, that is, one in which $a = 0$, could have a value for k that would bring the KG^{-1} locus p into tangency with the desired M circle. For the example chosen, $M = 1.18$ when $k = $ unity. Table 6·10, for which $a = 0$, shows that k may be 1.36 when $M = 1.3$. However, Figure 29b shows that the magnitude k in K_1G_1 must be much smaller when K_2G_2 has a finite value of a. Specifically, in order that the locus shown as q in Figure 29b shall be outside the circular locus r for $M = 1.3$, the value of k cannot exceed 0.4. Thus, from Equation 92, the velocity constant which would be 1.36 for $a = 0$ becomes, for $a = 1$,

$$K_v = \frac{0.4}{1 - 0.4} = 0.67$$

7   Example of Parallel Circuit for Specific G Function Shaping

The system of Figure 30 can be used to illustrate a constructive use of an element placed in the feedback path. Consider an amplifier of gain K_1 actuating a servomotor characterized by inertia J but having no appreciable viscous loss so that

$$K_2G_2(s) = \frac{K_2}{s^2} \tag{93}$$

A position loop closed around such a motor and amplifier will be unstable, as is shown immediately by the locus *a* in Figure 31.   Specifically this

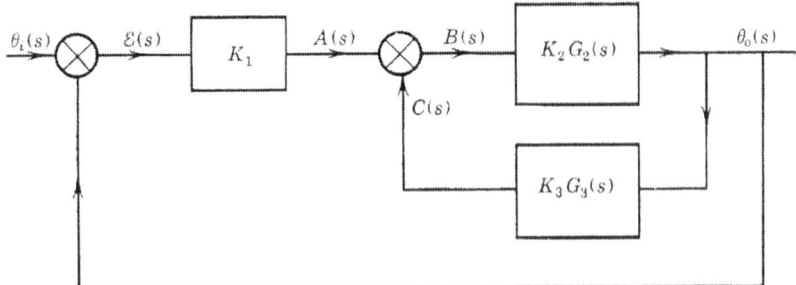

FIGURE 30.   A multiple loop block diagram.

locus is a straight line along the negative real axis.   However, the use of a tachometer as an auxiliary feedback loop can stabilize this system. Let this auxiliary loop feedback function be defined as

$$K_3 G_3(s) = K_3 s \qquad (94)$$

For the minor loop $\theta_o(s)/A(s)$ is

$$\frac{\theta_o(s)}{A(s)} = \frac{\dfrac{1}{K_3}}{s(\tau s + 1)} \qquad (95)$$

The addition of the tachometer feedback has in effect served to replace the motor without damping by a motor with damping but without

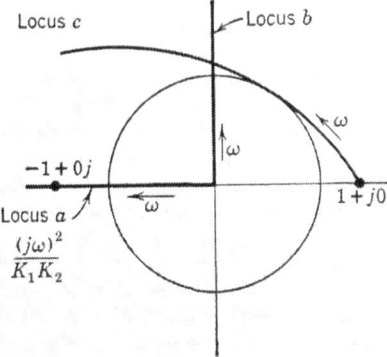

FIGURE 31.   Analysis of tachometric feedback KG^{-1} plane.

energy dissipation of a pure viscous kind.   It has given the effect of kinetic damping.

The overall response equation for this system becomes

$$\frac{\theta_i(s)}{\theta_o(s)} = \frac{1}{K_1 K_2} s^2 + \frac{K_3}{K_1} s + 1 \tag{96}$$

and the velocity constant for this system is simply K_1/K_3.

The locus for Equation 96 is shown in Figure 31. Locus a represents s^2/K_1K_2. Locus b represents $(K_3/K_1)s$. When these loci are added and plotted with respect to the point $1 + j0$, the result is locus c representing $\theta_i(s)/\theta_o(s)$. An inspection of the shape of the locus c shows that tachometric feedback in parallel with a servomotor defined by K_2G_2 gives a stable system with a finite velocity constant K_v.

The system of Figure 30 can, however, have infinite K_v and still be stable. Stability involves merely the shaping of locus c of Figure 31 to give a *tangency* with the M circle. If this shaping can be accomplished without introducing the degenerative effect of K_3G_3 at zero frequency for a velocity output, namely $K_3\omega_o$, K_v may be infinite. This is accomplished if the function K_3G_3 has zero magnitude and 180 degrees phase shift at zero frequency, but is substantially Ks at frequencies near resonance. Such reasoning represents an important property of the G locus concepts given in this chapter. Specifically, if the feedback function is of the form

$$K_3G_3(s) = \frac{K_3 s^2}{(as + 1)} \tag{97}$$

the velocity constant will be infinite as is shown by reference to Equation 87.

This condition can also be visualized from the relation

$$C(s) = \frac{K_3 s}{(\tau s + 1)} \Omega_o(s) \tag{98}$$

which indicates that for a steady velocity ω_o, $C(s)$ is zero at zero frequency. The effect of the feedback is then zero for a constant velocity input. There is no degeneration, and hence no error signal is required in order for the output to rotate at a constant velocity.

A numerical illustration of tachometric feedback through a high-pass filter network can be presented in a simplified manner. Consider the system of Figure 30, and choose the transfer function for a motor as

$$K_2G_2(ju) = \frac{\frac{1}{5}}{(ju)^2} \tag{99}$$

The tachometer and the network used with the motor can be chosen to have the transfer function

$$K_3 G_3(ju) = \frac{(ju6)^2}{(ju6 + 1)}$$ (100)

The form of Equation 100 follows from the relation giving the network output voltage in terms of the tachometer shaft motion θ_o for the circuit shown in Figure 32. The gain K_1 of the electronic amplifier external

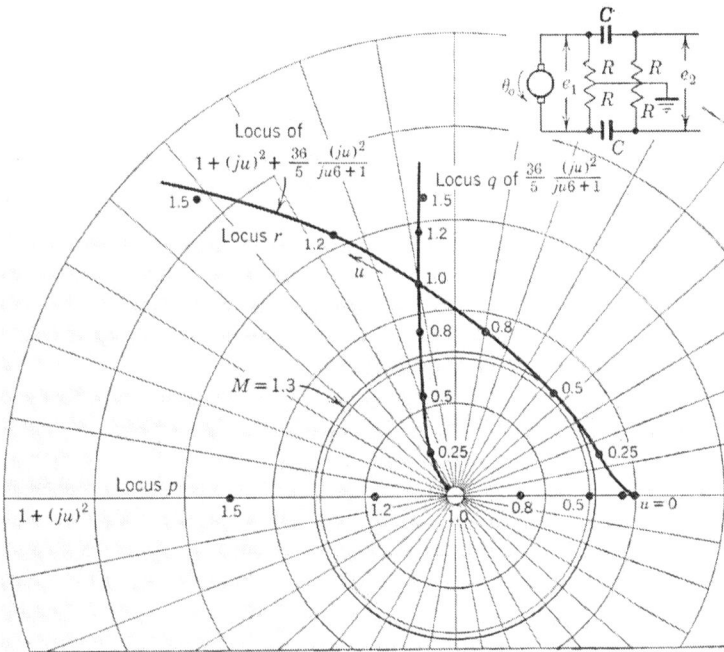

Figure 32. Study of tachometric feedback maintaining $K_v = \infty$.

to the tachometric feedback loop in Figure 30 may be varied to give a degree of stability for the overall system consistent with the value $M_p = 1.3$. The exact solution of this problem involves a trial-and-error procedure. The simplified version of the problem is given by the curves of Figure 32 without including the various trials that led to the final solution.

If the various numerical values for K_2, K_3, and $\tau = RC$ had not already been established, a full-fledged design problem involving complete parametric families of curves would have been needed to predict an optimum combination of motor, tachometer, and network. The procedure required to form the simple graphical study shown in Figure 32 is easier to follow than the more exhaustive problem.　Prior to adjusting K_1, the response function to be investigated is

$$\frac{\theta_i}{\theta_o}(ju) = 1 + \frac{1}{K_1}\left[\frac{(ju)^2}{\frac{1}{5}} + \frac{(j6u)^2}{(j6u)+1}\right]$$ (101)

For the particular numerical values chosen for the trials in this study, the quantity K_1 in Equation 101 has the value 5.　Thus, Equation 101 is rewritten as

$$\frac{\theta_i}{\theta_o}(ju) = 1 + (ju)^2 + \frac{36}{5}\frac{(ju)^2}{ju6+1}$$ (102)

The locus p in Figure 32 represents the motor locus $(ju)^2$ added to unity, giving $1 + (ju)^2$.　The locus q indicates the effect the tachometer and its high-pass network will have on the motor locus, since when these two vector loci are *added* at respective frequency points, the result is the composite locus r.　The locus r is indicative of the overall system performance.　The circle corresponding to $M_p = 1.3$ in the KG^{-1} plane is shown in the figure.　A tangency between the circle and the locus r occurs at the frequency $u = 0.5$.

It is important to notice that the parameters K_1, K_2, K_3, and τ cannot be independently varied without choosing new scales for the loci, p, q, and r.

The statement made earlier that a feedback procedure for stabilization need not result in a finite K_v can now be demonstrated.　The equivalent transfer function for the internal loop is formed by using Equation 79 and becomes

$$\frac{\theta_o(ju)}{A(ju)} = \frac{\dfrac{1}{5(ju)^2}}{1 + \dfrac{(6ju)^2}{5(ju)^2(6ju+1)}}$$ (103)

from which

$$\frac{\theta_o(ju)}{A(ju)} = \frac{(6ju+1)}{5(ju)^2(6ju+1+\frac{36}{5})}$$ (104)

Equation 104 indicates that the transfer function now has a second-order pole.　Thus, subject to the validity of the M_p criterion, a system having the desired order of dynamic stability and a velocity constant of infinity has been achieved.

8 Conclusion

Systems often have intermingled cascade and parallel arrangements of components. The compensation then required may comprise cascade and parallel arrangements of auxiliary equipment. For these reasons a person cannot always make a decisive choice as to whether the loci should be plotted on the G plane or on the G^{-1} plane. Often a parallel combination will be studied from loci on the G^{-1} plane. The results may then be converted to a form appropriate for their combination with other elements in cascade with the parallel combination. The overall results may then be presented by loci plotted on the G plane.

In Chapter 8, techniques are presented for plotting G functions to logarithmic coordinates. These methods offer advantages for *certain* studies. With the aid of a few master charts and templates, the designer can prepare function plots and readily interpret them. But the master charts are relatively complicated, being of the kind given in Figure 8·8. They are necessary whenever complete studies using the techniques of Chapter 8 are made. They are the equivalent of lines and circles used in the loci studies as shown in Figures 17, 18 and 19 of Chapter 6.

Frequently, the random nature of the disturbances and the inclusion of noise invalidate the simple criteria used herein for purposes of illustration. An evaluation of the problem by statistical methods [65] is then needed. A simple mean-square-error criterion is sometimes adequate. At all times considerations should be given to the power aspects of the mechanism.

In our opinion there is no such thing as an all-inclusive loci method or logarithmic method or even a frequency response method for closed-loop synthesis. Synthesis is the problem: the different graphical or analytical procedures are simply tools that a person may use to yield the answers desired by his problem. Some studies are most easily conducted using loci on the G plane, others by loci on the G^{-1} plane, still others by the logarithmic methods of Chapter 8. Occasions may arise where it is desirable to do portions of a comprehensive study by each of the methods outlined. This is particularly true when the study involves both experimental and calculated data. The final presentations of graphs, frequency functions, time functions, or tables of data will depend upon what is being sought. Frequently the audience to whom the presentation is given will determine the ultimate choice of procedures. Finally, in order to make a quick evaluation of the literature on this subject one should be familiar with all methods.

8

Methods of G Function Synthesis — Logarithmic Coordinates

1 General

The synthesis of linear closed-loop systems treated in Chapters 6 and 7 introduced various techniques which resulted in the plotting of transfer functions in the complex plane. A person who has carried through a few synthesis problems has probably become aware that one of the clues to a rapid solution of such problems is the systematization of the data and the method of attack employed. It is in this area that we again resort to techniques previously developed in the communications field. Reference to the literature on electronic feedback amplifier systems shows that the analysis of the problem has been greatly facilitated by representing various functions logarithmically. It is the purpose of this chapter to illustrate how the problem of closed-loop synthesis is systematized and aided by the application of logarithmic studies and appropriate organization of the functions into a few selected standard types.

The method outlined in the chapter, called the log modulus contour method,* is based upon three premises:

(1) All transfer functions representing linear systems are expressible in terms of one or more of the following factors; namely,

$$ju, \quad (ju + 1), \quad [(ju)^2 + j2\zeta u + 1]$$

(2) All manipulations of the functions in linear coordinates involving multiplication and division become addition and subtraction in logarithmic coordinates.

* The authors acknowledge the contributions to this work by the staff [4, 34, 35, 63] of the Bell Telephone Laboratories, the group under Mr. N. B. Nichols at the Radiation Laboratory,[65] the Massachusetts Institute of Technology, Cambridge, Mass., and the staff of the Servomechanisms Laboratory, also at M.I.T., Cambridge.

(3) The three primary factors of the transfer function may be constructed from memory any time, anywhere, with nothing more than a slide rule, straightedge, some transparent templates, and the applications of certain elementary techniques of analytic geometry.

Synthesis studies involving many trials before achieving proper compensation of a given system may be done quickly without destroying the graphical knowledge of the original function. In fact, this method lends itself to making several trial designs during the course of a few hours.

2 Log Magnitude and Angle Symbolism

Instead of plotting vector loci of the transfer function $KG(ju)$ to a linear scale, the contours are now plotted to a logarithmic scale. To exploit certain manipulative advantages, the modulus and argument graphs are made separately. The log of the magnitude is plotted versus log of the frequency; the phase is also plotted versus the log of frequency.

The log of the magnitude of $KG(ju)$ may be written

$$\log | KG(ju) | = \log K + \log | G(ju) | \tag{1}$$

The phase or angle of $KG(ju)$ is written as

$$\text{Ang } KG(ju) = \text{Ang } G(ju) \tag{2}$$

Because of a pattern established by authors of the literature treating communications circuits, logarithms to the base 10 are often used and the magnitudes are given as decibels. Thus the *log modulus of* $KG(ju)$, namely,

$$20 \log_{10} | KG(ju) | = 20 \log_{10} K + 20 \log_{10} | G(ju) | \tag{3}$$

is herein abbreviated to Lm $KG(ju)$. The units are given in decibels. The equation expressing the angle of the function, namely,

$$\text{Ang } KG(ju) = \text{Ang } G(ju) \tag{4}$$

usually has its value given in degrees.

More complicated transfer functions made up of several gain constants K and several complex functions $G(ju)$, as, for example,

$$KG(ju) = \frac{K_1 G_1(ju) K_2 G_2(ju)}{K_3 G_3(ju) K_4 G_4(ju)} \tag{5}$$

are readily handled. The log modulus of Equation 5 is written as

$$\text{Lm } KG(ju) = \text{Lm } K_1 + \text{Lm } K_2 - \text{Lm } K_3 - \text{Lm } K_4 + \text{Lm } G_1(ju)$$
$$+ \text{Lm } G_2(ju) - \text{Lm } G_3(ju) - \text{Lm } G_4(ju) \tag{6}$$

and the angle or phase is written

$$\text{Ang } KG(ju) = \text{Ang } G_1(ju) + \text{Ang } G_2(ju) - \text{Ang } G_3(ju)$$

$$- \text{Ang } G_4(ju) \quad (7)$$

A comparison of Equations 5 and 6 shows that calculations which formerly involved multiplication and division to a linear scale in order to yield vector moduli now involve the mere addition and subtraction of logarithms of numbers. No change occurs in the method of forming the phase of Equation 5 since the phase angles still add and subtract algebraically, depending upon whether the $G(ju)$ function appears in the numerator or denominator of Equation 5.

3   Simple Log Modulus and Phase Curves

Figure 1 illustrates the shape of a simple form of the functions under discussion. It shows the log modulus curve of the function $KG(ju) = (ju + 1)^{-1}$ which may be written as

$$\text{Lm } K = \text{Lm } 1 \cdot 0 = \text{zero}$$

and

$$\text{Lm } G(ju) = \text{Lm } (ju + 1)^{-1}$$

Certain unique features of the log modulus plot are shown by Figure 1. For example, when u is small compared with unity, the modulus of $G(ju)$ is unity, for which the value of the log modulus is zero. Likewise, when u is large compared with unity, the function approaches $(ju)^{-1}$ for which the magnitude varies inversely with frequency. Specifically, the magnitude $G(ju)$ halves each time the frequency u doubles. Since the $\log_{10} 2 = 0.301$, each doubling of frequency, or each octave change in u, involves a change in magnitude of 6 decibels in the magnitude function. This condition gives rise to the expression *the magnitude changes at a rate of 6 decibels per octave*.

The above conditions, namely, $u \ll 1$ and $u \gg 1$, set up two asymptotes to the true curve of $G(ju)$ which intersect at the frequency $u = 1$. In the neighborhood of the point $u = 1$, the true curve is readily located with respect to these asymptotes. For example, when $u = 1$, the magnitude of $KG(ju) = (\sqrt{2})^{-1}$, which expressed as a log modulus value equals -3 decibels. At the frequency $u = 2$, an octave above the frequency $u = 1$, the value of the magnitude of the function is $(\sqrt{5})^{-1}$ and its Lm $= -7$ decibels. However, at a frequency $u = 2$, the asymptote for $(ju)^{-1}$, starting at a zero decibel level at $u = 1$, would have the value -6 decibels. Likewise, at a frequency $u = 0.5$, one octave below the frequency $u = 1$, the value of the magnitude of the function $KG(ju)$ is $(\sqrt{1.25})^{-1}$ and its log modulus is -1 decibel. Again the asymptote for negligible u is at zero decibel. Thus, the two asymptotes drawn for the function $(ju + 1)^{-1}$, the first being at zero decibel and the second starting from the point zero decibel at $u = 1$ and having a slope of -6 decibels per octave for all frequencies greater than $u = 1$, lie on the true curve at low and high values of u. The true curve is 1 decibel below these asymptotes at an octave above and an octave below $u = 1$.

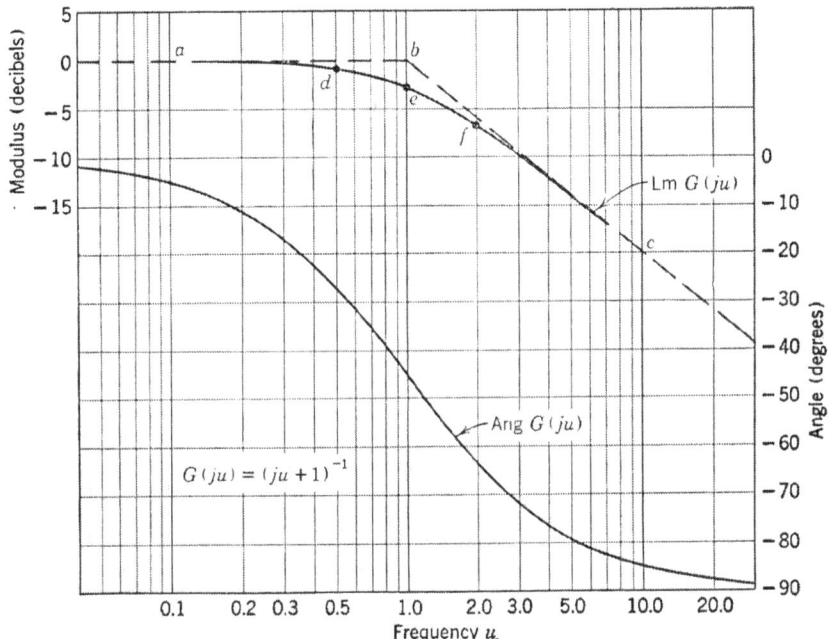

FIGURE 1. Log magnitude and angle graphs versus log frequency for $(ju + 1)^{-1}$.

It is 3 decibels below at the *break point* $u = 1$. Hence, for all practical purposes, the entire function $KG(ju) = (ju + 1)^{-1}$ can be drawn as in Figure 1, using two straight lines ab and bc and three corrective points d, e, f. The *break point* b occurs at the value of frequency u, which causes the real and imaginary parts of the function to be equal.

For the function $(ju + 1)^{-1}$, a simple construction yields a phase frequency diagram as shown in Figure 1. At values of u, small compared to unity, the phase is zero. For values of u large compared to unity, the phase is -90 degrees. For values of $u = 1$, the phase is -45 degrees. The phase function has symmetry on log coordinates at an octave above and an octave below $u = 1$ about the -45-degree line. Specifically at $u = 2$, an octave above $u = 1.0$, the phase is $-(45$ degrees $+ 18.5$ degrees$) = -63.5$ degrees, and at $u = 0.5$, an octave below $u = 1.0$, the phase is $-(45$ degrees $- 18.5$ degrees$) = -26.5$ degrees.

There are no straight line techniques for drawing the phase curve. However, a simple template for $\phi = \tan^{-1} u$ can be prepared for drawing the phase diagram quickly when once the user standardizes on the log paper used for the study. This template may also be used to give the phase curve of the function $(ju\tau + 1)^{\pm 1}$ or $\left(1 + \dfrac{\tau}{ju}\right)$.

4 Log Modulus Curves Including Gain Factors K

The gain constants K may be included in these studies in a simple manner. Consider $KG(ju) = 10(ju + 1)^{-1}$, giving $K = 10$, and $G(ju) = (ju + 1)^{-1}$. Thereby Equation 3 becomes

$$\text{Lm } KG(ju) \doteq 20 \log_{10} 10 - \text{Lm} \left| G(ju) \right| \text{ decibels}$$

$$\doteq 20 \text{ decibels} - \text{Lm} \left| G(ju) \right| \text{ decibels}$$

Thus, the presence of constants in the numerator or denominator of $KG(ju)$ add to or subtract their value in decibels from the ordinate of the log modulus curve of $G(ju)$. The presence of the gain K is accounted for merely by translating the zero decibel reference of the ordinate scale of Lm $G(ju)$ up or down by the amount $20 \log_{10} K$. It does not change the shape of the Lm $G(ju)$ graph. For this reason, all constants in the transfer functions may be neglected during initial work. At an appropriate place in the study, the specified values of K are inserted for analysis studies, or are determined numerically for synthesis studies. For convenience, K is initially chosen as unity corresponding to zero decibels. Later, in problems where the numerical value of K is known, the Lm $G(ju)$ curves, already plotted, need only have the zero decibel reference point reestablished to correct for the value of K.

In problems of synthesis, with which this chapter is more concerned, K is chosen initially as unity throughout all work until the shape of the Lm $G(ju)$ and the angle curves have been established. The correct numerical value of K is then determined in accordance with the M_p or associated criteria which make the response equations θ_o/θ_i or E/θ_i meet desired system specifications.

5 Components of the Generalized Transfer Function

The reader will recall from Chapter 6 that any transfer function $KG(ju)$ may be expressed by

$$KG(ju) = K \frac{A(ju)}{B(ju)} \tag{8}$$

where $A(ju)$ and $B(ju)$ are polynomials in the variable (ju). If only positive integer powers of (ju) appear in both $A(ju)$ and $B(ju)$, the

numerator and denominator of Equation 8 may always be factored into
three basic factors or product of factors, namely,

$$(ju)^m, \quad (ju + 1)^n, \quad [(ju)^2 + 2\zeta ju + 1]^p \Big\} \tag{9}$$
$$(ju\tau + 1)^{\pm 1}, \quad [(ju\tau)^2 + 2\zeta ju\tau + 1]^{\pm 1}$$

Both the numerator and the denominator of Equation 8 may contain
any or all the forms shown in Equation 9. The factor appears in the
numerator or denominator, depending upon whether the exponents
m, n, or p are positive or negative. Similarly, if any factor of either
polynomial is repeated, m, n, or p will have integer values greater than
unity.

Compound forms of transfer functions may always be broken down
into these elementary components. If modulus and angle studies are
made for them, subsequent closed-loop studies to any degree of complexity may be made with directness and clarity by adding together
logarithmically individual moduli to form the composite modulus $G(ju)$
and adding together linearly the corresponding angles to form the resulting angles of $G(ju)$.

Some of the more commonly used properties of these generalized functions are now prepared.

(1) The factor $(ju)^m$ is written symbolically as

$$\text{Lm } (ju)^m = 20m \log_{10} u \text{ decibels} \tag{10}$$

$$\text{Ang } (ju)^m = 90m \text{ degrees} \tag{11}$$

for all positive values of frequency. The plots of log modulus as a
function of log u are straight lines having a slope per octave of $6m$
decibels. The plots of phase as a function of log u have zero slope with
respect to frequency. Table 1 summarizes the variation of the modulus
slope and the phase as a function of the parameter m.

TABLE 1

THE FUNCTION $(ju)^m$

m	Lm	Ang in Degrees	Slope in Decibels per Octave
3	$60 \log u$	270	18
2	$40 \log u$	180	12
1	$20 \log u$	90	6
0	0	0	0
−1	$−20 \log u$	−90	−6
−2	$−40 \log u$	−180	−12
−3	$−60 \log u$	−270	−18

(2) The factor $(ju + 1)^n$ is written symbolically as

$$\text{Lm } (ju + 1)^n = 20n \log \sqrt{u^2 + 1} \tag{12}$$

and

$$\text{Ang } (ju + 1)^n = n \tan^{-1} u \tag{13}$$

Here, neither the modulus nor the phase functions as a function of log u are straight lines. Nevertheless, they may be plotted rapidly by determining high- and low-frequency asymptotes to the actual curve as indicated in Section 3. The agreement of the true curves having these asymptotes may be established in the middle frequency region by simple calculations.

The low-frequency asymptotes, that is, for $0 < u < 1$, may be found from

$$\text{Lm } (ju + 1)^n = \text{Lm } (1)^n = 20n \log_{10} 1 = 0 \text{ decibels} \tag{14}$$

$$\text{Ang } (ju + 1)^n = n \tan^{-1} 0 = 0 \text{ degrees} \tag{15}$$

The high-frequency asymptotes for $1 < u < \infty$ are

$$\text{Lm } (ju + 1)^n = 20n \log u \text{ decibels} \tag{16}$$

$$\text{Ang } (ju + 1)^n = n \tan^{-1} \infty = 90n \text{ degrees} \tag{17}$$

From Equations 14 and 16, it is noted that the plots of log modulus asymptotes as a function of log u of the function given in Equations 12 and 13 are straight lines. The low-frequency asymptote has a slope of zero decibels per octave. The high-frequency asymptote has a slope of $6n$ decibels per octave. When $u = 1$ these two asymptotes intersect. The statement that the modulus graph has a *break at u = 1 upward or downward with a slope 6n decibels per octave* is made because of this sharp slope change in the asymptote.

The general pattern of the plot of the function is similar to that of Figure 1. The true values of the modulus function in the middle frequency region may again be calculated by choosing values of u ranging an octave above and an octave below the so-called *critical* or *break frequency*. As in Section 3 and Figure 1, three points will suffice to establish the true curve:

$$\text{at } u = \tfrac{1}{2}, \quad \text{Lm } = 20n \log \sqrt{1.25} = n \text{ decibels} \tag{18}$$

$$\text{at } u = 1, \quad \text{Lm } = 20n \log \sqrt{2} = 3n \text{ decibels} \tag{19}$$

$$\text{at } u = 2, \quad \text{Lm } = 20n \log \sqrt{5} = 7n \text{ decibels} \tag{20}$$

Therefore, with respect to the asymptotes,

at $u = \frac{1}{2}$,   the true curve lies n decibels from the asymptote   (21)

at $u = 1$,   the true curve lies $3n$ decibels from the asymptote   (22)

at $u = 2$,   the true curve lies n decibels from the asymptote   (23)

The argument function, Equation 13, is not readily approximated by straight lines, but values selected from trigonometric tables covering a range from one decade below to one decade above the critical frequency will specify the $\tan^{-1} u$. The general procedure follows the pattern shown in Figure 1. When n has an integral value positive or negative, it is necessary only to multiply the ordinates of this angle curve by n to produce the desired argument curve. A template may be cut which will provide $\tan^{-1} u$ on a standard semilog scale or paper size, and no further calculations need be made to establish the argument values for this function.

(3) Quadratic factors $[(ju)^2 + 2\zeta(ju) + 1]$ having $\zeta < 1$, leading to conjugate complex factors, frequently occur in servo systems.

The difficulties of plotting the quadratic factor when its factors are complex are avoided by retaining its quadratic form. The modulus and phase for the general form are

$$\text{Lm } [(ju)^2 + 2\zeta(ju) + 1]^p = 20p \log \sqrt{(1 - u^2)^2 + (2\zeta u)^2} \quad (24)$$

$$\text{Ang } [(ju)^2 + 2\zeta(ju) + 1]^p = p \tan^{-1} \frac{2\zeta u}{1 - u^2} \quad (25)$$

No asymptote method for plotting the two families of curves of Equations 24 and 25 is suitable. Instead, a family of curves with ζ as a parameter is usually prepared. Such a family is shown in Figure 2. The modulus and phase graphs are given for a reasonable range of the parameter ζ for the value $p = -1$. When p has values other than -1 the desired log modulus and angle may easily be found by multiplying all ordinates of Lm and Ang of Figure 2 by the factor p.

6   Treatment of the Transfer Function

Transfer functions are usually sufficiently complicated to comprise many combinations of the basic factors described in Section 5. Rather than discuss the method for preparing $\text{Lm } G(ju)$ and $\text{Ang } G(ju)$ curves for a general transfer function, two transfer functions which typify familiar servos or components of servos will now be treated in detail.

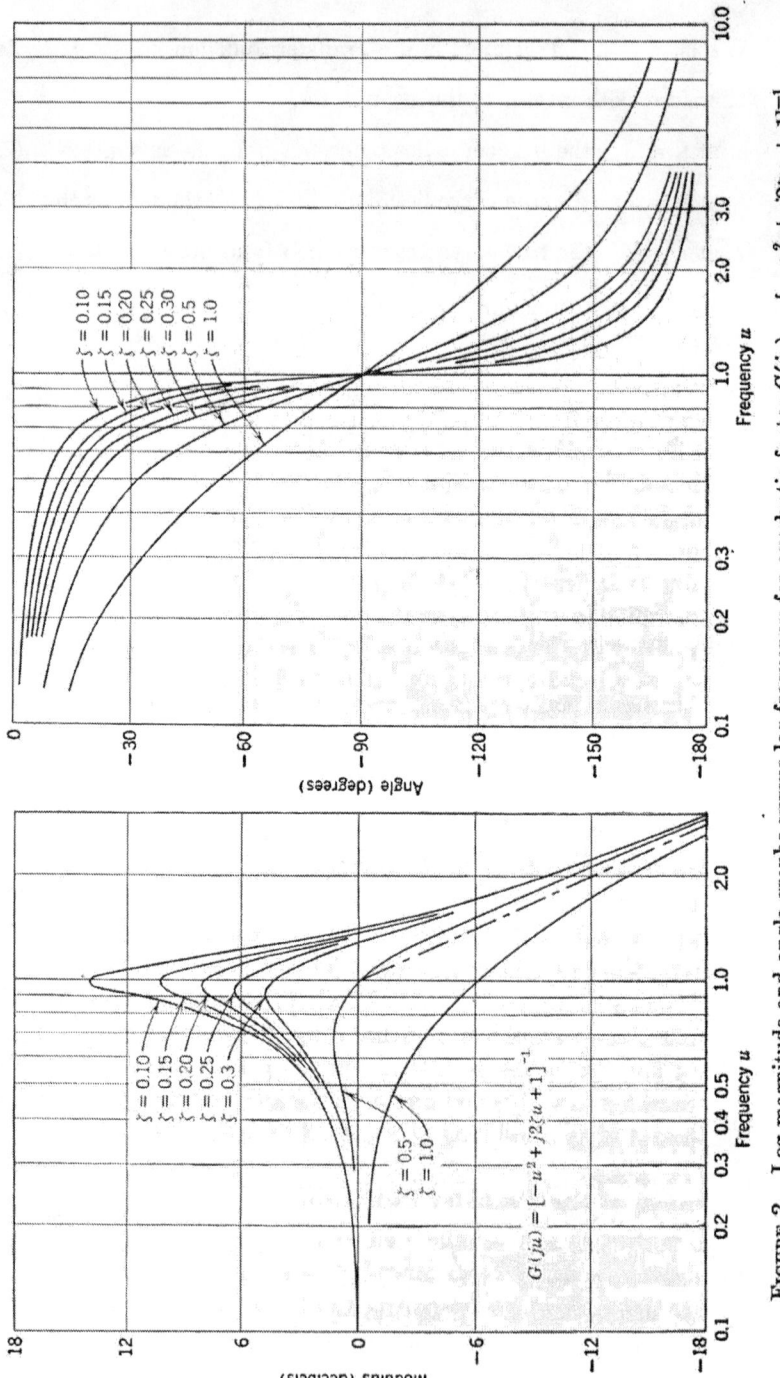

Figure 2. Log magnitude and angle graphs versus log frequency for quadratic factor $G(ju) = [-u^2 + j2\zeta u + 1]^{-1}$.

A closed-loop system comprising a motor and an amplifier unit shown in Figure 3 has the transfer functions expressing the open-loop behavior

$$\frac{\theta_o}{\phi_{ag}}(j\omega) = \frac{K_2}{j\omega(j\omega T_2 + 1)} \tag{26}$$

$$\frac{\phi_{ag}}{\varepsilon}(j\omega) = \frac{K_1}{(j\omega T_1 + 1)} \tag{27}$$

When these functions are combined, the overall opened-loop response is

$$\frac{\theta_o}{\varepsilon}(j\omega) = \frac{K_o}{j\omega(j\omega T_1 + 1)(j\omega T_2 + 1)} \tag{28}$$

where

$$K_o = K_1 K_2$$

The specific problem is to prepare the log modulus and angle curves for the transfer function. As usual, K_o is independent of frequency and can

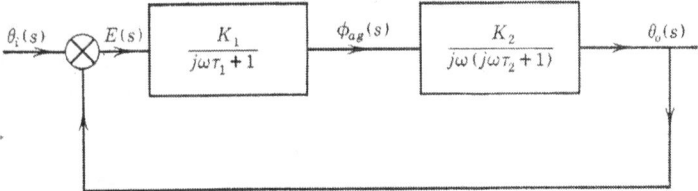

FIGURE 3.   Diagram of positional servomechanism.

be initially ignored. Methods for selecting K_o for a specific M_p are discussed later. In log magnitude form the transfer function of Equation 28 reads:

$$\mathrm{Lm}\left[\frac{\theta_o}{\varepsilon}(j\omega)\right] = \mathrm{Lm}\, K_o - \mathrm{Lm}\,(j\omega) - \mathrm{Lm}\,(j\omega T_1 + 1)$$
$$- \mathrm{Lm}\,(j\omega T_2 + 1) \tag{29}$$

$$\mathrm{Ang}\left[\frac{\theta_o}{\varepsilon}(j\omega)\right] = -\frac{\pi}{2} - \tan^{-1}\omega T_1 - \tan^{-1}\omega T_2 \tag{30}$$

Since K_o can be ignored for initial studies, only the $G(j\omega)$ function need be considered. Thus

$$\left.\begin{aligned}
\mathrm{Lm}\, G(j\omega) &= -\mathrm{Lm}\,(j\omega) - \mathrm{Lm}\,(j\omega T_1 + 1) - \mathrm{Lm}\,(j\omega T_2 + 1)\\
\mathrm{Ang}\, G(j\omega) &= -\frac{\pi}{2} - \tan^{-1}\omega T_1 - \tan^{-1}\omega T_2
\end{aligned}\right\} \tag{31}$$

The modulus and phase graphs for the component parts of Equation 31 have already been plotted and discussed in Sections 2 through 5 of this chapter. However, the procedure will be carried through to demonstrate some of the techniques which shorten the actual graphical work.

In order that numbers be used, choose $T_1 = 0.2$ second and $T_2 = 0.05$ second. Curves for the specific values T_1 and T_2 could be plotted but a change of variable can be made which will simplify the graph. If the first break frequency $\omega_1 = 1/T_1 = 5$ radians per second is selected for dimensionalization so that $u = \omega T_1 = 0.2\omega$, the graphs can be prepared for the frequency variable u. Thus the transfer function $K_oG(j\omega)$ changes to

$$K_u G(ju) = \frac{T_1 K_o}{ju(ju + 1)\left(ju\dfrac{T_2}{T_1} + 1\right)} \tag{32}$$

giving

$$G(ju) = \frac{1}{ju(ju + 1)\left(ju\dfrac{T_2}{T_1} + 1\right)} \tag{33}$$

The log vector forms are

$$\text{Lm } G(ju) = -\text{Lm } (ju) - \text{Lm } (ju + 1) - \text{Lm }\left(ju\dfrac{T_2}{T_1} + 1\right) \tag{34}$$

$$\text{Ang } G(ju) = -\frac{\pi}{2} - \tan^{-1} u - \tan^{-1}\frac{T_2}{T_1} u \tag{35}$$

or

$$\text{Lm } G(ju) = -\text{Lm } (u) - \text{Lm }\sqrt{u^2 + 1} - \text{Lm }\sqrt{(0.25u)^2 + 1} \tag{36}$$

$$\text{Ang } G(ju) = -\frac{\pi}{2} - \tan^{-1} u - \tan^{-1} 0.25u \tag{37}$$

The critical or break frequencies ω are

$$\left.\begin{array}{l} \omega_1 = \dfrac{1}{T_1} = \dfrac{1}{0.2} = 5 \\[3mm] \omega_2 = \dfrac{1}{T_2} = \dfrac{1}{0.05} = 20 \end{array}\right\} \tag{38}$$

Similarly, in the dimensionless frequency scale, the critical or break frequencies u are

$$\left.\begin{array}{l} u_1 = \dfrac{1}{1} = 1 \\[3mm] u_2 = \dfrac{1}{\left(\dfrac{T_2}{T_1}\right)} = \dfrac{T_1}{T_2} = 4 \end{array}\right\} \tag{39}$$

The modulus and argument curves for the individual factors of Equations 36 and 37 are prepared in Figure 4.   The individual curves of Figure 4 can be combined to form the composite log modulus and angle curve of Figure 5.

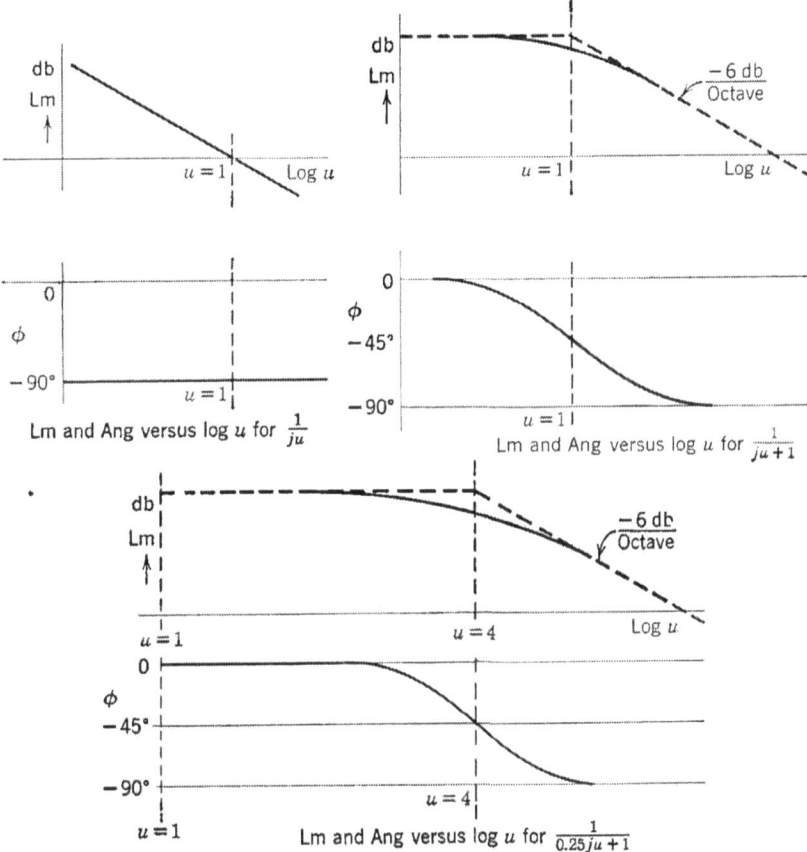

FIGURE 4.   Lm and Ang versus log u of individual components.

The composite modulus graph can be made up as outlined here.

(1) At very low frequencies, for example at $u = 0.01$, the value of Lm $G(ju)$ = Lm (100) = $+40$ decibels.   This value of 40 decibels at $u = 0.01$ locates the ordinate scale by providing a point on the graph for a specific value of frequency u.   The slope at this value of u is known to be -6 decibels per octave.   Thus the first asymptote of the function can be located on the plot.

(2) Throughout the frequency range $0 < u < 1.0$ establish an asymptote whose slope is the algebraic sum of the slopes of the three component parts of Lm $G(ju)$.   This line has -6 decibels per octave slope since

only the factor $-\text{Lm}\,(ju)$ contributes substantially to the value of the function.

(3) At the frequency $u = 1$, the first break occurs in the asymptote, specifically for the factor $-\text{Lm}\,(ju + 1)$. For values of $u > 1$ this factor contributes an additional -6 decibels per octave to the slope of the composite asymptote. Therefore, draw a line with -12 decibels per octave slope through $u = 1$ intersecting the line ab of the composite asymptote until the frequency $u = 4$ is reached.

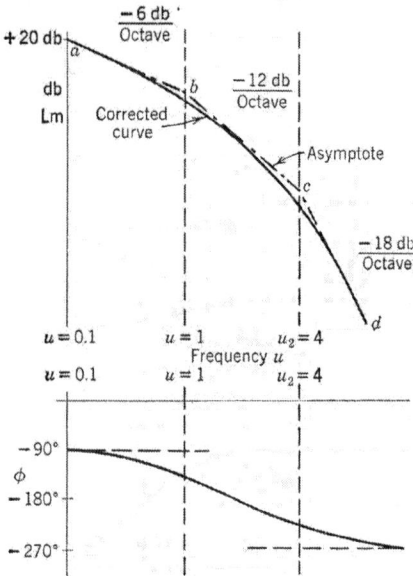

FIGURE 5.   Composite Lm and Ang versus log u for system of Figure 3.

(4) At $u = 4$, the second break in the asymptote occurs. The quantity $-\text{Lm}\,(0.25ju + 1)$ contributes an additional -6 decibels per octave to the slope of -12 decibels per octave which existed for frequencies $1 < u < 4$. Thus the third portion of the composite asymptote is a line having -18 decibels per octave drawn to intersect with the line of -12 decibels per octave at the frequency $u = 4$. No more changes in slope occur over the frequency range $4 < u < \infty$.

(5) The true log modulus of $G(ju)$ may be drawn now from the composite asymptote at the break frequencies and in the frequency region between breaks by algebraically summing the corrections resulting from each factor at various frequency points. The procedure is greatly

simplified if a pair of dividers is used to form the total correction as a distance by which the true curve is offset from the composite asymptote.

The composite asymptote can be prepared by establishing the two critical or break frequencies $u_1 = 1$ and $u_2 = 4$ and Lm $G(j0.01) = +40$ decibels in such a way that three straight lines can be drawn connecting these consecutive points with proper slopes. Figure 5 shows such a composite asymptote, where line ab has the -6 decibels per octave slope, and passes through $+40$ decibels at $u = 0.01$ and $+20$ decibels at $u = 0.1$. Line cd has the slope -18 decibels per octave and intersects the line bc at the frequency $u = 4$. The corrected curve is shown for the region of frequency about one octave above $u = 4$. Observe that the offset of the true curve from the asymptote in the region $1 < u < 4$ is made up of two parts. One came from the correction required for the lower break frequency and the other comes from that required by the upper break frequency. Care should be used in performing this correction when the values of the break frequencies are similar in magnitude because large corrections may arise from more than one factor.

The angle $G(ju)$ may be prepared in a similar manner to that outlined for the modulus. The details are illustrated in Figure 4. Specifically, $-$ Ang (ju) gives a $-(\pi/2)$ phase asymptote at low frequency. The Ang $(ju + 1)^{-1}$ contributes minus 45 degrees phase shift at $u = 1$. It contributes minus 26.5 degrees and minus 63.5 degrees at an octave below and an octave above $u = 1$. Likewise, the Ang $(0.25ju + 1)^{-1}$ contributes another -45 degrees phase shift at a point $u = 4$. It contributes -26.5 degrees and -63.5 degrees at an octave below and an octave above $u = 4$. The Ang $G(ju)$ is obtained by adding algebraically the three components. The composite angle graph is shown by Figure 5. No asymptote procedure is applicable.

A second example illustrating another form of transfer function is this. Consider the transfer function

$$\frac{\theta_o(j\omega)}{X(j\omega)} = KG(j\omega) = \frac{K}{j\omega[(j\omega)^2 T^2 + 2\zeta(j\omega)T + 1]} \tag{40}$$

which represents the output motion θ_o of the motor end of an hydraulic transmission with respect to the stroke motion X of the variable displacement pump. This transfer function was derived in Chapter 5, Equation 5·107.

The log modulus of Equation 40 becomes

$$\text{Lm } KG(j\omega) = \text{Lm } K - \text{Lm } (j\omega) - \text{Lm } [(j\omega)^2 T^2 + 2\zeta(j\omega)T + 1)] \tag{41}$$

The dimensionless form following a change in variable $\omega T = u$ is

$$\text{Lm } KG(ju) = \text{Lm } KT - \text{Lm } (ju) - \text{Lm } [(ju)^2 + 2\zeta(ju) + 1)] \quad (42)$$

Initially, only the frequency dependent part of Equation 42 is considered. The portion $\text{Lm } KT$ is introduced only during the final synthesis. A plot of the second and third portions of the modulus function can be made. The phase for the same function is given by

$$\text{Ang } KG(ju) = -\frac{\pi}{2} - \tan^{-1}\frac{2\zeta u}{1 - u^2} \quad (43)$$

If the procedure indicated in the previous example is followed, the Lm $G(ju)$ may first be approximated by a straight line of -6 decibels per octave for $0 < u < 1$. At $u = 1$, the asymptote breaks downward at -18 decibels per octave for $1 < u < \infty$. In the vicinity of $u = 1$ the true values of $G(ju)$ may be found by selecting corrections to the asymptote from Figure 2 for the value of ζ given in Equation 42.

The angle curve is established in much the same manner. The (ju) portion causes the angle graph to be asymptotic to -90 degrees, at low frequencies. The presence of the quadratic factor indicates that at high frequencies the angle curve will be asymptotic to -270 degrees. By selecting values from the plot of the quadratic factor, Figure 2, the composite angle curve of this $G(ju)$ function may be drawn. Figure 6 shows the nature of the two components, and Figure 7 shows the composite modulus and phase curves.

The log modulus and phase graphs thus far prepared for the two examples given by Equations 29 and 40 express the open-loop dynamical properties of the respective systems. The synthesis problem now requires that criteria be established which will permit the selection of the magnitude of both the frequency invariant factor K in the closed loop and the dynamical property of any compensating function, such as $G_c(j\omega)$, which may be introduced in cascade in the loop. The criteria on which the selection of K and $G_c(j\omega)$ are to be based must be consistent with system performance specifications. In the absence of any unusual performance requirements the same empirical basis is chosen for the log modulus method of making closed-loop synthesis studies as was used for the preparation of linear KG or KG^{-1} contour studies. The procedure for selecting the closed-loop sensitivity and for designing compensating networks using the logarithmic forms of curves therefore differs only in technique and not in principle.

In Chapter 6, contours of $\theta_o/\theta_i = M$ and Ang $\theta_o/\theta_i = N$ were established on the complex plane. It was shown that these contours could be superimposed on the $G(j\omega)$ plane where only the frequency variant portion of the transfer function was plotted. These two families of curves then became the basis for establishing system performance acceptable to present-day standards. The application of the same princi-

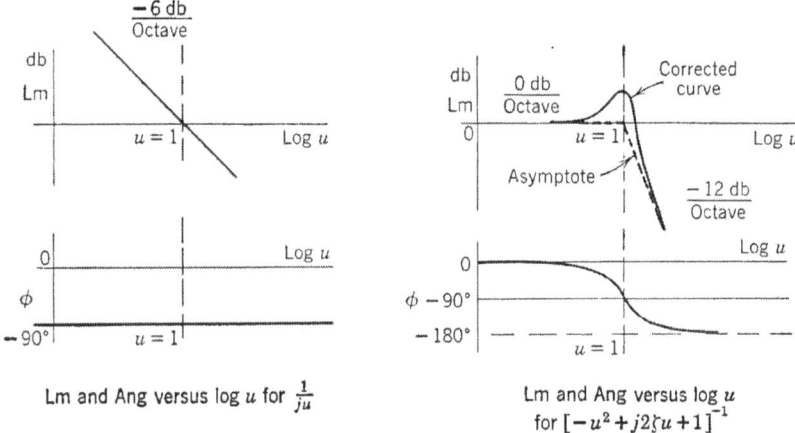

Lm and Ang versus log u for $\frac{1}{ju}$

Lm and Ang versus log u
for $[-u^2 + j2\zeta u + 1]^{-1}$

FIGURE 6.   Lm and Ang versus log u of individual components.

ples using the functions in logarithmic form requires the preparation of another chart called the *M-N* contour chart. Upon it are plotted contours of constant ratios of $\theta_o/\theta_i = M$ and constant Ang $\theta_o/\theta_i = N$, to an ordinate scale of decibels and abscissa scale of phase angle in degrees.

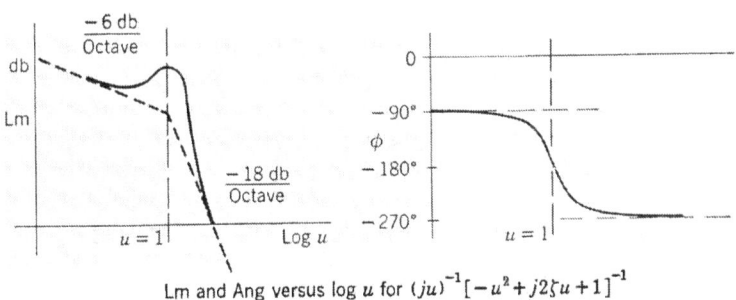

Lm and Ang versus log u for $(ju)^{-1}[-u^2 + j2\zeta u + 1]^{-1}$

FIGURE 7.   Composite Lm and Ang versus log u.

This chart then yields data for the system operating as a closed loop as contrasted with the Lm G versus log ω or Ang G versus log ω charts which yield only open-loop data. The two families of contours plotted in the Lm-Ang plane merge into a single chart as shown in Figure 8. The construction of this chart is treated in the next section.

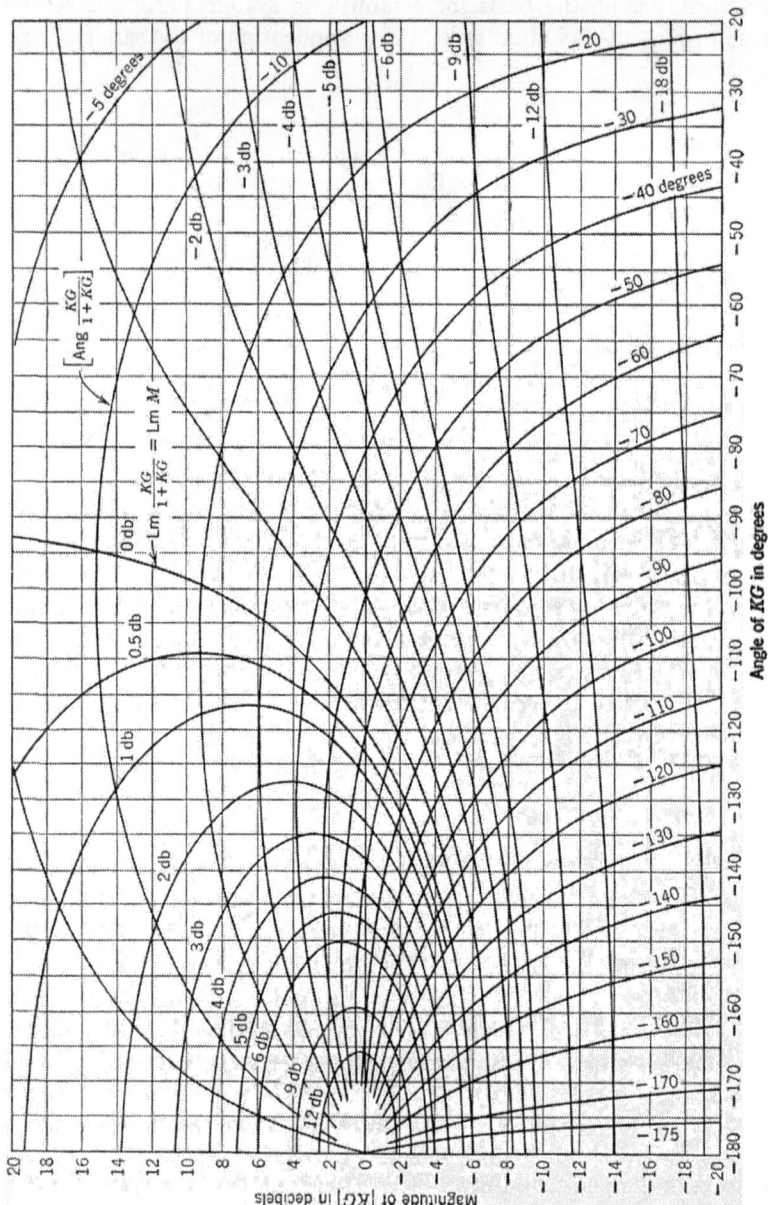

FIGURE 8.   Log modulus versus angle chart showing contours of constant magnitude and phase of θ_o/θ_i.

7   The *M-N* Contour Chart [65]

The contours for M and N could be prepared point by point. A suitable procedure would be first to draw M circles as shown in Figure 9, then to note the values of M versus phase, to compute the values of M in decibels, and finally to plot them as ordinate against phase in degrees

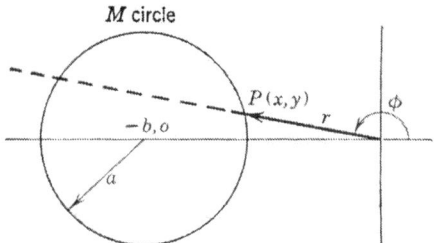

FIGURE 9.   Geometry for development of the chart of Figure 8.

as the abscissa. However, such a graphical procedure will lead to accumulated inaccuracies. The analytical expressions for the contours is therefore derived and used to plot the curves of Figure 8. The procedure is this.

The M circle shown in Figure 9 is defined by

$$a^2 = (x + b)^2 + y^2 \tag{44}$$

where the radius is

$$a = \frac{M}{M^2 - 1} \tag{45}$$

and the center is located at

$$b = \frac{M^2}{M^2 - 1} \tag{46}$$

The point $P(x, y)$ where an arbitrary vector $KG(j\omega)$ intersects the circle may be defined by

$$\left. \begin{aligned} x &= r \cos \phi \\ y &= r \sin \phi \end{aligned} \right\} \tag{47}$$

The relation between M, r, and phase ϕ becomes

$$r^2(M^2 - 1) + 2rM^2 \cos \phi + M^2 = 0 \tag{48}$$

When Equation 48 is solved for r, an expression defining the length and phase of $r = |\theta_o/E|$ results, which is consistent with $|\theta_o/\theta_i|_{\text{max}} = M$. This gives,

$$r = -\frac{M^2}{M^2 - 1} \cos \phi \pm \left[\frac{M^4}{(M^2 - 1)^2} \cos^2 \phi - \frac{M^2}{M^2 - 1} \right]^{\frac{1}{2}} \tag{49}$$

For convenience in plotting, Equation 48 is solved for the phase angle ϕ, giving

$$\phi = \cos^{-1} \frac{-M^2 - r^2(M^2 - 1)}{2rM^2} \tag{50}$$

In Equation 50, the value of M is not in decibels. It is given in regular numbers. Once the values of M for a particular contour is selected it may be converted to decibels for defining the particular contour on the Lm-Ang plane. The ordinate of this plane is Lm KG and the abscissa is Ang KG in degrees.

A similar set of contours for Ang $(\theta_o/\theta_i) = N$ may be plotted using the following equations. If

$$\text{Ang } \frac{\theta_o}{\theta_i} (j\omega) = \text{Ang } \frac{(KG)}{1 + KG} = N \tag{51}$$

then

$$\text{Ang } \frac{\theta_o}{\theta_i} (j\omega) = \text{Ang } \frac{(x + jy)}{1 + x + jy} = N \tag{52}$$

or

$$N = \tan^{-1} \frac{y}{x} - \tan^{-1} \frac{y}{1 + x} \tag{53}$$

Inserting values of x and y from Equation 47

$$N = \tan^{-1} \frac{r \sin \phi}{r \cos \phi} - \tan^{-1} \frac{r \sin \phi}{1 + r \cos \phi} \tag{54}$$

which may be written as

$$N = \phi - \tan^{-1} \frac{r \sin \phi}{1 + r \cos \phi} \tag{55}$$

When suitable constant values of N are selected, the second family of curves can be plotted on the M-N chart.

Figure 8 has been prepared where contours for M in decibels and N in degrees are plotted for ± 20 decibels of magnitude and -30 to -180 degrees of phase. However, transfer functions for servomechanisms systems frequently have phase shifts greater than -180 degrees for either low or high frequency regions. Symmetry exists in the Lm-Ang plane containing the contours of M and N. Hence, if functions involving angles greater than -180 degrees occur, the entire chart may be rotated about the -180-degree axis and a region covering angles from -180 to -330 degrees is available. The sketch of Figure 10 shows the

M and N contours for an Lm versus Ang plane extending from 0 to -360 degrees. Beyond these limits on either side, to the left of -360 degrees or to the right of 0 degrees, the contours are repeated for every zone of 360 degrees.

Sometimes, unusual problems in synthesis demand unusually large magnitudes of the ordinate. To use Figure 8 would necessitate an extension of the ordinate scale to plot larger positive or negative values.

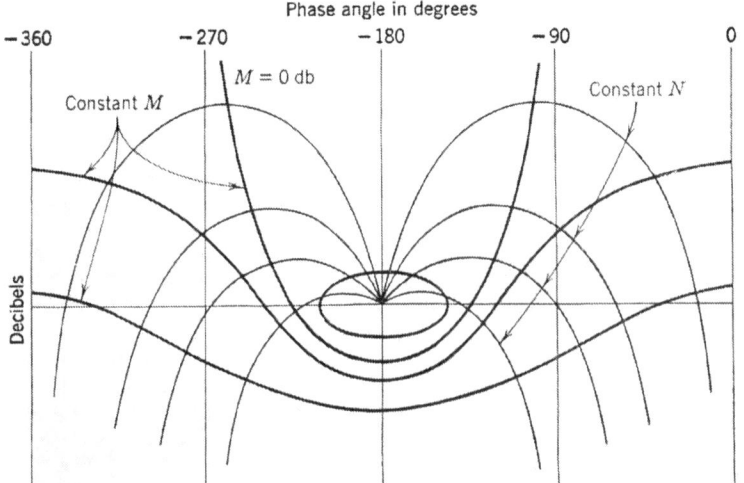

FIGURE 10.   Chart showing symmetry of *M-N* contours about phase of 180 degrees.

No symmetry exists for extending M and N curves in the ordinate direction. The user must extend the plots of M and N contours of Figure 8 by calculating enough new points to accommodate his problem.

8 System Synthesis Using *M-N* Contour Charts

The system synthesis generally involves (1) the determination of the frequency invariant term K of the transfer function for a system whose $G(j\omega)$ is known, or (2) the shaping of an overall $G(j\omega)$ function by the insertion of a compensation function such as $G_c(j\omega)$ to meet a desired K and system frequency behavior consistent with an M_p criterion.

If the value of $KG(j\omega)$ were known exactly for all values of frequency, the log modulus of $KG(j\omega)$ could be replotted as a function of Ang $KG(j\omega)$ on the Lm versus Ang plane at a number of frequency points, ω_1, ω_2, ω_3, etc. The Lm-Ang locus thus derived for $KG(j\omega)$ would cross the contours for constant values of M decibels and N degrees of the log vector contours of Figure 8. The values of θ_o/θ_i and Ang θ_o/θ_i as a function of ω for the closed-loop system could then be read directly from the chart. This operation would comprise merely *analysis*.

The problem of *synthesis* involves a revision of this procedure. The known $G(j\omega)$ function may be first plotted as an Lm versus Ang curve on the *M-N* contour chart of Figure 8. Then, remembering that the presence of a frequency invariant term K is to translate the $G(j\omega)$ function up or down the chart, the problem is to adjust the location of the curve of $G(j\omega)$ relative to the M and N contours in much the same manner as was used to adjust the location between the M circle and the $G(j\omega)$ locus on the $G(j\omega)$ plane in polar coordinates. Briefly, this adjustment comprises the addition of Lm K to the Lm $G(j\omega)$ function to locate a new contour as desired by the M criterion specified. The up or down translation of Lm $G(j\omega)$ required is then Lm K. The procedure is illustrated in detail for a problem that presupposes $G(j\omega)$ to be defined and calls for the magnitude of K to satisfy a given M_p criterion.

Since the problem illustrated by Equations 29 and 40 are good ones for a reader to complete, the above procedure will be outlined for a new example where

$$\frac{\theta_o}{E}(j\omega) = KG(j\omega) = \frac{K}{j\omega(j\omega T + 1)} \tag{56}$$

First convert Equation 56 to dimensionless form by the change of variable $j\omega T = ju$, giving

$$\frac{\theta_o}{E}(ju) = K_u G(ju) = \frac{KT}{ju(ju + 1)} \tag{57}$$

where

$$K_u = KT \tag{58}$$

The quantity KT is to be determined from the synthesis study. It is initially considered unity. The curves of Lm $G(ju)$ and Ang $G(ju)$ are then as shown in Figure 11, where the specific location of the ordinate scale for Lm $G(ju)$ is found from the condition that for $u = 0.1$ the function can be considered as equal to $1/ju$, for which Lm $(1/0.1) = +20$ decibels. The slope of the asymptote curve through the point $u = 0.1$ at $+20$ decibels is -6 decibels per octave. The break in the asymptote curve lies at zero decibels on the ordinate scale and $u = 1$ on the abscissa scale. The true curve is then sketched in, following the procedure outlined in Section 3.

The Lm-Ang curve for $G(ju)$ of Equation 57 is now found by replotting the data from the Lm and Ang curves versus log u onto a new sheet as

an Lm versus Ang curve having the same ordinate and abscissa scales
as the *M-N* chart of Figure 8.   Figure 12 shows the Lm-Ang curve for
$G(ju)$ with the values of u marked off along the contour.   If $M_p = 1.3$
is to be the basis for selecting K_u, the contour for $M = 2.28$ decibels on

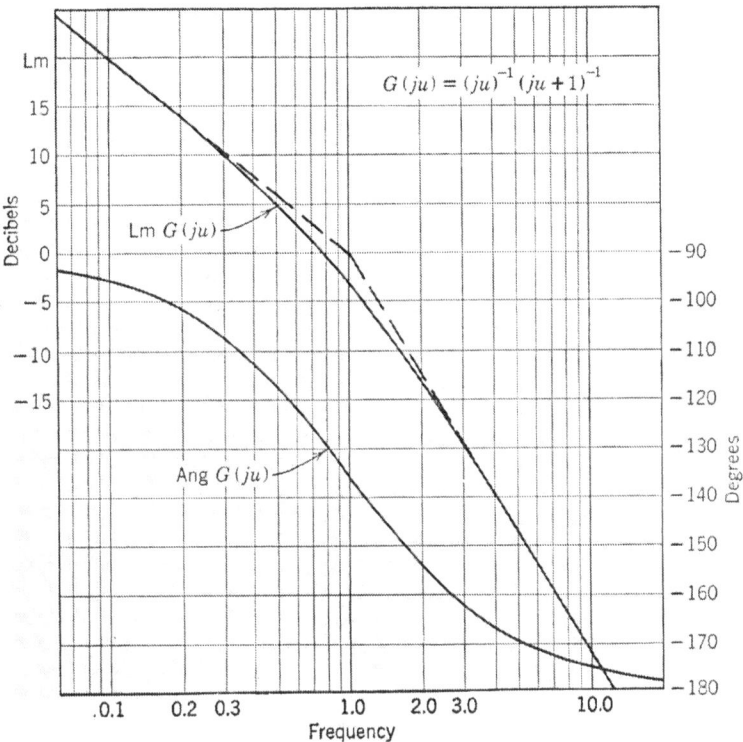

FIGURE 11.   Lm and Ang versus log u for the function $(ju)^{-1}(ju + 1)^{-1}$.

the *M-N* chart of Figure 8 is to be tangent to the $K_u G(ju)$ Lm-Ang contour of Figure 12 if the two are superposed.   Figure 12 shows that the
$G(ju)$ locus (curve *a*) lies below the $M = 2.28$-decibel contour (curve *b*).
The $G(ju)$ locus must be raised by the amount Lm K_u to give a tangency.
A practical technique in these problems is to have a transparent template
of the $M = 2.28$-decibel contour which is placed on the sheet and translated up or down to give a tangency as shown by curve *c*.   The amount
of movement of the template from the 0-decibel reference is Lm K_u.
For the example shown, Lm $K_u = 2.6$, which means that the value of
K_u can be increased to $+2.6$ decibels before the $K_u G(ju)$ trace would

pass inside the $M = 2.28$-decibel contour if plotted on Figure 8, and violate the condition that $|\theta_o/\theta_i|_{max} = 1.3$.

The value K_u may be found as follows:

$$20 \log K_u = 2.6 \text{ decibels}$$

$$K_u = 1.35$$

The dimensionless resonant frequency for the closed loop having this value of K_u is $u_R = 0.9$, as indicated by the tangency of the $M = 2.28$-decibel contour with the $K_u G(ju)$ locus.

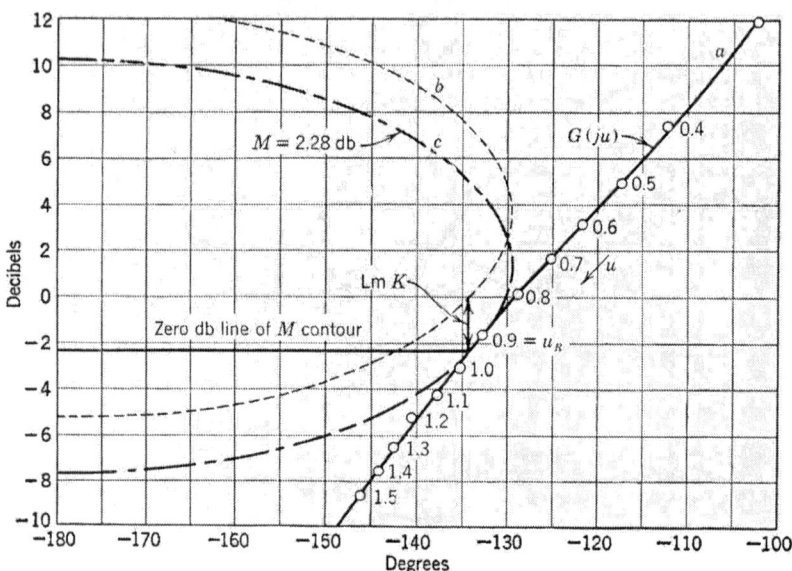

FIGURE 12.   Lm-Ang chart showing M contour superposed.

If the time constant T had been 0.05 second, the values for K and ω_R become

$$K = \frac{1.35}{0.05} = 27 \text{ seconds}^{-1}$$

$$\omega_R = \frac{0.9}{0.05} = 18 \text{ radians per second}$$

A check can be made for these values by recalling that the system being studied is defined by a second-order characteristic equation.   It was also used as the example of Chapter 6, Section 13. The value $|\theta_o/\theta_i|_{max} = 1.3$ is consistent with $\zeta = 0.43$. Therefore,

$$\zeta = \frac{1}{2\sqrt{Ku}}, \text{ giving } K_u = \frac{1}{(0.84)^2} = 1.33$$

$$u_r = u_n\sqrt{1 - 2\zeta^2} = \sqrt{K_u(1 - 2\zeta^2)} = 0.92$$

These values of ζ and u_r, calculated from the characteristic equation, check those derived graphically in this chapter and those derived in Chapter 6, within good limits.

When the $M = 1.3$ contour has been located with respect to the $G(ju)$ trace on Figure 12, the values for Lm θ_o/θ_i and Ang θ_o/θ_i may be found. To accomplish this, superpose the $G(ju)$ trace of Figure 12 on the plot of Lm KG versus Ang KG of Figure 8 by making the zero decibel line located at -2.6 decibels on the Lm G scale of Figure 12 coincide with the zero decibel line of the Lm KG scale of Figure 8. The $G(ju)$ locus has now become a $KG(ju)$ locus. It crosses the various M and N contours in such a way that values for Lm (θ_o/θ_i) decibels and Ang (θ_o/θ_i) degrees may be read for each frequency point. The data procured may be plotted on decibel log u coordinates and degree log u coordinates as before. For the $G(ju)$ locus of Figure 12, the values are as tabulated:

Frequency, u	Lm $\frac{\theta_o}{\theta_i}$, Decibels	Ang $\frac{\theta_o}{\theta_i}$, Degrees
0.25	0.2	−12
0.40	0.60	−18
0.50	1.00	−25
0.60	1.40	−31
0.70	1.70	−38
0.80	2.00	−48
0.90	2.28	−60
1.00	2.0	−71
1.10	1.8	−83
1.20	1.2	−92
1.30	0.0	−104
1.40	−1.0	−112

These data plotted in Figure 13 show the frequency response θ_o/θ_i of the closed-loop system.* The plot shows that the closure of the loop eliminates the low-frequency attenuation originally present in the transfer function by virtue of the integration in the loop. It makes a system that is a low-pass filter with a band width $u = 1$. The attenuation above $u = 1$ becomes -12 decibels per octave.

* See pages 282, 285 and 291 for an asymptote method of approximating θ_o/θ_i.

A careful examination of the contour of the system function on Figure 12 shows that the frequency invariant term K could be materially increased if the shape of the contour of $G(ju)$ could be modified in the region of phase shift near 135 degrees. Specifically, if the shape could be adjusted downward, the term K could be increased. The basis for

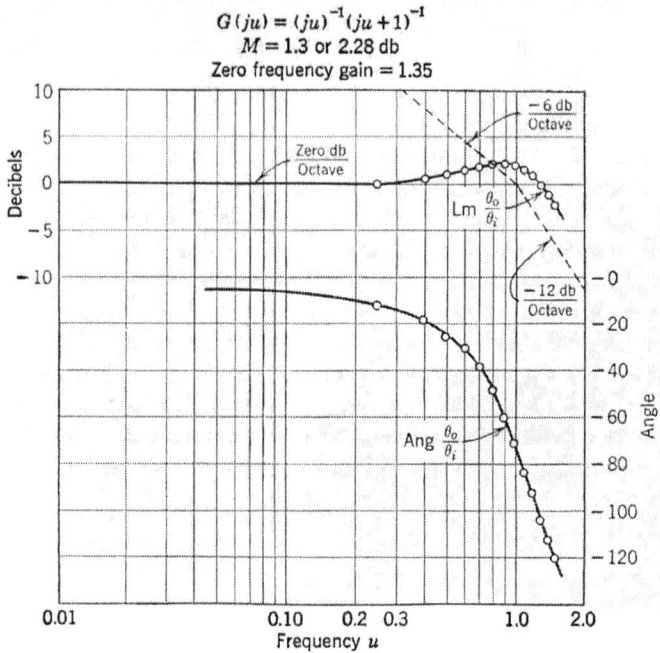

$$G(ju) = (ju)^{-1}(ju+1)^{-1}$$
$$M = 1.3 \text{ or } 2.28 \text{ db}$$
$$\text{Zero frequency gain} = 1.35$$

FIGURE 13.   Lm and Ang of θ_o/θ_i versus log u.

changing the shape of the locus of the transfer function is something that is imposed by requirements or obtained by experience, although certain helpful procedures can be outlined.

9   Gain Margin and Phase Margin (See Chapter 6, Section 12, p. 189.)

Frequently, two quantities related to the $KG(j\omega)$ locus are used as criteria in closed-loop synthesis. One of these quantities is designated as the *phase margin* and is commonly defined as the value of the angle [180 degrees $+$ Ang $G(j\omega)$] for the frequency ω at which $KG(j\omega) = 1$. The other quantity, designated as the *gain margin*, is defined as the minus log modulus of $KG(j\omega)$ when the frequency ω is such that Ang $G(j\omega)$ $= -180$ degrees. While both quantities give useful information pertaining to the selection of the $KG(j\omega)$ function of a closed-loop system, they do not, individually or collectively, provide sufficient basis for synthesis.

An estimate of the value of using the gain and phase margin as criteria for adjustment of closed-loop systems can be obtained from a study of Figure 14. The magnitude of a in the KG plane is the gain margin. It is often given in decibels below the zero decibel level. The angle ψ is the phase margin. It is usually given in degrees. The frequency ω_2 for which the gain margin a is defined is not uniquely related to the frequency ω_1 for which the phase margin ψ is defined. Both the gain margin and the phase margin could have prescribed values and yet the system response could be unsatisfactory. A consideration of loci similar to those shown in Figures 7·1 and 7·2 will demonstrate this point.

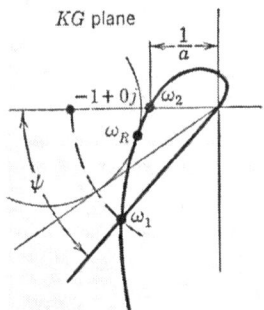
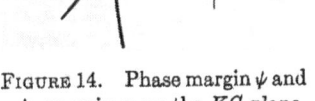

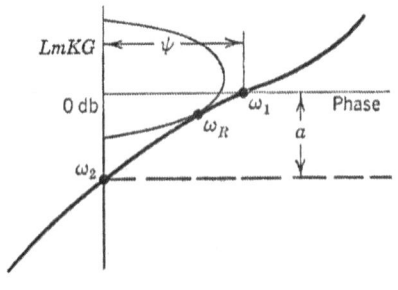

FIGURE 14.   Phase margin ψ and gain margin a on the KG plane.

FIGURE 15.   Phase margin ψ and gain margin a on the Lm-Ang chart.

Figure 15 shows the $KG(j\omega)$ locus of Figure 14 replotted in the Lm-Ang plane for the condition giving a tangency with a specific M_p contour. The distance a marks off the gain margin in decibels. The angle ψ is the phase margin. Neither value is directly related to the tangency of the locus with the M_p contour at $\omega = \omega_R$, but it should be apparent to the reader that phase margin and $\sin^{-1}(1/M)$ do not differ greatly as criteria for setting the gain K.

Synthesis is a broader problem than can be defined by selecting particular values of gain margin, phase margin, or even M_p. The criterion that the *shape* of the $G(j\omega)$ locus and the value of gain K must be such that the G locus and the M_p contour have the proper grazing intersection is but one of many that must be recognized. Not only is the intersection itself important, but the *slopes* of the two curves at the intersection must be appropriate. Furthermore, the general curvature and location of the $KG(j\omega)$ locus on the Lm-Ang plane with respect to the lines of M and N are of *interest for all frequencies*. The reader can easily demonstrate the importance of this broader view by referring to the loci of Figures 7·1 and 7·2.

10 Reshaping the $G(ju)$ Locus on the Lm-Ang Plane

A direct procedure for altering the shape of the $G(ju)$ contour for a given system is to place additional dynamic elements appropriately inside the loop. These elements are to have a transfer function which will give the desired location and shape to the resulting system locus as it crosses the M and N contours on the Lm-Ang chart. Sometimes the characteristics required of the elements become apparent from an observation of the shape of the Lm and Ang curves of the original system plotted as a function of log u, as for example in Figure 5. This characteristic may become apparent prior to plotting the Lm-Ang graph. However, it is often dangerous to rely wholly on this method to guide the entire synthesis, because the relative curvatures of the M contour and the $G(ju)$ contour on the Lm-Ang chart permit errors in the Lm K which, while small in decibels, are large numerically. Too often guesswork replaces accurate synthesis unless care is taken during the final preparation of the charts. Since the likely extent of these errors can rarely be detected when working with the log modulus and angle curves plotted with respect to the log u, the only sound basis for synthesis is to carry the study through the preparation of the Lm-Ang chart. Frequently, small variations in curvature of the original G contour on the Lm G-Ang plane may be obscured by inaccurate plotting. These variations often prevent careful adjustment of the relative shape of the compensating functions necessary to obtain the best results. Reference to the curves of Figure 2 will show that in the region near the resonant frequency, the mere substitution of the log modulus asymptote values of the function for the true log modulus values will lead to gross inaccuracies. However, the asymptotes are very useful for getting a quick survey of the problem preparatory to an accurate study.

The gist of the technique for reshaping the G locus using the logarithmic asymptote may be explained by reference to the simple illustration of Figure 16. Consider the transfer function $1/(ju)^2$. It represents a system having only a second-order pole. It is shown plotted as the line oa in Figure 16a. The corresponding phase curve for this function is the straight line at -180 degrees phase for all values of u. When these data are transferred to the Lm-Ang plane in Figure 16b, the locus is the straight line at an angle of -180 degrees. No value of gain K can be selected for this system which will permit a tangency between the locus fg and an M_p contour. The phase margin is zero and the gain margin cannot be defined.

The objective is now to reshape the G locus so that it will bulge to the right around a selected M contour in the Lm-Ang plane.   Let the selected M contour be shown as M in Figure 16b.   The reshaping can be accomplished by inserting a function in series with $G(ju)$ which will introduce phase lead to the G function in the region where its magnitude ranges from about 14 decibels to about -6 decibels.   Without resorting to quantitative numbers, it should be apparent that a new modulus curve obc and a new phase curve for the positive bulge dge can be formed to

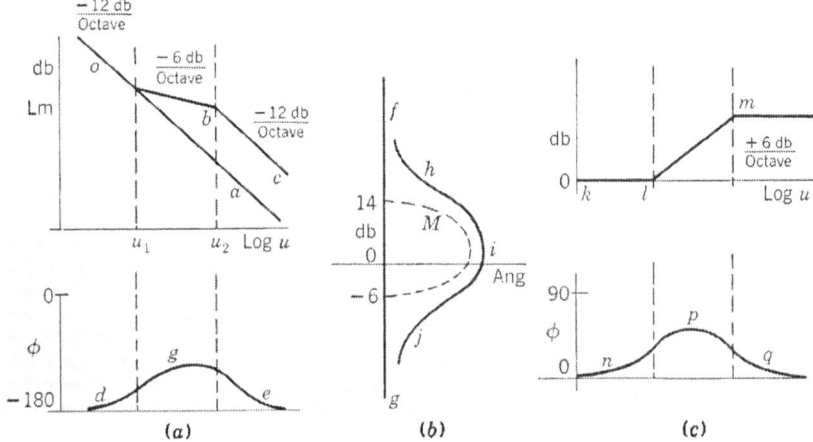

FIGURE 16.   Reshaping the G function.

give the new system locus hij.   This new locus then has the properties which permit the setting of a gain K_1 for a system that will be stable to the desired degree and have the velocity constant of infinity.   Figure 16c shows the G function required of the compensation equipment.   The modulus curve klm and the phase curve npq represent, respectively, the magnitude and angle difference between the original G function vector locus and the new vector locus.   The phase margin can be about 50 degrees if u_2 is $10u_1$, but the gain margin cannot be defined.

As another illustration of the usefulness of a quick but approximate asymptote study, consider the system whose Lm versus log u and phase versus log u plots are shown on Figure 17a.   These plots are representative of a system defined by a single-order pole and a first-order lag such that $G(ju) = (ju)^{-1}[ju + 1]^{-1}$.   The system can have a limited value K for a given M_p criterion.   Consequently, the velocity constant K_v is limited.

If it is assumed desirable to make the velocity constant infinite, the break appearing in Figure 17a at the frequency u_2 could be completely eliminated by making the modulus locus a straight line of −12 decibels per octave. The treatment would then be identical with the previous example, and the question of stability would require consideration. A more enlightened approach to the problem of obtaining an infinite

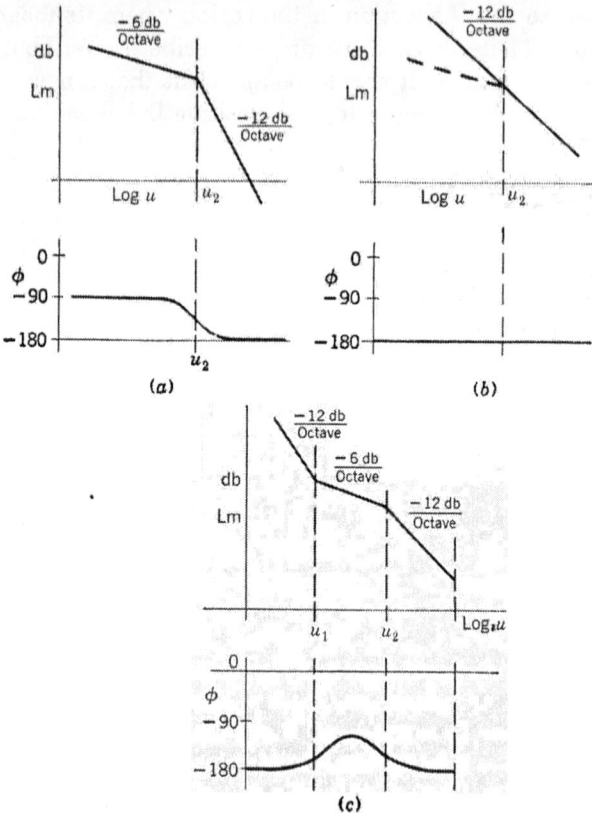

FIGURE 17. Reshaping the G function.

velocity constant and at the same time obtaining a good measure of stability for the closed-loop system would be to allow a segment of the modulus locus to continue to have a slope −6 decibels per octave, as shown in Figure 17c. This segment of −6 decibels per octave slope lying between the frequencies u_1 and u_2 gives the necessary positive phase bulge to accomplish the adjustment indicated in Figure 16b.

It is of interest to contrast the philosophy behind these two examples. The first example involved the improvement of a system by means of an auxiliary device that introduced positive phase shift; the second example accomplished identically the same result by using an auxiliary device that gave appropriate negative phase shift. The aim of synthesis in using the modulus and phase curves jointly with the Lm-Ang contour chart is to pick consistent techniques which are now available for altering these shapes over any portion of the frequency spectrum.

11 Reshaping the $G(ju)$ Locus Using Passive Networks

To Give Improved Low-Frequency Performance. The so-called undercompensated integral circuit of Figure 18 is often used to increase

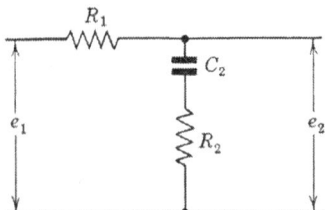

FIGURE 18. Passive network for approximating integral control.

the velocity constant K_v. This circuit has the transfer function

$$\frac{E_2}{E_1}(j\omega) = \frac{1 + j\omega\tau_i}{1 + j\omega\alpha_i\tau_i} \tag{59}$$

or, in dimensionless form,

$$\frac{E_2}{E_1}(ju) = \frac{1 + ju}{1 + j\alpha_i u} = G_i(ju) \tag{60}$$

where

$$\left.\begin{aligned}\alpha_i &= \frac{R_1 + R_2}{R_2}\\[2mm]\tau_i &= R_2 C\end{aligned}\right\} \tag{61}$$

For which the Lm and Arg equations become

$$\text{Lm } G_i(ju) = \text{Lm } (ju + 1) - \text{Lm } (ju\alpha_i + 1) \tag{62}$$

$$\text{Arg } G_i(ju) = \tan^{-1} u - \tan^{-1} \alpha_i u \tag{63}$$

The graph of Equations 62 and 63 are a parametric family of curves for discrete values of the constant α_i similar to those shown in Figure 19. This circuit attenuates by the factor α_i all signals passing through the cascade system at frequencies much above $u = 1$ so that the entire high-frequency portion of the Lm-Ang contour of the original function is translated downward. Unfortunately a negative phase occurs in the frequency region between $u = 1/\alpha_i$ and $u = 1$. The phase shift, even at the break frequencies 1 and $1/\alpha_i$, is often appreciable. The maximum phase shift occurs at the geometric mean of these two frequencies. The phase shift may tend to translate the contour toward regions of less stability than can be tolerated even though the attenuation is moving it down to the region of increased stability. If the element in the under-compensated integral circuit is properly selected so that the phase shift

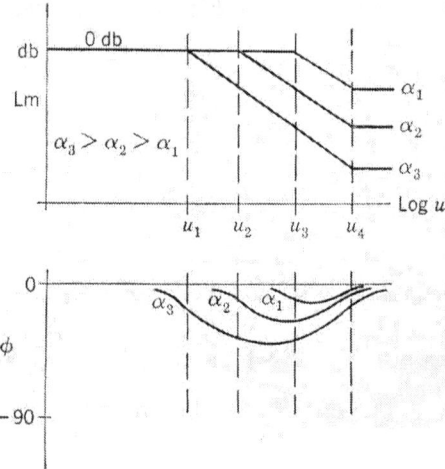

FIGURE 19.   Lm and Ang versus log u for passive integral network.

is located appropriately in the frequency range of the original transfer function, these opposing effects can be minimized to the extent that the magnitude of K in the composite system can be increased almost by the magnitude of α_i over that of the uncompensated system.

The shape of the modulus and phase curves for the $G(ju)$ is shown by the lines abc in Figure 20. When the undercompensated integral function $G_i(ju)$ is introduced, the composite function $G(ju)G_i(ju)$ modulus and phase curves become as shown by the lines ade of Figure 20. The entire portion of the composite curve beyond the second break point at $u = u_2$ is shifted downward by Lm α_i decibels. This downward shift is the adjustment of the locus sought in this synthesis. The composite argument curve must accept the negative phase bulge caused by the network designed to accomplish the attenuation. Therefore the problem of obtaining the best location along the frequency spectrum for the compensating network involves a compromise which must be resolved by trial and error.

The Lm-Ang chart for an undercompensated integral in cascade with the original system is shown in Figure 21. After the addition of the undercompensated integral control, two different resonant frequencies are often possible for different values of K, both conditions satisfying the specification that $M = 2.28$ decibels. These two frequencies are illustr ted as u_{r1} and u_{r2} in Figure 21. Experience in design shows that the low-frequency resonance u_{r2} must be kept from occurring not only by maintaining a satisfactorily high value for K but also by a sufficient

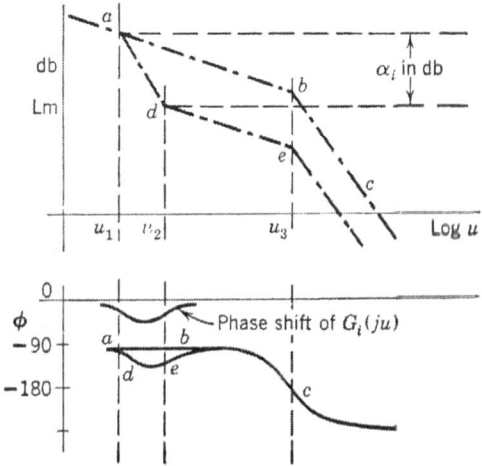

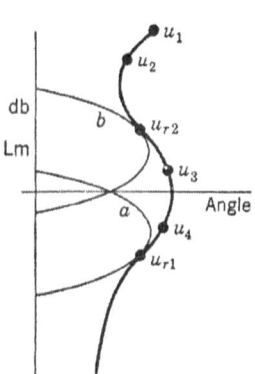

FIGURE 20.   Integral network applied to a typical system.

FIGURE 21.   Illustrating multiple choice of gain setting.

margin of safety in the adjustment of the system constants to prevent the closed loop from operating at this low frequency should the constants of the components change with age or by malfunction. This statement will be justified if the reader calculates the transient response of the system. Generally, the transient response will be satisfactory when the value of K corresponds to the high-frequency resonance u_{r1}, whereas when the value of K permits the low-frequency resonance u_{r2} the system tends to be very sluggish and relatively useless.

To Give Improved High-Frequency Performance. A system may often be required to respond to frequency components of data in the input signal higher than can be accomplished if K is selected merely by closing the loop and adjusting for $M = 2.28$ decibels. Alternatively the phase of θ_o/θ_i over a given frequency band may have to be small.

Such requirements impose a problem of synthesis involving the addition of compensation networks that exhibit positive phase shifts over portions of the frequency range to widen the band of frequency response and increase K commensurate with a given stability criteria.

One network which will accomplish this form of compensation is shown in Figure 22. It has the transfer functions.

$$\frac{E_2}{E_1}(j\omega) = KG_\ell(j\omega) = \frac{1}{\alpha_\ell}\frac{1 + j\alpha_\ell\tau_\ell\omega}{1 + j\tau_\ell\omega} \tag{64}$$

$$\frac{E_2}{E_1}(ju) = K_uG_\ell(ju) = \frac{1}{\alpha_\ell}\left[\frac{1 + j\alpha_\ell u}{1 + ju}\right] \tag{65}$$

where

$$\left.\begin{aligned}\alpha_\ell &= \frac{R_1 + R_2}{R_2}\\[2mm]\tau_l &= \frac{R_1R_2C}{R_1 + R_2}\end{aligned}\right\} \tag{66}$$

The log modulus and argument equations are

$$\text{Lm } G_\ell(ju) = \text{Lm }(ju\alpha_\ell + 1) - \text{Lm }(ju + 1) \tag{67}$$

$$\text{Arg } G_\ell(ju) = \tan^{-1}\alpha_\ell u - \tan^{-1} u \tag{68}$$

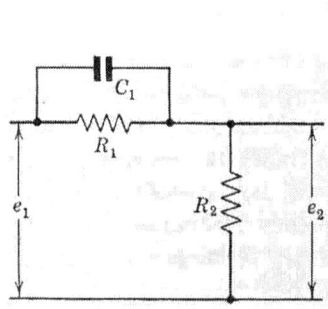

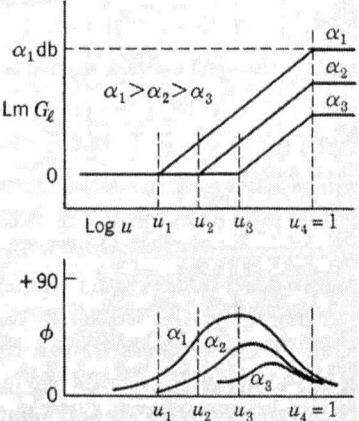

FIGURE 22. Passive lead network giving high gain and positive phase shift at high frequency.

FIGURE 23. Lm and angle versus log u graphs of lead network.

The Lm and Arg graphs of Equations 67 and 68 are given in Figure 23. Again there is a parametric family of curves for the constant α_ℓ. If the lower break frequency $1/\alpha_\ell$ of the Lm curve for the compensating network is adjusted to occur near the first break in the Lm curve of the original function $G(ju)$, the composite modulus and argument curves of $G(ju)G_\ell(ju)$ appear as in Figure 24. The curves *oab* represent the original system. Curves *ocd* show the effect of adding the compensating network. The positive phase contribution of the compensating system, shown as curve *e*, offsets the high negative phase shift of the original system function for a limited frequency range as shown by the composite phase curve. When the curves *ocd* of Figure 24 are used to form a

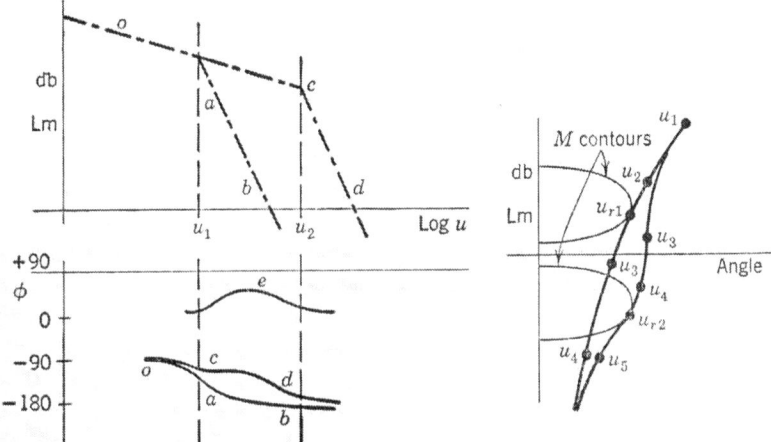

FIGURE 24. Lead network for the improvement of system performance.

FIGURE 25. Reshaping the G locus by lead control.

Lm-Ang chart, the M contour selected for the adjustment of K may be moved several decibels in a negative direction compared with the location of the former uncompensated system before a tangency occurs as shown in Figure 25. The resonant condition now occurs at a value of frequency u_{r2}, higher than the frequency u_{r1} originally obtained. The band of frequency within which θ_o/θ_i is approximately unity and within which Ang θ_o/θ_i is small is therefore widened. The gain K is increased. Here, as with the integral network, the exact location of the compensating network along the frequency axis is determined by experience.

12   Reshaping the $G(ju)$ Function by the Insertion of Feedback Functions

Frequently another method is used for providing compensation to the transfer function of a closed-loop dynamical system. A minor feedback loop is introduced around certain portions of the apparatus. The log modulus method for performing the synthesis study can still be applied to this problem, but special techniques must be employed to provide an accurate graphical study.

The gist of this problem can be clarified by reference to Figure 26, where a minor loop containing the elements $K_m G_m$ and $K_t G_t$ exists within the main loop. The procedure is first to consider the problem of minor

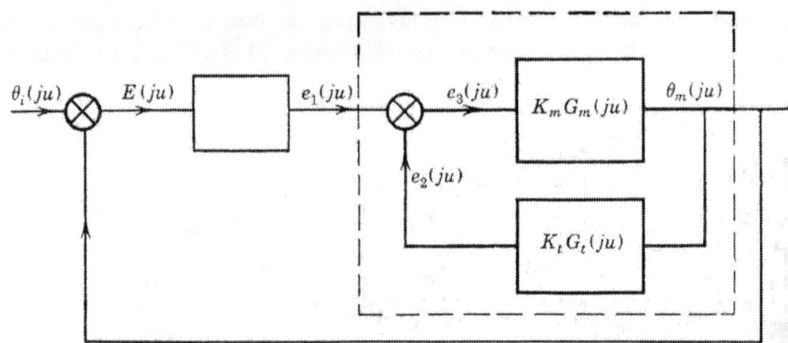

FIGURE 26. Multiple loop block diagram.

loop synthesis by performing certain algebraic and graphical manipulations on the minor loop transfer function. To make this work clearer, the minor loop is shown separately in Figure 27. Next, this loop is assumed to be opened at the error-measuring means and a transfer function e_2/e_3 is formed for the series connection of the two dynamic components. This transfer function is then prepared as a locus on the Lm-Ang plane. The minor loop is then closed for a specific M_p value and the response e_1/e_2 is obtained. All the steps follow the straight-forward procedure thus far given for closed-loop synthesis, except that

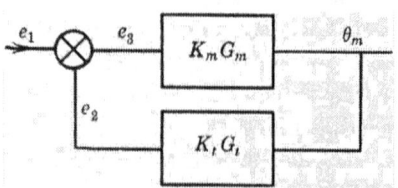

FIGURE 27. System with tachometric feedback.

new criteria now establish the value of M_p. The quantity e_1/e_2 is not the quantity explicitly desired. The quantity θ_m/e_1 can be derived from the quantity e_2/e_1 by multiplying e_2/e_1 by a modification factor. The minor loop may then be considered as a single equivalent block, as embraced by the dotted lines of Figure 26. The procedure may be clear in terms of the action to be taken, but the technique for executing the steps is not simple. A detailed description of the method follows.

If the dynamical element in the feedback path of the closed-loop system of Figure 27 has the transfer function $K_t G_t(ju)$, whereas the elements in the direct path are defined by $K_m G_m(ju)$, the relation for the minor loop or equivalent block of Figure 26 is

$$\frac{\theta_m}{e_1}(ju) = \frac{K_m G_m(ju)}{1 + K_m G_m(ju) K_t G_t(ju)} \tag{69}$$

By multiplying and dividing by $K_t G_t(ju)$, this function may be put into a form $A/(1 + A)$, giving

$$\frac{\theta_m}{e_1}(ju) = \left[\frac{1}{K_t G_t(ju)}\right]\left[\frac{K_m G_m(ju) K_t G_t(ju)}{1 + K_m G_m(ju) K_t G_t(ju)}\right] \tag{70}$$

Many different procedures may be used to prepare the logarithmic graphs for transfer functions which permit multiple loop synthesis studies. The complexity of the problem renders a general treatment somewhat indefinite, whereas the study of a typically difficult problem becomes too tedious and long to present. As a simplified example, consider that a tachometer is used to form a feedback loop around an ideal electric motor as shown in Figure 27. The electric motor is specifically defined by the transfer function

$$\frac{\theta_m}{e_3}(ju) = K_m G_m(ju) = K_m \frac{1}{(ju)^2} \tag{71}$$

The tachometer is defined by the transfer function

$$\frac{e_2}{\theta_m}(ju) = K_t G_t(ju) = ju K_t \tag{72}$$

The cascade transfer function formed from Equations 71 and 72 becomes

$$\frac{e_2}{e_3}(ju) = K_m G_m(ju) K_t G_t(ju) = K_m K_t \frac{1}{ju} \tag{73}$$

This cascade transfer function may now be treated mathematically and graphically as has been illustrated in previous examples. Figure 28 shows the individual modulus and angle graph for the cascade transfer function given in Equation 73. When the Lm-Ang chart is prepared for the cascade transfer function of Equation 73, the locus becomes a straight line along the constant angle value of -90 degrees, as shown in Figure 29. This locus crosses only M contour values less than zero decibels and N contour values less than -90 degrees. When actual values for the magnitude and phase e_2/e_3 are read from the Lm-Ang chart, the resulting curves for Lm e_2/e_1 and Ang e_2/e_1 appear in Figure 30.

The modulus and argument curves plotted in Figure 30 represent a mathematical function of the form $(ju + 1)^{-1}$, which, incidentally, is

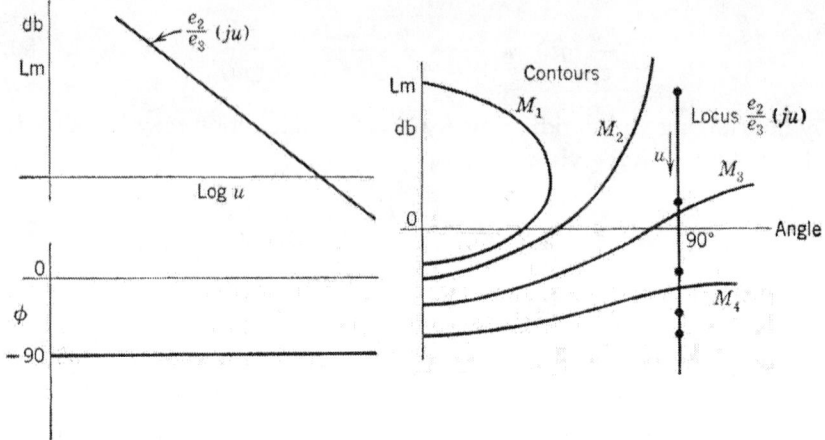

FIGURE 28.   Lm and Ang versus log u for $\dfrac{e_2}{e_3} (ju)$.

FIGURE 29.   Lm-Ang chart for $\dfrac{e_2}{e_3} (ju)$.

easily derived for this particular problem because of its simplified nature.   For example,

$$\frac{e_2}{e_1} (ju) = \frac{K_m K_t \dfrac{1}{ju}}{1 + K_m K_t \dfrac{1}{ju}} \tag{74}$$

$$= \frac{1}{ju \dfrac{1}{K_m K_t} + 1} \tag{75}$$

Equation 75 verifies the shape of the curves in Figure 30.
     The quantity really desired is

$$\frac{\theta_m}{e_1} (ju) = \frac{\theta_m}{e_2} (ju) \frac{e_2}{e_1} (ju) \tag{76}$$

It may be obtained by altering the graph of Figure 30 by the reciprocal of the transfer function defining the tachometer.   This transfer function

$$\frac{\theta_m}{e_2} (ju) = \frac{1}{K_t(ju)} \tag{77}$$

is shown as Figure 31.   The two loci, Figures 30 and 31, merge to give
the locus shown as Figure 32.   The modulus locus in Figure 32 is nothing

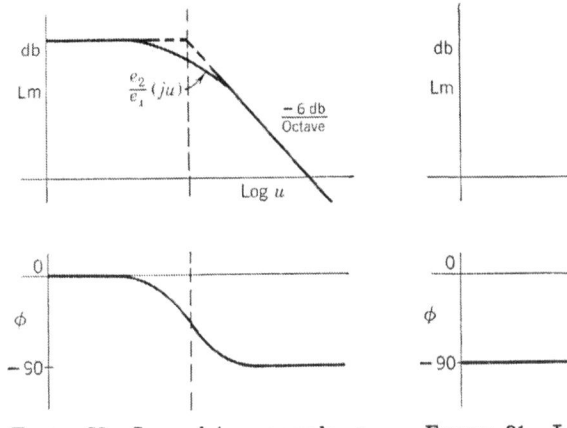

FIGURE 30.   Lm and Ang versus log u
for $\dfrac{e_2}{e_1}(ju)$.

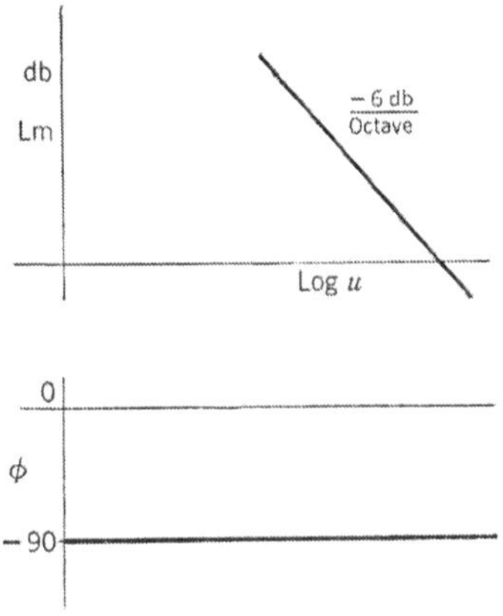

FIGURE 31.   Lm and Ang versus
log u for $\dfrac{\theta_m}{e_2}(ju)$.

more than a -6 decibels per octave slope added to the slopes of the
modulus asymptote curve of Figure 30.   An angle of -90 degrees is

added to the phase curve of Figure 30 over its entire frequency
range. The location of the break
point and the corrections to the
asymptote to the true curve for
θ_m/e_1 in this region of frequency
are not altered. However, in the
process of merging the two functions, the constant Lm $(K_m K_t)^{-1}$
must be considered when setting
the Lm scale for the overall composite function of the motor tachometer loop.

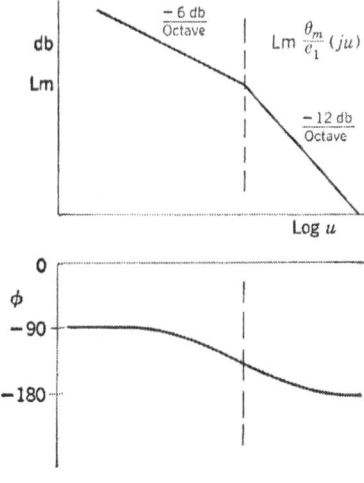

    The problem chosen for the pre-
vious illustration is so simple that
it may impair and obscure the true
importance of the detailed procedure necessary to carry out the
solution of servomechanism synthesis problems when multiple

FIGURE 32.   Lm and Ang versus log u
for $\dfrac{\theta_m}{e_1}(ju)$.

loops are involved. For this reason, the designer must consider the situation which arises if the transfer functions of the components found in both the direct and the feedback paths are sufficiently complicated to cause a locus for the quantity Z/W shown in Figure 33.

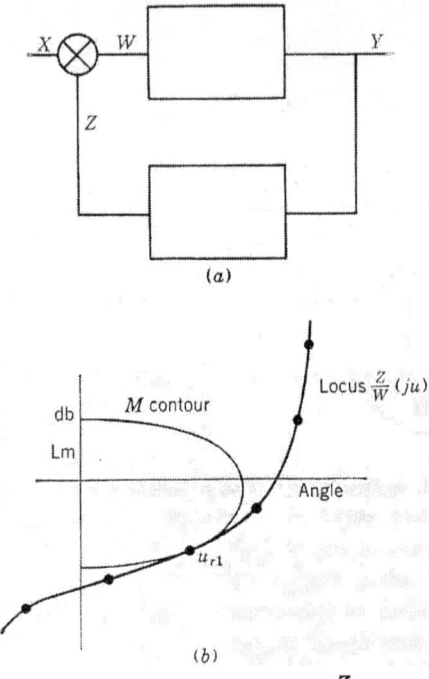

Figure 33.   Lm-Ang chart for $\dfrac{Z}{W}\,(ju)$.

The gain of the loop as shown in Figure 33 cannot be increased to extremely large values without the loop becoming oscillatory. A basis for the selection of M_p, which establishes the performance of the minor loop now being closed and adjusted, is required. Therefore, some criterion must be accepted for choosing the degree of stability that should be present in the minor loop. This must be done before the value of gain for the main loop is established. Another problem that makes the adjustment somewhat difficult relates to the various fractions of the loop gain which may be in the forward or the feedback paths. In other words, it is not possible always to locate the total gain for the loop with respect to any single component in the loop. Specific parts of the minor loop gain may necessarily be related to specific blocks in the loop. Furthermore, this problem gets to be important when considered for large chemical plants or large turbo electric stations. In particular, the chemical process may dictate a specific gain for a specific element. Here many minor loops may be encountered. Such studies become rather momentous engineering enterprises. Nevertheless, a clearly defined approach to this problem has been cited even though the solution of a specific problem is beyond the scope of this book.

One important problem to consider when adjusting minor loops is to take care that the various components do not saturate when large signals circulate in the minor loop. This situation can often arise when the minor loop stability is consistent with a much larger value of M_p than that for overall θ_o/θ_i performance. The method for closing the minor loop is a direct one, but the procedure has not been sufficiently well explored to warrant the presentation of generalizations. The M value of the minor loop must be carefully considered in terms of the behavior of the minor loop relative to the performance of the major loop.

Granting the difficulties of selecting suitable M_p values for a minor loop, a value of M_p is chosen so that the resonance conditions of the minor loop are not too violent. The value of loop sensitivity K_{minor} is then adjusted by making the specific M_p contour in Figure 33 tangent to the transfer function locus Z/W. The specific value of K_{minor} is then read directly from the Lm-Ang chart. Next the modulus and angle graphs of Z/X versus log ω are formed for this minor loop. The procedure is the same as outlined in the previous example. These modulus and angle curves are shown in Figure 34. The resonant tendencies present in the minor loop are made prominent in the graph of Z/X. The reciprocal function Y/Z for the dynamical element in the feedback path is now merged graphically with the values plotted in Figure 34. The overall transfer function Y/X is obtained as in Figure 35. Usually by the time this many graphical operations have been performed, the asymptote values for the resulting modulus function are completely missing and often not readily found. This is not a serious drawback, for by this time the asymptote approximation is not important to the solution.

The graph in Figure 35 is finally combined with whatever other transfer functions are in cascade with the elements defined by Y/X making up the closed loop for the system. The resulting Lm and Ang graphs are again transferred to the Lm-Ang plane as shown in Figure 36. This contour is adjusted to have a tangency with a prescribed M contour to set the value for the overall K of the system. The overall K must be established without altering the gain of any minor loop. If necessary, other compensation elements may be added to the major loop after minor loops have been closed and adjusted.

Since the locus shown in Figure 35 indicates the total system performance of the dynamical elements in both the feedforward and feed-

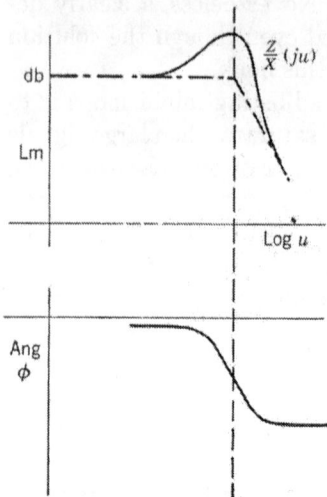

Figure 34. Lm and Ang versus
$\log u$ of $\dfrac{Z}{X}(ju)$.

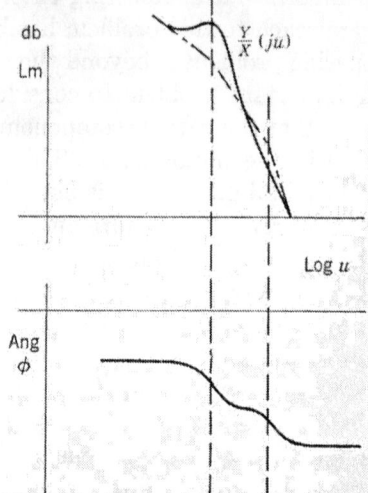

Figure 35. Lm and Ang versus log
u of $\dfrac{Y}{X}(ju)$.

back path, the modulus and angle curves must exhibit the prominent dynamical features of both paths. The curves of Figure 35 can be shaped in any manner which preserves their realizability. They can be altered by all the synthesis techniques thus far treated in the book. Furthermore, a completely generalized approach to the problem can be made which permits the location of the specific mathematical function in specific boxes to create poles and zeros at definite places at the complex plane. This subject could be a complete treatment in itself. Network synthesis theorems can be brought into play to establish ladder structures for the dynamical hardware within the boxes.[61, 62]

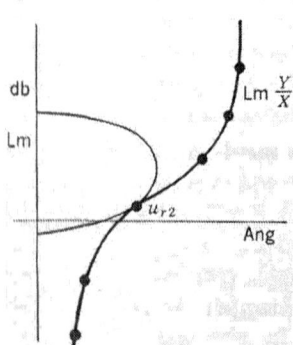

Figure 36. Lm-Ang chart for
$\dfrac{Y}{X}(ju)$.

It is important to note that, as the designer goes farther into the problem of synthesis, using minor loops for altering loci shapes, the necessary mathematical tools become scarce.

Likewise, the complete generalization which tends to exist in this purely mathematical approach to synthesis leads to abstractions which, only in few instances, permit translation into the engineering language. Complicated techniques using lattice structures, matrices, and expansion of representation of physical equipment by ladder structures, and the insertion of dissipative function tend to become only techniques of organization.

13 Illustrative Examples

It has been stated previously that the material presented in this chapter introduces no new principle. It represents merely a different method from that presented in Chapter 7 for accomplishing a particular result which, because of a systematization of method, lends itself to a quick exploration of the problem. To illustrate these facts, certain problems solved in Chapter 7 using polar plots are again solved using the methods of this chapter. The same problem is treated rather than a new one, specifically to aid the reader in comparing the two techniques. Four examples are given: (1) a simple system with ideal integral control, (2) the motor generator with a passive integral network added in cascade, (3) the motor generator with a passive lead network added in cascade, and (4) tachometric feedback in parallel with a motor having no friction. In this example, certain short-cut procedures involving the asymptotes of the functions, the break frequencies, and the slopes are emphasized.

Example 1. Ideal Integral Control (Chapter 7, Equation 32). The procedure is, first, to plot the asymptotic approximation for the principal part of the system, namely $K/ju(ju + 1)$ with $K = 1$, and, second, to plot the corrected composite modulus and phase curves. Figure 37 shows the result of these steps as curves ADE and FGH, respectively. If the solution from Chapter 7 had not been available, the loop would first be closed without integral control in order to establish a basis for criteria on which to select the integral time constant. This step would lead to curve A of Figure 38 where the tangency of curve B with curve A confirms the initial work of Chapter 7. In this problem, the time constant τ_i is to be selected to result in an overall G function whose Lm-Ang curve would yield the desired shape with relation to the M contour on the M-N chart of Figure 8.

Ideal integral control added to this system makes possible the change in the slope of part of the line AB from minus 6 decibels per octave to minus 12 decibels per octave in the low-frequency region. The presence of a second-order pole in the overall $G(ju)$ for $u = 0$ established an initial minus 12 decibels per octave slope. The introduction of *integral control*, however, must be done in a way that permits sufficient *phase margin* for system operation with a reasonable M_p value. A poor choice of the integral circuit parameters may make it impossible to locate properly the Lm-Ang curve with the desired M_p contour of the M-N chart of Figure 8.

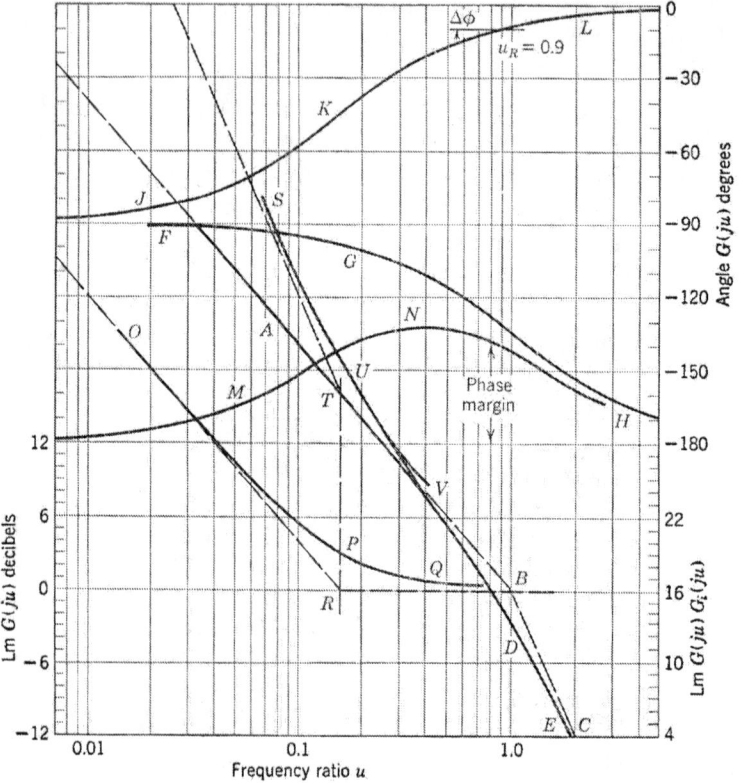

Figure 37. Lm $G(ju)$ and Ang $G(ju)$ versus log u for Example 1.

Criteria for choosing the integral time constant were suggested in Chapter 7, Equation 7·38. They would normally be applicable here also. The 10-degree negative phase shift at a frequency $u = 0.9$ selected as a means of calculating the integral system parameters did not permit $M_p = 1.3$ for the system. The experience gained in Chapter 7 indicates that a smaller value of phase shift should be chosen as a first approximation. However, the criterion of 10 degree phase shift will still be used to find the integral system constants in order to compare the two methods. The parameters for the integral network are found in Figure 37 by sliding a phase template, computed * for Ang $[ju + 1]^{-1}$ and shaped like curve JKL, along the frequency axis until the value $\Delta\phi$ is 10 degrees at the frequency $u = 0.9$. The phase curve JKL is then added to the original system phase curve FGH to give the composite phase curve MNH for the Ang $G(ju)$, Equation 7·40, for the overall system.

Since the shape of $G_i(ju)$ is known, the value for α_i locates the Lm $G_i(ju)$ curve shown as OPQ. The asymptote approximation curve ORQ

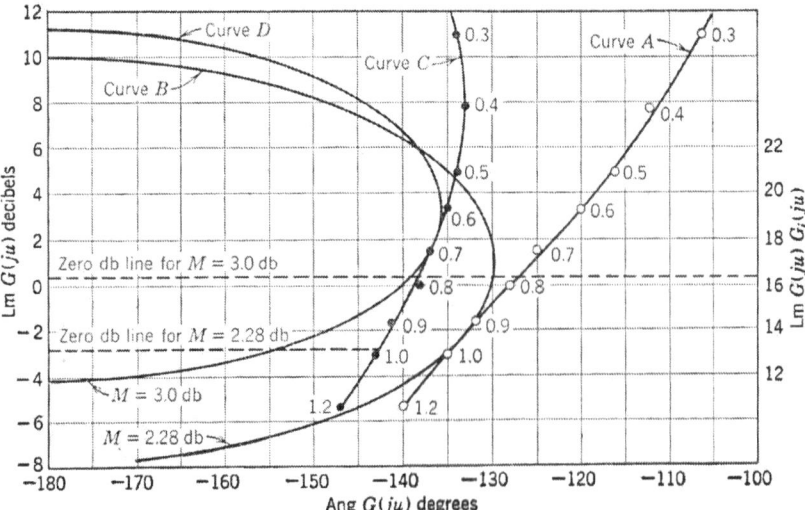

FIGURE 38.   Lm $G(ju)$ versus Ang $G(ju)$ for Example 1.

is established once the break frequency $u = 0.155$ is found. The frequency $u = 0.155$ is the reciprocal of the constant $\alpha_i = 6.5$ (Equation 7·37) required for $\Delta\phi$ to be 10 degrees at $u = 0.9$. Above this frequency the integral element will have but little effect on the original system or on the asymptote ABC. The asymptote approximation to the composite system is curve $STBC$. The curve $SUVDE$ is the true modulus, being the sum of curves OPQ and ADE.

As soon as the graphs of Figure 37 are ready, the general observation that the *phase margin* is about 40 degrees can be made. However, the mere existence of a 40-degree *phase margin* does not insure that satisfactory performance can be obtained for this system. The two curves $SUVDE$ and MNH must be transferred to the Lm-Ang plane in order to finish the study with accuracy.

* This is merely a quick way to represent Ang $\left(1 + \dfrac{1}{ju}\right)$.

Curve A, Figure 38, is the Lm-Ang plot of $[ju(ju + 1)]^{-1}$. The contour for $M_p = 2.28$ decibels is curve B. Curve C shows the Lm-Ang plot of the overall system $G(ju)$ for $\alpha_i = 6.5$. An $M_p = 2.28$ decibel contour can never lie to the left of curve C. Therefore no value of gain K can establish an $M_p = 1.3$ for the particular value of integral constant $\alpha_i = 6.5$, as was shown in Chapter 7. Superposing curve C on

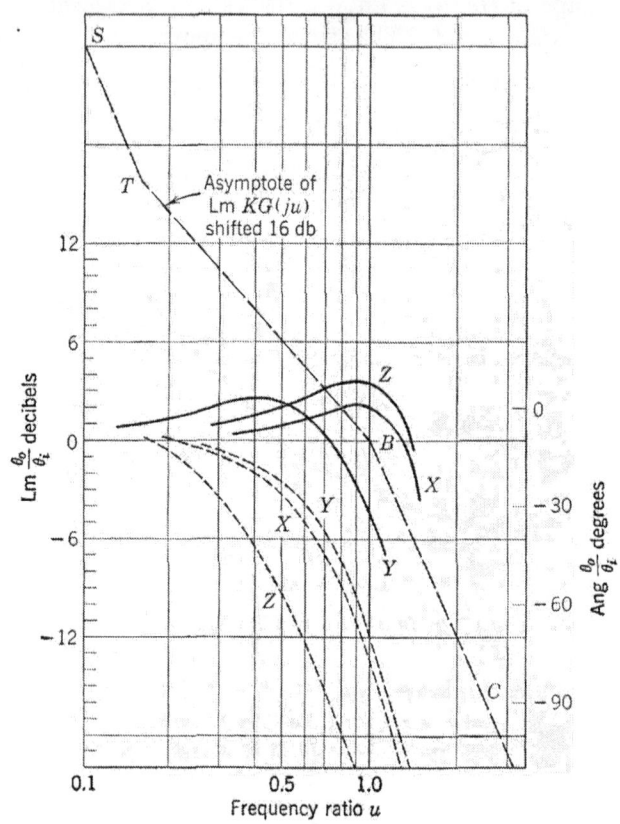

FIGURE 39.   Lm of θ_o/θ_i versus log u for Example 1.

the M-N contour chart, Figure 8, gives the overall performance of the system. Table 7·1 tabulates the essential data of this study for $M_p = 1.4$.

Figure 38 shows the solution to the problem for the value $\alpha_i = 6.5$ and for an $M_p = 3$ decibels. The selection of $M_p = 3$ decibels does not represent a unique solution. It is used only to show how the problem is completed. The steepness of curve C indicates that the system resonant frequency increases more rapidly as gain is increased now that

integral control is added.   The smallest M_p that will fall within the
boundary of curve C gives a resonant frequency $u_R = 0.4$.

Figure 39 illustrates the significance of M_p upon the frequency response of the system.   Curves X show magnitude and phase for θ_o/θ_i
of the original system for $M_p = 2.28$.   Curves Y are for the smallest
value of M_p obtainable for the overall system, and show $u_R = 0.4$.
Curves Z show that, by tolerating an $M_p = 3.8$ decibels, the band width
of the overall system is substantially the same as that for the original
system.   Thus integral control narrows the frequency band of operation
of the system when a given M_p is maintained even though the increase
in K_v is obtained.

Example 2.   Passive Integral Network.   The motor generator system
described in Chapter 5, Figure 5·9, has the transfer function (Equation
7·44)

$$G(ju) = \frac{1}{ju(0.086ju + 1)(1.61ju + 1)(0.61ju + 1)} \tag{78}$$

The critical frequencies, namely, the reciprocal values of the time constants, are $u_1 = 0.62$, $u_2 = 1.63$, and $u_3 = 11.7$.   Curve A, Figure 40,
is the graph of the asymptote representation of Lm $G(ju)$.   Curve B
is the graph of the true function Lm $G(ju)$.   Curve C shows the angle of
$G(ju)$.

Prior to making a design study of the motor generator system, where
integral or lead networks are introduced, the loop is first closed using
control signals at the generator fields proportional to error.   This
procedure determines the closed-loop performance of the basic system.
The Lm-Ang curve of this G function can then be examined with relation
to the M contour on the M-N chart in order to indicate the properties
of the auxiliary equipment to give the desired shape for the overall
Lm-Ang curve.

When the magnitude and angle data of Figure 40 are transferred to
the Lm-Ang plane, to study the closed-loop prior to the insertion of compensation, the result is curve X of Figure 41.   The contour for $M_p = $
2.28 decibels, shown as curve Y, is made tangent with the $G(ju)$ function
locus.   For the particular gain adjustment corresponding to the location
of curve Y, the closed-loop system has a dimensionless gain K_u of minus
5.7 decibels or the value 0.52, a velocity constant K_v of 31.6 seconds^{-1},
a dimensionless resonant frequency u_r of 0.45, and a resonant frequency
ω_r of 27.2 radians per second.   The value of the velocity constant K_v
which would cause sustained oscillation is found to be 129 seconds^{-1}
by observing that the magnitude of Lm $G(ju)$ is minus 6.5 decibels when
the phase lag is 180 degrees (see point Z).   The dimensionless gain for

sustained oscillation is therefore 6.5 decibels, and the dimensionless frequency u_R is approximately unity.

The vector ratio θ_o/θ_i is found for this system by superposing the curves of Figure 41 appropriately on the M-N contour chart. Curves D

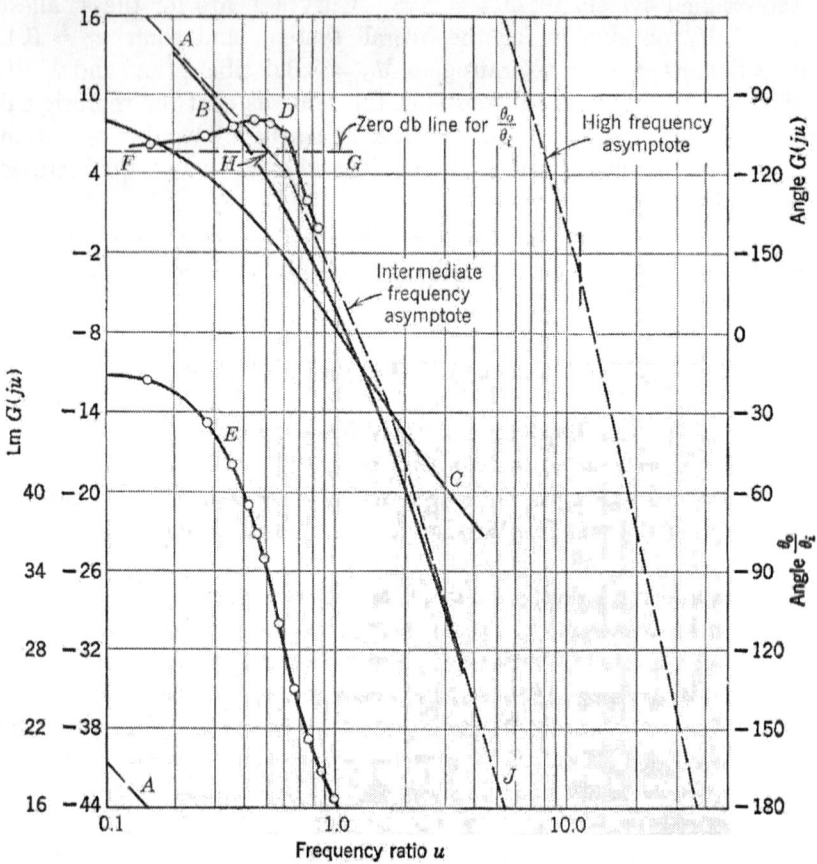

FIGURE 40.   Lm $G(ju)$ and Ang $G(ju)$ versus log u for Example 2.

and E of Figure 40 show the magnitude and phase response respectively for $M_p = 2.28$ decibels. The line FG is the zero decibel reference for θ_o/θ_i shown by curve D. It will be noted that FG is drawn at 5.7 decibels on the $G(ju)$ scale. This procedure then gives FHJ as an asymptotic approximation to θ_o/θ_i and follows from the fact that *for a servomechanism $KG/(1 + KG)$ is approximately zero decibels at low frequencies and KG decibels at high frequencies.* Thus, when a line is drawn at zero decibels on the Lm KG versus log u diagram it will represent the low-frequency asymptote response for θ_o/θ_i up to the frequency where it intersects the KG asymptote. For frequencies above this intersection the KG and the θ_o/θ_i asymptotes superpose. The asymptote FHJ represents this procedure and the location of FG at 5.7 decibels on Figure 40 serves to rescale the asymptote AHJ from Lm G to Lm KG.

A passive network can now be used to increase the velocity constant K_v of the basic motor generator system. The network of Figure 7·14 will again be used with the intention of increasing the gain for low-frequency operation by about a factor of 20 decibels. This requires an integral network with an $\alpha_i \cong 10$. In Chapter 7, a discussion was

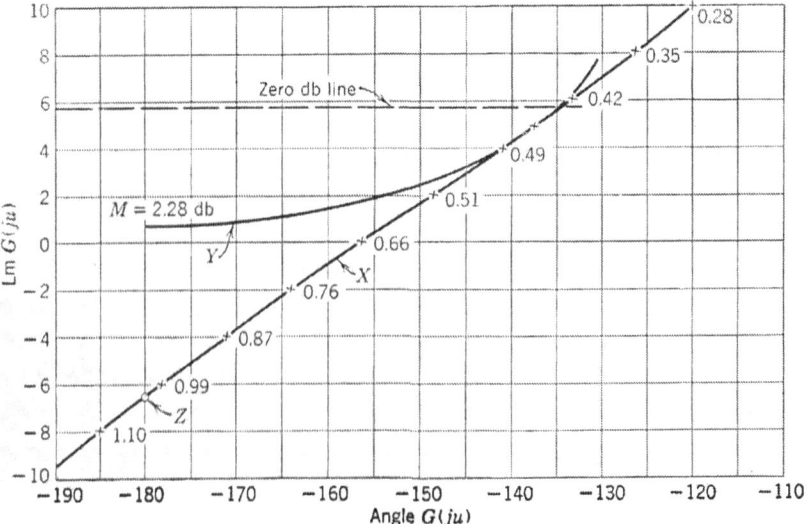

FIGURE 41.   Lm $G(ju)$ versus Ang $G(ju)$ for Example 2.

presented which led to a selection of integral time constant that would cause the integral network to contribute a phase lag of about 10 degrees at the resonant frequency when the loop was closed without compensation. In the adjustment selected for this particular problem, about 7 degrees phase lag at a frequency $u \cong 0.4$ is used to establish the influence of the integral circuit at the higher frequencies. Figure 42 shows the various curves which were constructed to give the overall system function.

The procedure for the construction of Figure 42 is as follows:

The modulus asymptote of the uncompensated system is redrawn as curve $ABCDE$ from Figure 40. The angle curve is redrawn as curve F.

The phase curve of the integral network with $\alpha_i = 10$ but with no specific time constant τ_i has the shape G, being constructed from curves

H and K for the lower and upper break frequencies $1/10\tau_i$ and $1/\tau_i$, respectively (see Figure 19). The composite phase curve L is ob-

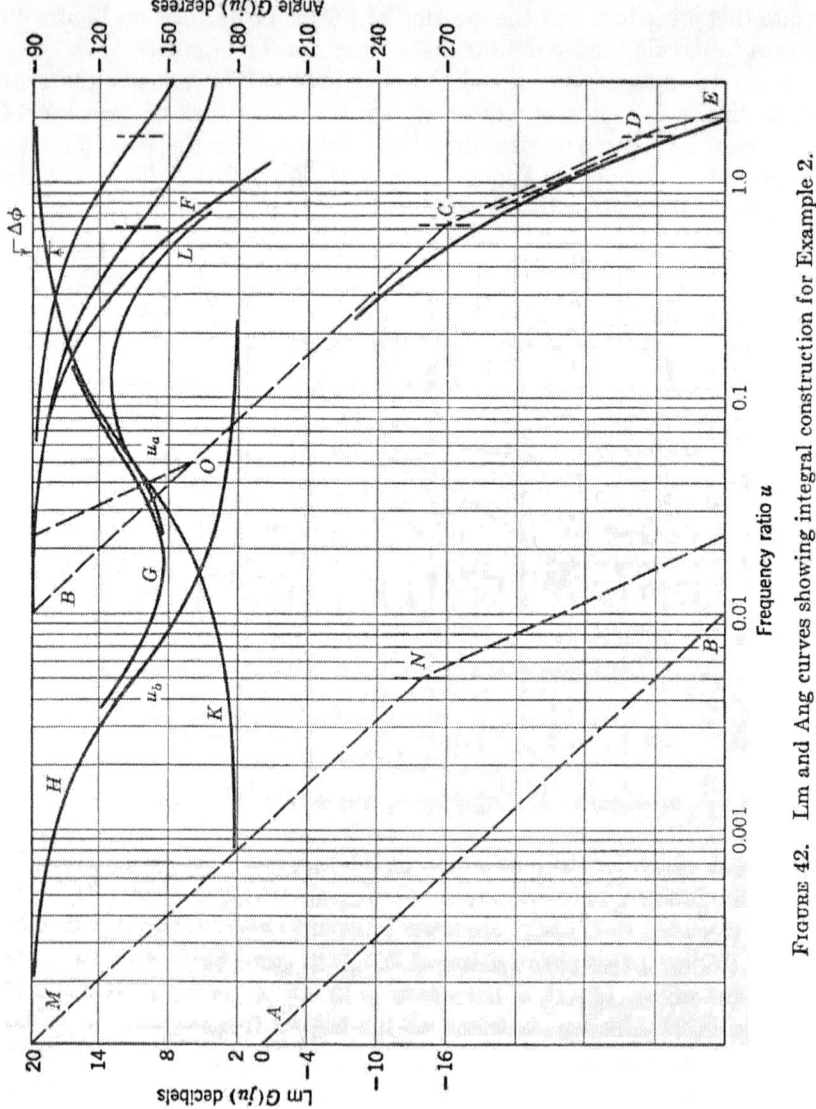

FIGURE 42. Lm and Ang curves showing integral construction for Example 2.

tained, first by moving curve G along the frequency scale until $\Delta\phi$ is 7 degrees at $u = 0.4$, and then adding curve G to curve F.

The location of curve G on the frequency scale establishes the break points O and N for adding the integral effect to the modulus asymptote. The composite modulus is then given by curve $MNOCDE$.

The composite modulus and phase curves are next drawn on the Lm-Ang plane as curve R on Figure 43. The M contour for $M_p =$

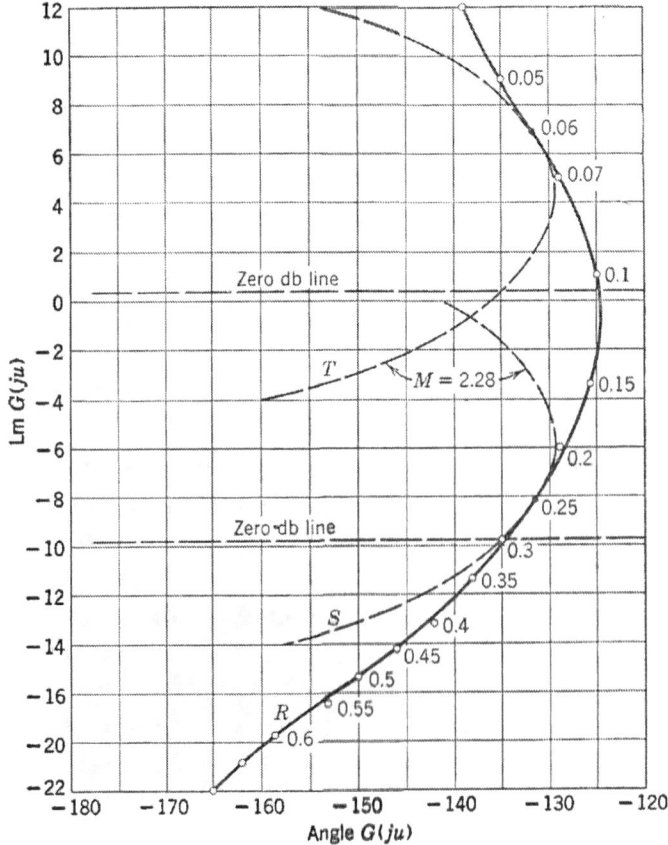

FIGURE 43. Lm-Ang curve with integral control added for Example 2.

2.28 decibels is curve S. For the adjustments established by the location of curve S, the dimensionless gain $K_u = 9.6$ decibels $= 3.02$; the velocity constant $K_v = 183$ seconds^{-1}; the dimensionless resonant frequency $u_r = 0.25$; the resonant frequency $\omega_r = 15.25$ radians per second; the time constant $\tau_i = \frac{20}{61} = 0.33$ second; since $61u = \omega$.

As shown by curve T, a gain $K_u \cong 0.04$ decibel will also permit $M_p = 2.28$ at $u_R = 0.06$, giving $K_v = 61$ seconds^{-1} and $\omega_R = 3.66$ radians per second. The response for the two gain settings can be compared by drawing the asymptotes for θ_o/θ_i. The reader may do this on Figure 42 by drawing horizontal lines at -9.6 decibels for the larger gain and at 0.04 decibel for the smaller gain. These lines will be the zero decibel asymptotes of θ_o/θ_i for the respective gain settings for frequencies up to their intersection with asymptote $OCDE$. For higher frequencies, $OCDE$ is the θ_o/θ_i asymptote.

Example 3. Passive Lead Network with Motor Generator System (Chapter 7, Equation 72). An illustration of the use of a passive lead

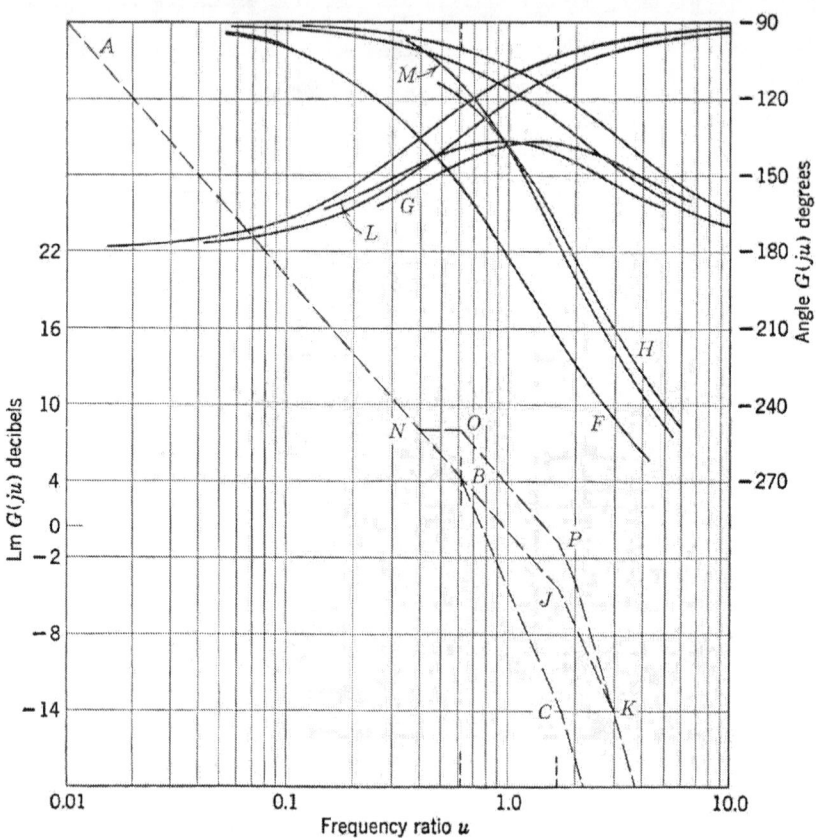

FIGURE 44. Lm $G(ju)$ and Ang $G(ju)$ as a function of log u for Example 3.

network with the objective of improving *the frequency response* for the motor generator system is now presented. If the procedure of Chapter 7 is followed, the lead network will have an α_ℓ of 5. Among the various problems is the selection of the time constant τ_ℓ. While we might first assume that the lead network time constant should be chosen to cancel the largest time constant of the denominator of $G(ju)$, it does not necessarily follow that doing so will automatically give an optimum solution to the problem.   Once again it must be emphasized that any real problem may specify velocity constant, frequency band, phase shift, or transient behavior, or any or all of these performance criteria.   This example illustrates merely the procedure to initiate a design program by showing one solution where the lead canceled a lag in the original system and a repeat solution where the lead time constant was increased approximately 50 per cent.

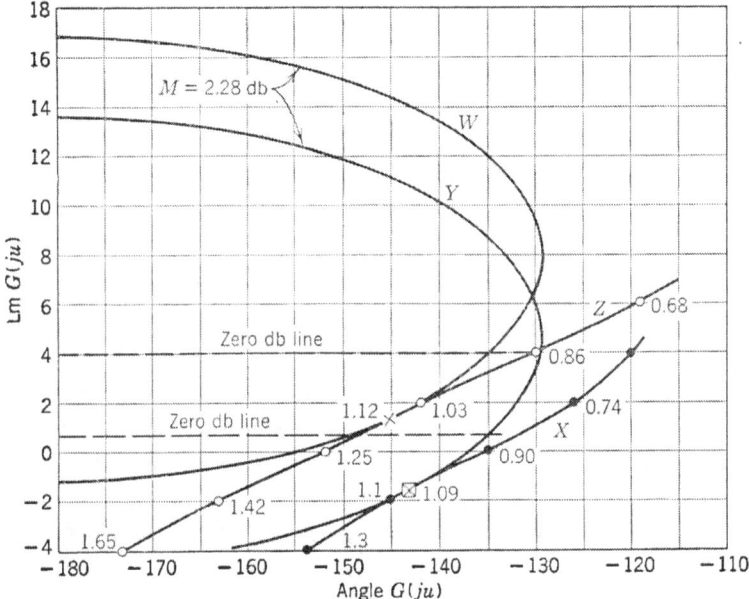

FIGURE 45.   Lm-Ang curve with lead control added for Example 3.

The modulus asymptote of the uncompensated system is redrawn on Figure 44 as curve $ABCD$ from Figure 40.   The corresponding angle curve is redrawn as curve F.

For the adjustment which makes $[1 + \alpha_\ell \tau_i ju]$ of the lead network cancel the term $[1 + 1.61ju]$ of the original system, the angle of the lead network is represented by curve G.   The composite phase for the cascade connection is then curve H.   The composite modulus asymptote is curve $ABJK$.   For the adjustment of the lead network which makes τ_ℓ approximately 50 per cent greater than the value just considered, the phase of the lead network is given by curve L.   The composite phase is given by curve M.   The composite modulus asymptote is given by the curve $ANOPK$.

The composite true modulus and phase curves for these two values of lead time constant are next drawn on the Lm-Ang plane as curves X

and Z, respectively, as shown on Figure 45. Curve X applies to the value of time constant that canceled the lag in the motor generator system.

The M contours for an $M_p = 2.28$ decibels are shown as curves Y and W. For the adjustments of the system established by the location of curves Y and W, the principal performance data are:

$(1 + \alpha\tau_\ell ju) = 1 + 1.6(ju)$	$(1 + \alpha\tau_\ell ju) = (1 + 2.5ju)$

Dimensionless gain K_u	= 0.92	Dimensionless gain K_u	= 0.63
K_v	= 56	K_v	= 38
Dimensionless frequency u_R	= 1.0	Dimensionless frequency u_R	= 1.1
Angular frequency ω_R	= 60 radians per second	Angular frequency ω_R	= 66 radians per second
Dimensionless time constant	= 0.32	Dimensionless time constant	= 0.5
$\tau_\ell = \dfrac{0.32}{61}$	= 0.005 second	$\tau_\ell = \dfrac{0.5}{61}$	= 0.008 second

The discrepancy between the numerical values of the solution given for this example and the numerical values tabulated in Table 7·2 is the result of one or the other method making it easier to read certain data from the curves. It does not result from differences in fundamental philosophy.

The example indicates that the selection of a lead time constant that cancels the principal lag in the motor generator transfer function gives a good solution. The selection of a larger lead time constant tended to give a slightly higher resonant frequency and a lower velocity constant. We cannot at this stage say that any particular selection is optimum. Any full-scale study would examine the behavior with respect to transients, or $\theta_o(j\omega)/\theta_i(j\omega)$ or phase shift versus frequency and so forth before reaching a decision. Even when this has been done, the system may be changed when constructed because of factors present in practice but ignored in analysis because of the difficulty of representing them.

Example 4. Parallel Circuit Method for Shaping the G Function (see Chapter 7, Section 7). The study of the motor with tachometric feedback given in Chapter 7, Section 7, can be repeated using logarithmic graphs. The block diagram in Figure 7·30 described the system. Figure 7·32 showed the steps in the analysis, but the curves were presented on the G^{-1} plane. An inverse plane is not used for the logarithmic study; hence direct correlation with the steps leading to Figure 7·32 cannot be made.

The transfer functions that define the three blocks in Figure 7·30 are

$$K_1G_1(ju) = K_1 = 5 \tag{79}$$

$$K_2G_2(ju) = \frac{1}{5(ju)^2} \tag{80}$$

$$K_3G_3(ju) = \frac{(6ju)^2}{6ju + 1} \tag{81}$$

The minor loop graphs must be made first. This permits the closure of the major loop. Figure 46 shows the complete construction of the

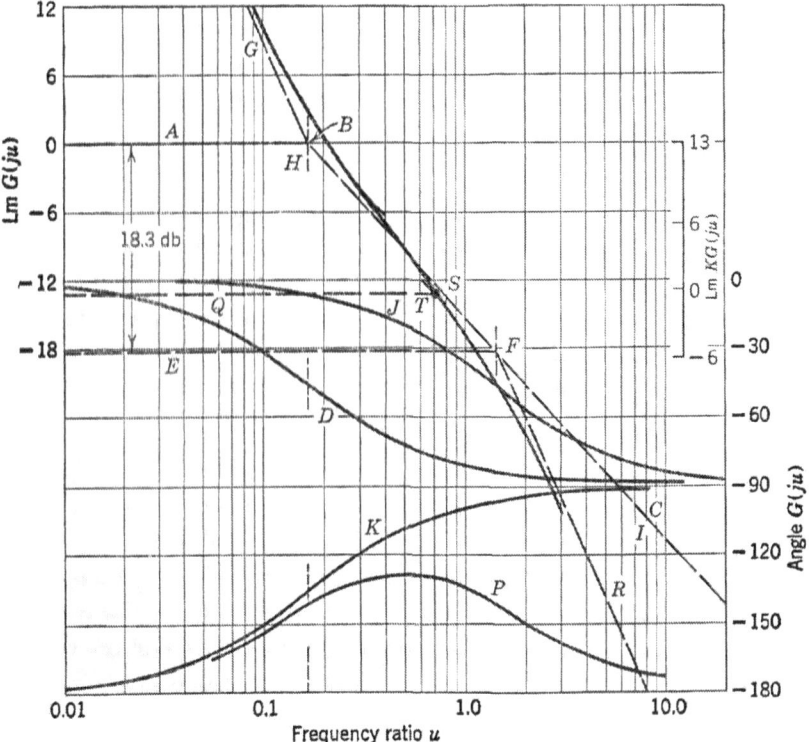

FIGURE 46.   Lm $G(ju)$ and Ang $G(ju)$ as a function of log u for Example 4.

Lm and Ang curves. The asymptote representation of the G portion of the transfer function, $G_2(ju)G_3(ju)$, that relates $C(s)$ to $B(s)$ in Figure 7·30 is the line ABC. The angle for this transfer function is shown by curve D. The gain in the minor loop has already been selected; therefore, no synthesis is involved. In the general problem, this step would be one of cut and try with an overall system performance as a criterion for the gain setting. The opened minor loop considered as having input $B(s)$ and output $C(s)$ has a gain of $\frac{36}{5}$ or 17.2 decibels. Since unit closure around a dynamic element results in an overall gain reduction of $1/(1 + K)$ and a time constant reduction of $1/(1 + K)$ (see Figure 5·27), the minor loop system response $C(ju)/A(ju)$ of Figure 7·30 is given by a horizontal line 18.3 decibels $= 20 \log_{10} (1 + K)$ down from AB and having a break to minus 6 decibels per octave where it intersects the line BC. The asymptote curve EFC gives the performance of the closed minor loop.* The procedure is simple in this particular problem because the minor loop characteristic equation is only first order. Higher order characteristic equations would require a transfer of the true Lm curve for which ABC is the asymptote and D is the phase curve, to the Lm-Ang Chart. Then the intersections of the M-N contours with the locus would give modulus and phase curves similar to EFC and J.

The graphs relating $\theta_o(ju)/A(ju)$ instead of $C(ju)/A(ju)$ must be found. Specifically $\theta_o(ju)/A(ju)$ equals $[C(ju)/A(ju)]K_3G_3{}^{-1}$. Equation 70 shows how the mathematics can be prepared to make this an easy graphical procedure. If the total minor loop transfer function $C(s)/B(s)$ is $KG(s)$, curves EFC and J represent $KG/1 + KG$. These curves must then be modified by the reciprocal of the transfer function $G_3(ju)$ of the element in the feedback path in order to obtain the relation between $\theta_o(ju)$ and $A(ju)$. (See Equations 70 through 77 for the detailed mathematical steps.)

The reciprocal of $K_3G_3(ju)$ is the line GHI in Figure 46, plotted to the original zero decibel reference. This line has the same high-frequency asymptote as the overall G function of the opened minor loop. A study will show that BC and HI must superpose. Below the frequency $u = \frac{1}{6}$, the asymptote for $1/K_3G_3$ has a slope of minus 12 decibels per octave. The phase for $1/K_3G_3$ is given by curve K. The composite modulus curve $\theta_o(ju)/A(ju)$ for the minor loop has the *shape GHFR*. It is obtained by adding the two asymptote curves EFC and GHI. The composite phase curve P is obtained by adding the two phase curves K and J.

The final adjustment of the main loop for the performance desired in this particular problem does not call for any change in the shape of the

---

* The asymptote construction for overall response given on page 282 applied to servomechanisms, or specifically to systems with at least one integration in KG. The minor loop C/A here considered has no integration, hence its low-frequency asymptote would be at $K/(1 + K)$ decibels. However since the asymptote ABC is only the G portion of C/B, the closed minor loop low-frequency asymptote is at Lm $(1 + K)^{-1} = -18.3$ decibels on the $G(ju)$ scale and not at $K/(1 + K)$ decibels The high-frequency asymptote is the original open-loop asymptote FC of C/B.

main loop transfer function.   The numerical value for K_1 had already been chosen.   Therefore the asymptotes $GHFR$ can be corrected at the break points H and F to give the true curve.   Then the whole construction can be moved up by $20 \log_{10} (5 \times 36)/41 = 12.9$ decibels where 5 is the gain K_1 and $\frac{36}{41}$ is the zero frequency gain across the minor loop. This is conveniently done by rescaling the modulus graph as shown by the right-hand decibel scale in Figure 46.   The point B formerly at zero decibel now locates at 12.9 decibels.   The curves $GHFR$ and P are now transferred to the Lm-Ang chart.

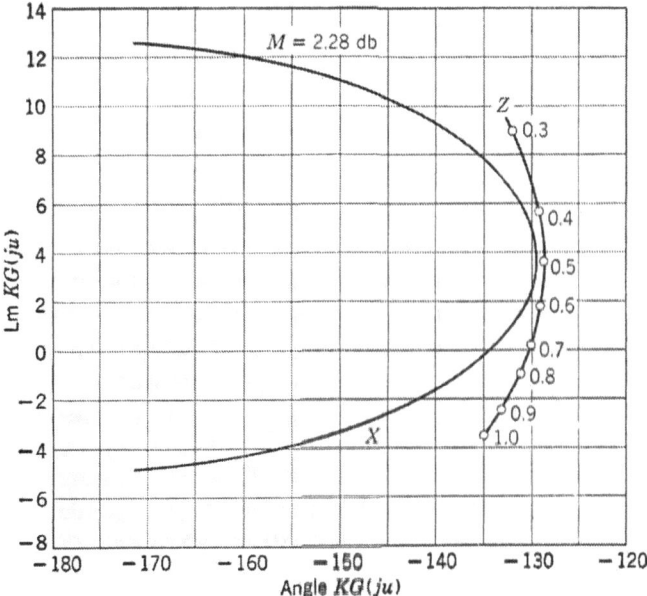

FIGURE 47.   Lm $G(ju)$ as a function of Ang $G(ju)$ for Example 4.

Curve Z, Figure 47, is the locus of the transfer function of the major loop.   The curve X shows an M contour for $M_p = 2.28$ decibels.   Although this curve does not quite intersect the locus Z, the results are adequate confirmation of the former study in Chapter 7.

Figure 47 shows that the zero decibel value for the M_p contour and the system locus, curve Z, superpose.   Therefore, on Figure 46 a line QT starting at zero decibels on the Lm KG scale and continuing as $QSFR$ gives the asymptote for θ_o/θ_i.   Notice also that $u = 0.7$ and $\psi = 50$ degrees at zero decibels on curve Z of Figure 47.   This observation points to another procedure for estimating the θ_o/θ_i asymptote. For example, for frequencies below which $\psi = $ about 50 degrees, θ_o/θ_i ranges between 0.7 and 1.3.   Hence the frequency point at which

$\psi = 50$ degrees allows one to select K and hence Lm KG. The *shape* of the phase curve serves also as the principal criterion for inserting integral or lead networks into the loop. Another helpful observation is that u_R occurs for values of Lm KG that range between zero and -6 decibels. Finally the *true* value of θ_o/θ_i at the frequency u_R is M_p and is one point on the θ_o/θ_i curve. A freehand approximation to the curve can then be drawn.

The use of only asymptotes enables a designer to estimate the general performance of a closed-loop system but when supported by the above related criteria a more comprehensive picture is available. Thus, as a sound background of approximation methods for studying feedback systems is built up, new designs can be quickly explored.

14 Conclusion

This chapter has presented a method of synthesis using logarithmic techniques in the manipulations. The preliminary work involved the establishment of elementary forms of $G(ju)$ which often repeat themselves in servo system transfer functions. The second portion of the chapter involved the graphical representation of these functions and their merging into combinations which are typical in closed-loop synthesis. After preparing the necessary master graphs, the third portion of the presentation involved preparation of Lm-Ang charts for the study of sensitivity adjustments in closed loops and for the design procedures necessary to alter the shape of the $G(ju)$ functions.

The theme of the presentation has been directed toward establishing rapidity of synthesis and high utility of the graphs so that the user can prepare preliminary designs of rather complex mechanisms in a few hours and can proceed to alter these designs without losing the identity of his problem.

The discussion dealing with compensation techniques, and, in particular, the discussion of multiple loop systems, is hardly more than a sketch of the total material which can be studied and which should necessarily be part of a complete engineering investigation. However, the curves and procedures for accomplishing complicated designs are not easy to present in writing because of their size and the difficulty of describing, step by step, procedures necessary for their formation.

Finally, it should be remembered that all conclusions reached only after a frequency study should be reexamined in the light of the transient behavior of the system before any job of synthesis can be called complete. This work can be aided by use of the material presented in Chapter 11

9

Systems Subjected to Multiple Disturbances

1 General

The principal function of many servomechanisms is to provide at a remote point a follow-up of the command specifically under circumstances where the follow-up member may be represented by a lumped inertia. The output member is often an inertia element that is acted upon only by forces or torques established within the loop by the control. On the other hand, many systems operate under conditions where the output member experiences signals or disturbances not only as a result of the control operation but also as a result of numerous random factors that establish the need of or the existence of the control.

Many instrument servomechanisms fall within the category of systems subjected only to input disturbances. The loads that the output must overcome are negligible. The inertia of the output behaves merely as an energy storage element rigidly attached to the output drive motor. It may be assumed to be inside the loop. Its effect is correctly considered in the analysis by the techniques outlined in the previous chapters because the controlled quantity has the same instantaneous value on the driven side of the inertia as on the output side. On the average, no work is done in moving the mass because all the kinetic energy possessed by it is returned to the system when the mass is brought to rest.

The presence of true viscous friction or drag at the output member likewise introduces no complication into the analyses heretofore presented. The linearizing assumptions established as a basis for the studies permit the inclusion of the viscous effects, and hence the energy dissipation, inside the loop.

When the control is intended to operate against the opposing action of spurious or applied disturbances at the output, the analytical techniques given in previous chapters need extension in order to establish a design that will meet prescribed specifications. The various factors that may be represented as output disturbances of one kind or another are coulomb forces or loads or a torque against which the output member must work during the operation of the system. Figure 1 shows a block representation of this condition. Examples of disturbances of this kind are pulsating loads resulting from the recoil action of a gun on firing; the cyclic load of a compressor drive; the steady or cyclically

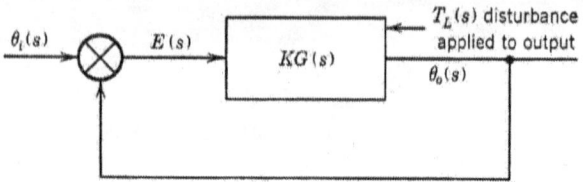

FIGURE 1.   Diagram showing disturbances at input and output.

varying friction on a gear drive that binds or has eccentricity; the varying load on a voltage-regulating system for an electric generator, or the varying load of a turbine regulated for speed. There are many other problems. They arise whenever the device must perform useful work at the controlled station.

The presence of dynamical systems that are lumped outside the point of closure of the loop sometimes make the closed loop act as though it is excited externally. Factors that give rise to this condition are typified by a mass attached to the controlled member by a spring as shown by Figure 2. Sometimes a controlled member that comprises distributed stiffness and mass outside the point where the controlled quantity is measured also exerts this effect. Factors such as these are frequently the result of poor design of the controlled member or of circumstances

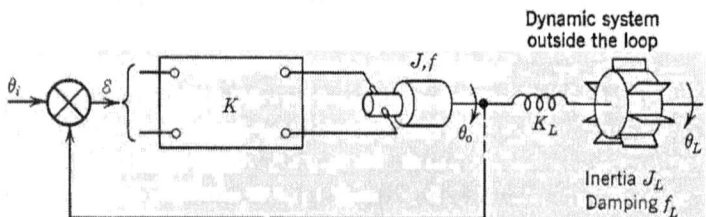

FIGURE 2.   Dynamic elements inside and outside the closed loop.

peculiar to the particular problem being studied. They arise often in gun drives or turrets, where the mounts must be allowed to have a certain degree of flexibility because of size or weight considerations. In such circumstances, the positional feedback to the error-measuring element is often driven by the shaft of the motor that drives the turret. The mass and elasticity of the driven member are therefore external to the closed loop. Finally, a matter often given little attention, perhaps because little is known about its effect, is the interaction of power source dynamics with system dynamics. Sometimes a source of power is used to energize the low-energy section as well as the high-energy section of the system. Because of poor regulating properties the power source voltage may vary on account of large power demands by the output drive. This variation may cause the introduction of spurious signals of a transient or cyclic character at various parts within the loop.

When the closed loops are servomechanisms, the requirement that they perform useful work at the controlled station makes them subjected to input and to load disturbances. Both disturbances may occur simultaneously. Much has been written about the treatment of analysis and synthesis of a servomechanism subjected only to time variation of the input. However, little material exists to guide the synthesis of the same servomechanism when it is to have a specified performance under time variation of disturbances on the output. On the other hand, regulators are intended to regulate against disturbances only on their output. Their synthesis and design are aimed at meeting specifications of performance for only this condition.

The following sections of this chapter aim to present a few guides to the synthesis and design of servomechanisms intended for the dual function of follow-up and regulation. The last section treats briefly the extension of the analysis to those problems in which dynamical elements at the output are located outside the feedback loop.

2   Systems Involving Simultaneous Application of Input and Load Disturbances

Consider the situation in which a disturbance, such as a load torque $T_L(t)$, is applied to the system simultaneously with the application of

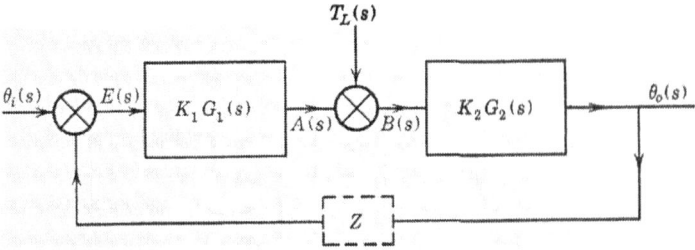

FIGURE 3.   Diagram for representing simultaneous disturbances on a closed-loop system.

an input $\theta_i(t)$. A block diagram such as the one shown in Figure 3 is often helpful when the study involves these simultaneous disturbances.

It is not necessary that the system have unity feedback from θ_o to θ_i. Dynamic elements, as shown by the dotted block Z, may be present. In this treatment, however, they will be neglected in the interest of simplicity.

Provided the principle of linear superposition is applicable, certain transfer functions inside the loop may be defined, and used in the formulation of system relations that allow useful system generalizations. The transfer functions applicable to a system subjected only to the two disturbances $\theta_i(t)$ and $T_L(t)$ are defined as follows for the block diagram of Figure 3.

$$
\left. \begin{aligned}
A(s) &= K_1 G_1(s) E(s) \\
\theta_o(s) &= K_2 G_2(s) B(s) \\
B(s) &= A(s) - T_L(s) \\
E(s) &= \theta_i(s) - \theta_o(s)
\end{aligned} \right\} \tag{1}
$$

The output response for the simultaneous application of the two disturbances $\theta_i(s)$ and $T_L(s)$ is

$$
\theta_o(s) = \frac{K_1 G_1(s) K_2 G_2(s)}{1 + K_1 G_1(s) K_2 G_2(s)} \theta_i(s) - \frac{K_2 G_2(s)}{1 + K_1 G_1(s) K_2 G_2(s)} T_L(s) \tag{2}
$$

and the error response is

$$
E(s) = \frac{1}{1 + K_1 G_1(s) K_2 G_2(s)} \theta_i(s) + \frac{K_2 G_2(s)}{1 + K_1 G_1(s) K_2 G_2(s)} T_L(s) \tag{3}
$$

Observe the two portions to each response equation. As written, the first portion is associated with the input disturbance $\theta_i(s)$ while the second is associated with the load disturbance $T_L(s)$. This follows from the principle of linear superposition. Provided the "at rest" condition can be established as zero for the individual disturbances, the response caused by θ_i and T_L may be analyzed separately. The net response is then given by the instantaneous sum of the two separate responses. It is noted that when a load T_L is applied alone, the output response is not the same as that when an input θ_i is applied alone. The same is true for the error response when calculated for each separate disturbance.

Equations 2 and 3 are in a form useful for the prediction of the general response of the system considered as a regulator as well as considered as a servomechanism. Regulator theory that ties back to servomechanisms theory can be built upon a modification to the response of servomechanisms for only input disturbances. Stated in other words, the regulator performance with respect to a load disturbance acting alone

can be given in terms of the performance with respect to a time variation of command in the form of a change to its set point. For example,
if the load $T_L(s)$ on the system is initially assumed to be zero, Equations 2 and 3 reduce to

$$\frac{\theta_o(s)}{\theta_i(s)} = \frac{K_1 G_1(s) K_2 G_2(s)}{1 + K_1 G_1(s) K_2 G_2(s)} = \mathcal{C}(s) \qquad (4)$$

and

$$\frac{E(s)}{\theta_i(s)} = \frac{1}{1 + K_1 G_1(s) K_2 G_2(s)} = \mathcal{B}(s) \qquad (5)$$

Similarly, if the input $\theta_i(s)$ is zero, the equations reduce to

$$\frac{\theta_o(s)}{T_L(s)} = -\frac{K_2 G_2(s)}{1 + K_1 G_1(s) K_2 G_2(s)} = \mathcal{D}(s) \qquad (6)$$

and

$$\frac{E(s)}{T_L(s)} = +\frac{K_2 G_2(s)}{1 + K_1 G_1(s) K_2 G_2(s)} = -\mathcal{D}(s) \qquad (7)$$

from which

$$\mathcal{D}(s) = -\frac{\mathcal{C}(s)}{K_1 G_1(s)} = -\mathcal{B}(s) K_2 G_2(s) \qquad (8)$$

Equation 8 states that the performance of the system when acted
upon only by a load, as in regulation, is related to its performance when
acted upon only by an input disturbance, as in a servomechanism, by
the simple relation that

$$\frac{E(s)}{T_L(s)}\bigg|_{\substack{\text{as a regulator} \\ \text{when } \theta_i = 0}} = \frac{1}{K_1 G_1(s)} \left\{ \frac{\theta_o(s)}{\theta_i(s)} \bigg|_{\substack{\text{as a servomechanism} \\ \text{when } T_L = 0}} \right\} \qquad (9)$$

where $K_1 G_1(s)$ is the transfer function of the part of the system between
the error and the summing point with respect to the load. For systems
which must exhibit the combined features of follow-up and regulation,
that is, must accept random time variations of inputs and loads, Equations 2, 3, and 9 furnish in compact form a complete picture of their
behavior. These equations show that much may be learned about the
regulator behavior once the servomechanism behavior $\theta_o(s)/\theta_i(s)$ is
formulated. The formulation of this $\theta_o(s)/\theta_i(s)$ behavior does not in
general involve unnecessary effort because the degree of stability as a
regulator is often established in terms of the response of the system to
a variation in its set point.[8]

3 Example of a System Subjected to Load and Input Disturbances

The significance of Equation 9 is made clearer by consideration of a specific example. Assume that the hydraulic transmission treated in Chapter 5, Equation 93, is to be used in a closed loop and is to be subjected to time variations of command $\theta_i(t)$ and load torque $T_L(t)$. The derivation of the transfer function relating the output shaft motion $\theta_o(t)$ to the stroke motion $X(t)$, as given in Chapter 5, neglected load torque. However, to include load torque the relation expressing hydraulic pressure and output motion, as given in Equation 5·102, may be rewritten as

$$d_m P = J_m \frac{d^2\theta_o}{dt^2} + T_L(t) \tag{10}$$

giving

$$P = \frac{J_m}{d_m}\frac{d^2\theta_o}{dt^2} + \frac{T_L(t)}{d_m} \tag{11}$$

and

$$\frac{dP}{dt} = \frac{J_m}{d_m}\frac{d^3\theta_o}{dt^3} + \frac{1}{d_m}\frac{dT_L(t)}{dt} \tag{12}$$

The substitution of P and dP/dt from Equation 12 in Equation 5·101 now gives

$$d_p n x = \frac{d_m}{dt}\frac{d\theta_o}{dt} + \frac{LJ_m}{d_m}\frac{d^2\theta_o}{dt^2} + \frac{LT_L(t)}{d_m} + \frac{VJ_m}{Bd_m}\frac{d^3\theta_o}{dt^3} + \frac{V}{Bd_m}\frac{dT_L(t)}{dt} \tag{13}$$

which, when separated into factors involving θ_o and T_L and transformed under the assumption that the initial conditions are zero, may be written as

$$d_p n X(s) = \left(d_m s + \frac{LJ_m}{d_m}s^2 + \frac{VJ_m}{Bd_m}s^3\right)\theta_o(s) + \left(\frac{L}{d_m} + \frac{V}{Bd_m}s\right)T_L(s) \tag{14}$$

The information given by Equation 14 may be represented in the form of a block diagram shown in Figure 4. The procedure for deriving the functions in the blocks is to assume first that $\theta_o(t)$ is held zero while the relation between stroke and torque is determined, and second to hold stroke zero while the relation between torque and output motion is determined. The torque is established in the device by a pressure in the hydraulic system. In terms of the diagram of Figure 4, $E(s)$ represents stroke, and $\alpha(s)$ and $\mathcal{B}(s)$ represent torque. The summing point

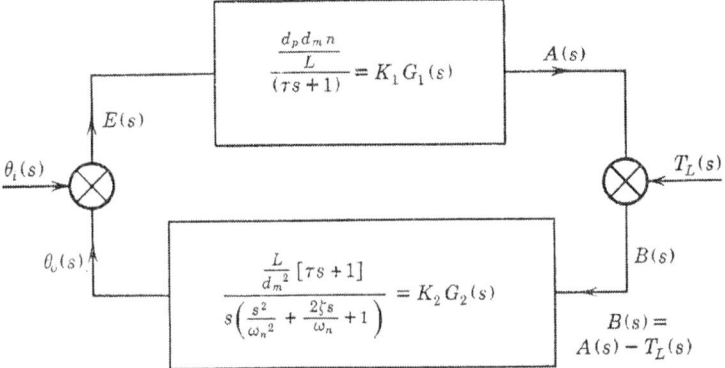

FIGURE 4. Diagram of hydraulic transmission with input θ_i and load torque T_L.

for the load has pressure as a parameter. Thus, if $\theta_o(t)$ is zero, Equation 14 reduces to

$$d_p n X(s) = \left(\frac{V}{Bd_m} s + \frac{L}{d_m} \right) T_L(s) \tag{15}$$

giving

$$\frac{T_L(s)}{X(s)} = \frac{Q(s)}{E(s)} = K_1 G_1(s) \tag{16}$$

$$= \frac{d_p n}{\left(\dfrac{V}{Bd_m} s + \dfrac{L}{d_m} \right)} \tag{17}$$

or

$$K_1 G_1(s) = \frac{\dfrac{d_p d_m}{L} n}{(\tau s + 1)} \tag{18}$$

where

$$\tau = \frac{V}{LB} \tag{19}$$

Likewise, if $X(s)$ is held zero, Equation 14 reduces to

$$\left(\frac{VJ_m}{Bd_m} s^3 + \frac{LJ_m}{d_m} s^2 + d_m s \right) \theta_o(s) = - \left[\frac{V}{Bd_m} s + \frac{L}{d_m} \right] T_L(s) \tag{20}$$

Since $B(s) = A(s) - T_L(s)$, the transfer function $K_2 G_2(s)$ equals

$$K_2 G_2(s) = \frac{\theta_o(s)}{B(s)} = \frac{\theta_o(s)}{-T_L(s)} \tag{21}$$

$$= \frac{\left[\dfrac{V}{Bd_m}s + \dfrac{L}{d_m}\right]}{s\left[\dfrac{V}{B}\dfrac{J_m}{d_m}s^2 + \dfrac{LJ_m}{d_m}s + d_m\right]} \tag{22}$$

or in nondimensional form

$$K_2 G_2(s) = \frac{\dfrac{L}{d_m^2}[\tau s + 1]}{s\left[\dfrac{s^2}{\omega_n^2} + \dfrac{2\zeta}{\omega_n}s + 1\right]} \tag{23}$$

where

$$\left. \begin{array}{c} \dfrac{1}{\omega_n^2} = \dfrac{VJ_m}{Bd_m^2} \\[3ex] \dfrac{2\zeta}{\omega_n} = \dfrac{LJ_m}{d_m^2} \\[3ex] \tau = \dfrac{V}{LB} \end{array} \right\} \tag{24}$$

As a check on Equations 18 and 23, the load T_L may be assumed zero. The equivalent function for the cascade connection of $K_1 G_1(s)$ and $K_2 G_2(s)$ is then

$$\frac{\theta_o(s)}{X(s)} = \frac{\theta_o(s)}{E(s)} = K_1 G_1(s) K_2 G_2(s) = KG(s) \tag{25}$$

$$= \frac{\dfrac{d_p d_m}{L}n}{(\tau s + 1)} \frac{\dfrac{L}{d_m^2}[\tau s + 1]}{s\left[\dfrac{s^2}{\omega_n^2} + \dfrac{2\zeta s}{\omega_n} + 1\right]} \tag{26}$$

$$= \frac{\dfrac{d_p n}{d_m}}{s\left[\dfrac{s^2}{\omega_n^2} + \dfrac{2\zeta s}{\omega_n} + 1\right]} \tag{27}$$

$$= \frac{K_v}{s\left[\dfrac{s^2}{\omega_n^2} + \dfrac{2\zeta s}{\omega_n} + 1\right]} \tag{28}$$

Equation 28 for the overall $KG(s)$ for the transmission is the same as that derived for Equation 5·107.

Figure 4 shows the block diagram for this hydraulic transmission and shows the appropriate functions in the blocks. It now follows from Equation 9 that the ability of this system to hold small errors when subjected to load torques, that is, when operated as a regulator, is given by

$$-\frac{\theta_o(s)}{T_L(s)} = \left[\frac{\theta_o(s)}{\theta_i(s)}\right] \left.\frac{(\tau s + 1)}{\dfrac{d_p d_m}{L}n}\right|_{\text{for } \theta_i = 0} \tag{29}$$

Thus, at zero frequency the steady-state output θ_{oss} or the steady-state error $\mathcal{E}_{ss}$ is equal to

$$-\theta_{oss} = +\mathcal{E}_{ss} = \frac{L}{d_p d_m n}\,|\,T_L\,| \tag{30}$$

Equations 29 and 30 show that the steady-state error is proportional to load and to the leakage L and inversely proportional to the displacement of pump and motor. The dynamic error is a function of the magnitude and phase of $K_1 G_1 (j\omega)$ versus frequency and the magnitude and phase of θ_o/θ_i versus frequency operating as a servomechanism in the absence of load. The loci plots of the functions θ_o/θ_i and $K_1 G_1$ given in Figure 5 show that an integration is necessary in the function $K_1 G_1$

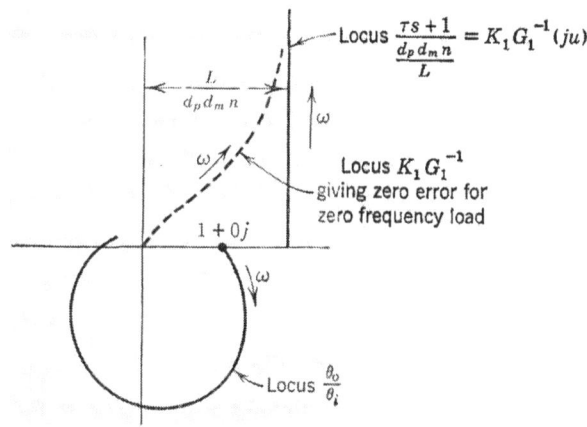

FIGURE 5.   Loci plot of transfer functions of Figure 4.

if the system is to operate as a regulator with zero error in the steady state. A typical locus of $K_1 G_1{}^{-1}$ permitting zero error in the steady state is shown by the dotted line in the figure. Such a locus could be obtained by modifying the closed loop in a manner that would provide an additional integration in series with the box now shown as K_1G_1 in Figure 3. Alternatively, if a new K_1G_1 function of the form

$$K_1G_1(s) \text{ (new)} = \frac{1}{s} K_1G_1(s) \text{ (old)} \tag{31}$$

could be synthesized and used in the loop in place of the existing K_1G_1, zero error for a steady load would be established. However, the stability of the system may no longer be acceptable.

Clearly it is immaterial from the standpoint of the θ_o/θ_i performance whether the $1/s$ integration in the overall function KG is in K_1G_1 or K_2G_2. Thus a study of the kind here presented gives in the general case

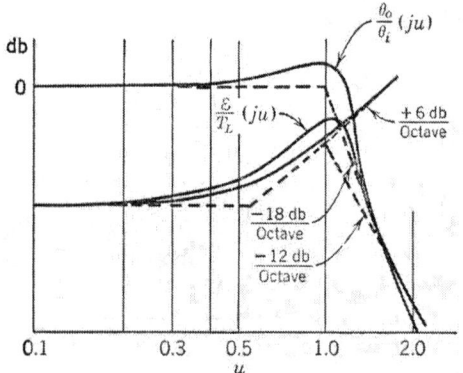

FIGURE 6. Plot of functions of Figure 4 to log coordinates.

a direct indication of where in the array of elements in the system those having integrating properties must be located with respect to the various outputs or places where disturbances are applied.

Numerical values for the dimensionless parameters in Equation 23 for a typical hydraulic transmission are

$$\omega_n = 120 \text{ radians per second}$$

$$\zeta = 0.3$$

$$\tau = 0.015 \text{ second}$$

When the system functions are plotted with respect to ω_n as unit frequency, that is, in terms of $\mu = \omega/\omega_n$, and when the loop closed for an $M_p = 1.3$, typical data are

$$K_u = 0.3$$

$$\mu_R = 0.9$$

$$\tau_u = 0.015 \times 120 = 1.8$$

The superposed plots to log coordinates showing θ_o/θ_i and the error response $\mathcal{E}/T_L$ to load disturbance are given in Figure 6, both in terms of the frequency variable u. The simplicity of the analysis based on the background of Chapter 8 makes possible a freehand study of the problem with usable results.

4 Effects of Integration at Various Places within the Loop

At this point in the discussion a matter that was treated lightly in Chapter 2 can be given elaboration. The analysis relative to Figure 2·7 showed that the insertion of the integrating element in the closed-loop mechanical system made it fulfill the requirements for a servomechanism. At the same time, it performed as a high performance regulator in the steady state, that is, with zero error for steady load torque. These matters are shown by Equations 2·56 and 2·57. Similarly, the analysis of the system of Figure 2·8 showed the system to fulfill the requirement of a servomechanism, but its performance as a regulator in the steady state was inferior to that of Figure 2·7. These matters are shown by Equations 2·69 and 2·70. Its steady error was proportional to the steady load torque. Nothing has yet been stated relative to its dynamic error as a regulator.

The point that may not have been immediately apparent at the time of the discussion of Figures 2·7 and 2·8 is that, although both systems have an integration in the loop, each has it in different locations. In the mechanical system, the integration is given by a specific component where

$$\theta_k = \frac{1}{\tau} \int \mathcal{E}\, dt \tag{32}$$

In the electrical system the integration is given by the property of the motor, that

$$\frac{d\theta_o}{dt} = \frac{k\mathcal{E}}{f} \tag{33}$$

or

$$\theta_o = \frac{k}{f} \int \mathcal{E}\, dt \tag{34}$$

In the mechanical system the integrating element is located with respect to the appearance of a torque at a point between where error occurs and where the torque is effective. On the other hand, in the electrical system the integration is between the point where torque is effective and where output occurs. Hence in the electrical system the integration cannot affect the zero frequency or steady-load error because it is not physically located between error and torque. These considerations, however, do not tell much about the dynamic error.

The dynamic behavior is made clearer by reviewing Equations 2·56 and 2·67 and deriving from them the functions K_1G_1 and K_2G_2 in the manner shown by Equations 1, 2, and 3, relative to T_L in Figure 3. Equation 2·56 can be rewritten as

$$f\frac{d^2\theta_o(t)}{dt^2} + k\frac{d\theta_o(t)}{dt} + \frac{k}{\tau_i}\theta_o(t) = \frac{k}{\tau_i}\mathcal{E}(t) + \frac{k\theta_o(t)}{\tau_i} - \frac{dT_L(t)}{dt} \tag{35}$$

which gives

$$K_1G_1(s) = \frac{T_L(s)}{E(s)} = \frac{1}{s}\frac{k}{\tau_i}\bigg|_{\text{for }\theta_o=0} \tag{36}$$

$$K_2G_2(s) = \frac{\theta_o(s)}{-T_L(s)} = \frac{1}{(fs+k)}\bigg|_{\text{for }\mathcal{E}=0} \tag{37}$$

Likewise, Equation 2·67 may be rewritten as

$$J\frac{d^2\theta_o(t)}{dt^2} + f\frac{d\theta_o(t)}{dt} + k\theta_o(t) = k\mathcal{E}(t) + k\theta_o(t) - T_L(t) \tag{38}$$

which gives

$$K_1G_1(s) = \frac{T_L(s)}{E(s)} = k\bigg|_{\text{for }\theta_o=0} \tag{39}$$

$$K_2G_2(s) = \frac{\theta_o(s)}{-T_L(s)} = \frac{1}{s(Js+f)}\bigg|_{\text{for }\mathcal{E}=0} \tag{40}$$

The equivalent block diagram for the system of Figure 2·7 in terms of the KG functions of Equations 36 and 37 is shown in Figure 7. The

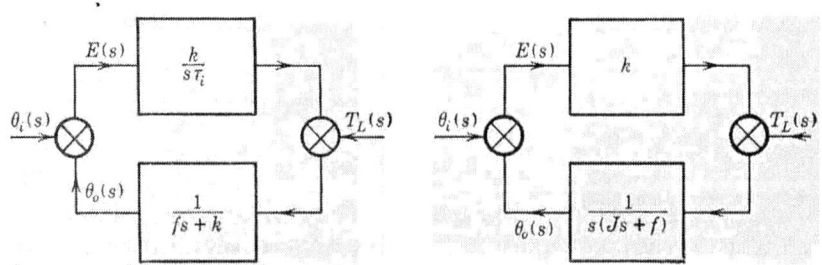

FIGURE 7. Diagram for system of   FIGURE 8. Diagram for system of
Figure 2·7.   Figure 2·8.

corresponding block diagram for the system of Figure 2·8, in terms of Equations 39 and 40, is shown in Figure 8.

Plots of the function $\mathcal{E}/T_L$ to logarithmic coordinates for these two systems are given in Figures 9a and 9b. It is noted that whereas the function θ_o/θ_i is the same for each system, the plots of $\mathcal{E}/T_L$ differ appreciably. Equations 2·56 and 2·67 indicate that the function θ_o/θ_i attenuates at -12 decibels per octave in the upper frequency region. However, because of the 6 decibels per octave rise of K_1G_1 of Figure 9a, the

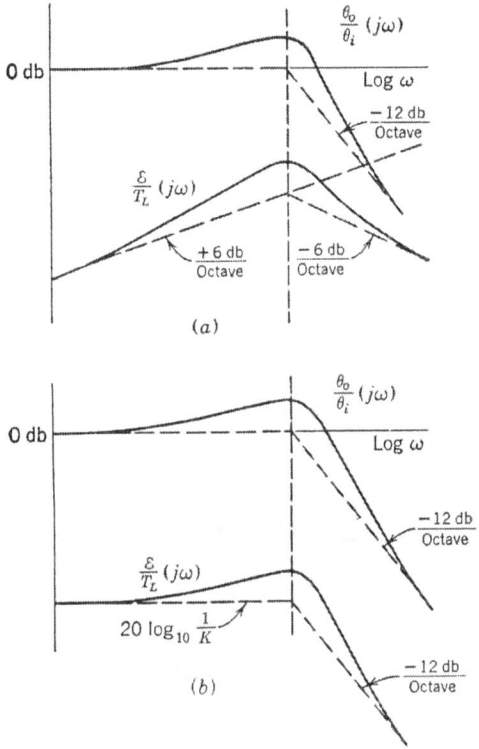

FIGURE 9.   (a) Plot of functions of Figure 7 to log coordinates.   (b) Plot of functions of Figure 8 to log coordinates.

final attenuation of the $\mathcal{E}/T_L$ function of the closed-loop mechanical system is only -6 decibels per octave, whereas that of the closed-loop electrical system is -12 decibels per octave. Thus, the location of the integrating property within the loop affects not only the width of the frequency band, throughout which the errors may be considerable, but also the rate of attenuation of error after the maximum has been reached. This means that a regulator having zero error at zero frequency may not be so useful as one having a small error at zero frequency. This is because error magnification that occurs in a system typified by Figure 9a may be more objectionable at some particular frequency than the relatively constant error with sharp cutoff in the system, such as Figure 9b.

To conclude this section, it seems appropriate to mention that if the overall system can be defined as a frequency function θ_o/θ_i, the algebraic investigations indicated by Equation 9 lead quickly to a statement of the general system requirements. Most persons working with closed-loop systems have a qualitative idea of the behavior of θ_o/θ_i. They therefore have a ready means for gaining a qualitative loci plot of the function $\mathcal{E}/T_L$ once the equivalent block diagram is formed. In particular, the significance of integration in various places within the system and the effect of feedback elements of one kind or another from various parts of the system to other parts are readily recognized. At least we can quickly ascertain whether the particular component affects the system stability by virtue of its frequency variant property or whether it merely affects the zero frequency or steady-state behavior.

5   Effects of Dynamical Elements outside the Loop

Sometimes the effect of dynamic elements outside the loop can be included in the analysis by an appropriate change to the function KG that otherwise would represent the equipment inside the loop. Consider, for purposes of illustration, the system shown in Figure 2. Let $K\mathcal{E}$ be the torque applied by the controller to the output member included within the loop. Let the stiffness of the spring, the damping, and the inertia external to the loop be represented respectively by K_L, f_L, and J_L. The equations of motion for the system between $\mathcal{E}$ and θ_L of Figure 2 are

$$K\mathcal{E} = \frac{J\, d^2\theta_o}{dt^2} + f\frac{d\theta_o}{dt} + T_L \tag{41}$$

where T_L is the reaction torque of the spring and may be written as

$$T_L = (\theta_o - \theta_L)K_L = \frac{J_L\, d^2\theta_L}{dt^2} + f_L\frac{d\theta_L}{dt} \tag{42}$$

If Equations 41 and 42 are transformed subject to all initial conditions being zero, the result is

$$KE(s) = (Js^2 + fs)\theta_o(s) + T_L(s) \tag{41a}$$

$$T_L(s) = [\theta_o(s) - \theta_L(s)]K_L = (J_L s^2 + f_L s)\theta_L(s) \tag{42a}$$

giving

$$KE(s) = (Js^2 + fs + K_L)\theta_o(s) - K_L\theta_L(s) \tag{43}$$

From Equation 42a

$$\theta_L(s) = \frac{K_L\theta_o(s)}{J_Ls^2 + f_Ls + K_L} \tag{44}$$

which, substituted in Equation 43, gives

$$KE(s) = (Js^2 + fs + K_L)\theta_o(s) - \frac{K_L^2\theta_o(s)}{J_Ls^2 + f_Ls + K_L} \tag{45}$$

which may be rewritten as

$$K[J_Ls^2 + f_Ls + K_L]E(s)$$

$$= [(Js^2 + fs + K_L)(J_Ls^2 + f_Ls + K_L) - K_L^2]\theta_o(s) \tag{46}$$

or

$$\frac{\theta_o(s)}{E(s)} = \frac{K(J_Ls^2 + f_Ls + K_L)}{(Js^2 + fs + K_L)(J_Ls^2 + f_Ls + K_L) - K_L^2} \tag{47}$$

Equation 47 now expresses an equivalent transfer function for the entire assembly. The block diagram of the system, now equivalent to Equation 47 and Figure 2, is shown in Figure 10. Notice that the quantity

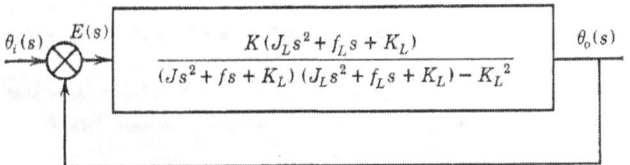

FIGURE 10.   Diagram of Figure 2 when K_L is finite.

θ_L is no longer specifically identified in the block diagram. It can, however, be derived from Equation 44.

When K_L = zero, Equation 47 reduces to

$$\frac{\theta_o(s)}{E(s)} = \frac{K}{s(Js + f)} \tag{48}$$

which is the form for a system comprising inertia J and damping f wholly inside the loop. Also when $K_L = \infty$, Equation 47 reduces to

$$\frac{\theta_o(s)}{E(s)} = \frac{K}{s[(J + J_L)s + (f + f_L)]} \tag{49}$$

which merely has the effect of adding the external inertia and damping to the internal inertia and damping, respectively, as would have been expected and as is shown in Figure 11.

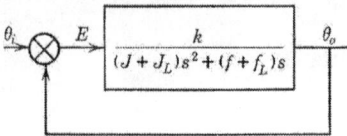

FIGURE 11. Diagram of Figure 2 when K_L is infinite.

The output member conditions treated in this section may sometimes be created deliberately. At other times they may occur accidentally. Hence the conclusions that we should draw from an examination of the transfer function of Equation 47 depends upon the objective of the study. For example, the performance of some servos may be improved by deliberately adding the spring, inertia, and damping and by tuning the elements to a certain frequency. If this is the objective, the analysis should be extended to develop the analytical forms of the function θ_o/θ_i, so that the effect of K_L, f_L, and J_L on θ_o/θ_i can be investigated. This situation may be particularly important when certain frequency phenomena in the overall system behavior are to be neutralized. It is similar in some respects to the problem that is often effectively treated by the well-known Lanchester damper or vibration absorber. It should be mentioned that the damping f_L may be caused by a drag referred to the frame of reference of the system or it may be caused by a drag referred only to the other * inertia J. These matters are illustrated by Figure 12. The analysis given above is applicable only to the system

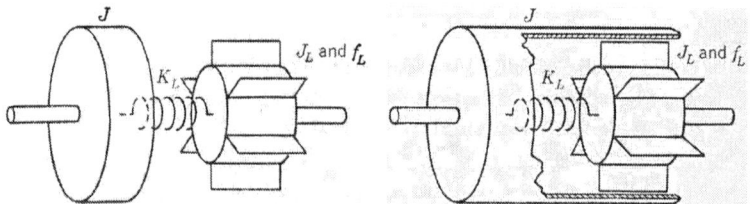

FIGURE 12. Damping with respect to fixed and moving references.

in which the drag is referred to the frame of reference of the system. It therefore is representative of a situation involving energy dissipation for a constant velocity ω_o. The analysis would necessitate modification

* A small servomechanism for instrument purposes that used this principle was developed about 1943 by Dr. A. C. Hall of the Servomechanisms Laboratory at the Massachusetts Institute of Technology.

if f_L were of the other kind, where there would be energy dissipation only during motion of J_L relative to J. That is, there is only relative damping and no energy dissipation when the system is operating at a constant velocity. Synchros are frequently damped in this manner.[38]

When the so-called outboard elements exist even though the designer does not desire them, for example, when it is not feasible to measure the response at the extreme outward end of the system, a different philosophy is needed. Sometimes it may be feasible to measure the output quantity at the extreme end of the system, but it may still be inadvisable to do so. The effects of backlash can often be avoided or minimized by attaching the output measuring device such as a synchro to the output drive motor shaft and by driving the synchro through high-quality instrument gearing. The actual output load may then be driven through high-power gearing in which backlash and elasticity may be present and difficult to control. One objective of a study might then be to introduce into the main loop a mode of compensation to the internal G function that would nullify the effects of the outboard element. In fact, the study may take a variety of forms.

6 Conclusion

A large number of closed-loop control problems can best be treated according to the general procedure outlined in this chapter. The wide variety of typical problems makes difficult their extensive illustration. The objective has been to indicate the pattern of a comprehensive study in the event that one should become necessary. It should be clear, however, that the load disturbances T_L need not always be a torque applied to the output of a positional system. Feedback systems, especially those encountered in industry, may have external disturbances resulting from environment or interaction of other machines or portions of the plant. These disturbances may be the important factor in determining the quality of operation of the feedback system. For such problems an investigation of the error ε may be more desirable than an investigation of the response θ_o. The entire pattern of the general theory in Chapters 6, 7, and 8 can be recast in terms of ε/θ_i or ε/T_L. A quantitative study can then be made of the errors in systems subjected to multiple disturbances. Use of the linear superposition theorem can enable the designer to seek a minimization of error under the multiple disturbances.

10

Experimental Studies in Servomechanisms

1 Introduction

Measurements are performed on closed-loop systems or parts of closed-loop systems to obtain data which confirm designs, permit comparison of different designs, and enhance new designs. The selection of measuring equipment and the data to be taken for each measurement require individual emphasis.

To confirm a closed-loop system design both transient and frequency response tests should be made to compare the actual response and the predicted response. Frequently, extensive testing is necessary to obtain reliable comparisons when selecting one system from many others designed for a particular task. Another aspect of measurement relates to new designs when a choice of proper components to make up the closed loop involves measurement of the dynamic performance of each component. Often direct measurement provides the only feasible method for obtaining quantitative data about such components.

Response measurements of closed-loop system performance have been conducted primarily in the laboratory, but now they must be conducted equally often and with comparable accuracy in the field. The characteristics being measured may refer to components and to systems of relatively low power rating, but they may refer as well to entire processes or controlled members of high intrinsic energy level such as a reaction vat or an aircraft in flight. Measurement problems upon high-power level systems are usually encountered when control is to be applied to a specified process or load member whose design is well known and standardized and the apparatus is already built. Frequently the choice of a component is a problem of economy or procurement. Intricate equipment such as amplifiers or hydraulic transmissions may already be available. Although the engineer can learn nothing about their inner ramification or workings, nevertheless he must use them. Complexity of the components, complexity of their environment, distributed interactions arising between components from invalidity of the lumped-parameter simplification and other factors, prevent the writing of differential equations to represent these systems. Only by measurement can we gain quantitative data about their behavior.

The broadest approach to the problem of performance measurement utilizes the frequency response philosophy, that is, by measuring the vector quantities $\theta_o(j\omega)$ and $\mathcal{E}(j\omega)$ for sinusoidally applied external disturbances $\theta_i(j\omega)$ and $T_L(j\omega)$. The resulting data can be reduced to dimensionless frequency scales and plotted as vector loci. The manner whereby these data were obtained then becomes insignificant because mixtures of measured data and mathematically derived data are used in synthesis.

Because of the wide variety of control problems encountered, and because of the relative newness of the frequency response method applied to the design problem, neither standard instruments nor standard techniques exist for performing frequency response measurements. Improvised instruments and procedures are usually required for each new situation. If measurements are conducted in a well-equipped laboratory, the task of improvising is not difficult. However, there is usually little opportunity to improvise during a test program in the field. Unless carefully designed test equipment is used, the data may not be usable.

Experimental frequency response investigations can be conducted on complicated plants, processes, and control systems without closing the plant down or withdrawing the equipment from its normal duty or operation. However, a careful plan must be adopted for selecting instruments to give sinusoidally varying signals of small amplitude to the system. The disturbances must be of a kind that may be injected into the closed loop without disturbing its normal operation. Considerable ingenuity may be required to devise such instruments and to select the appropriate place in the system where they can be connected. Although the measurement of vector functions for electrical systems and for certain mechanical systems has been obtained with a high degree of accuracy in the laboratory without complicated apparatus, it may not be easy to perform similar measurements in chemical plants or industrial processes. However, the improvement in control made possible by the additional knowledge gained from the measurements will often amply repay the cost and effort of making them.

Inconsistencies will appear in test data. Nonlinearities in the equipment caused by excessive strain, or an excessively large amplitude of test signal, may contribute to them. The data might also show negligible response at relatively low frequencies. Some of these results immediately indicate a lack of suitability of the equipment for any possible application where increased performance calls for an increase in the frequency band width over which $0.7 < M_p < 1.3$. Preliminary or trial results may indicate a grave danger of system instability. In some cases measurements will show that no suitable control can be devised which lies within reasonable range of economy and good engineering judgment.

Data carefully taken may often be difficult to interpret; data containing inconsistencies are almost impossible to interpret. Careful supervision must be given continually to the problems of measurement. The sinusoidal signals applied to the physical system must be sufficiently small to insure approximately linear system operation. The component parts must not exhibit backlash or hysteresis effects to the extent that these undesirable properties cause high harmonic content in the quantities being measured. All these difficulties cited might tend to discourage extensive measurements on closed-loop systems. Fortunately, the difficulty of performing measurements is often offset by the considerable value the designer gains from them.

The following sections of this chapter discuss certain experimental techniques developed at the Massachusetts Institute of Technology for the use of students when conducting frequency response studies on servomechanisms.[27, 72]

2   The Servomechanism Used for Experimental Investigations

An experimental servomechanism especially designed to facilitate dynamical measurements is shown in Figure 1. The components are:

(1) A synchro generator driven by the input θ_i and a synchro control transformer driven by the output θ_o. A voltage, e, proportional to the error, ε, appears at the secondary terminals of the control transformer.

(2) A vacuum tube phase-sensitive demodulator and a filter to convert the alternating error signal, e, to a direct signal and filter it, reducing the ripple voltage caused by rectification. Since the carrier frequency is 400 cycles per second, the time constant of this filter is usually small enough to have negligible effect on dynamic behavior of the system and still provide usable filtering of ripple.

(3) An electronic push-pull power amplifier.

(4) A direct current generator driven at constant speed and having dual control fields excited by the push-pull amplifier.

(5) A servomotor identical in electrical characteristics to the generator.

(6) A gear train connecting the motor to the synchro transformer.

Secondary equipment such as power supplies, 400-cycle voltage sources for the data system, and voltage gain controls are not included in the schematic diagram of Figure 1. The second synchro and a

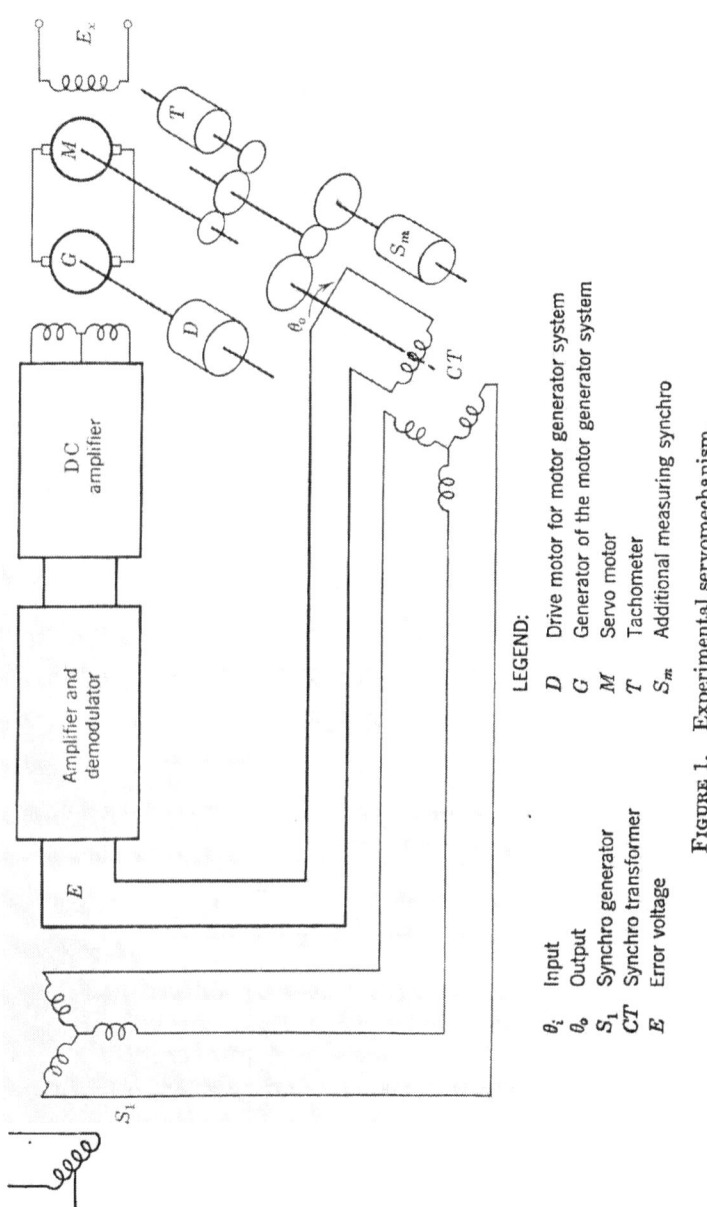

LEGEND:

θ_i	Input	D Drive motor for motor generator system
θ_o	Output	G Generator of the motor generator system
S_1	Synchro generator	M Servo motor
CT	Synchro transformer	T Tachometer
E	Error voltage	S_m Additional measuring synchro

FIGURE 1.   Experimental servomechanism.

tachometer attached to the output gear train are used for auxiliary outout position and output speed indication, respectively.

3 Experimental Procedures

General. The frequency response of a servomechanism can be measured experimentally in various ways, depending upon the information

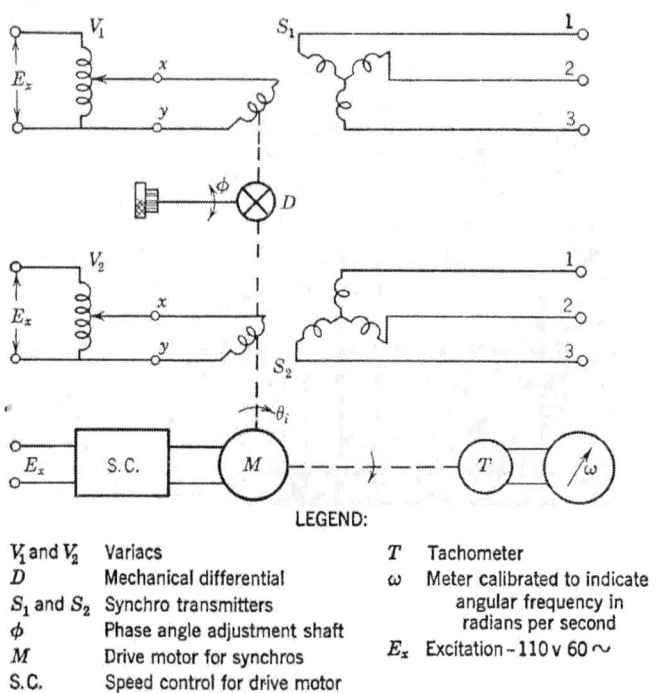

LEGEND:

V_1 and V_2	Variacs	T	Tachometer
D	Mechanical differential	ω	Meter calibrated to indicate
S_1 and S_2	Synchro transmitters		angular frequency in
ϕ	Phase angle adjustment shaft		radians per second
M	Drive motor for synchros	E_x	Excitation – 110 v 60 $\sim$
S.C.	Speed control for drive motor		

FIGURE 2. Sinusoidal signal generator.

desired. If the system is already satisfactorily adjusted, or if it has been made sufficiently stable for preliminary study, the tests may be conducted with the loop closed. Data then obtained are $|\theta_o/\theta_i|$ and Ang θ_o/θ_i. If the system is in a state of development the loop may be open pending changes in design. Useful tests would then determine the overall transfer function $KG(j\omega)$. Finally the loop may never have been closed and all components may not be interconnected. The tests may then be for the purpose of defining the transfer function $KG(j\omega)$ of various isolated components.

Although no basic differences exist between the measuring techniques used when the loop is open and when it is closed, the kind of measuring

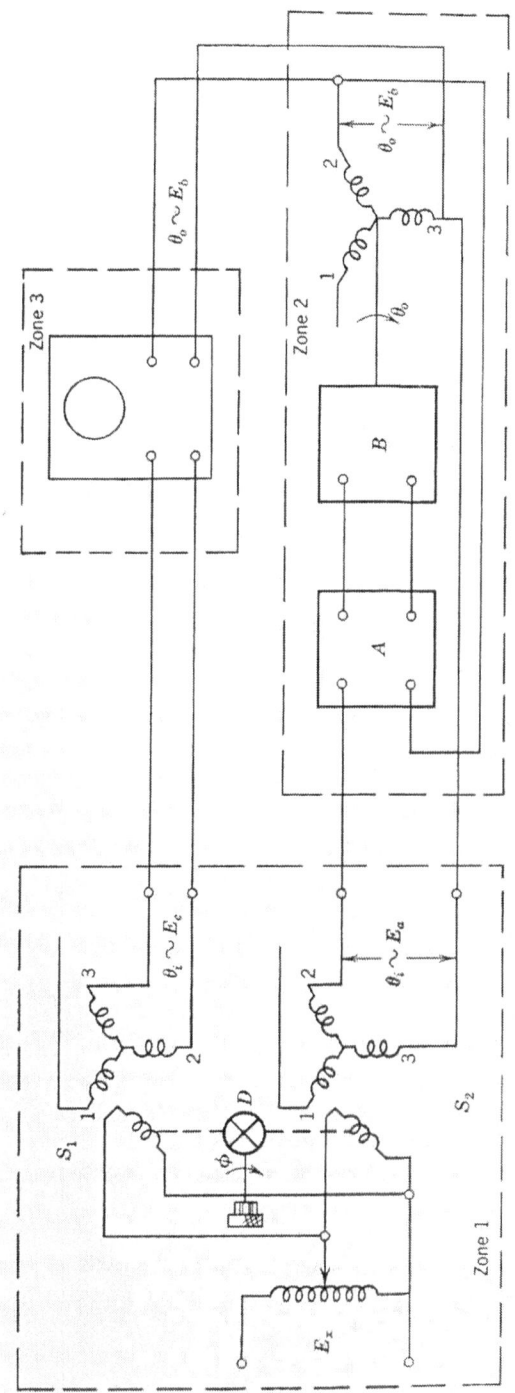

Zone 1. Sine wave generator described in Figure 2.

Zone 2. Servomechanism, except that its input member has been replaced by the synchro S_2 which appears in the sine generator. See Figure 2.

Zone 3. Measuring apparatus which includes a cathode ray oscilloscope.

FIGURE 3.   Diagram of connections for the measurement of θ_o/θ_i.

equipment required depends upon the type of data to be obtained. The skill and patience needed also vary with the type of tests. Whereas closed-loop testing of approximately adjusted systems may not be too difficult, open-loop testing of all systems, whether totally defined or only partially defined, is likely to be quite difficult to perform. Extreme care must be taken in order (1) to use a *small input signal* to hold the operation of all parts of the system within their linear range, (2) to maintain calibration of both the closed-loop and the measuring system during extended test periods.

A mechanism is required to provide the vector excitation signals $\theta_i(j\omega)$ and $T_L(j\omega)$. Usually this part of the test equipment is referred to as a *sine wave generator*. A measuring instrument must also be available to indicate numerical values for the ratio of the magnitudes of the input and output vector quantities, and their relative phase angle. The sine wave generator and a cathode ray oscilloscope appropriately used with electronic instruments to measure angular position and magnitude of input and output can accomplish all the desired measurements. The apparatus and its interconnection to perform the frequency response test are shown in Figures 2, 3, and 4.

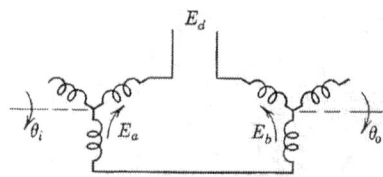

FIGURE 4. · Connections of synchros to give sinusoidally varying voltage from continuous rotation of the rotor.

The apparatus shown schematically in Figure 2 is a sine wave generator. It consists of two conventional synchros, two variacs for control of excitation voltage to the synchros, and a source of rotary motion of adjustable speed to rotate the synchros. One synchro is used to generate the input signal $\theta_i(j\omega)$ of the servomechanism. The other synchro is used to send similar input signal $\theta_i(j\omega + \phi)$ to the cathode ray oscilloscope. The shaft of each synchro rotor is connected to a shaft of a mechanical differential whose third shaft rotates an amount ϕ degrees, equal to the difference in rotation of the two rotor shafts. The dial attached to the third shaft is calibrated in degrees. It therefore reads the phase displacement ϕ between the two signals transmitted by the synchros. Attached to the driving shaft of the synchros is a tachometer for measuring angular frequency or angular speed of rotation of the synchro rotor.

Appropriate connections of the synchros in the sine wave generator and the synchros in the servomechanism (S_2 and S_3, Figure 3) establish voltages E_a and E_b, respectively, proportional to the quantities θ_i and θ_o. When the source of variable speed is adjusted to give proper motions simultaneously to the rotors of the synchros, the vectors quantities $\theta_i(j\omega)$, $\theta_o(j\omega)$, and $\mathcal{E}(j\omega)$ are obtained as voltages. These voltages are amplitude modulations superposed upon a 60 or 400 cycles per second carrier. Thus sinusoidally varying voltages can be compared upon the screen of a cathode ray oscilloscope to measure relative modulation-voltage magnitudes and relative phase shift between the modulation voltages.

Closed-Loop Response Measurements of θ_o/θ_i. The manner in which the test apparatus is used for the determination of a frequency characteristic θ_o/θ_i is shown by the diagram of Figure 3. Notice that windings of the synchro S_2 in the sine wave generator are connected in series with the windings of the synchro transformer driven by the servomotor. This establishes a series connection of the voltages E_a and E_b as shown in Figure 4. The vector voltage difference E_d is then applied to the amplifier input. The excitation voltage of each synchro is adjusted for equal maximum value of voltages E_a and E_b so that when they are 180 degrees out of phase the amplifier voltage E_d is zero. This is the zero error condition. As the synchro rotors S_2 and S_3 are turned, pulsating voltages appear across the terminals of the windings. The servomechanism output member rotates in response to the error voltage signal E_d so that the output motion θ_o causes the voltage E_b exactly to nullify the voltages E_a vectorially.

The terminals of one winding of the synchro S_1 in the sine wave generator are connected to one pair of plates of a cathode ray oscilloscope. The terminals of the synchro S_3 driven by the output motor are connected to the other pair of plates of the oscilloscope. In this manner Lissajous figures are made to appear on the screen whenever the phase of the voltages E_a and E_b differ. Thus, as the phase of the output with respect to the input varies with frequency, the configuration of the Lissajous figure changes. The magnitude of the phase ϕ is obtained by reducing the Lissajous figure to a straight line on the screen by rotating the shaft of the mechanical differential in the sine generator. The amount of shaft rotation indicated on the calibrated dial is the phase difference between the input $\theta_i(j\omega)$ and the output $\theta_o(j\omega)$.

The use of a cathode ray oscilloscope for the measurement of the vector quantities θ_o, θ_i, and $\mathcal{E}$ eliminates the need for additional measuring instruments. The oscilloscope can be calibrated as a voltmeter to measure the magnitudes $|\theta_o|$, $|\theta_i|$, and $|\mathcal{E}|$, or the magnitude ratio $|\theta_o/\theta_i|$. The phase dial on the sine generator can be calibrated directly in degrees of phase difference $\phi = \text{Ang } \theta_o - \text{Ang } \theta_i = \text{Ang } \theta_o/\theta_i$.

The magnitude calibration of the test is established by applying a disturbance $\theta_i(j\omega)$ small enough to make the output response $\theta_o(j\omega)$ free of saturation effects and large enough to prevent slow jerky operation.

At a very low value of frequency, the output response θ_o can be considered identical in magnitude to the input. This response can be chosen as *unity*. The voltage representing it is put on to the vertical plates of the oscilloscope, and the deflection y_o on the screen is initially set at unity or, for example, 10 units. As the frequency of input is varied, the magnitude of output $|\theta_o|$ is obtained for any subsequent value of ω merely by bringing to zero the gain of the amplifier exciting the x axis plates, and then reading the voltage indicated by the y axis deflection for that value of ω.

The phase calibration is obtained from the behavior of the Lissajous figure. When $\theta_o(j\omega)$ is placed upon the y axis and $\theta_i(j\omega)$ upon the x axis of the oscilloscope, a Lissajous figure as shown in Figure 6, item 4, is obtained. Since the voltages applied to the plates are 100 per cent modulated, the carrier shape of figure in the scope is a random ellipse until calibrated. To establish a reference phase, it is assumed that the output and input are in phase when the system is operated at very low frequency. The indicating system is made to agree with this condition by rotating the mechanical differential to cause the elliptical shape to collapse into a straight line. The dial then indicates zero relative phase for Ang θ_o/θ_i. For each higher frequency of input signal, the Lissajous figure first takes the form of an ellipse which is collapsed to a straight line by rotating the mechanical differential dial. The dial rotation gives the relative phase reading directly.

Open-Loop Response Measurements $\theta_o/\mathcal{E}$. The response of the equipment of Figure 1, operated as an open loop, can be obtained by connecting the test apparatus as shown in Figure 5. The windings of synchro S_2 in the sine wave generator are connected directly to the amplifier and now furnish the *input signal* to the opened loop. This signal is in the form of a voltage proportional to a fictitious angular error $\mathcal{E}(j\omega)$. The excitation of the synchro S_2 is reduced to a low value by adjustment of the variac V_2. The terminals of the synchro S_1 are connected to one pair of plates of the cathode ray oscilloscope. The output velocity $\omega_o(j\omega)$ of the system is indicated by a tachometer that gives its information in the form of a modulated carrier. Attached to the output shaft of the servomechanism is a two-phase drag-cup motor serving as a tachometer with one winding excited from a source of voltage of the same frequency as that used to excite the synchros. The other winding of the tachometer furnishes an alternating voltage whose envelope is a measure of the velocity of the motor armature. The terminals of the winding are connected to the other set of plates of the cathode ray oscilloscope. This arrangement gives a Lissajous figure on the screen of the oscilloscope, as indicated by item 5 of Figure 6.

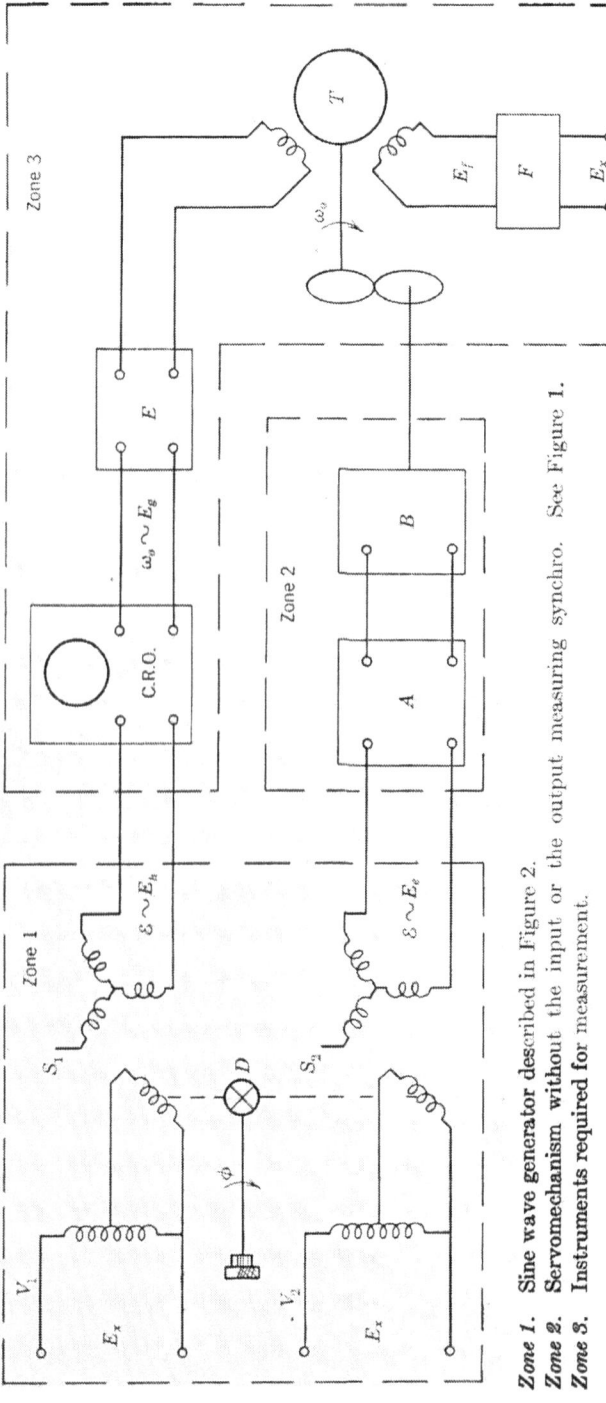

FIGURE 5. Measuring open-loop transfer function.

Zone 1. Sine wave generator described in Figure 2.

Zone 2. Servomechanism without the input or the output measuring synchro. See Figure 1.

Zone 3. Instruments required for measurement.

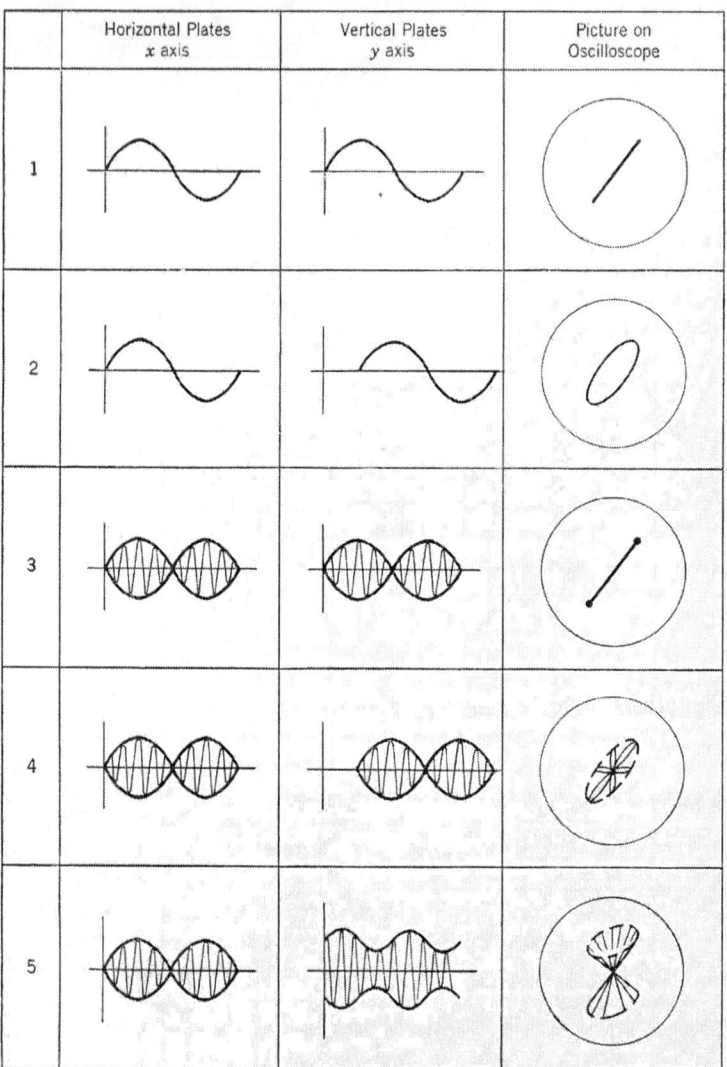

FIGURE 6. Lissajous figures.

The calibration of the open-loop system for test is particularly difficult and tedious. Furthermore, the selection of the speed of operation of the equipment during the sinusoidal test is important. For example, the open-loop operation of the system of Figure 1 may exhibit very poor wave shape of the velocity vector $\omega_o(j\omega)$ when the sinusoidal operation cycles about the standstill or zero velocity point. Furthermore, the system may exhibit very different properties when operated about the standstill condition from those exhibited when operated about a mean speed somewhere within the operating range. This means that open-loop testing must be conducted throughout the regions of operating speed that are encountered in normal use of the system as a closed loop. Operation about a mean speed other than zero may be obtained by unbalancing the electronic system so that a bias speed ω_{oss} is obtained for zero test signal.

The test procedure applicable with Figure 5 permits a complete exploration of the characteristics of the opened-loop equipment over a wide range of speeds and a wide range of loading. The apparent advantages of the broad testing possibilities with the opened loop may be quickly lost if there is a tendency for the operating point to drift during long periods of testing. Also unbalancing the electronic components to give the bias speed effect may cause nonlinear operations of the overall equipment.

The excitation of synchro S_2 establishes the magnitude of the voltage E_e, which in turn determines the sinusoidal component of the output velocity ω_o. The voltages E_h and E_g are therefore respectively proportional to error ε, and velocity ω_o. They may require amplification or attenuation at the oscilloscope to provide easily recognized Lissajous patterns.

The phase calibration problem is made difficult in the open-loop measurement because the voltage E_h is essentially a 100 per cent modulated voltage whereas the voltage E_g is less than 100 per cent modulated because of the finite average velocity being measured by the tachometer. Furthermore, the ratio of the magnitude of the sinusoidal velocity component to the magnitude of the average velocity influences the precision of phase measurement. Before the Lissajous figures given by such voltages may be interpreted, E_g must be carefully adjusted.

The carrier frequency of E_g and E_h must be nearly in phase. Also the -90-degree phase shift in the voltage E_g with respect to the reference voltage introduced by the tachometer must be nullified in order to compare the modulation component of the two voltages. Item 5, Figure 6, shows the voltage forms which should appear at the oscilloscope terminals to permit phase measurements. When the modulating frequency is very low, the elliptically shaped bases of the hour-glass figure may be collapsed by rotating the mechanical differential shaft. This rotation will zero the phase dial. As new values of modulating frequency are applied, the rotation of the phase dial gives directly the phase angle in degrees between the modulation signals.

When the test data for ω_o/ε are obtained, it becomes necessary to convert them by actual calculation into data for θ_o/ε. The relation which gives the conversion is

$$\frac{\theta_o(j\omega)}{\varepsilon(j\omega)} = \frac{1}{j\omega}\frac{\omega_o(j\omega)}{\varepsilon(j\omega)} = KG(j\omega) \tag{1}$$

The value for $KG(j\omega)$ can also be obtained graphically by plotting the data for ω_o/ε in decibels as offsets from a -6 decibels per octave line and a -90-degree phase line as indicated in Figure 7.

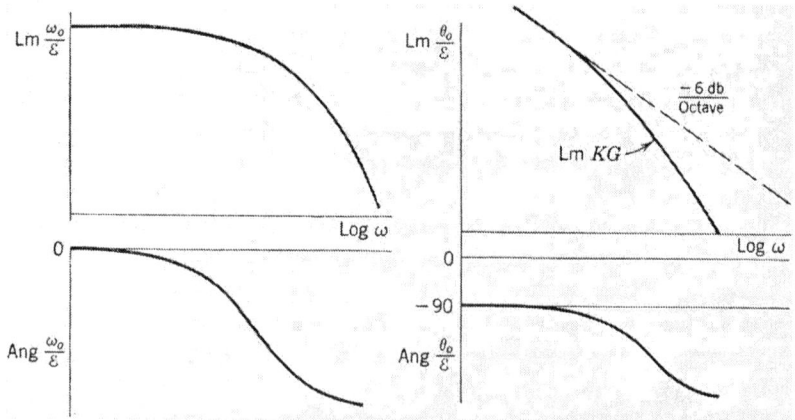

Figure 7. Method for converting open-loop measured data into transfer function form.

Closed-Loop Testing to Obtain $KG(j\omega)$. The transfer function KG can also be obtained from the closed-loop measurement of θ_o/θ_i. A graphical procedure for doing this is outlined in Figure 8.

4 Tabulation of Measured Data

The measured data for θ_o/θ_i appears in Table 1. The graphs for these data are plotted in Figure 10, where they are compared with the calculated performance of the system for the identical adjustment. These calculated data are presented in Table 2. The analysis which substantiates them is given in Section 5.

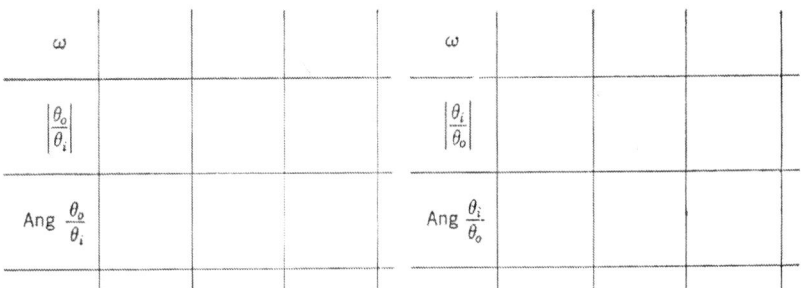

1. Measure Data   2. Form Reciprocal

$$\frac{\theta_o}{\theta_i} = \frac{KG}{1 + KG}$$

$$\frac{\theta_o}{\mathcal{E}} = KG$$

$$\frac{\theta_i}{\theta_o} = \frac{1}{KG} + 1$$

$$\frac{\mathcal{E}}{\theta_o} = \frac{1}{KG}$$

3. Formulas for Reciprocal Studies

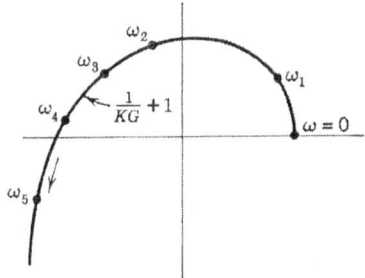

4. Graph of Reciprocal $\frac{\theta_i}{\theta_o}$

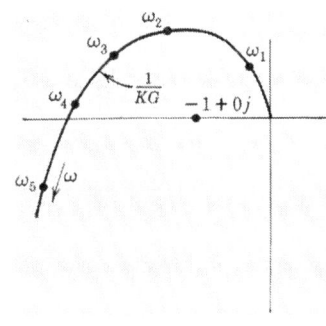

5. Graph for KG^{-1}

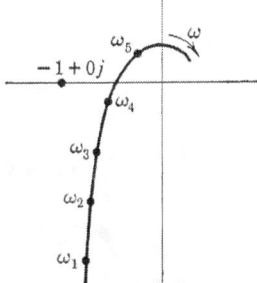

6. Graph for KG

FIGURE 8. Obtaining $KG(j\omega)$ from closed-loop measurements.

The measured data for $\omega_o/\mathcal{E}$ is given in Table 3. The graph for the transfer function is plotted in Figure 11. The measured values are compared with the calculated values for the transfer function KG as shown in Table 4.

TABLE 1

EXPERIMENTAL SERVOMECHANISM MEASURED RESPONSE $\dfrac{\theta_o}{\theta_i}(j\omega)$

u	ω	$\left\|\dfrac{\theta_o}{\theta_i}\right\|$	Ang $\dfrac{\theta_o}{\theta_i}$	$\left\|\dfrac{\theta_o}{\theta_i}\right\|$ Decibels
0.0375	2	1.00	0.0	0.00
0.075	4	1.00	0.0	0.00
0.112	6	1.01	−5.0	0.09
0.150	8	1.04	−21.0	0.34
0.187	10	1.10	−33.0	0.83
0.225	12	1.20	−41.0	1.58
0.262	14	1.25	−53.0	1.94
0.300	16	1.28	−63.0	2.14
0.338	18	1.30	−72.0	2.28
0.375	20	1.28	−93.0	2.14
0.412	22	1.22	−105.0	1.73
0.449	24	1.10	−120.0	0.83
0.486	26	1.00	−127.0	0.00
0.523	28	0.85	−136.0	−1.41
0.560	30	0.78	−143.0	−2.16
0.656	35	0.55	−159.0	−5.19
0.750	40	0.40	−173.0	−7.96

TABLE 2

EXPERIMENTAL SERVOMECHANISM CALCULATED RESPONSE $\dfrac{\theta_o}{\theta_i}(j\omega)$

(From data of Table 5.)

u	ω	$\dfrac{\theta_o}{\theta_i}$	Ang $\dfrac{\theta_o}{\theta_i}$	$\dfrac{\theta_o}{\theta_i}$ Decibels
0.120	6.4	1.10	−20.0	0.8
0.186	10.0	1.15	−36.0	1.2
0.25	13.4	1.25	−55.0	1.9
0.32	17.1	1.30	−85.0	2.28
0.39	20.9	1.12	−115.0	1.0
0.47	25.2	0.79	−145.0	−2.0
0.53	28.4	0.52	−164.0	−5.6
0.65	34.8	0.35	−180.0	−9.0

TABLE 3

MEASURED VALUES FOR THE OPEN-LOOP RESPONSE $\frac{\theta_o}{\varepsilon}$ (ju)

Angular Frequency, ω	Dimensionless Frequency, u	Magnitude of $\frac{\omega_o}{\varepsilon}$ (ju)	Angle of $\frac{\omega_o}{\varepsilon}$ (ju)	Magnitude of $\frac{\theta_o}{\varepsilon}$ (ju)*	Angle of $\frac{\theta_o}{\varepsilon}$ (ju)*	Magnitude † $\frac{\theta_o}{\varepsilon}$ (ju)* db
1	0.0187	1.00	0	1.00	−90	0
2	0.0375	0.98	−2	0.49	−92	−6.56
3	0.0562	0.94	−8	0.31	−98	−10.1
5	0.0937	0.90	−14	0.18	−104	−14.9
7	0.131	0.86	−18	0.12	−108	−18.4
9	0.168	0.83	−21	0.09	−111	−20.9
11	0.206	0.81	−27	0.07	−117	−23.1
13	0.244	0.79	−33	0.06	−123	−24.4
15	0.281	0.76	−39	0.051	−129	−25.8
17	0.318	0.72	−43	0.042	−133	−27.5
19	0.356	0.66	−49	0.035	−139	−29.1
21	0.393	0.61	−53	0.029	−143	−30.8
24	0.450	0.56	−60	0.023	−150	−32.8
28	0.524	0.51	−64	0.018	−154	−34.9
32	0.600	0.45	−71	0.014	−161	−37.0
36	0.674	0.40	−75	0.011	−165	−39.2
40	0.750	0.38	−82	0.0095	−172	−40.9
50	0.936	0.29	−92	0.0057	−182	−44.4

* Calculated from $\frac{\omega_o}{\varepsilon}$ (ju).   † Calibration factor plus 35 db.

TABLE 4

CALCULATED VALUES OPEN-LOOP RESPONSE $\dfrac{\theta_o}{\mathcal{E}}(ju)$

(From data of Table 5.)

Dimensionless Frequency, u	Magnitude $\dfrac{\theta_o}{\mathcal{E}}(ju)$, in Decibels	Angle $\dfrac{\theta_o}{\mathcal{E}}(ju)$, Degrees
0.1	+20	−107
0.2	+13	−124
0.3	+9.0	−137
0.4	+5.0	−151
0.5	+2.0	−164
0.6	−1.0	−175
0.7	−3.3	−185
0.8	−5.5	−194
0.9	−7.7	−201
1.0	−9.3	−208

5 Analytical Checks

To provide a check on the accuracy of the experimental frequency response measurements, an analytical study was undertaken utilizing a differential equation approach and definite values for individual parameters. Experimental methods were used to determine the value of these parameters as tabulated in Table 5.

To systematize the mathematical analysis for the system, the block diagram of Figure 9 was used. The differential equations and the transfer function KG were formulated following the procedure shown in Chapter 5. The transfer function $KG(s)$ is calculated as follows:

$$\mathcal{E}(s) = \theta_i(s) - \theta_o(s) \tag{2}$$

$$E_o(s) = E_m \mathcal{E}(s) \tag{3}$$

$$E_1(s) = K_1 E_m \mathcal{E}(s) \tag{4}$$

$$E_2(s) = K_c G_c(s) E_1(s) \tag{5}$$

$$I_f(s) = \frac{\mu E_2(s)}{(R_p + R_f)(\tau_f s + 1)} \tag{6}$$

where

$$\tau_f = \frac{L_f}{R_p + R_f} \tag{7}$$

$$E_g(s) = K_2 I_f(s) \tag{8}$$

$$I_a(s) = \frac{E_g(s) - E_b(s)}{(R_g + R_m) + s(L_m + L_g)} \tag{9}$$

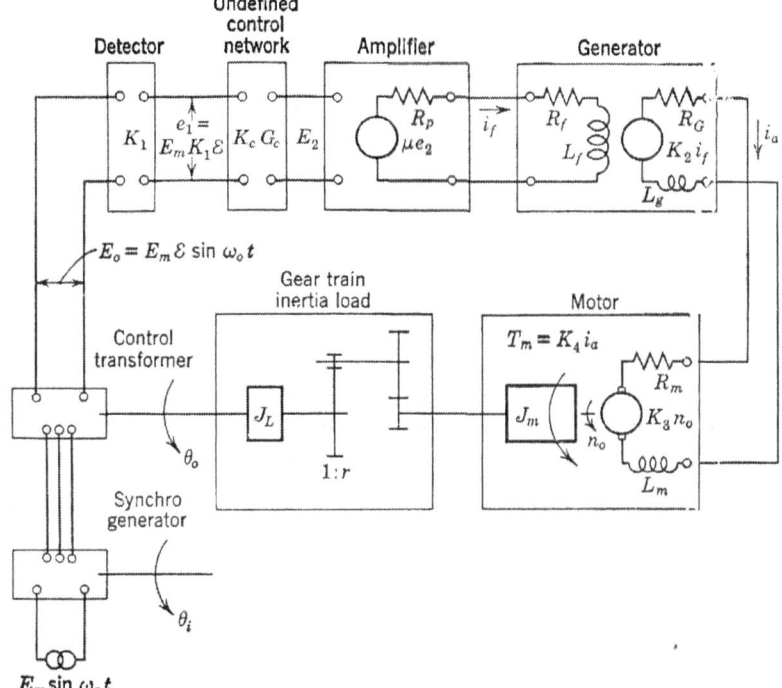

FIGURE 9. Block diagram of system used for experimental stud.

$$E_b(s) = K_3\omega_m(s) = K_3 s\theta_m(s) \tag{10}$$

$$\left[J_m + \frac{J_L}{r^2}\right] s^2\theta_m(s) = T_m(s) = K_4 I_a(s) \tag{11}$$

$$\left.\begin{aligned} \theta_o(s) &= \frac{1}{r}\theta_m(s) \\[2mm] T_o(s) &= rT_m(s) \end{aligned}\right\} \tag{12}$$

giving

$$\frac{\theta_o(s)}{\mathcal{E}(s)} = \frac{\mu K_1 E_m K_4 K_2}{(R_p + R_f)(R_m + R_g)} [K_c G_c(s)] \frac{r}{\tau_{mg}(r^2 J_m + J_L)}$$

$$\frac{1}{s(\tau_f s + 1)\left[s^2 + \dfrac{1}{\tau_{mg}}s + \dfrac{K_4 r^2 K_3}{\tau_{mg}(R_m + R_g)(r^2 J_m + J_L)}\right]} \tag{13}$$

where

$$\tau_{mg} = \frac{L_m + L_g}{R_m + R_g}$$

TABLE 5

NUMERICAL PARAMETERS FOR AN EXPERIMENTAL SERVOMECHANISM SYSTEM

K_1	(detector constant) = 0.9 volt per volt	
μ	(amplifier gain) = adjustable	
R_p	(amplifier resistance) = 10,000 ohms	
R_f	(generator field resistance) = 1380 ohms	Measured value T_f = 0.01 second
L_f	(generator field inductance) = 16 henries	
τ_f	(measured time constant) = 0.01 second	
K_2	(generator constant) = 1500 volts per ampere	
R_g	(generator armature resistance) = 56 ohms	
R_m	(motor armature resistance) = 34 ohms	
n_o	(motor shaft speed expressed in rpm)	
K_3	(motor back voltage constant) = 2.06 volts per motor rps	
K_4 ·	(motor torque constant) = 46.4 in ounces per ampere	
J_m	(motor armature inertia) = 0.151 in.^{2} lb	
r	(gear ratio; negligible inertia) = 100	
J_L	(load inertia) = 0.156 slug feet^2	
E_m	(peak value of supply voltage) = 81.2 volts	
$L_m + L_g$	(M-G armature circuit self ind.) = 0.58 henry	

The individual values of R_p, R_f, L_f, in Table 5, are not used to calculate the generator time constant τ_f because they are obtained using static permeability values for the generator magnetic circuit. This fact, coupled with an incorrect prediction of the dynamic plate impedance of the vacuum tubes by use of straight load lines intersecting the tube characteristics, gave a calculated value of τ_f much lower than the measured value.

The measured value of R_g includes the effect of armature resistance and armature reaction in the generator. The static value of the resistance is 34 ohms, identical with the motor.

The groups of terms in Equation 13 have the following numerical values:

$$r^2 J_m + J_L = 3.91 + 1.87 = 5.78 \text{ in. lb sec}^2$$

$$\frac{K_4 r^2 K_3}{2\pi(R_m + R_g)} = 106$$

$$\frac{K_4 r^2 K_3}{\tau_{mg} 2\pi(R_m + R_g)(r^2 J_m + J_L)} = \frac{\dfrac{46.4}{16} \times (100)^2 \times \dfrac{2.06}{6.28}}{0.0065 \times 90 \times 5.78} = 2850 \text{ seconds}^{-2}$$

$$\frac{1}{\tau_{mg}} = \frac{R_m + R_g}{L_m + L_g} = \frac{90}{0.58} = 155 \text{ seconds}^{-1}$$

These values inserted in Equation 13 give

$$\frac{\theta_o(s)}{\mathcal{E}(s)} = K_{\text{overall}}G_c(s)\,\frac{1}{s(0.01s + 1)(s^2 + 155s + 2850)} \tag{14}$$

where $G_c(s)$ is an unspecified block in the diagram of Figure 9. By considering $G_c(s) = 1$ and setting the overall gain K consistent with M_p = 1.3 the curves of Figure 10 and 11 result. The details of the mathe-

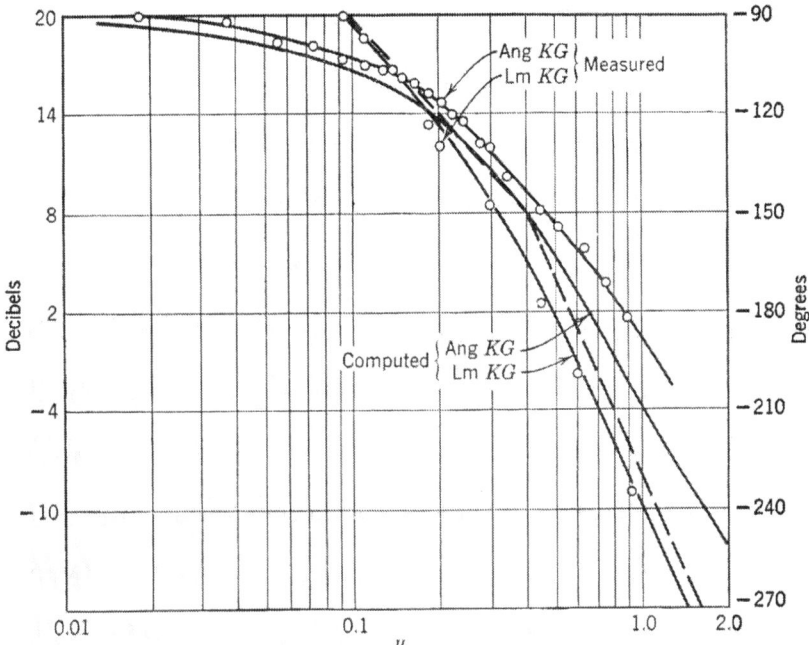

FIGURE 10.   Comparison of computed and measured transfer function.

matics follow the procedure developed in Chapter 8. When the loop is closed, the value of K_{overall} equals 6.5×10^4.

One of a series of calculations giving the transient response of this system used the transfer function

$$KG(s) = \frac{5 \times 10^4}{s(0.01s + 1)(s^2 + 155s + 2850)} \tag{15}$$

The output response $\theta_o(t)$ calculated from Equation 15 for a step disturbance of angle θ_i gives as a dimensionless response

$$\frac{\theta_o(t)}{\theta_i} = 1.00 - 3.08te^{-120t} - 0.79e^{-120t}$$
$$+ 1.18e^{-6.9t}\cos(17.7t - 218.9°) \tag{16}$$

Figure 12 is a plot of Equation 16; the corresponding M_p was 1.13.

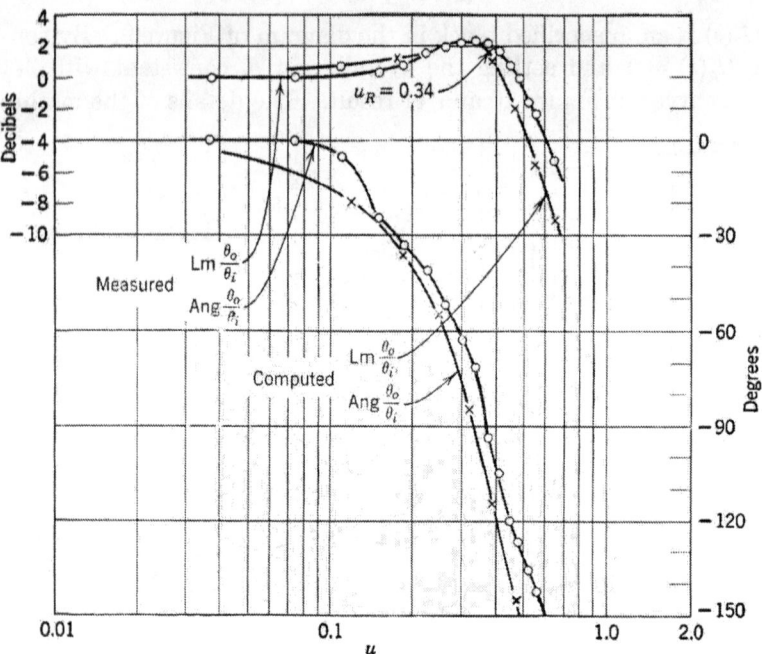

FIGURE 11.   Comparison of computed and measured overall response θ_o/θ_i.

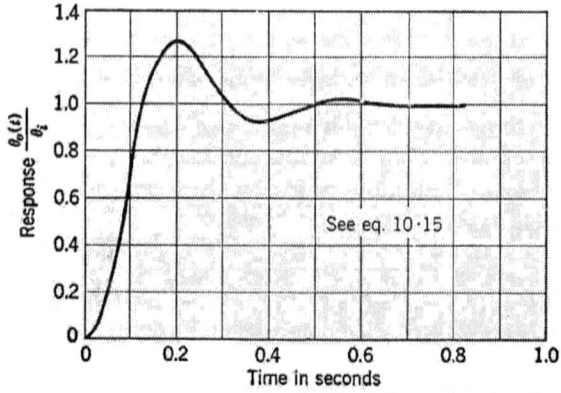

FIGURE 12.   Typical angle transient of experimental servomechanism for $M_p = 1.13$

6 Conclusion

Figures 10 and 11 show the general agreement between the computed and measured data. The observed departure between measured and calculated data results from the difficulty of obtaining a good zero phase point during the calibration of the instruments. At low frequencies, coulomb friction in the motor bearings and armature commutation causes a distorted wave form and makes equivalent phase measurement difficult.

The results obtained are believed to be consistent with good engineering practice. The measurements can be repeated by independent operators. The measured values are sufficiently accurate to be used jointly with partially calculated information as a means of synthesis.

Perhaps more important than the actual measured results is the tendency of the measurement methods herein indicated gradually to widen the field of dynamical measurements. In aerodynamics, process control, turbine governing, hydraulic-machine design, and, strangely enough, in new electrical designs, where the method originated and was supposed to be quite thoroughly explored, measurement techniques are continually being extended.

11

Method for Approximating the Transient Response from the Frequency Response

Author's Note

The extension of synthesis and design techniques in closed-loop control problems by the frequency response methods frequently relegated the transient analysis to background status. Often it was ignored entirely with the result that the transient response of some designs was not satisfactory.

Many attempts have been made to correlate closely the transient behavior and the frequency behavior. In Chapter 4 a criterion of correlation based on observed phenomena was given. Particular significance was attached to the quantity M_p, and its value in the region $1.2 < M_p < 1.6$ was established as a working basis for many problems. Unfortunately this criterion bounds the frequency function only throughout a small range of frequencies in the neighborhood of resonance. In Chapter 8 phase margin and gain margin as design criteria were also described. These quantities also bound the behavior of the function near the resonant frequency.

To simplify the analytical problem of relating the frequency and transient response, a thesis investigation made by Mr. George F. Floyd under the supervision of the authors was conducted at the Massachusetts Institute of Technology. The basis of the investigation was the inverse transform of the frequency function. The specific aim was to obtain a relatively quick approximate method for performing both the direct and inverse transformation.

The result obtained is believed to be easier to use than another approximation procedure developed by Bedford and Fredendall.[67] It is certainly easier to use than any exact methods [48] when the differential equation associated with the function is greater than fourth order. In general, the accuracy of the method is better than 5 per cent and may be increased by the use of sufficient terms in the series expansions involved.

Mr. Floyd has generously permitted the inclusion of his work in this book. It should be a great help in many design studies. Because it is not possible for the authors to improve upon the treatment given by Mr. Floyd, his work is given herewith with only slight rearrangement of text and unification of symbols.

1 General

At the present time, techniques for the synthesis of closed-loop systems are based on system frequency response rather than system transient response. On the other hand, since closed-loop systems are subjected to inputs which cause transients, we must have a knowledge of the general manner in which the system settles down when subjected to a discontinuous input. In many instances, the transient response of the system is calculated on the assumption that the input was a Heaviside step of position or velocity. Often the response of the system to these test inputs is used as a criterion for the response to arbitrary inputs. If the input contains spurious signals or noise it has been shown [35, 65] that the step function response may be misleading, and that when noise inputs are of importance, it is preferable to study the time response of the system to typical, rather than test, inputs.

It is shown in Section 7 that the time response of a system to an arbitrary input may be broken up into the sum of two terms. One of these terms depends on the particular initial conditions of the system and may always be made identically zero by a proper choice of the initial conditions. The other term depends on the driving function. It does not depend on the initial conditions but it may be thought of as the forced response of the system to the particular driving function. The forced response of the system expressed symbolically as $\theta_{of}(t)$ to an input function $\theta_i(t)$ is given by [48]

$$\theta_{of}(t) = \int_0^t h(t - x)\theta_i(x) \, dx \tag{1}$$

where $h(t)$ is the response of the system to a unit impulse applied at $t = 0$ with the system at rest. The impulse is taken as the limit of a positive pulse enclosing unit area as the duration of the pulse tends to zero. (See Section 7.) The overall system transfer function $H(s)$ is,

$$H(s) = \frac{\theta_o(s)}{\theta_i(s)} \tag{2}$$

Since the transform of a unit impulse is unity, $h(t)$ is the inverse transform of $H(s)$.

When determining the time response of the system to typical inputs, it is convenient to neglect the initial condition transient and determine only the forced response as given by Equation 1. The reader will recall that the treatment of initial conditions was given in Chapter 3, Section 8. The reasons for not attempting to determine the exact initial condition transient are:

1. In actual practice the exact initial state of the system may vary widely.
2. During the initial condition transient, the system may have a large error, which introduces nonlinearities and so forth.

3. The duration and general nature of a small initial condition transient may be determined qualitatively by inspection of $h(t)$ as is shown in Section 7.

In general, if the design is carried out on the frequency response basis, the impulse response $h(t)$ may be determined in order to give both the forced response to typical inputs and also the duration and general nature of the initial condition transient. The step function is the time integral of the impulse. Therefore the response to the step is the time integral of the response to the impulse.

The determination of $h(t)$ by classical, operational, or transform methods involves the conventional solution of a differential equation. This requires solution of the characteristic equation. When its order is greater than four, the determination of its roots is quite tedious.[68] Once the roots are obtained it is still necessary to determine the multiplying constants appearing in the function $h(t)$. Therefore, an exact determination of $h(t)$ will in general require a large amount of work. However, since the differential equation of a system usually attempts to describe only the most important characteristics of the mechanism, it is more or less approximate. Therefore, an approximate determination of $h(t)$ may be perfectly satisfactory in many problems.

The purpose of this chapter is to develop an *approximate method of calculating $h(t)$ when the frequency response $H(j\omega)$ is known*. The method involves only routine calculations. Its degree of accuracy depends on the number of terms used in the approximation procedure and thus may be varied depending on the degree of accuracy which is needed. The general approximation method was suggested during a conference with Professor E. A. Guillemin of the Massachusetts Institute of Technology.

2 Derivation of the Approximate Inverse Transformation

The general problem of determining $h(t)$, knowing $H(s)$, is performing the inverse Laplace transformation. Throughout this treatment, it is assumed that:

1. $H(s)$ may be written as the ratio of two rational polynomials in s with real and constant coefficients.
2. $\lim\limits_{s \to \infty} H(s) = 0$
3. $H(s)$ has no poles in the right half s plane or on the imaginary axis.

In general, the inverse transform $h(t)$ of $H(s)$ is given by the integral

$$h(t) = \frac{1}{2\pi j} \int_{c-j\infty}^{c+j\infty} H(s)e^{ts}\, ds \tag{3}$$

where the path of integration is parallel to the imaginary axis and to the right of all poles of $H(s)$.

Since all the poles of $H(s)$ are in the left-hand plane, the path of integration may be made the imaginary axis. Thus

$$h(t) = \frac{1}{2\pi j} \int_{-j\infty}^{j\infty} H(s)e^{ts} \, ds \tag{4}$$

The substitution of

$$\left. \begin{aligned} s &= (j\omega) \\ H(s) &= \operatorname{Re} H(j\omega) + j \operatorname{Im} H(j\omega) \\ e^{ts} &= e^{j\omega t} = \cos \omega t + j \sin \omega t \end{aligned} \right\} \tag{5}$$

in Equation 4 gives it a form that permits desirable simplification. In Equation 5 the symbols Re and Im mean "real part of" and "imaginary part of" respectively. With these substitutions, Equation 4 becomes

$$h(t) = \frac{1}{2\pi} \int_{-\infty}^{+\infty} \{\operatorname{Re} H(j\omega) \cos t\omega - \operatorname{Im} H(j\omega) \sin t\omega\} \, d\omega$$

$$+ \frac{j}{2\pi} \int_{-\infty}^{+\infty} \{\operatorname{Re} H(j\omega) \sin t\omega + \operatorname{Im} H(j\omega) \cos t\omega\} \, d\omega \tag{6}$$

Since $H(s)$ is the ratio of polynomials in s having only real and constant coefficients, it follows that $\operatorname{Re} H(j\omega)$ is an even function in ω and $\operatorname{Im} H(j\omega)$ is an odd function in ω. Then since $\cos t\omega$ is even and $\sin t\omega$ is odd, the integrand of the first integral of Equation 6 is even in ω while that of the second integral is odd in ω. Since the range of integration is from $-\infty$ to $+\infty$, the value of the first integral is twice that from 0 to ∞, whereas the value of the second is zero. Thus Equation 6 reduces to the form

$$h(t) = \frac{1}{\pi} \int_0^\infty [\operatorname{Re} H(j\omega) \cos t\omega] \, d\omega - \frac{1}{\pi} \int_0^\infty [\operatorname{Im} H(j\omega) \sin t\omega] \, d\omega \tag{7}$$

In Equation 7, both integrals represent functions of time t. Since t enters only in the cosine and sine terms, the first integral is an even function of time while the second is an odd function of time.

By taking the integration indicated in Equation 4 along a closed path which includes the imaginary axis from $-j\infty$ to $j\infty$, and a semicircle of a large radius in the right-hand plane, the value $h(t)$ can be shown to be equal to zero for all negative values of time. The proof follows from the fact that the sum of the residues at the poles of $H(s)e^{ts}$ within this contour is zero, because $H(s)$ has no poles in the right half plane. This means that *numerically* the two functions of time in Equation 7 are equal for all values of t. Therefore for all positive values of time [62]

$$h(t) = \frac{2}{\pi} \int_0^\infty [\text{Re } H(j\omega) \cos t\omega] \, d\omega \qquad (8)$$

Equation 8 is the *exact inverse transformation* for an $H(s)$ that fulfills the previously stated conditions 1, 2, and 3. It will be the basis for the approximate inverse transformation.

It is well known that performing the integration of Equation 8 is difficult because few practical engineering problems yield functions, Re $H(j\omega)$, which are sufficiently simple. The time function resulting from the evaluation of the integral of even these simple functions is not always recognized. However, a simplified example can be chosen to illustrate the steps necessary in the exact evaluation of the integral of Equation 8. Then approximate methods for performing the same integration can be discussed with greater clarity. The example to be considered involves predicting the transient response of a two-phase motor. A control field voltage e_c is suddenly applied to this motor. The problem is to find the time variation of the motor speed when the transfer function relating the rotor angular velocity ω_m to the control voltage e_c is known. The specific transfer function for the motor is assumed to be

$$\frac{\omega_m}{e_c}(j\omega) = \frac{K_m}{j\omega\tau_m + 1} \qquad (9)$$

From Equation 9, the real part of the transfer function becomes

$$\text{Re}\left[\frac{\omega_m}{e_c}(j\omega)\right] = \text{Re}\left[\frac{K_m}{j\omega\tau_m + 1}\right] \qquad (10)$$

$$= \frac{K_m}{\sqrt{\omega^2\tau_m^2 + 1}} \cos \phi \qquad (11)$$

The value of $\cos \phi$ is known to be

$$\cos \phi = \frac{1}{\sqrt{\omega^2\tau_m^2 + 1}} \qquad (12)$$

Therefore, the integral of Equation 8 can be written to give the impulse response $h(t)$ of the motor. The value is

$$h(t) = \frac{2}{\pi} \int_0^\infty \frac{K_m \cos t\omega}{(\omega^2\tau_m^2 + 1)} \, d\omega \qquad (13)$$

A change of variable $\omega \tau_m = u$ permits the change of Equation 13 to a simpler form, thus

$$h(t) = \frac{2}{\pi} \int_0^\infty \frac{K_m \dfrac{1}{\tau_m}}{(u^2 + 1)} \cos \frac{t}{\tau_m} u \, du \qquad (14)$$

The exact impulse response of the motor can be found from Equation 14 because this particular equation is integrable.* Thus the value $h(t)$ is

$$h(t) = \frac{2}{\pi} \frac{K_m}{\tau_m} \left[\frac{\pi}{2} e^{-(t/\tau_m)} \right] \qquad (15)$$

The integral of $h(t)$ for Equation 15 gives the response of the motor to a step function of voltage on the control field. Thus

$$\omega_m(t) = \int h(t) \, dt \qquad (16)$$

$$= \frac{K_m}{\tau_m} \int e^{-(t/\tau_m)} \, dt \qquad (17)$$

$$= -K_m e^{-(t/\tau_m)} + C \qquad (18)$$

The constant of integration, C, is found by putting $t = 0$ in Equation 18. The motor speed ω_m is zero for $t = 0$ because the rotor, being characterized by inertia, cannot acquire a finite speed during the application of the step function disturbance of voltage. Hence $C = K_m$ and the motor speed is

$$\omega_m(t) = [1 - e^{-(t/\tau_m)}] K_m e_c \qquad (19)$$

The motor speed transient predicted by Equation 19 is known to be correct. This verifies the exact evaluation of the integral in Equation 8 for the simple illustration.

The general approximate procedure for performing the integration is to plot Re $H(j\omega)$ versus ω and then approximate the exact shape with a series of straight line segments. The straight line approximation is written as a sum of trapezoidal functions. Equation 8 is applied to each of the trapezoids. The resulting time functions are added to obtain the approximation to $h(t)$. The addition of the individual functions is justified by the superposition property of Equation 8.

The general trapezoidal function used to approximate Re $H(j\omega)$ is

---

* See Equation 490, *A Short Table of Integrals*, Pierce.

shown in Figure 1. Specifically, Figure 1 represents an Re $H(j\omega)$ that is a simple trapezoid. Therefore,

$$h(t) = \frac{2}{\pi} \int_0^\infty \text{Re } H(j\omega) \cos \omega t \, d\omega \qquad (20)$$

where the two straight line segments may be individually written as

$$= \frac{2}{\pi} \int_0^{\omega_1-\Delta_1} r_1 \cos \omega t \, d\omega + \frac{2}{\pi} \int_{\omega_1-\Delta_1}^{\omega_1+\Delta_1} r_1 \frac{\omega_1 + \Delta_1 - \omega}{2\Delta_1} \cos \omega t \, d\omega \qquad (21)$$

where r_1 is the altitude of the trapezoid out to ω_a, and where ω_a, ω_1, ω_b, and Δ_1 are as shown in Figure 1. The two integrals of Equation 21 are

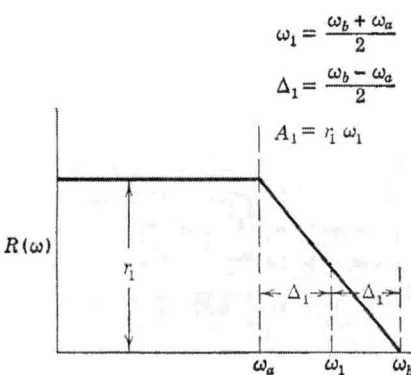

$$\omega_1 = \frac{\omega_b + \omega_a}{2}$$

$$\Delta_1 = \frac{\omega_b - \omega_a}{2}$$

$$A_1 = r_1 \omega_1$$

FIGURE 1.   Geometry of a trapezoid for approximating the real part of response function.

the only two which have any value for $0 < \omega < \infty$ because the integrand is zero for all other values of ω.

The evaluation of Equation 21 is performed by first expanding the second integral into two parts, giving

$$h(t) = \frac{2r_1}{\pi} \int_0^{\omega_1-\Delta_1} \cos t\omega \, d\omega + \frac{2r_1(\omega_1 + \Delta_1)}{2\pi\Delta_1} \int_{\omega_1-\Delta_1}^{\omega_1+\Delta_1} \cos t\omega \, d\omega$$

$$- \frac{2r_1}{2\pi\Delta_1} \int_{\omega_1-\Delta_1}^{\omega_1+\Delta_1} \omega \cos t\omega \, d\omega$$

$$= \frac{2r_1}{\pi t} \sin t\omega \Big]_0^{\omega_1-\Delta_1} + \frac{r_1(\omega_1 + \Delta_1)}{\pi\Delta_1 t} \sin t\omega \Big]_{\omega_1-\Delta_1}^{\omega_1+\Delta_1} - \frac{r_1\omega}{\pi\Delta_1 t} \sin t\omega \Big]_{\omega_1-\Delta_1}^{\omega_1+\Delta_1}$$

$$- \frac{r_1}{\pi\Delta_1 t^2} \cos t\omega \Big]_{\omega_1-\Delta_1}^{\omega_1+\Delta_1} \qquad (22)$$

When the limits are substituted in Equation 22, the sine terms cancel, and all that is left is

$$h(t) = -\frac{r_1}{\pi \Delta_1 t^2} [\cos (\omega_1 + \Delta_1)t - \cos (\omega_1 - \Delta_1)t]$$

$$= \frac{2r_1 \sin \omega_1 t \sin \Delta_1 t}{\pi \Delta_1 t^2} \tag{23}$$

or

$$h(t) = \frac{2r_1\omega_1}{\pi} \left(\frac{\sin \omega_1 t}{\omega_1 t}\right)\left(\frac{\sin \Delta_1 t}{\Delta_1 t}\right) \tag{24}$$

If $r_1\omega_1 = A_1$ is substituted in Equation 24, the result is

$$h_1(t) = \frac{2}{\pi} A_1 \left(\frac{\sin \omega_1 t}{\omega_1 t}\right)\left(\frac{\sin \Delta_1 t}{\Delta_1 t}\right) \tag{25}$$

where $A_1 = $ area, and the subscript 1 denotes the first trapezoid.

For a general function Re $H(j\omega)$, the particular time function $h(t)$ is

$$h(t) = \sum_{n=1}^{k} h_n(t) \tag{26}$$

where $h_n(t)$ is the contribution from the integration of the nth trapezoid. That is,

$$h(t) = \sum_{n=1}^{k} \frac{2}{\pi} A_n \left(\frac{\sin \omega_n t}{\omega_n t}\right)\left(\frac{\sin \Delta_n t}{\Delta_n t}\right) \tag{27}$$

and is the approximate inverse transformation.

Tables of $\sin x/x$ are given at the end of this chapter as Table 1.

3   Methods for Obtaining Re $\left(\frac{\theta_o}{\theta_i}(j\omega)\right)$

The work of Chapters 7 and 8 give both analytical and graphical methods for determining the frequency function θ_o/θ_i for prescribed performance. Such performance was uniquely selected in accordance with M_p criteria for closed-loop adjustments wholly in terms of frequency functions. By the work of this section, the real part of the frequency function can be prepared. Then by the application of Equation 27, the specific behavior in the time domain of the impulse response $h(t)$ for the system initially at rest is obtained. The behavior to a step disturbance is obtained by graphical integration of this impulse response.

If the system may be regarded as a single loop with unity feedback, a Lm-Ang plot of the transfer function KG may be used to find $\mathrm{Re}\,\dfrac{\theta_o}{\theta_i}\,(j\omega)$. If the system does not have a unit feedback, the analysis is more easily done with a loci plot in the KG^{-1} plane. Since the analysis in this plane yields $\dfrac{\theta_i}{\theta_o}\,(j\omega)$, the $\mathrm{Re}\,\dfrac{\theta_o}{\theta_i}\,(j\omega) = \mathrm{Re}\,H(j\omega)$ is found by dividing the cosine of the angle of $\dfrac{\theta_i}{\theta_o}\,(j\omega)$ by the magnitude of $\dfrac{\theta_i}{\theta_o}\,(j\omega)$. The reader should pay some attention to the matter of algebraic sign. It will be helpful to note that because the cosine is an even function, the cosine of $\mathrm{Ang}\,\dfrac{\theta_i}{\theta_o}$ equals the cosine of $\mathrm{Ang}\,\dfrac{\theta_o}{\theta_i}$.

Since many designs involve only the unity feedback, an auxiliary chart of contours can be formed which will make it easy to determine the $\mathrm{Re}\,H(j\omega)$ when the log modulus contour of $KG(j\omega)$ is known. The locus can be established for any number which defines the real part of the system response, namely $\mathrm{Re}\left(\dfrac{KG}{1+KG}\right)$. The analytic derivation of the function that will give this locus for the $\mathrm{Re}\left(\dfrac{KG}{1+KG}\right)$ as a complete family of contours is as follows. Let $|KG| \triangleq A$, and let the angle of $|KG| \triangleq \phi$. Then

$$KG = A \cos \phi + jA \sin \phi \tag{28}$$

Therefore,

$$\mathrm{Re}\left(\frac{KG}{1+KG}\right)$$

$$= \mathrm{Re}\left\{\frac{A \cos \phi + jA \sin \phi}{1 + A \cos \phi + jA \sin \phi}\right\} \tag{29}$$

$$= \mathrm{Re}\left\{\frac{(A \cos \phi + jA \sin \phi)(1 + A \cos \phi - jA \sin \phi)}{(1 + A \cos \phi)^2 + A^2 \sin^2 \phi}\right\} \tag{30}$$

$$= \frac{A \cos \phi(1 + A \cos \phi) + A^2 \sin^2 \phi}{1 + 2A \cos \phi + A^2 \cos^2 \phi + A^2 \sin^2 \phi} \tag{31}$$

$$= \frac{A^2 + A \cos \phi}{A^2 + 2A \cos \phi + 1} \tag{32}$$

The locus $\operatorname{Re}\left(\dfrac{KG}{1+KG}\right) = $ constant $\triangleq R$ is then given by the equation

$$\frac{A^2 + A\cos\phi}{A^2 + 2A\cos\phi + 1} = R \tag{33}$$

which may be written as

$$A\cos\phi(1 - 2R) = A^2(R - 1) + R \tag{34}$$

The general structure of the locus is indicated by evaluating Equation 34 for particular values of R. Specifically if

$$R = \tfrac{1}{2}, \quad A = 1 \text{ for all values of } \phi \tag{35}$$

Also, if

$$R \neq \tfrac{1}{2}, \quad \cos\phi = \frac{A^2(R - 1) + R}{A(1 - 2R)} \tag{36}$$

Finally, if

$$R = \tfrac{1}{2} + P, \quad \cos\phi = \frac{A^2(P - \tfrac{1}{2}) + (P + \tfrac{1}{2})}{-2AP} \tag{37}$$

where $P \neq 0$, but may be positive or negative.

The symmetry in the loci plot is shown by replacing A by $1/A$ and P by $-P$, giving

$$\left.\begin{aligned}\cos\phi &= \frac{\dfrac{1}{A^2}(-P - \tfrac{1}{2}) + (-P + \tfrac{1}{2})}{2\dfrac{1}{A}P} \\[2mm] &= \frac{A^2(P - \tfrac{1}{2}) + (P + \tfrac{1}{2})}{-2AP}\end{aligned}\right\} \tag{38}$$

Therefore, if A is plotted in decibels as a function of phase ϕ in degrees, the loci for positive and negative values of P are symmetrical about the 0 decibel line. A plot of $\operatorname{Re}\left(\dfrac{KG}{1+KG}\right) = \operatorname{Re}\left(\dfrac{\theta_o}{\theta_i}\right)$ is shown in Figure 2. When the chart has the same scales as the M-N chart of Chapter 8, Figure 8, the two charts may be superposed, giving the real part directly from the overall transfer function locus.

4 Graphical Evaluation of the Integral

The real part of θ_o/θ_i, derived graphically from Figure 2 or from the KG^{-1} loci, is next plotted as shown by the solid line in Figure 3. The problem now becomes one of curve fitting. Straight line approxima-

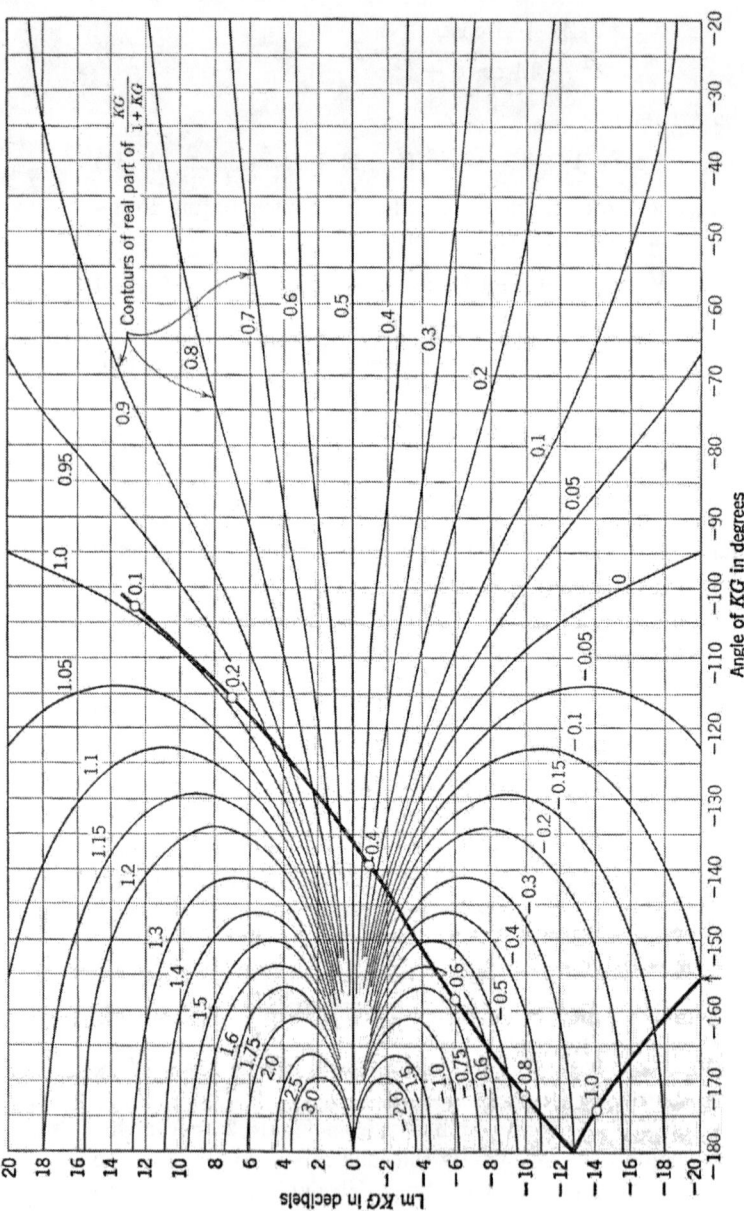

FIGURE 2.   Chart for obtaining the real part of the response function.

tions to the $\mathrm{Re}\left(\dfrac{\theta_o}{\theta_i}(j\omega)\right)$ are good enough if carefully applied. These approximations also lead to the use of trapezoidal shapes which gave the result of Equation 27.

The question of the number of straight line segments to use in the approximation of $\mathrm{Re}\left(\dfrac{\theta_o}{\theta_i}(j\omega)\right)$ is difficult to answer. Naturally, better results will be achieved if more terms are used. However, experience shows that it is more important to approximate $\mathrm{Re}\left(\dfrac{\theta_o}{\theta_i}(j\omega)\right)$ closely at

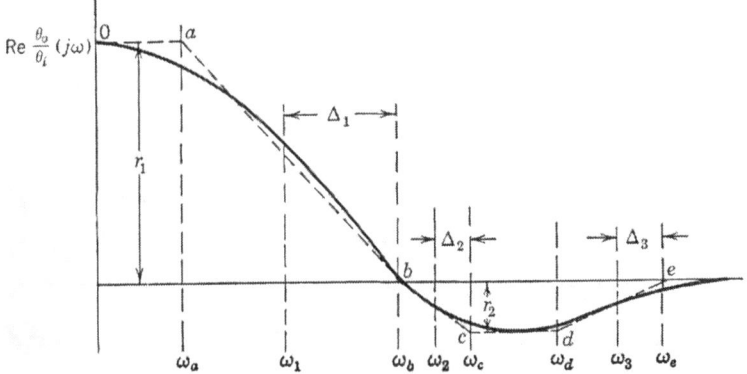

FIGURE 3. Approximating real part of θ_o/θ_i by several trapezoids.

low frequencies than at high frequencies, and that rather rough approximations still lead to results which are useful.

To illustrate the evaluation procedure, consider the curve of Figure 3. This curve is the plot of a particular $\mathrm{Re}\left(\dfrac{\theta_o}{\theta_i}(j\omega)\right)$. It is approximated by five straight line segments. The individual segments oa, ab, bc, cd, and de define the frequencies ω_a, ω_b, ω_c, ω_d, and ω_e, which are critical in evaluating the integral of Equation 20 or in finding terms for Equation 27. Once the straight lines are established, the values for ω_1, Δ_1, ω_2, Δ_2, A_2, and ω_3, Δ_3, and A_3 are determined. For example,

$$\left.\begin{aligned}
\omega_1 &= \frac{\omega_a + \omega_b}{2}\\[2mm]
\Delta_1 &= \frac{\omega_b - \omega_a}{2}\\[2mm]
A_1 &= r_1\omega_1
\end{aligned}\right\} \tag{39}$$

and are associated with the first trapezoid shown in Figure 4a. Similarly,

$$\omega_2 = \frac{\omega_b + \omega_c}{2}$$

$$\Delta_2 = \frac{\omega_c - \omega_b}{2}$$

$$A_2 = r_2\omega_2$$

(40)

are associated with the second trapezoid shown in Figure 4b. Notice however, that the second trapezoid is used to offset an area in a third

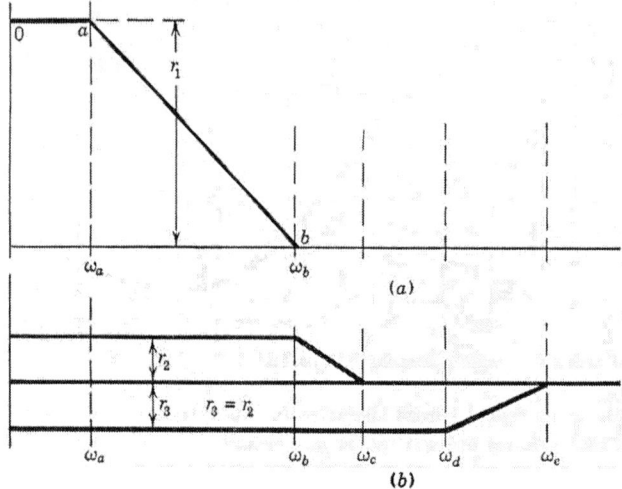

FIGURE 4. Individual trapezoids required to approximate the function of Figure 3.

trapezoid which represents at its upper frequency end the portion of the curve c from ω_b to ω_e. For trapezoid number 3,

$$\omega_3 = \frac{\omega_e + \omega_d}{2}$$

$$\Delta_3 = \frac{\omega_e - \omega_d}{2}$$

$$A_3 = -r_3\omega_3$$

(41)

Notice that r_3 always equals r_2. The contribution to $h(t)$ from trapezoid 3 minus the contribution from trapezoid 2 gives the contribution from the true curve ω_b to ω_e. Thus the series expansion of $h(t)$ has three terms, namely,

$$h_1(t) = \frac{2}{\pi} A_1 \left(\frac{\sin \omega_1 t}{\omega_1 t} \right) \left(\frac{\sin \Delta_1 t}{\Delta_1 t} \right) \tag{42}$$

$$h_2(t) = \frac{2}{\pi} A_2 \left(\frac{\sin \omega_2 t}{\omega_2 t} \right) \left(\frac{\sin \Delta_2 t}{\Delta_2 t} \right) \tag{43}$$

$$h_3(t) = \frac{2}{\pi} A_3 \left(\frac{\sin \omega_3 t}{\omega_3 t} \right) \left(\frac{\sin \Delta_3 t}{\Delta_3 t} \right) \tag{44}$$

$$\text{The system } h(t) = h_1(t) + h_2(t) + h_3(t) \tag{45}$$

The impulse response $h(t)$ from Equation 45 must now be computed for a range of time sufficient to insure that the transient has reached a

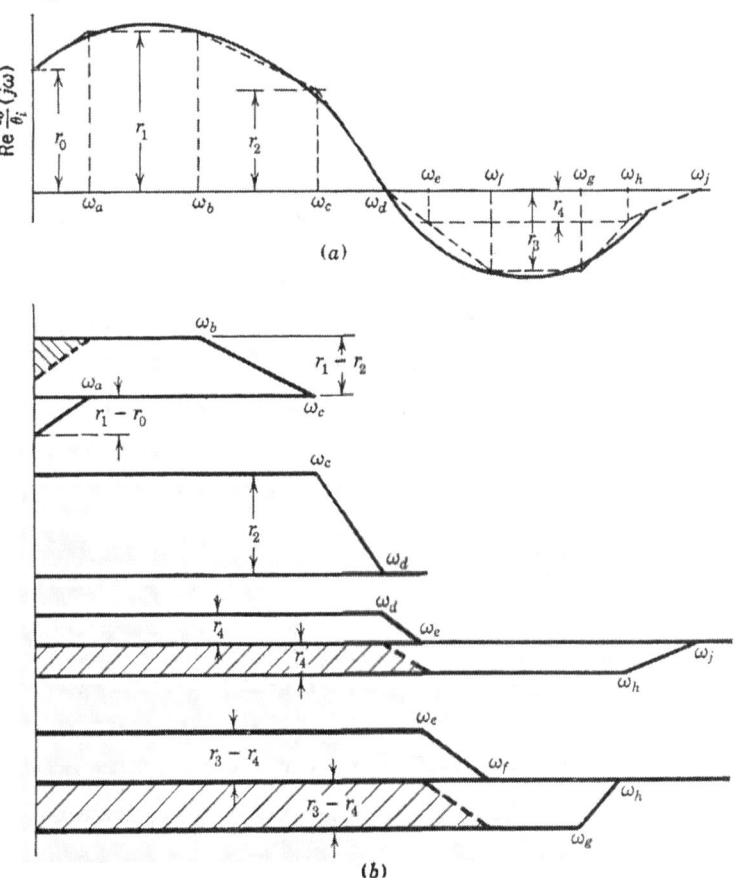

FIGURE 5.   (a) Trapezoidal approximation for a complicated real part.   (b) Individual trapezoids required for approximation.

few per cent of its final value. An approximate method for determining the duration of $h(t)$ is given in Section 6. Specifically, if $t \cong 4t_{bu}$

$$t > \frac{4\pi}{\omega_b} \tag{46}$$

a satisfactory result will have been obtained.

A curve such as is encountered in a problem where more than five straight line segments are required to represent $\mathrm{Re}\left(\dfrac{\theta_o}{\theta_i}\right)$ is shown in Figure 5a. In this figure, eight straight lines are used. Figure 5b shows the various trapezoids used to evaluate the integral. The positive and negative values of the quantity A are determined by the respective positive or negative trapezoidal areas in Figure 5b.

5   Illustrative Numerical Problems

The first numerical example will be to determine $h(t)$ knowing $H(s)$ analytically. Assume the function for $H(s)$ to be

$$H(s) \triangleq \frac{18.72}{[(s+1)^2+1][(s+0.6)^2+9]} \tag{47}$$

Figure 6 shows a plot of the real part of $H(j\omega)$. The values used for ω, Δ, and A of the series were, respectively,

$$\omega_1 = \frac{1.2 + 0.5}{2} \qquad\qquad \omega_2 = \frac{2.0 + 1.2}{2}$$

$$\Delta_1 = \frac{1.2 - 0.5}{2} \qquad\qquad \Delta_2 = \frac{2.0 - 1.2}{2}$$

$$A_1 = 0.85 \qquad\qquad A_2 = 0.66 \times 1.6$$

$$\omega_3 = \frac{3.50 + 2.6}{2} \qquad\qquad \omega_4 = \frac{7.2 + 3.6}{2}$$

$$\Delta_3 = \frac{3.50 - 2.6}{2} \qquad\qquad \Delta_4 = \frac{7.2 - 3.6}{2}$$

$$A_3 = -0.66 \times 3.05 \qquad\qquad A_4 = 0.07 \times 5.40$$

$$\omega_5 = \frac{3.60 + 3.50}{2}$$

$$\Delta_5 = \frac{3.60 - 3.50}{2}$$

$$A_5 = -0.07 \times 3.55$$

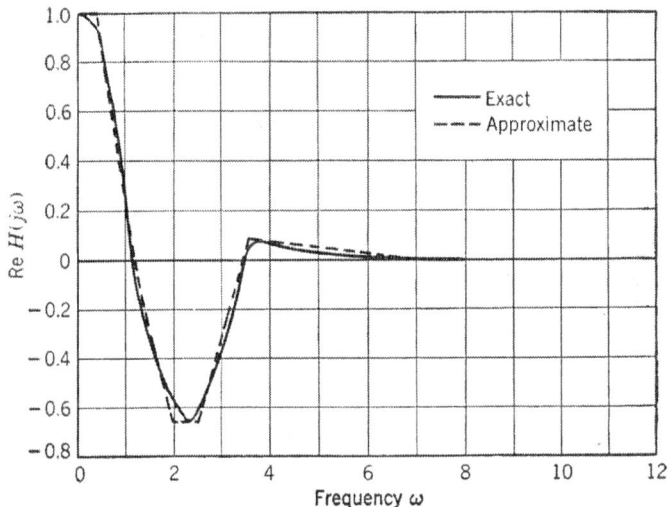

FIGURE 6.   Real part of the response function—Illustrative Problem 1.

The evaluation of Equation 45 gives the following result:

$$h(t) \cong \frac{2}{\pi}\left[0.85\left(\frac{\sin 0.85t}{0.85t}\right)\left(\frac{\sin 0.35t}{0.35t}\right) + 1.07\left(\frac{\sin 1.6t}{1.6t}\right)\left(\frac{\sin 0.4t}{0.4t}\right)\right.$$

$$- 2.01\left(\frac{\sin 3.05t}{3.05t}\right)\left(\frac{\sin 0.45t}{0.45t}\right) + 0.38\left(\frac{\sin 5.40t}{5.40t}\right)\left(\frac{\sin 1.8t}{1.8t}\right)$$

$$\left.- 0.25\left(\frac{\sin 3.55t}{3.55t}\right)\left(\frac{\sin 0.05t}{0.05t}\right)\right] \tag{48}$$

The calculation of $h(t)$ by the inverse Laplace transformation gives this exact result:

$$h(t) = 2.28e^{-t} \sin (t + 5.6 \text{ degrees})$$

$$- 0.761e^{-0.6t} \sin (3t + 17 \text{ degrees}) \tag{49}$$

The exact and approximate solutions are plotted in Figure 7.

As a second example, consider a system having unity feedback and a transfer function defined as

$$KG(ju) = \frac{K}{ju\left(1 + j\dfrac{u}{10.6}\right)\left(1 + j\dfrac{u}{0.615}\right)\left(1 + j\dfrac{u}{1.62}\right)} \tag{50}$$

where

$$u \triangleq \frac{\omega}{61}$$

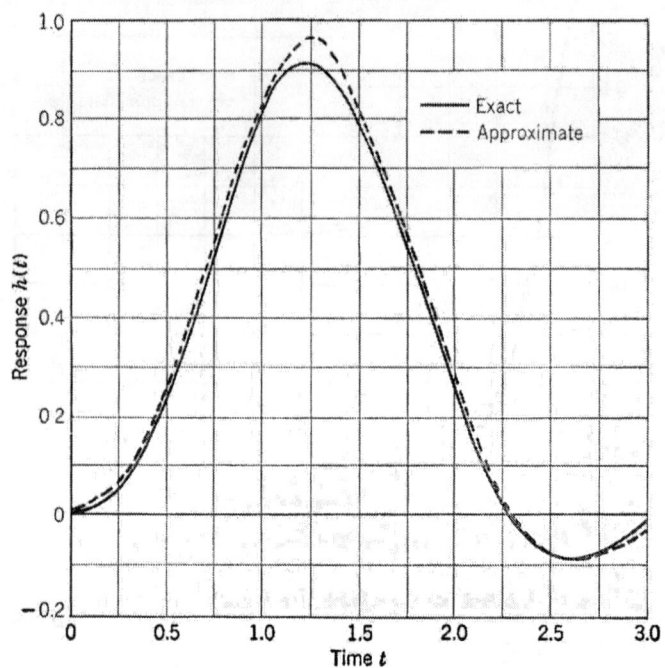

FIGURE 7.   Transient response for Illustrative Problem 1.

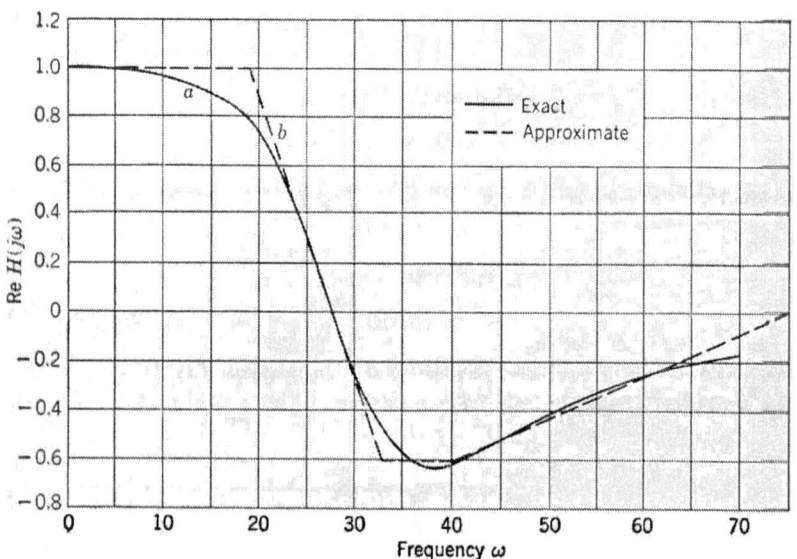

FIGURE 8.   Real part of the response function—Illustrative Problem 2.

The exact function for $h(t)$ using the inverse Laplace transform is

$$h(t) = -0.244e^{-710t} + 10.92e^{-112t}$$

$$+ 35.86e^{-12.1t} \cos (27.4t - 107.6 \text{ degrees})$$

This is the transfer function of a motor generator system as used in previous chapters. The numerical values apply for a specific selection of components. A value for $K = -7$ decibels corresponds to $M_p = 1.3$. A plot of the KG locus is shown as the heavy line in Figure 2. The values of the real part of θ_o/θ_i are read from this plot and are redrawn as curve a in Figure 8. The approximation of this curve, shown dotted as the straight line segments b, lead to the following approximation to $h(t)$:

$$h(t) \cong 14.9S(4.4t)S(23t) + 11.6S(2.6t)S(30.2t) - 22.1S(18t)S(58t)$$

where

$$S(xt) = \left(\frac{\sin xt}{xt}\right)$$

The exact and approximate time responses are plotted in Figure 9.

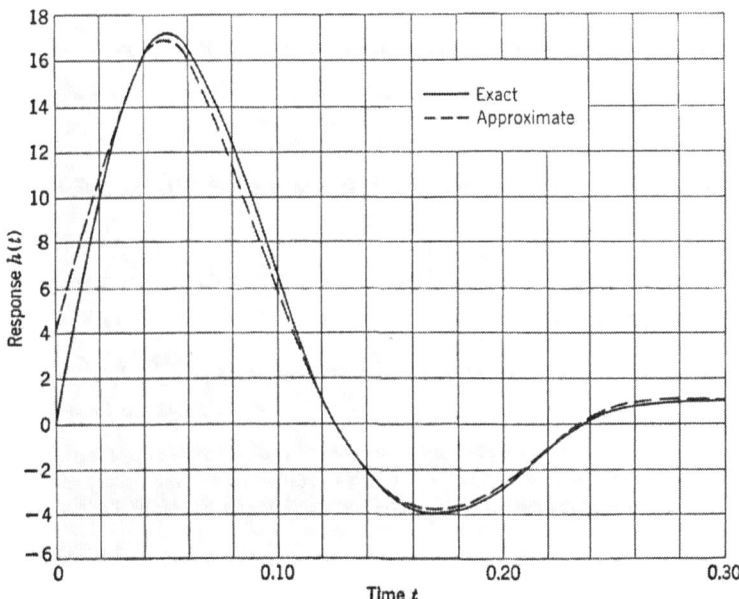

FIGURE 9.   Transient response for Illustrative Problem 2.

It is worth while to mention that because of the neglect of high-frequency terms in the approximation of Re $H(j\omega)$, the graphical integration to give $h(t)$ will not, in general, converge to zero at $t = 0$. This matter is not serious because any small value of $h(t)$ at $t = 0$ will not contribute appreciably to the response following a step if the solution for $h(t)$ to the impulse is integrated. Alternatively, it can be made zero arbitrarily. At intermediate values of time, the convergence for $h(t)$ is rapid. Since the designer is mainly interested in the response when the transients are large, that is, for intermediate values of time, the graphical solution is believed to be quite good.

6 Approximate Transformations from Time Domain to the Frequency Domain

The general procedure used for obtaining $h(t)$ from Re $H(j\omega)$ may also be used to obtain Re $H(j\omega)$ from $h(t)$. Then, by the use of the Bode curves,[61] the amplitude and phase of $H(j\omega)$ may be found from Re $H(j\omega)$, if the function is assumed to be minimum phase.

Let $h(t)$ satisfy the following conditions:

$$\left. \begin{aligned} h(t) &= 0 \text{ for } t = 0 \\ h(t) &\to 0 \text{ as } t \to \infty \end{aligned} \right\} \tag{51}$$

Under these conditions the transform of $h(t) = H(s)$ is given as:

$$H(s) = \int_0^\infty h(t)e^{-st}\,dt \tag{52}$$

From Equation 51, it follows that s may be replaced by $j\omega$, giving

$$H(j\omega) = \int_0^\infty h(t)e^{-j\omega t}\,dt = \int_0^\infty h(t)\cos\omega t\,dt - j\int_0^\infty h(t)\sin\omega t\,dt \tag{53}$$

of which the real part is

$$\text{Re } H(j\omega) = \int_0^\infty h(t)\cos\omega t\,dt \tag{54}$$

Equation 54 is of the same form as that for the inverse transformation, namely, Equation 8. Therefore, Re $H(j\omega)$ may be approximated graphically by a procedure similar to that used in Section 2.

A useful example of the direct transformation, which is sufficiently simple to treat exactly, is given to illustrate the significance of the operation rather than the method. Sections 2, 3, and 4 illustrate the graphical method. This example determines the system frequency response required to realize an idealized response to a unit step function, where the step is the time integral of the impulse. Plots of the step and the desired response are shown as Figures 10a and 10b, respectively.

A system which has the response of Figure 10b to a step of Figure 10a would have a response to an impulse that is merely the time derivative of Figure 10b. If the time of build-up specified for the response of Figure 10b is t_{bu} and its maximum amplitude is unity, the response to the impulse is as shown in Figure 10c, where the magnitude is $1/t_{bu}$.

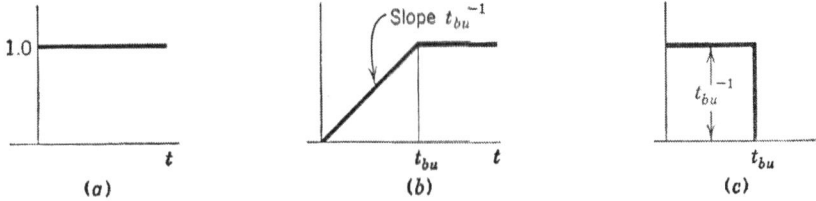

FIGURE 10. (a) Graph of a step disturbance. (b) Graph of desired response. (c) Graph of response to an impulse for a system giving (b) as response to a step.

The response of Figure 10c now becomes $h(t)$ for the system under consideration. The real part of $H(j\omega)$ is then given directly by Equation 54, that is,

$$\text{Re } H(j\omega) = \int_0^\infty h(t) \cos \omega t \, dt \tag{54}$$

$$= \int_0^{t_{bu}} \frac{1}{t_{bu}} \cos \omega t \, dt \tag{55}$$

$$= \frac{\sin \omega t}{\omega t_{bu}}\Big|_0^{t_{bu}} \tag{56}$$

$$= \frac{\sin \omega t_{bu}}{\omega t_{bu}} \tag{57}$$

Thus, for the system whose behavior corresponds to the responses shown by Figure 10b,

$$\text{Re } H(j\omega) = \frac{\sin \omega t_{bu}}{\omega t_{bu}} \tag{58}$$

This relation may be used to determine an approximate relation between cutoff frequency * and the time of build-up of the system response to a unit step. In general, Re $H(j\omega)$ will pass through zero at the lowest value of ω for which the angle of $H(j\omega)$ is $\pi/2$. Let this frequency be

* When $\dfrac{\theta_o}{\theta_i} (j\omega)$ has -90 degrees of phase shift.

called ω_1. This general rule also holds for Equation 58, which states that Re $H(j\omega)$ is zero when $\omega t_{bu} = \pi$.

Therefore

$$\frac{\sin \omega t_{bu}}{\omega t_{bu}} = 0 \quad \text{when} \quad \omega t_{bu} = \pi \tag{59}$$

But from the general case

$$\text{Re } H(j\omega) = 0 \quad \text{when} \quad \omega = \omega_1$$

giving

$$\omega_1 = \frac{\pi}{t_{bu}} \quad \text{or} \quad t_{bu} = \frac{\pi}{\omega_1} \tag{60}$$

where t_{bu} is the value for the built-up time expressed in terms of the frequency ω_1 at which $H(j\omega)$ has a phase angle of 90 degrees.

Equation 59 is also of use when performing the approximate inverse transformation since it gives an indication of the range of values of time which will be of most importance in the time response. An equivalent relation is given by MacColl [4] in the form $2f_{co}t_{bu} = 1$ if one recognizes the difference in the definitions of f_{co} and t_{bu}.

7 General Use of System Impulse Response

Strictly speaking, the unit impulse function is of infinite height and zero duration. A close approximation to the response of a physical system to an impulse may be obtained experimentally, however, by using a pulse of short duration and finite height. As long as the duration of the pulse is much shorter than the response time of the system being tested, the response obtained will be indistinguishable from the theoretical impulse response. In this connection, the magnitude of the pulse should be such that the area enclosed is unity.

From a mathematical point of view, the unit impulse function is more convenient to use than the step function. It is the purpose of this section to point out some of the uses to which the impulse response may be put. In order to do so, it is necessary to recall from Chapter 2 that, for a linear system, the general form of the differential equation relating output $\theta_o(t)$ to input $\theta_i(t)$ is

$$\sum_{n=0}^{n=M} A_n \frac{d^n\theta_o(t)}{dt^n} = \sum_{n=0}^{n=K} B_n \frac{d^n\theta_i(t)}{dt^n} \tag{61}$$

where A_n and B_n are constants and $M \geq K$. Furthermore, when Equation 61 is transformed, the general result comprises the system transform and an initial condition transform as shown in Chapter 3, Sections 7 and 9. It follows, therefore, that in transform notation, Equation 61 may be written as

$$\theta_o(s) = \frac{\sum_{n=0}^{n=K} B_n s^n}{\sum_{n=0}^{n=M} A_n s^n} \theta_i(s) + \frac{\text{Transforms of initial conditions}}{\sum_{n=0}^{n=M} A_n s^n} \tag{62}$$

If the output function $\theta_o(t)$ is written as the sum of a forced response $\theta_{of}(t)$ caused by $\theta_i(t)$, and a transient response $\theta_{ot}(t)$ caused by the initial state, it follows from Equation 62 that

$$\theta_{of}(t) = \mathcal{L}^{-1} H(s)\theta_i(s) \tag{63}$$

where

$$H(s) = \frac{\sum_{n=0}^{n=K} B_n s^n}{\sum_{n=0}^{n=M} A_n s^n} \tag{64}$$

and

$$\theta_{ot}(t) = \mathcal{L}^{-1} \frac{\text{Transforms of initial conditions}}{\sum_{n=0}^{n=M} A_n s^n} \tag{65}$$

The function $H(s)$ is called the system function. It completely defines the general nature of the system. It alone tells nothing of the general state of the system.

If the inverse transform of the system function $H(s)$ is called $h(t)$, where $h(t)$ is physically the time response to a unit impulse with the system initially at rest, it follows from the real convolution integral that

$$\theta_{of}(t) = \int_0^t h(t - x)\theta_i(x) \, dx \tag{66}$$

where $\theta_i(x)$ is the arbitrary forcing function with t replaced by x. Therefore, if the function $h(t)$ can be found from a knowledge of $H(s)$, the forced response $\theta_{of}(t)$ to a driving function $\theta_i(t)$ may be found through the use of Equation 66, using graphical integration if necessary. A procedure for evaluating Equation 66 will be described in the next section.

In any particular problem, the total response $\theta_o(t)$ will also contain the term $\theta_{ot}(t)$ caused by the particular initial conditions. Equation

62 shows, however, that the denominators of both $\theta_{of}(s)$ and $\theta_{ot}(s)$ are identical. Because the denominator of a transform completely determines the time function except for magnitude constants, both $h(t)$ and $\theta_{ot}(t)$ will have similar exponential forms. Therefore, from a knowledge of $h(t)$, the *general* form of $\theta_{ot}(t)$ is also known, irrespective of the particular initial state of the system. In a stable system $h(t) \cong 0$, when t is greater than some value T, called the settling time. Because $\theta_{ot}(s)$ has the same denominator as $H(s)$, it then follows that $\theta_{ot}(t) \cong 0$ for $t > T$. Consequently, by inspection of $h(t)$, the duration and general nature of the transient caused by the initial state of the system may be found, and then for values of $t > T$, $\theta_o(t) \cong \theta_{of}(t)$. Therefore, Equation 66 gives $\theta_o(t)$ for $t > T$. Finally, since $H(s)$ completely determines the differential equation of the system and $h(t)$ is the transform of $H(s)$, it follows that $h(t)$ also completely describes the system.

The following summarizes the properties of the time function $h(t)$:

1. It is the system response to a unit impulse when the system is initially at rest.
2. It completely determines the system response.
3. It makes possible the statement that the transient response due to the initial state of the system is of the same general form as $h(t)$.
4. It makes possible the determination of the forced response to an input $\theta_i(t)$ by means of Equation 66.
5. It is the Fourier transform of the system frequency response function $H(j\omega)$.

8   Response to an Arbitrary Forcing Function

It is shown in Section 7 that the forced response of the system to a driving function $\theta_i(t)$ is given by

$$\theta_{of}(t) = \int_0^t h(t - x)\theta_i(x)\, dx \qquad (66)$$

where

$$\left.\begin{array}{l} \theta_{of}(t) \text{ is the forced or dynamic system response} \\ \theta_i(t) \text{ is the forcing function} \\ h(t) \text{ is the system impulse response} \end{array}\right\} \qquad (67)$$

In order to develop a formula which will permit an approximate evaluation of Equation 66, let $h(x)$ be as shown in Figure 11a; then $h(-x)$ and $h(t - x)$ will be as shown in Figure 11b and 11c. Note that to increase t, the whole plot of $h(t - x)$, shown in Figure 11c, is simply shifted to the right by the amount t. Also let $\theta_i(t)$ be as shown in

Figure 12a. Then, if the quantity $h(t - x)\theta_i(x)$ is formed, the result is as shown in Figure 12b.

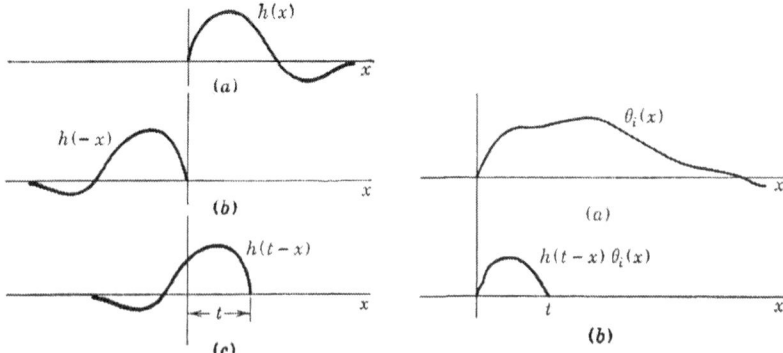

FIGURE 11. Development of $h(t - x)$ from $h(x)$.

FIGURE 12. Method for forming $h(t - x)\theta_i(x)$.

In terms of the graphical solution to Equation 66, $\theta_{of}(t)$ is simply the area under the $h(t - x)\theta_i(x)$ curve of Figure 12 between the limits 0 and t. To approximate this integral, divide the range of integration into the segments Δ as shown in Figure 13. It is assumed that the sum

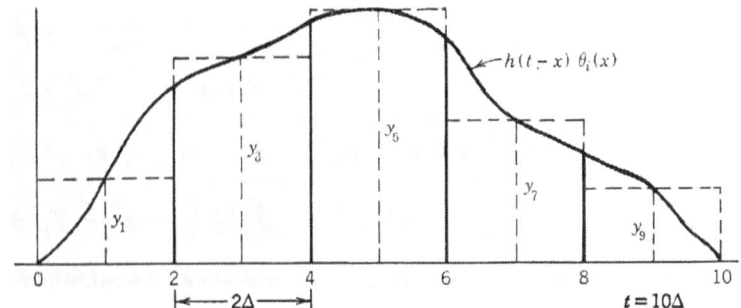

FIGURE 13. Method of representing $h(t - x)\theta_i(x)$ by means of rectangles.

of the areas under the dotted line equals the area under the curve. For the Figure 13, it is assumed that $t = 10\Delta$. The sum of the area is then

$$\theta_{of}(t) = \Sigma \text{ shaded area} \cong \int_0^t h(t - x)\theta_i(x)\, dx$$

$$= y_1 2\Delta + y_3 2\Delta + y_5 2\Delta + y_7 2\Delta + y_9 2\Delta \qquad (68)$$

$$= 2\Delta(y_1 + y_3 + y_5 + y_7 + y_9) \qquad (69)$$

But since $t = 10\Delta$,

$$y_1 = h(10\Delta - \Delta)\theta_i(\Delta)$$

$$y_3 = h(10\Delta - 3\Delta)\theta_i(3\Delta)$$

$$y_5 = h(10\Delta - 5\Delta)\theta_i(5\Delta) \tag{70}$$

$$y_7 = h(10\Delta - 7\Delta)\theta_i(7\Delta)$$

$$y_9 = h(10\Delta - 9\Delta)\theta_i(9\Delta)$$

Consequently,

$$\theta_{of}(10\Delta) \cong 2\Delta \sum_{n=1,\,3,\,5,\,\cdots}^{9} h[(10-n)\Delta]\theta_i(n\Delta) \tag{71}$$

If, in general, $t = k\Delta$,

$$\theta_{of}(k\Delta) = 2\Delta \sum_{n=1,\,3,\,5,\,\cdots}^{k-1} h[(k-n)\Delta]\theta_i(n\Delta) \tag{72}$$

where both k and n are even.

In order to make the process clear, a sample table of the expansion of Equation 72 for the graphical solution of a typical problem is as follows.

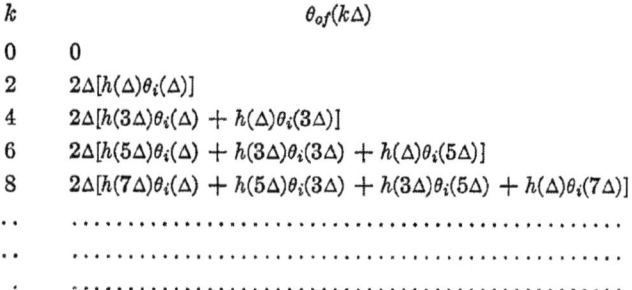

k	$\theta_{of}(k\Delta)$
0	0
2	$2\Delta[h(\Delta)\theta_i(\Delta)]$
4	$2\Delta[h(3\Delta)\theta_i(\Delta) + h(\Delta)\theta_i(3\Delta)]$
6	$2\Delta[h(5\Delta)\theta_i(\Delta) + h(3\Delta)\theta_i(3\Delta) + h(\Delta)\theta_i(5\Delta)]$
8	$2\Delta[h(7\Delta)\theta_i(\Delta) + h(5\Delta)\theta_i(3\Delta) + h(3\Delta)\theta_i(5\Delta) + h(\Delta)\theta_i(7\Delta)]$
..	....
..	....
.	....

A FOUR PLACE TABLE OF $\dfrac{\sin x}{x}$

TABLE 1

Values of $\dfrac{\sin x}{x}$ appearing in the main body are multiplied by 10,000 and are given for x expressed in radians at intervals of 0.01 up to $x = 20$ and intervals of 0.02 for $20 < x < 40$. Where the sign of the function is not given, it is understood to be the same as that last indicated.

This table, published in *Zeitschrift für Kristallographie*, Vol. 85, p. 404, Berlin, 1933, was prepared by Dr. J. Sherman, formerly of Gates Chemical Laboratory, California Institute of Technology, and now of The Texas Company Research Laboratories, Beacon, N. Y. The authors are indebted to Dr. Sherman for permission to reproduce this table.

x	0	1	2	3	4	5	6	7	8	9
0.0	+10000	10000	9999	9999	9997	9996	9994	9992	9989	9987
0.1	9983	9980	9976	9972	9967	9963	9957	9952	9946	9940
0.2	9933	9927	9919	9912	9904	9896	9889	9879	9870	9860
0.3	9851	9840	9830	9820	9808	9797	9785	9774	9761	9748
0.4	9735	9722	9709	9695	9680	9666	9651	9636	9620	9605
0.5	+9589	9572	9555	9538	9521	9503	9486	9467	9449	9430
0.6	9411	9391	9372	9351	9331	9311	9290	9269	9247	9225
0.7	9203	9181	9158	9135	9112	9089	9065	9041	9016	8992
0.8	8967	8942	8916	8891	8865	8839	8812	8785	8758	8731
0.9	8704	8676	8648	8620	8591	8562	8533	8504	8474	8445
1.0	+8415	8384	8354	8323	8292	8261	8230	8198	8166	8134
1.1	8102	8069	8037	8004	7970	7937	7903	7870	7836	7801
1.2	7767	7732	7698	7663	7627	7592	7556	7520	7484	7448
1.3	7412	7375	7339	7302	7265	7228	7190	7153	7115	7077
1.4	7039	7001	6962	6924	6885	6846	6807	6768	6729	6690
1.5	+6650	6610	6570	6530	6490	6450	6410	6369	6328	6288
1.6	6247	6206	6165	6124	6083	6042	6000	5959	5917	5875
1.7	5833	5791	5749	5707	5665	5623	5580	5538	5495	5453
1.8	5410	5368	5325	5282	5239	5196	5153	5110	5067	5024
1.9	4981	4937	4894	4851	4807	4764	4720	4677	4634	4590
2.0	+4546	4503	4459	4416	4372	4329	4285	4241	4198	4153
2.1	4111	4067	4023	3980	3936	3893	3849	3805	3762	3718
2.2	3675	3632	3588	3545	3501	3458	3415	3372	3328	3285
2.3	3242	3199	3156	3113	3070	3028	2984	2942	2899	2857
2.4	2814	2772	2730	2687	2645	2603	2561	2519	2477	2436
x	0	1	2	3	4	5	6	7	8	9

TABLE 1   (*Continued*)

x	0	1	2	3	4	5	6	7	8	9
2.5	+2394	2352	2311	2269	2228	2187	2146	2105	2064	2023
2.6	1983	1942	1902	1861	1821	1781	1741	1702	1662	1622
2.7	1583	1544	1504	1465	1427	1388	1349	1311	1273	1234
2.8	1196	1159	1121	1083	1046	1009	972	935	898	861
2.9	825	789	753	717	681	646	610	575	540	505
3.0	+470	436	402	368	334	300	266	233	200	167
3.1	+134	+102	+69	+37	+5	−27	−58	−90	−121	−152
3.2	−182	213	243	273	303	333	362	392	421	449
3.3	478	506	535	562	590	618	645	672	699	725
3.4	752	778	804	829	855	880	905	930	954	978
3.5	−1002	1026	1050	1073	1096	1119	1141	1164	1186	1208
3.6	1229	1251	1272	1293	1313	1334	1354	1374	1393	1413
3.7	1432	1451	1470	1488	1506	1524	1542	1559	1576	1593
3.8	1610	1627	1643	1659	1675	1690	1705	1720	1735	1749
3.9	1764	1777	1791	1805	1818	1831	1844	1856	1868	1880
4.0	−1892	1903	1915	1926	1936	1947	1957	1967	1977	1987
4.1	1996	2005	2014	2022	2030	2039	2046	2054	2061	2068
4.2	2075	2082	2088	2094	2100	2106	2111	2116	2121	2126
4.3	2131	2135	2139	2143	2146	2150	2153	2156	2158	2161
4.4	2163	2165	2166	2168	2169	2170	2171	2172	2172	2172
4.5	−2172	2172	2172	2171	2170	2169	2168	2166	2164	2162
4.6	2160	2158	2155	2152	2150	2146	2143	2139	2136	2132
4.7	2127	2123	2119	2114	2109	2104	2098	2093	2087	2081
4.8	2075	2069	2063	2056	2049	2042	2035	2028	2020	2013
4.9	2005	1997	1989	1981	1972	1963	1955	1946	1937	1927
5.0	−1918	1908	1899	1889	1879	1868	1858	1848	1837	1826
5.1	1815	1804	1793	1782	1770	1759	1747	1735	1723	1711
5.2	1699	1687	1674	1662	1649	1636	1623	1610	1597	1584
5.3	1570	1557	1543	1530	1516	1502	1488	1474	1460	1445
5.4	1431	1417	1402	1387	1373	1358	1343	1328	1313	1298
5.5	−1283	1268	1252	1237	1221	1206	1190	1175	1159	1143
5.6	1127	1111	1095	1079	1063	1047	1031	1015	999	982
5.7	966	950	933	917	900	884	867	851	834	818
5.8	800	784	768	751	734	718	701	684	667	650
5.9	634	617	600	583	567	550	533	516	499	482
x	0	1	2	3	4	5	6	7	8	9

TABLE 1   (*Continued*)

x	0	1	2	3	4	5	6	7	8	9
6.0	−466	449	432	416	399	382	365	348	332	315
6.1	299	282	265	249	232	216	200	183	167	150
6.2	−134	−118	−102	−85	−69	−53	−37	−21	−5	+11
6.3	+27	43	58	74	90	105	121	136	152	167
6.4	182	197	212	227	242	257	272	287	302	316
6.5	+331	346	360	374	388	403	417	431	445	458
6.6	472	486	499	513	526	539	552	566	579	591
6.7	604	617	630	642	654	667	679	691	703	715
6.8	727	738	750	761	773	784	795	806	817	828
6.9	838	849	859	870	880	890	900	910	919	929
7.0	+939	948	957	966	975	984	993	1002	1010	1019
7.1	1027	1035	1043	1051	1058	1066	1074	1081	1088	1095
7.2	1102	1109	1116	1123	1129	1135	1142	1148	1153	1159
7.3	1165	1171	1176	1181	1186	1191	1196	1201	1206	1210
7.4	1214	1219	1223	1227	1231	1234	1238	1241	1244	1248
7.5	+1251	1254	1256	1259	1261	1264	1266	1268	1270	1272
7.6	1274	1275	1277	1278	1279	1280	1281	1282	1282	1283
7.7	1283	1284	1284	1284	1284	1283	1283	1282	1282	1281
7.8	1280	1279	1278	1277	1275	1274	1272	1270	1269	1267
7.9	1264	1262	1259	1257	1255	1252	1249	1246	1243	1240
8.0	+1237	1233	1230	1226	1222	1218	1214	1210	1206	1202
8.1	1197	1193	1188	1183	1179	1174	1169	1163	1158	1153
8.2	1147	1142	1136	1130	1124	1118	1112	1106	1100	1093
8.3	1087	1080	1074	1067	1060	1053	1046	1039	1032	1025
8.4	1017	1010	1102	995	987	979	972	964	956	948
8.5	+939	931	923	915	906	898	889	880	872	863
8.6	854	845	836	827	818	809	800	790	781	771
8.7	762	752	743	733	724	714	704	694	684	675
8.8	665	655	645	635	625	614	604	594	584	573
8.9	563	552	542	532	521	511	500	490	479	469
9.0	+458	447	437	426	415	404	394	383	372	361
9.1	351	340	329	318	307	296	286	275	264	253
9.2	242	231	220	210	199	188	177	166	156	145
9.3	134	123	112	101	91	80	69	58	48	37
9.4	+26	+16	+5	−6	−16	−27	−37	−48	−58	−69
x	0	1	2	3	4	5	6	7	8	9

TABLE 1   (*Continued*)

x	0	1	2	3	4	5	6	7	8	9
9.5	−79	89	100	110	120	131	141	151	161	172
9.6	182	192	202	212	222	231	241	251	261	271
9.7	280	290	299	309	318	328	337	346	356	365
9.8	374	383	392	401	410	419	428	436	445	454
9.9	462	471	479	487	496	504	512	520	528	536
10.0	−544	552	560	567	575	582	590	597	604	612
10.1	619	626	633	640	647	653	660	667	673	680
10.2	686	692	699	705	711	717	723	728	734	740
10.3	745	751	756	761	767	772	777	782	787	791
10.4	796	801	805	809	814	818	822	826	830	834
10.5	−838	842	845	849	852	855	859	862	865	868
10.6	871	873	876	879	881	883	886	888	890	892
10.7	894	896	898	899	901	902	904	905	906	907
10.8	908	909	910	911	911	912	912	913	913	913
10.9	913	913	913	913	913	912	912	911	911	910
11.0	−909	908	907	906	905	904	902	901	899	898
11.1	896	894	892	890	888	886	884	882	879	877
11.2	874	872	869	866	863	860	857	854	851	848
11.3	844	841	837	834	830	826	822	819	815	811
11.4	806	802	798	794	789	785	780	776	771	766
11.5	−761	756	751	746	741	736	731	726	720	715
11.6	709	704	698	693	687	681	675	669	663	657
11.7	651	645	639	633	626	620	614	607	601	594
11.8	588	581	574	568	561	554	547	540	533	526
11.9	519	512	505	498	491	484	476	469	462	454
12.0	−447	440	432	425	417	410	402	395	387	379
12.1	372	364	356	348	341	333	325	317	309	301
12.2	294	286	278	270	262	254	246	238	230	222
12.3	214	206	198	190	182	174	166	158	150	142
12.4	134	125	117	109	101	93	85	77	69	61
12.5	−53	−45	−37	−29	−21	−13	−5	+3	+11	+19
12.6	+27	35	42	50	58	66	74	82	89	97
12.7	105	113	120	128	136	143	151	158	166	173
12.8	181	188	196	203	210	218	225	232	240	247
12.9	254	261	268	275	282	289	296	303	310	316
x	0	1	2	3	4	5	6	7	8	9

TABLE 1   (*Continued*)

x	0	1	2	3	4	5	6	7	8	9
13.0	+323	330	337	343	350	356	363	369	376	382
13.1	388	395	401	407	413	419	425	431	437	443
13.2	448	454	460	466	471	477	482	488	493	498
13.3	503	509	514	519	524	529	534	538	543	548
13.4	552	557	562	566	570	575	579	583	587	591
13.5	+595	599	603	607	611	614	618	622	625	628
13.6	632	635	638	641	644	647	650	653	656	659
13.7	661	664	666	669	671	673	676	678	680	682
13.8	684	686	688	689	691	692	694	695	697	698
13.9	699	700	702	703	703	704	705	706	706	707
14.0	+708	708	708	709	709	709	709	709	709	709
14.1	709	708	708	708	707	707	706	705	705	704
14.2	703	702	701	700	699	697	696	695	693	692
14.3	690	688	687	685	683	681	679	677	675	673
14.4	671	668	666	663	661	658	656	653	650	648
14.5	+645	642	639	636	633	630	626	623	620	616
14.6	613	609	606	602	599	595	591	587	583	579
14.7	575	571	567	563	559	555	550	546	542	537
14.8	533	528	524	519	514	509	505	500	495	490
14.9	485	480	475	470	465	460	455	449	444	439
15.0	+434	428	423	417	412	406	401	395	390	384
15.1	378	373	367	361	355	349	344	338	332	326
15.2	320	314	308	302	296	290	284	278	272	265
15.3	259	253	247	241	234	228	222	216	209	203
15.4	197	190	184	178	171	165	159	152	146	140
15.5	+133	127	120	114	108	101	95	88	82	76
15.6	69	63	56	50	43	37	31	24	18	11
15.7	+5	−1	−8	−14	−20	−27	−33	−39	−46	−52
15.8	58	64	71	77	83	89	95	102	108	114
15.9	120	126	132	138	144	150	156	162	168	174
16.0	−180	186	192	197	203	209	215	220	226	232
16.1	237	243	248	254	259	265	270	276	281	286
16.2	292	297	302	307	312	318	323	328	333	337
16.3	342	347	352	357	362	366	371	376	380	385
16.4	389	393	398	402	407	411	415	419	423	427
x	0	1	2	3	4	5	6	7	8	9

Table 1   (*Continued*)

x	0	1	2	3	4	5	6	7	8	9
16.5	−431	435	439	443	447	451	454	458	462	465
16.6	469	472	476	479	482	486	489	492	495	498
16.7	501	504	507	510	513	515	518	521	523	526
16.8	528	531	533	535	538	540	542	544	546	548
16.9	550	552	553	555	557	558	560	561	563	564
17.0	−566	567	568	569	570	571	572	573	574	575
17.1	575	576	577	577	578	578	579	579	579	579
17.2	580	580	580	580	580	579	579	579	579	578
17.3	578	577	577	576	576	575	574	573	572	571
17.4	570	569	568	567	566	565	563	562	561	559
17.5	−557	556	554	553	551	549	547	545	543	541
17.6	539	537	535	533	530	528	526	523	521	518
17.7	516	513	510	508	505	502	499	496	493	490
17.8	487	484	481	478	475	471	468	465	461	458
17.9	454	451	447	444	440	436	433	429	425	421
18.0	−417	413	409	405	401	397	393	389	385	381
18.1	376	372	368	364	359	355	350	346	341	337
18.2	332	328	323	319	314	309	304	300	295	290
18.3	285	281	276	271	266	261	256	251	246	241
18.4	236	231	226	221	216	211	206	201	195	190
18.5	−185	180	175	170	164	159	154	149	143	138
18.6	133	128	122	117	112	106	101	96	90	85
18.7	80	74	69	64	58	53	48	42	37	32
18.8	−26	−21	−16	−10	−5	+0	+6	+11	+16	+21
18.9	+27	32	37	42	48	53	58	63	68	74
19.0	+79	84	89	94	99	104	110	115	120	125
19.1	130	135	140	145	150	155	159	164	169	174
19.2	179	184	188	193	198	202	207	212	216	221
19.3	226	230	235	239	244	248	252	257	261	265
19.4	270	274	278	282	286	290	295	299	303	307
19.5	+311	314	318	322	326	330	333	337	341	344
19.6	348	351	355	358	362	365	369	372	375	378
19.7	382	385	388	391	394	397	400	403	405	408
19.8	411	414	416	419	422	424	427	429	431	434
19.9	436	438	440	443	445	447	449	451	453	455
x	0	1	2	3	4	5	6	7	8	9

TABLE 2

x	0	2	4	6	8	x	0	2	4	6	8
20.0	+456	460	463	466	469	23.5	−425	425	425	424	424
20.1	472	475	477	479	481	23.6	423	423	422	421	419
20.2	483	485	486	487	488	23.7	418	416	415	413	411
20.6	489	490	490	490	490	23.8	408	406	403	401	398
20.4	490	490	489	488	487	23.9	395	392	388	385	381
20.5	+486	485	483	482	480	24.0	−377	373	369	365	361
20.6	478	475	473	470	467	24.1	356	352	347	342	337
20.7	464	461	458	454	450	24.2	332	327	321	316	310
20.8	447	442	438	434	429	24.3	304	299	293	287	280
20.9	424	420	415	409	404	24.4	274	268	261	255	248
21.0	+398	393	387	381	375	24.5	−241	235	228	221	214
21.1	369	362	356	349	342	24.6	206	199	192	185	177
21.2	335	328	321	314	307	24.7	170	162	155	147	139
21.3	299	292	284	276	268	24.8	132	124	116	108	100
21.4	260	252	244	236	228	24.9	93	85	77	69	61
21.5	+219	211	202	194	185	25.0	−53	45	37	29	21
21.6	176	168	159	150	141	25.1	−13	−5	+3	+11	+19
21.7	132	123	114	105	96	25.2	+27	35	42	50	58
21.8	87	78	69	60	51	25.3	66	74	81	89	96
21.9	42	32	23	14	5	25.4	104	111	119	126	134
22.0	−4	13	22	31	40	25.5	+141	148	155	162	169
22.1	49	58	67	76	85	25.6	176	183	189	196	203
22.2	93	102	111	119	128	25.7	209	215	222	228	234
22.3	136	145	153	161	169	25.8	240	246	251	257	263
22.4	178	185	193	201	209	25.9	268	273	278	284	288
22.5	−217	224	231	239	246	26.0	+293	298	303	307	311
22.6	253	260	267	274	280	26.1	315	320	323	327	331
22.7	287	293	299	305	311	26.2	334	338	341	344	347
22.8	317	323	329	334	339	26.3	350	352	355	357	359
22.9	344	349	354	359	364	26.4	361	363	365	367	368
23.0	−368	372	376	380	384	26.5	+370	371	372	373	373
23.1	388	391	394	397	400	26.6	374	374	375	375	375
23.2	403	406	408	410	413	26.7	375	374	374	373	372
23.3	415	416	418	419	421	26.8	371	370	369	368	366
23.4	422	423	423	424	424	26.9	365	363	361	359	357
x	0	2	4	6	8	x	0	2	4	6	8

TABLE 2 (*Continued*)

x	0	2	4	6	8	x	0	2	4	6	8
27.0	+354	352	349	346	343	30.5	−260	256	252	247	243
27.1	340	337	334	331	327	30.6	238	233	229	224	219
27.2	323	319	316	312	307	30.7	214	209	204	198	193
27.3	303	299	294	290	285	30.8	188	182	177	171	165
27.4	280	275	270	265	260	30.9	160	154	148	142	136
27.5	+254	249	243	238	232	31.0	−130	124	118	112	106
27.6	226	220	214	208	202	31.1	100	94	87	81	75
27.7	196	190	184	177	171	31.2	69	62	56	50	43
27.8	164	158	151	145	138	31.3	37	31	24	18	11
27.9	131	124	117	111	104	31.4	−5	+1	+8	+14	+20
28.0	+97	90	83	76	69	31.5	+27	33	39	45	52
28.1	62	55	48	41	34	31.6	58	64	70	76	82
28.2	+26	+19	+12	+5	−2	31.7	88	94	100	106	112
28.3	−9	16	23	30	37	31.8	118	124	129	135	140
28.4	44	51	58	65	72	31.9	146	151	157	162	167
28.5	−79	85	92	99	105	32.0	+172	177	182	187	192
28.6	112	118	125	131	138	32.1	197	202	206	211	215
28.7	144	150	156	162	168	32.2	219	224	228	232	236
28.8	174	180	186	192	197	32.3	239	243	247	250	254
28.9	203	208	213	219	224	32.4	257	260	263	266	269
29.0	−229	234	239	243	248	32.5	+272	275	277	280	282
29.1	253	257	261	266	270	32.6	284	286	288	290	292
29.2	274	278	281	285	288	32.7	293	295	296	297	299
29.3	292	295	298	301	304	32.8	300	300	301	302	302
29.4	307	310	312	315	317	32.9	303	303	303	303	303
29.5	−319	321	323	325	326	33.0	+303	303	302	302	301
29.6	328	329	330	331	332	33.1	300	299	298	297	296
29.7	333	334	334	335	335	33.2	294	293	291	290	288
29.8	335	335	335	335	334	33.3	286	284	281	279	277
29.9	334	333	332	332	331	33.4	274	272	269	266	263
30.0	−329	328	327	325	323	33.5	+260	257	254	250	247
30.1	321	320	317	315	313	33.6	243	240	236	232	228
30.2	311	308	305	302	300	33.7	224	220	216	212	208
30.3	296	293	290	287	283	33.8	203	199	194	190	185
30.4	280	276	272	268	264	33.9	180	175	171	166	161
x	0	2	4	6	8	x	0	2	4	6	8

Table 2   (Continued)

x	0	2	4	6	8	x	0	2	4	6	8
34.0	+156	151	145	140	135	37.0	−174	170	165	161	156
34.1	130	124	119	113	108	37.1	152	147	143	138	133
34.2	102	97	91	86	80	37.2	129	124	119	114	109
34.3	74	69	63	57	51	37.3	104	99	94	89	84
34.4	46	40	34	28	22	37.4	79	74	68	63	58
34.5	+17	+11	+5	−1	−7	37.5	−53	47	42	37	32
34.6	−12	18	24	30	35	37.6	26	21	16	10	5
34.7	41	47	52	58	63	37.7	+0	6	11	16	21
34.8	69	75	80	85	91	37.8	27	32	37	42	47
34.9	96	102	107	112	117	37.9	53	58	63	68	73
35.0	−122	127	132	137	142	38.0	+78	83	88	93	98
35.1	147	152	157	161	166	38.1	102	107	112	117	121
35.2	170	175	179	183	187	38.2	126	130	135	139	143
35.3	192	196	199	203	207	38.3	148	152	156	160	164
35.4	211	214	218	221	225	38.4	168	172	176	179	183
35.5	−228	231	234	237	240	38.5	+186	190	193	197	200
35.6	243	245	248	250	253	38.6	203	206	209	212	215
35.7	255	257	259	261	263	38.7	218	220	223	225	228
35.8	264	266	268	269	270	38.8	230	232	234	236	238
35.9	271	272	273	274	275	38.9	240	241	243	244	246
36.0	−275	276	276	277	277	39.0	+247	248	249	250	251
36.1	277	277	277	276	276	39.1	252	253	253	254	254
36.2	276	275	274	273	272	39.2	254	255	255	255	255
36.3	271	270	269	268	266	39.3	254	254	254	253	252
36.4	265	263	261	259	257	39.4	252	251	250	249	248
36.5	−255	253	251	248	246	39.5	+246	245	244	242	241
36.6	243	241	238	235	232	39.6	239	237	235	233	231
36.7	229	226	223	220	216	39.7	229	227	224	222	219
36.8	213	209	206	202	198	39.8	217	214	211	208	206
36.9	194	190	186	182	178	39.9	203	199	196	193	190
x	0	2	4	6	8	x	0	2	4	6	8

Problems

Chapter 2

1. The input signal $e_1(t)$ to an amplifier is a square wave form of amplitude 0.01 volt applied for periods of 0.01 second with intervals of 0.01 second when $e_1(t)$ is zero.

The amplifier is defined by the equation

$$80e_1(t) = 0.003 \frac{de_2(t)}{dt} + e_2(t)$$

Draw the response $e_2(t)$ for this square wave of input.

In order to improve the response of the amplifier, it is proposed to make it a negative feedback system having a gain K_b in the feedback path. The input to the amplifier itself is now a voltage $\varepsilon(t)$ defined by the relation

$$\varepsilon(t) = e_1(t) - e_3(t)$$
$$= e_1(t) - K_b e_2(t)$$

The transient response $e_2(t)$ for the system must be over in 0.002 second for each sudden disturbance caused by the application of the square wave $e_1(t)$. What is the value for K_b. Draw this transient response superposed on the graph for the system response having no feedback. Compare the results.

If a lag is introduced into the feedback path so that the voltage $e_3(t)$ fed back to the summing device at the input is

$$K_b e_2(t) = 0.001 \frac{de_3(t)}{dt} + e_3(t)$$

draw a graph of the response and comment on the quality of system performance with respect to the simple feedback where

$$K_b e_2(t) = e_3(t)$$

2. Three types of closed-loop systems, each defined by the same output member, are subjected to the same input disturbance. If all the systems were at rest prior to the application of a step function input disturbance, θ_i, draw the θ_o/θ_i response curves as a function of time for each of the following:

(a) A *continuous* control system for controller torque proportional to error.
(b) An *off-on* controller having a fixed magnitude torque applied whenever the error exists. (See reference 1 of Bibliography.)
(c) A *step-by-step* controller having torque of fixed magnitude applied for a time duration proportional to the error.

3. An elementary servomechanism is characterized by an output member of inertia J, and a viscous friction coefficient f. It has a control torque or stiffness k propor- .

tional to error. The stiffness k is to be selected. If the output member is a steel assembly 3 inches long and 1.5 inches in diameter, determine the stiffness constant k in order that the steady-state error shall not exceed 0.01 radian when the steady velocity is one radian per second for different degrees of dynamic stability corresponding to damping ratios, ζ, of 0.2, 0.6, 0.9, and 1.5. What are the undamped angular frequency ω_n, the frequency of oscillation ω_o, the viscous damping coefficient f, and the time for the transient to decay to 2 per cent of final value for each value of damping ratio?

4. For the closed-loop system shown in the accompanying illustration, determine the differential equations relating the output $\theta_o(t)$ to the error $\varepsilon(t)$, and the output $\theta_o(t)$, to the input $\theta_i(t)$.

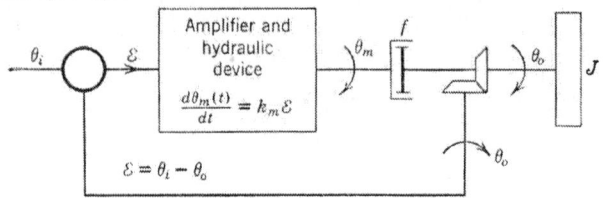

PROBLEM 2·4.

Assume that the gears have negligible inertia and that the load torque on the output shaft is zero.

5. Measurements conducted on a servomechanism show that a good approximation to the error response is

$$\frac{\varepsilon(t)}{\theta_i} = 1.66e^{-8t} \sin (6t + 37°)$$

when the input is given a sudden displacement θ_i.

For the system as adjusted, determine the natural frequency ω_n, the damping ratio ζ, and the damped angular frequency ω_0.

The inertia of the output member is known to be 0.01 pound-foot second squared, and the viscous friction coefficient f of the output is estimated to be 0.16 pound-foot second. What is the loop gain K or static stiffness k? How much can the loop gain be increased if the damping ratio ζ cannot be less than 0.4?

Chapter 3

1. Transform the following time functions by the Laplace integral into functions of the variable s:

      (a) $\theta(t) = 10u(t)$

      (b) $\theta(t) = 10t$

      (c) $\theta(t) = 3(1 - e^{-0.1t})$

      (d) $\theta(t) = 5 \sin \omega t$

      (e) $\theta(t) = 5 \cos \left(3t + \frac{\pi}{4} \right)$

2. Expand by partial fraction methods and evaluate the coefficients of the expansion for

$$(a) \quad \frac{1}{(s+3)(s+4)}$$

$$(b) \quad \frac{(s+2)}{(s+1)^2(s+3)}$$

$$(c) \quad \frac{(s+1)}{s^2+4s+16}$$

$$(d) \quad \frac{(s+2)}{s(s+1)(s^2+9)}$$

3. Convert the transforms represented by the functions in question 2 into the time domain by means of the inverse Laplace transformation.

4. Indicate the stability for the closed-loop systems having the following characteristic equations. Find the roots of these equations:

(a) $\qquad\qquad s^3 + 250s^2 + 14{,}665s + 144{,}250 = 0$

(b) $\qquad\qquad s^4 + 10.65s^3 + 89s^2 + 15.5s + 27 = 0$

(c) $s^5 + 35.5s^4 + 473.5s^3 + 2848s^2 + 6910s + 2800 = 0$

5. A servomechanism represented by the following equations is in the steady state with the input rotating at a speed ω_i.

$$J_o \frac{d^2\theta_o}{dt^2} + f_o \frac{d\theta_o}{dt} = K_T \varepsilon + n_3 \int \varepsilon \, dt$$

$$\varepsilon = \theta_i - \theta_o$$

(a) Write the expression for $\theta_o(s)$ after θ_i has suddenly been brought to a standstill. The expression should be in terms of the operator s, the input angular velocity ω_i, and the system coefficients.

(b) Write the transfer function $KG(s)$ of this system.

6. A servomechanism represented by the equations

$$J \frac{d^2\theta_o}{dt^2} = K_1 \varepsilon + K_2 \frac{d\varepsilon}{dt} + K_3 \int \varepsilon \, dt$$

$$\varepsilon = \theta_i - \theta_o$$

is operating in a steady state with its input rotating at a constant angular velocity ω_i. The input is suddenly brought to a standstill.

(a) By means of the Laplace transform method, determine $\theta_o(s)$ in terms of the system constants K_1, K_2, K_3, J, and ω_i. All initial conditions are to be evaluated.

(b) Write the transfer function $\theta_o(s)/\varepsilon(s) = KG(s)$.

7. A direct current generator supplies armature power to a shunt motor, as shown in the accompanying illustration. The generator armature is rotated at constant angular velocity and the motor field flux is assumed constant. The principle assumption upon which the analysis is based is linearity of both the electric circuit and the magnetic circuit found in each machine. The generator induced voltage is proportional to the generator field current. The airgap torque of the motor is proportional to armature current. The motor chosen for this study is mechanically characterized

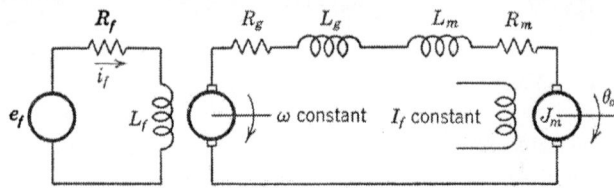

PROBLEM 3·7.

by inertia J, but is considered to have no viscous friction torque applied on its shaft. Use the machine constants listed in Table 5 of Chapter 10.

(a) If a voltage e_f of 69 volts is suddenly applied to the field winding of the generator, derive an equation which will predict the instantaneous angular velocity of the motor armature.

(b) Solve the equation and plot the solution as a function of time.

(c) If e_f is zero and a torque T_L is applied to the output shaft θ_o, determine the effort required to turn the shaft as a function of velocity ω_o.

8. A simple closed-loop system is defined by the relation

$$\tau_m \frac{d^2\theta_o}{dt^2} + \frac{d\theta_o}{dt} = K_v \varepsilon$$

and

$$\varepsilon = \theta_i - \theta_o$$

in which τ_m is the motor time constant (second) and K_v is the velocity constant in radians per second per radian.

The system defined as above is subjected to an input $\theta_i u(t)$. The response to this disturbance was found to be

$$\theta_o = \theta_i(1 + 0.207e^{-60.6t} - 1.207e^{-10.4t})$$

(a) Determine the damping ratio ζ, the velocity constant K_v, the motor time constant, τ_m.

(b) Suppose the velocity constant K_v were increased until the damping ratio ζ became 0.707. Find the new natural frequency ω_n and velocity constant K_v.

(c) Write the time solution of the new system response to a step function $\theta_i u(t)$. Plot the original and the new response to the same scale on a single piece of coordinate paper. Note the relative duration of the transient for the values of K_v.

Chapter 4

1. A servomechanism is defined by the differential equation

$$\frac{d^2\theta_o}{dt^2} + 5\frac{d\theta_o}{dt} = 25\varepsilon$$

and

$$\varepsilon = \theta_i - \theta_o$$

(a) Determine the steady-state complex ratio $\theta_o(j\omega)/\varepsilon$ for the open-loop system excited by the forcing function $\varepsilon = \Re E e^{j\omega t}$.

(b) Determine the steady-state complex ratio $\theta_o(j\omega)/\theta_i$ for the closed-loop system excited by the forcing function $\theta_i = \Re \theta e^{j\omega t}$.

(c) What are the natural frequency, damping ratio, and damped frequency characteristic of a transient following a step disturbance θ_i?

(d) Plot the magnitude and phase relation as a function of ω for the solutions to parts a and b.

2. A closed-loop system is to be used as a speed control so that the error equation is

$$\varepsilon_\omega(t) = \omega_i(t) - \omega_o(t)$$

The control torque applied to the mechanical output member is

$$T(t) = K_i \int \varepsilon_\omega(t)\, dt$$

and the mechanical output member is characterized by inertia and friction in such a way that

$$J\frac{d\omega(t)}{dt} + f\omega(t) = T(t)$$

(a) Derive the transfer functions for the dynamical components comprising the controller and the output member.

(b) Write the transfer function relating the output speed to the speed error.

(c) If the output inertia J is 5 in.^{2} pounds and the mechanical system time constant is 0.05 second, adjust the integral constant K_i so that the system has an undamped natural angular frequency $\omega_n = 20$, and a damping ratio $\zeta = 0.5$.

(d) For a sudden change of input speed, estimate the time required for the output speed transient to decay to within 10 per cent of its final value.

(e) If sinusoidal fluctuations of input speed are applied to the system adjusted as above, at what frequency will resonance occur?

(f) Approximately what value would be found for the maximum output speed with respect to a unit speed at the resonant frequency?

(g) Repeat parts d, e, and f for a torque disturbance $T_L \sin \omega t$ applied to the output shaft with the input reference speed held constant.

3. A particular servomechanism is defined by the relation

$$\frac{\theta_o(s)}{\varepsilon(s)} = \frac{K_v}{s(\tau_m s + 1)}$$

and

$$\varepsilon(s) = \theta_i(s) - \theta_o(s)$$

If the system is designed to have a resonant undamped frequency ω_n of 10 radians per second and a damping ratio ζ of 0.5:

(a) What is the velocity constant K_v?

(b) What is the time constant τ_m?

(c) What is the steady-state error for a constant input velocity of 20 degrees per second?

(d) What is the actual frequency of the damped oscillation?

(e) What is the time required for a transient to attenuate to within 2 per cent of its final value?

(f) At what angular frequency ω_f for $\theta_i(t) = \theta_i \sin \omega_f t$ does the ratio $\theta_o/\theta_i(j\omega)$ have its maximum value? What is this value? What is the phase of $\theta_o/\theta_i(j\omega)$ at this value of ω_f?

4. Assume a torque $T_L \sin \omega t$ is applied to the motor shaft of the motor generator system described in Problem 7 of Chapter 3. Determine the output angle $\theta_o(t)$ and output velocity $\omega_o(t)$ for values of ω from zero to 50 radians per second.

Chapter 5

1. Compare the methods for controlling an electric servomotor in a closed-loop position system in terms of the type and complexity of auxiliary equipment for:

(a) A field-controlled motor, that is, field current controls the motor torque.

(b) An armature-controlled motor, that is, adjustable armature current is supplied to the motor.

2. Determine the numerical value for the transfer function of an hydraulic transmission when the parameters described in Equation 5.93 have the following values:

Pump displacement	= 0.4 cubic inch per revolution
Motor displacement	= 0.4 cubic inch per revolution
Motor inertia	= 1.35×10^{-3} slug ft^2
Leakage coefficient	= 1.1×10^{-3} cubic inch per second per pound per square inch
Pump speed	= 3500 rpm
Volume of oil in system under compression	= 4.0 cubic inches

Investigate the effects on the dynamic properties of the transmission, of increasing the pump or motor displacement or the pump speed to increase the power rating.

3. The hydraulic amplifier shown schematically in the accompanying figure has the feature that negligible motion X_v of the pilot piston is required in the steady-state operation of the device. The input quantity is a force $F(t)$. The output quantity is a displacement $X_p(t)$ of the power piston. The purpose of the device is to displace the power piston from neutral proportional to the force F applied to the pilot piston.

For the system as defined by the symbols given below, assuming that coercion forces on valve may be neglected, determine

(a) The analytical expression for $X_p(s)/F(s)$.
(b) Compare the stability of the system when the damping coefficient f is finite and zero.

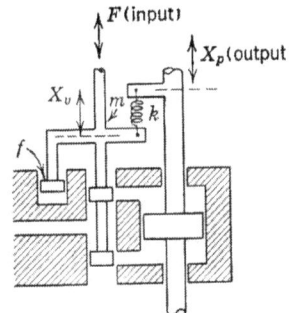

PROBLEM 5·3.

F = input force

X_v = pilot piston displacement

X_p = power piston displacement

$X_p = K \int X_v \, dt$

k = spring constant (lb/in.)

f = damping coefficient (lb/in./sec)

m = mass of pilot valve and associated parts

4. A. A two-phase, two-pole induction motor has the equivalent circuit (for balanced operation) of the accompanying illustration. Plot the torque-speed characteristics of this motor from minus synchronous speed to plus synchronous speed for:

$$(a) \quad \begin{cases} V_1 = 100 \cos 400t \\ V_3 = 100 \sin 400t \end{cases}$$

$$(b) \quad \begin{cases} V_1 = 100 \cos 400t \\ V_3 = 50 \sin 400t \end{cases}$$

$$(c) \quad \begin{cases} V_1 = 100 \cos 400t \\ V_3 = 0 \sin 400t \end{cases}$$

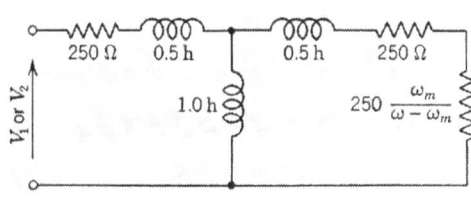

PROBLEM 5·4.

B. When the machine of part A is operated as a tachometer, plot the phase ψ and amplitude V_3 of the output voltage $V_3 \sin (400t + \psi)$ for speeds of -400 to $+400$ radians per second when $V_1 = 100 \cos 400t$ and $i_3 = 0$.

5. A two-phase induction motor is to be used for a control application, and for this purpose the winding of one phase is excited continuously while the second winding has a variable control voltage e_c applied to it. The motor internal torque is approximately proportional to this control voltage, that is, torque $\tau \approx k e_c$.

The data for the torque-speed curve, for rated voltage on both windings, are:

Full-Load Torque, Per Cent	Synchronous Speed, Per Cent
0	98.5
100	94.5
200	89.5
300	81.5
360	70.0
400	54.0
425	36.0
450	0

(a) Plot the torque-speed data, and on the same sheet plot similar curves for 50 and 150 per cent rated voltage on the control phase.

(b) From the curves plotted in (a) derive a set of curves relating torque τ to the control voltage e_c as the independent variable, for zero, 20, 40, and 60 per cent of synchronous speed.

(c) Write the differential equations with numerical coefficients, relating motor speed to control voltage when the motor delivers 100 and 75 per cent of the maximum output obtainable for each value of control voltage. Assume a particular value of rotor inertia and utilize the torque-speed curves and a plot of power versus torque to obtain numerical values for the equivalent viscous damping coefficient.

(d) For each value of load and for each value of voltage, determine the time required for the motor to reach a speed within 10 per cent of its final value following a sudden small change in the control voltage.

6. A dynamic temperature study is to be made on the physical system shown in the accompanying figure. The system comprises a heat exchanger located in an air-

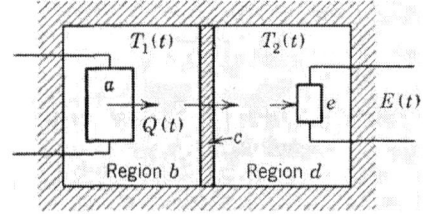

PROBLEM 5·6.

filled region b and an adjacent air-filled region d, which contains a thermal-measuring device e. A wall c of semi-insulating material is between the two regions b and d. Heat passes from region b to d through thermal resistance of this wall, but the wall may be assumed to have no thermal storage.

For the quantities listed and defined below, prepare the differential equation which relates the voltage $E(t)$ to the quantity of heat $Q(t)$:

$Q(t)$ = heat added to region b in Btu per minute

$T_1(t)$ = temperature of region b in degrees F

$T_2'(t)$ = temperature of region d in degrees F

$T_3(t)$ = temperature of thermometer element in degrees F

$E(t) = KT_3$ where K = thermometer sensitivity in volts per degree F

A_1 = thermal capacity of region b, Btu per degree F

A_2 = thermal capacity of region d, Btu per degree F

A_3 = thermal capacity of thermometer element, Btu per degree F

R_{12} = thermal resistance between regions b and d in degrees F per Btu per minute

R_{23} = thermal resistance between regions d and the thermometer element, degrees F per Btu per minute

It is helpful to assume that no distributed parameters exist anywhere in the system, that is, perfect circulation of air occurs in both chambers b and d. There are no boundary layer temperature effects at the wall c.

7. Two transmitter synchros are wired to a synchro differential. (See Bibliography, reference 38.) The differential synchro rotor, having an inertia J_R, is mechanically attached to a linkage as shown in the accompanying figure.

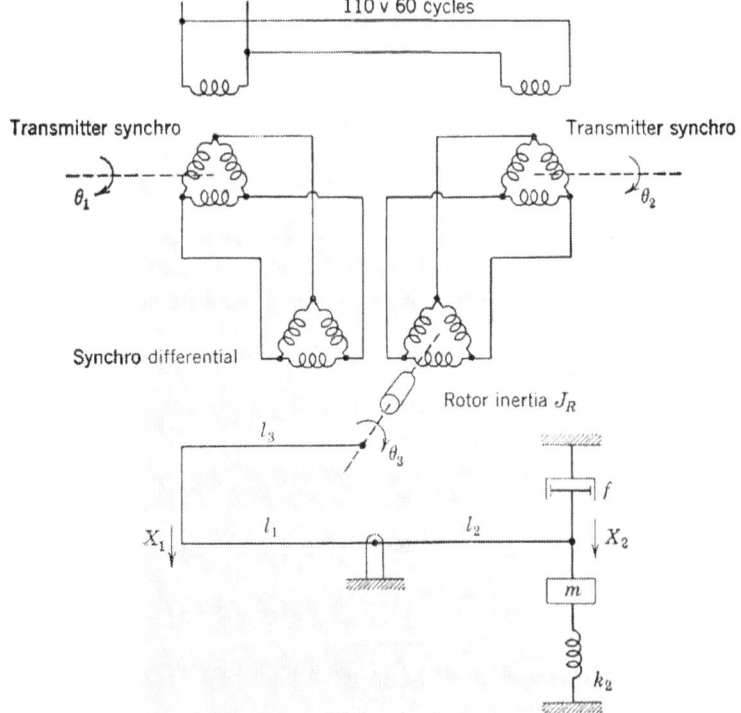

PROBLEM 5·7.

Assume for purpose of analysis that all rotary motions of the differential synchro rotor are small enough to consider the linear displacement $X_1(s)$ proportional to the angular deflection $\theta_3(s)$ in radians. Let the torque gradient or static sensitivity of the synchro differential be k_1 units of torque per radian difference in transmitter angular positions.

If no viscous damping is present at the differential synchro shaft, derive an expression for the motion $X_2(s)$ with respect to the difference of transmitter shaft motions $\theta_1(s) - \theta_2(s)$. Ignore all initial conditions.

Derive the transfer function relating motion at X_2 to $\theta_1 - \theta_2$.

8. The accompanying diagram illustrates a simplified voltage regulator. It comprises an electronic amplifier for error-measuring means and for excitation of a pilot

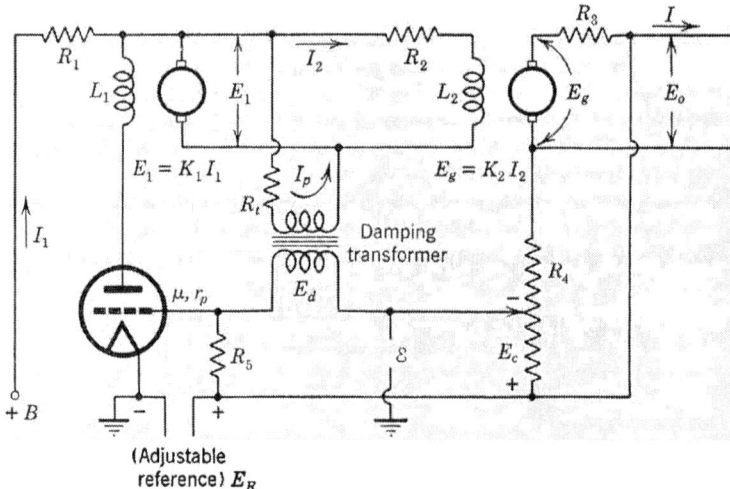

PROBLEM 5·8.

generator. The pilot generator furnishes field current for the main generator. A damping transformer is introduced as shown to assist the stabilization of the system. Use the symbols indicated in the figure. Assume for purposes of simplification that $R_5 \gg R_4$, $I_p \ll I_2$, and that the damping transformer is defined by the relation $E_d = M\, dI_p/dt$, $I_p = E_1/R_t$.

What is a block diagram for this system? Indicate the transfer functions in the boxes.

Chapter 6

1. For a system defined by the transfer function

$$KG(s) = \frac{K}{s\left(\dfrac{s^2}{\omega_n{}^2} + \dfrac{2\zeta s}{\omega_n} + 1\right)}$$

and

$$\mathcal{E}(s) = \theta_i(s) - \theta_o(s)$$

determine the constants K_v and ω_R of the closed-loop system when $\zeta = 0.3, 0.6$, and 1.0 for an M_p of 1.3, 1.6, and 2.0. What value of K will make the system oscillate indefinitely?

Calculate the transient error response following a sudden input disturbance θ_i or ω_i for any of the above conditions.

2. The transfer function for a furnace is given approximately by the relation

$$\frac{T_F(s)}{H(s)} = \frac{K_1}{(50s + 1)(100s + 1)}$$

where $T_F(s)$ is the transform of furnace temperature $T_F(t)$, and $H(s)$ is the transform of heat input $H(t)$.

A regulator or a process controller supplies heat to the furnace according to the relation

$$\frac{H(s)}{T_R(s) - T_F(s)} = \frac{K_2}{(10s + 1)}$$

where $T_R(s)$ is the transform of the reference temperature $T_R(t)$. This latter equation allows for the dynamical effects or imperfections in the controller or regulator.

Find the resonant frequency for the closed-loop system for $M_p = 1.5$, and give the value for the sensitivity of the opened loop in terms of the degrees temperature rise per unit error in temperature.

3. An hydraulic transmission is to drive the rotary member of a large printing press. When the inertia effects of the rotating parts of the press are included with the hydraulic motor, the transfer function is

$$\frac{\theta_o(s)}{X_s(s)} = \frac{K_1}{s(s^2 + 60s + 10,000)}$$

If the mechanism that strokes the pump is considered perfect, that is, $\mathcal{E}(s) = X(s)$, where $\mathcal{E}(s) = \theta_i(s) - \theta_o(s)$ and $X(s)$ is pump stroke, and $M_p = 1.5$ is chosen for the adjustment of the closed loop, determine the velocity constant K_v and resonant frequency ω_R of the closed-loop system.

If the stroke control should be truly represented by the relation

$$\frac{X(s)}{\mathcal{E}(s)} = \frac{K_2}{(0.05s + 1)}$$

instead of being ideal, what would be the new performance in the system assuming $M_p = 1.5$ as before?

4. The motor generator given in Problem 7 of Chapter 3 is made into a closed-loop system. The error-to-field voltage sensitivity may be assumed an adjustable constant. The field winding of the generator is in the plate circuit of a vacuum tube having $r_p = 10,000$ ohms. The gear reduction between the motor and a load inertia of 0.156 slug ft^2 is 100:1.

(a) Write the transfer function $KG(s) = \theta_o(s)/\mathcal{E}(s)$ for the servomechanism in terms of the system parameters.

(b) Using the numbers given, plot the frequency variant portion of the transfer function $G(ju)$. Nondimensionalize the frequency variable using $u = \omega/\omega_{nq}$ as the base frequency. [ω_{nq} is the undamped natural angular frequency of the quadratic factor appearing in the transfer function $KG(j\omega)$.]

(c) At what value of static sensitivity K will the system start to oscillate? What
is the corresponding value of the amplification factor of the error-field voltage
sensitivity? At what frequency will the system oscillate?

(d) What is the velocity constant K_v of the system, if M_p is to be 1.6? At what
frequency is θ_o/θ_i a maximum?

(e) Derive and plot the solution for $\varepsilon(t)/\varepsilon_{ss}$, for this servomechanism for a suddenly applied velocity input ω_i.

5. A positional servomechanism comprising a split field servomotor with viscous
damping in the load is synthesized as below with tachometric feedback. All parameters are given in volts, milliamperes, ounces, inches, radians, and seconds.

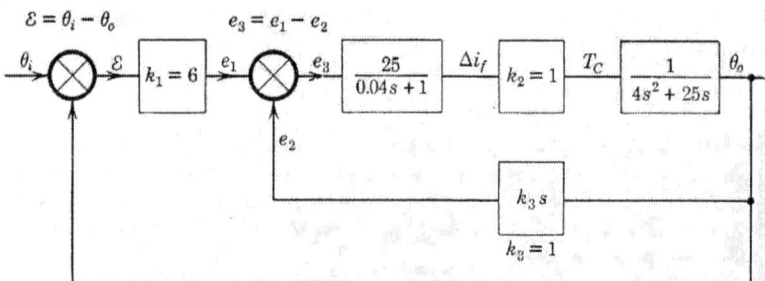

PROBLEM 6·5.

Determine the transfer function of the closed-loop system. Determine the velocity
error of the system for an input velocity of 1 radian per second. Determine the
steady-state error for a load torque of 10 ounce-inches on the output shaft. Is the
value of M_p reasonable?

Assume that the viscous damping in the output member is reduced to zero. Adjust
the gain k_1 and the gain in the tachometric loop to give the same value of M_p as
existed in the former adjustment. Compare the new performance with the old.
Adjust for a more desirable value of M_p.

Chapter 7

1. Prepare a study of a closed-loop system with passive integral compensation for
contrast with the results presented in Table 7·1. Use the physical system shown
in Figure 7·15 but replace the amplifier K by a passive integral network combined
with an amplifier. Choose $M_p = 1.3$ to 1.4, $\alpha_i = 10$, and $\tau_m = 0.1$ second for this
study.

2. Investigate the effect that the magnitude of the integral time constant τ_i has
upon the closed-loop system performance in Problem 1. Select values of τ_i that are
double and half the value obtained for τ_i when $M_p = 1.4$ and $\alpha_i = 10$. Compare the
magnitude and phase response θ_o/θ_i for the three values of τ_i. Prepare a study of the
characteristic equation $1 + KG(j\omega) = 0$ that shows the influence of the integral time
constant τ_i upon the speed with which transients subside when the system is disturbed.

3. A carrier-type lead network and amplifier are cascaded as shown in the figure for Problem 7·3a.

(a) Find the values of k, C, L, R_2 if R_1 is 10,000 ohms and f_c is 400 cycles per second, and if the performance is to provide about +50 degrees maximum phase shift for the modulation signal on the carrier.

(b) What is the minimum Q at the frequency f_c that a coil for this network could have?

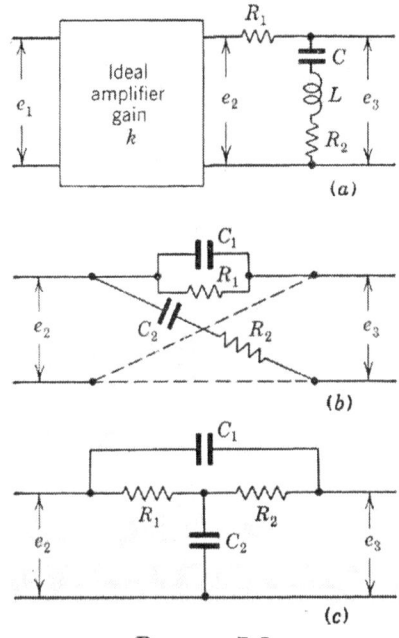

(a)

(b)

(c)

PROBLEM 7·3.

The symmetrical lattice network shown in the figure for Problem 7·3b is used in lieu of the network following the amplifier in the figure for Problem 7·3a.

(c) Determine the constants C_2, C_1, R_1 of the figure for Problem 7·3b, when $R_2 = $ 10,000 ohms and $f_c = $ 400 cycles per second.

The Bridge T network shown in the figure for Problem 7·3c is now substituted for the figure of Problem 7·3b.

(d) Determine the relationship between the frequency ratio ω_m/ω_c and the maximum lead angle that must exist for realizability. (ω_m is the frequency for maximum phase shift.)

4. (a) Prepare a study of the dynamic response of a servomechanism described in the figure for Problem 7·4a on the KG^{-1} plane if $M_p = 1.3$ and if the tachometer signal is made zero by opening the tachometer loop at B. Determine the velocity constant K_v, the torque per unit error constant K_t, and the frequency at which the system tends to show its resonant peak for θ_o/θ_i.

(b) For the same system as shown in the figure for Problem 7·4a add the tachometric feedback loop. Let the capacitor C shown in the figure for Problem
7·4b be shorted, making τ_g infinite. If $K_g = 0.0287$ volt-second, determine
the value of μ, K_v, torque per unit error constant K_t, and the frequency at
which the system tends to show its resonant peak when $M_p = 1.3$.

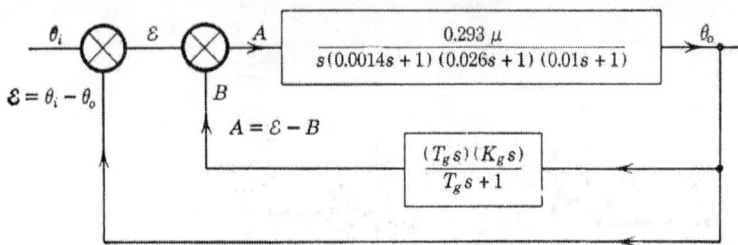

PROBLEM 7·4a.

Refer to Table 5, Chapter 10.

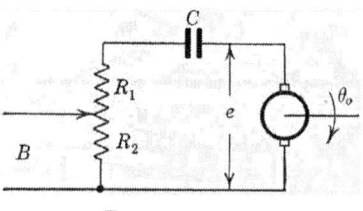

PROBLEM 7·4b.

(c) Repeat the study of part b with the tachometric feedback network (the figure
for Problem 7·4b), having the capacitor C set to a finite value. For $T_g = 0.23$
second and $K_g = 0.0287$ volt-second, determine K_v, μ, torque constant, and
the frequency at which $M_p = 1.3$.

(d) Compare the results obtained in parts a, b, and c. What are the limitations
upon the use of tachometric feedback such as described?

5. The hydraulic transmission whose numerical characteristics were given in Problem 3, Chapter 6, is controlled by the stroke amplifier also described. The combination is used as a servomechanism for positioning the cutting head of a contour milling
machine. The operation of the system is as follows: a stylus traces the master pattern $x_i(t)$; the position of the tool cutting the actual object $x_2(t)$ is compared with the
stylus position $x_i(t)$; the error signal ε_x in inches of motion actuates the stroke control; the stroke amplifier in turn controls the variable stroke pump of the hydraulic
transmission; the motor of the transmission drives through a lead screw to position
the cutting tool.

The cutting head weighs 100 pounds. It is driven through a 20-pitch lead screw
with an additional gear reduction of 10:1 between the hydraulic motor and the lead
screw. The table holding the model and the piece to be machined is driven at a
constant traverse velocity. The maximum vertical speed which can be obtained
because of the cutting tool material and the stock being machined is 4 inches per
minute.

The servo system should have a transient performance consistent with $M_p = 1.3$ and a steady-state error at the cutting tool of not more than 0.002 inch when the stylus is tracing over an incline of 30 degrees. Find the velocity constant K_v required for the closure of the loop. What is the maximum possible table speed with this value of K_v? How much increase in production could be obtained with this milling machine if the limitation of maximum vertical speed (4 inches per second) were eliminated by the use of special tools and special lubricants. Demonstrate, by redesigning the control system, how to turn out five to six times as many objects per hour, maintaining the same M_p.

Compare the two systems quantitatively, giving the values for K_v, ω_R, etc.

6. The accompanying figure shows a servomechanism block diagram containing a field-controlled servomotor which has a negligible field time constant. A device for

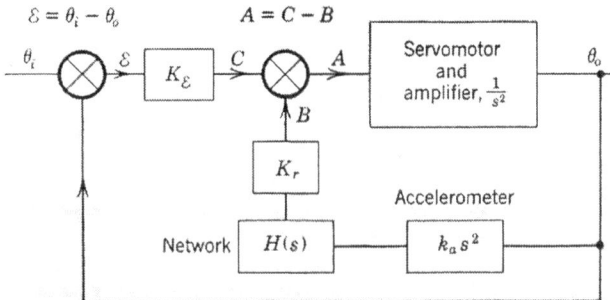

PROBLEM 7·6.

generating an electrical signal proportional to the output acceleration is attached to the output shaft. It is proposed to use the acceleration signal as a means for stabilizing the servo, but a network may be needed to modify the acceleration signal.

(a) For the case of $H(s) = 1$, show that this feedback scheme will not stabilize the servomechanism.

(b) Determine an $H(s)$ that will permit acceleration feedback to stabilize the servomechanism.

(c) Assuming zero source impedance and infinite load impedance for the network used in conjunction with the accelerometer, determine how you would arrange one resistor and one condenser to form an appropriate network for modifying the acceleration signal to make it effective as a stabilizing means. Support your answer by analysis.

Chapter 8

1. Discuss the relationship between gain margin and phase margin and transient stability for a closed-loop system.

Discuss the relative soundness of using one or the other of these as the sole criterion for setting the design constants of a closed-loop system. What is the justification for their use in closed-loop synthesis? State what other data may be needed to assure good system performance.

2. The asymptote plot of $G(j\omega)$ for a servomechanism is shown in the accompanying figure.

(a) Write at least one algebraic form of the transfer function that would permit system stability.

(b) Draw the phase curve as a function of log ω.

(c) Draw the locus in the G plane for the system that is stable.

(d) Show the closure of the locus in the KG plane when ω varies from $-j\infty$ to $+j\infty$. Is the system stable or unstable? Why?

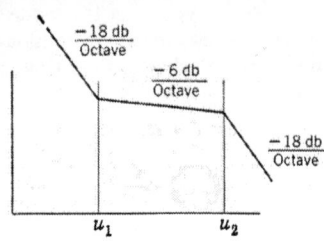

· PROBLEM 8·2.

(e) If M_p is to be 1.3, how many values of gain K will give a solution to the design problem? Show by a diagram.

(f) How far apart should the frequencies u_1 and u_2 be for the system to be stable? What is a reasonable value for u_R, assuming $M_p = 2.28$ decibels for the closed loop?

3. Prepare a dimensionless study to log coordinates of the *tuned* compensation network defined by

$$\frac{E_2(s)}{E_1(s)} = \frac{s^2 + 2\zeta_1\omega_{n1}s + \omega_{n1}^2}{s^2 + 2\zeta_2\omega_{n2}s + \omega_{n2}^2}$$

(a) Under what conditions can it be considered a lead network, an integral network, or both?

(b) What physical, electrical, or mechanical equipment is required to produce this transfer function by utilizing the feedback principle? Can it be realized without the use of a feedback system?

4. A positioning servomechanism is to be designed with a direct current motor drive. The load specifications are:

Minimum load velocity	= 1.5 radians per second
Minimum acceleration of load at any speed	= 5 radians per second per second
Load inertia	= 1000 pound-inches^2
Maximum positioning error	= 0.1 degree
Maximum velocity error	= 0.5 degree
Maximum load dry friction torque	= 3 pound-feet
Resonant frequency	= 0.5 cycle per second, with an $M_p = 1.3$

Two motors, respectively A or B (see figure), whose torque speed curves and rotor inertia are as given in the accompanying figure, are available for the drive member.

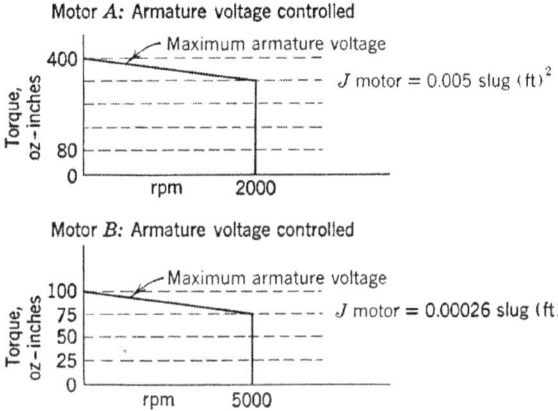

Motor A: Armature voltage controlled

Maximum armature voltage

J motor = 0.005 slug (ft)^2

Motor B: Armature voltage controlled

Maximum armature voltage

J motor = 0.00026 slug (ft)^2

PROBLEM 8·4.

For which of these motors may a gear ratio be found to satisfy the specifications? Discuss your results.

5. A common method of improving the performance of a servomechanism using a motor-generator system is to feed back negatively a portion of the armature terminal voltage in such a way that the current in the generator field is more or less proportional to the difference between the error signal and armature voltage under dynamic conditions. This permits increasing the zero frequency gain without adversely

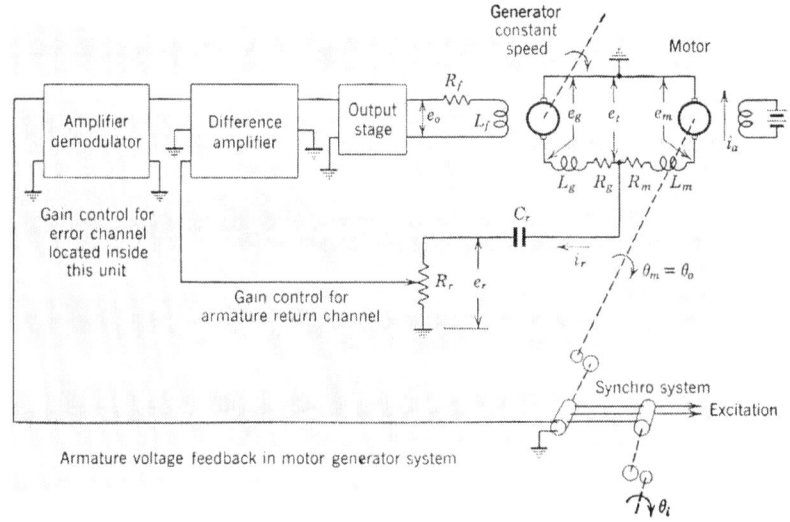

Armature voltage feedback in motor generator system

PROBLEM 8·5.

affecting the stability; the higher gain results in a stiffer servo with a larger torque constant. To avoid the effect of armature feedback on the velocity error, a high-pass filter is ordinarily used in the armature feedback circuit.

The figure of this problem shows schematically a system with armature feedback The gain controls for error signal and armature signal are arranged to be independent of one another. In working this problem use the constants and defining equations given below. The object of this problem will be to investigate the improvement possible with a specified amount of armature feedback.

Values of Constants

$K_3 = 0.328$ volt-second per radian $\tau_g = 0.00737$ second
$K_4 = 46.4$ inch-ounces per ampere $\tau_{ma} = 0.00737$ second
$R_g = 30.0$ ohms $\tau_f = 0.00408$ second
$R_m = 30.0$ ohms $J_o = 3.15$ in.^{2}-ounces

Defining Equations

$\varepsilon = \theta_i - \theta_o$

$e_o = k_e \varepsilon - k_r e_r$

$e_g = K_1 i_f$

$e_m = K_3 \omega_m$

$\dfrac{i_r}{i_a} = $ negligible fraction

$\tau_g = \dfrac{L_g}{R_g}, \quad \tau_{ma} = \dfrac{L_m}{R_m}, \quad \tau_f = \dfrac{L_f}{R_f}$

$\tau_r = C_r R_r$

Motor torque $= T_m = K_4 i_a$

Load torque $= T_L$, only other load is motor + load inertia, J_o

(a) Determine the general relationship between angle θ_m, torque T_L, and error ε. Use nondimensional gains and parameters involving time only, whenever possible.

(b) Determine the velocity constant for the condition of no armature feedback. Adjust system for $M_p = 1.3$.

(c) Determine the velocity constant for the condition of $\tau_r = 0.5$ second and the armature return gain adjusted so that the velocity constant is 0.25 that of part b if the error gain were kept the same as in part b and the condenser, C_r, is shorted. Again adjust for $M_p = 1.3$.

(d) Determine, for the settings of parts b and c, the coefficients for the approximate expression:

$$\varepsilon = a_1 \frac{d\theta_1}{dt} + a_2 \frac{d^2 \theta_1}{dt^2}$$

6. Repeat the studies of Problems 1, 2, 4, 5, or 6 of Chapter 7, using the methods of Chapter 8.

Chapter 9

1. What properties distinguish an elementary positional servomechanism from an elementary positional regulator?

Why are these properties necessary? Draw the locus of $KG(j\omega)$ for each elementary system as described in part a above, first in the KG plane and second as log magnitude and phase versus log frequency.

A closed-loop positional system is defined by the following relations:

> Error $\varepsilon = \theta_i - \theta_o$
> Torque developed by control on the output member $= k_1\varepsilon$
> Output member defined by an inertia J, viscous friction f, and load torque $T_L(t)$

Derive the block diagram representative of this system considered both as a servomechanism and as a regulator. Plot θ_o/θ_i when $T_L =$ zero and ε/T_L when $\theta_i =$ zero as log magnitude versus log ω, on the assumption that as a servomechanism $M_p = 2.28$ decibels. Indicate clearly the slopes of the asymptotes.

An undercompensated integral network defined by the relation

$$\frac{V_o(s)}{V_i(s)} = \frac{1 + \tau_i s}{1 + 10\tau_i s}$$

is inserted in the loop. Assuming the total gain in the loop is still such that the servo performance gives $M_p = 2.28$ decibels, replot the resulting θ_o/θ_i for $T_L =$ zero and ε/T_L for $\theta_i =$ zero, as log magnitude versus log ω to contrast with the plots of the uncompensated system.

2. A closed-loop system is arranged to have a torque proportional to error brought to bear on an output member of inertia J_1. An external inertia J_2 is coupled to the inertia J_1 by viscous friction B. The second inertia is elastically coupled to a fixed reference. The feedback is from the position of inertia J_1 and is identified as θ_o. The closed-loop error relation is given by $\varepsilon = \theta_i - \theta_o$.

(a) Derive the differential equation which relates the output motion of the servo loop $\theta_o(s)$ to the input motion $\theta_i(s)$. (Initial conditions may be omitted.)

(b) Discuss the merits of the externally coupled mass, spring, and damping as a method for stabilizing the closed loop.

3. The servo system described in the figure of this problem is used to control the tension of steel strip coming from a slitting machine. In this simplified problem the tension is controlled by controlling the motor torque. The motor speed is determined by the velocity of the strip as delivered from the slitting machine.

The net torque T_o available for tensioning the strip is established by controlling the motor armature current. This current is measured as the voltage drop e_3 in a resistor (αR_a in the figure, where α is less than unity). The difference e_2 between input voltage e_1 and the feedback voltage e_3 is applied to an amplifier which controls the generator field current i_f. This current in turn controls the armature circuit current i_a. The motor torque is assumed proportional to i_a. The generator voltage e_g is assumed proportional to i_f. The generated voltage e_m of the motor is proportional to speed $d\theta_m/dt$. If the total inertia on the motor armature shaft is J_o and there is no mechanical damping or rotational loss;

(a) Determine the Laplace transform relating e_1 and θ_m and T_o in terms of the system parameters (neglect all initial conditions). Draw the block diagram for the system.

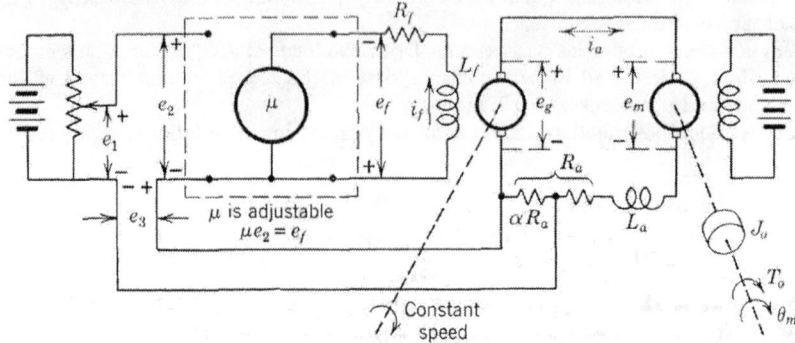

PROBLEM 9·3.

(b) Determine the value of μ permissible when $M_p = 1.1$ must be maintained. M_p may be defined as the maximum value of

$$\frac{\left|\dfrac{T_o}{e_1}\right|_{\max}}{\left|\dfrac{T_o}{e_1}\right|_{\omega=0}}$$

The values of the system parameters are:

$$\alpha = 0.1$$
$$L_f = 10 \text{ henries}$$
$$R_f = 1000 \text{ ohms}$$
$$L_a = 0.01 \text{ henry}$$
$$R_a = 1 \text{ ohm}$$
$$k_g = 1000 \text{ volts per ampere}$$
$$K_4 = 0.738 \text{ foot-pounds per ampere}$$
$$K_3 = 1 \text{ volt per radian per second}$$

(c) Determine the torque error per unit angular velocity of the motor under steady-state conditions for the setting of μ and the circuit constants of part b.

(d) Show a circuit modification to reduce the torque error caused by constant speed operation.

4. The figure of this problem shows a method for stabilizing a servomechanism which uses a field-controlled servomotor. A small auxiliary flywheel, J_d, is coupled to the output shaft through a viscous damper, f_d. The torque required to turn the damper-flywheel assembly may be neglected in comparison with the torque required to accelerate the combined load and motor inertia, J_o. A stabilizing signal voltage e_2 proportional to the difference in output shaft position θ_o and the auxiliary flywheel position θ_d is subtracted from the error signal voltage e_1 and the difference

is amplified and used to control the motor field current. The torque developed by the amplifier-motor combination may be assumed equal to $K_3(e_1 - e_2)$. There is no mechanical damping on the output shaft.

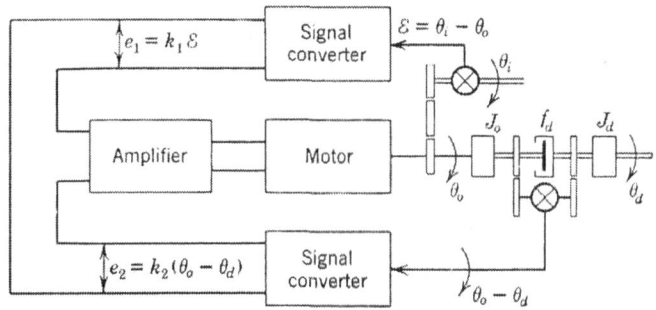

PROBLEM 9·4.

(a) Determine either the transfer function θ_o/ε or the reciprocal transfer function ε/θ_o.

(b) Sketch a representative locus for θ_o/ε or ε/θ_o.

(c) What is the velocity constant in terms of the system parameters? Explain physically what it means.

(d) Show how you would install a single mechanical spring in the diagram of the figure in such a manner as to make the velocity constant infinite. (Appropriate gearing may be used.)

5. For the control system shown in the accompanying figure compute the power absorbed by the member whose transfer function is K/s^2 when $T_L = 0$ and the input motion is $\theta_i(t) = \theta_i \sin \omega_f t$.

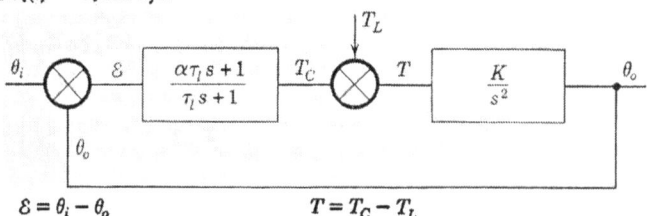

PROBLEM 9·5.

Calculate the power supplied to the same member when $\theta_i = 0$ and the torque $T_L(t) = T_L \sin \omega_f t$.

Plot the power functions $P(\omega_f)$ for each disturbance on semilogarithmic coordinates, following the procedure of Chapter 8.

Compare the power required by the *regulator* with that required by the *servomechanism*.

6. For a fixed reference voltage e_R in Problem 8, Chapter 5, perform a study which relates the output voltage deviation ΔE to load current I as a function of frequency.

What modifications would you make to the system to give it the properties of a servomechanism? How would you introduce these modifications?

Bibliography

The following references are listed approximately in the order they are introduced in the text. References of one type or those related to one phase of the topic are grouped together. The list does not pretend to be complete. The authors of the references are noted in the index to aid the identification of a reference known only by author and not by title.

1. "Theory of Servomechanisms," by H. L. Hazen, *Jour. Franklin Inst.*, Vol. 218, No. 3, pp. 279–330, September 1934.
2. *Governors and the Governing of Prime Movers*, by Willibald Trinks, D. Van Nostrand Company, 1919.
   "On Governors," by James Clerk Maxwell, *Proc. Royal Soc. London*, 16–1868, pp. 270–283.
3. *The Introduction to Non-linear Mechanics*, by N. Minorsky, J. W. Edwards Bros., Ann Arbor, Mich.
4. *Fundamental Theory of Servomechanisms*, by LeRoy A. MacColl, D. Van Nostrand Company, New York, 1945.
5. "Analysis of Relay Servomechanisms," by H. K. Weiss, *Jour. Aero. Sciences*, Vol. 13, No. 7, July 1946.
6. *Analysis and Synthesis of Linear Servomechanisms*, by Albert C. Hall, Technology Press, Cambridge, Mass., 1943.
   "Application of Circuit Theory to Design of Servomechanisms," by Albert C. Hall, *Jour. Franklin Inst.*, Vol. 242, No. 4, October 1946.
7. *Servomechanism Fundamentals*, by Henri Lauer, Robert Lesnick, and Leslie E. Matson, McGraw-Hill Book Company, New York, 1947.
8. *Automatic Regulation*, by W. R. Ahrendt and John F. Taplin, P. O. Box 4673, Washington, D. C.
9. *Automatic Control Engineering*, by Ed. S. Smith, McGraw-Hill Book Company, New York, 1944.
10. *Principles of Industrial Process Control*, by Donald P. Eckman, John Wiley & Sons, New York, 1945.
11. *Technical Memoranda on Automatic Control*, published by Industrial Instruments Division, Scientific Apparatus Makers of America, 1938.
12. "Direct-Acting Generator Voltage Regulator," by W. K. Boice, S. B. Crary, G. Kron, and L. Thompson, *Trans. AIEE*, p. 149, March 1940.
13. "Solution of the General Voltage Regulator Problem by Electrical Analogy," by E. L. Harder, *Trans. AIEE*, Vol. 66, pp. 815–825, 1947.
14. "Recent Developments in Generator Voltage Regulation," by C. R. Hanna, K. A. Oplinger, and C. E. Valentine, *Trans. AIEE*, Vol. 58, pp. 838–844, 1939.
   "Recent Developments in Speed Regulation," by C. R. Hanna, K. A. Oplinger and S. J. Mikina, *Trans. AIEE*, Vol. 59, pp. 692–700, 1940.

15. "General Analysis of Speed Regulators under Impact Loads," by G. D. McCann, W. O. Osbon, and H. S. Kirschbaum, *Trans. AIEE*, Vol. 66, 1947.
16. "Constant Speed Control Theory," by H. K. Weiss, *Jour. Aero. Sciences*, Vol. 6, No. 4, February 1939.
17. "Directional Stability of Automatically Steered Bodies," by N. Minorsky, *Jour. Am. Soc. Naval Engrs.*, Vol. 34, No. 2, May 1922.
    "Automatic Steering Tests," by N. Minorsky, *Jour. Am. Soc. Naval Engrs.*, Vol. 42, No. 2, May 1930.
18. "Electric Automatic Pilots for Aircraft," by P. Halpert and O. E. Esval, *Trans. AIEE*, Vol. 63, 1944.
    "The Gyrosyn Compass," by O. E. Esval, *Trans. AIEE*, Vol. 63, 1944.
19. "A New Type of Differential Analyzer," by V. Bush and S. H. Caldwell, *Jour. Franklin Inst.*, Vol. 240, October 1945.
20. "Tracer Controlled Position Regulator for Propeller Milling Machine," by C. R. Hanna, W. O. Osbon, and R. A. Hartley, *Trans. AIEE*, Vol. 64, p. 201, 1945.
    "Application of Electric Equipment for Ship-Propeller Milling Machine," by H. E. Morton and O. G. Rutemiller, *Trans. AIEE*, Vol. 64, p. 207, 1945.
21. "The Cinema Integraph," by H. L. Hazen and G. S. Brown, *Jour. Franklin Inst.*, Vol. 230, July–August 1940.
22. "An Automatic Curve Follower," by H. L. Hazen, J. J. Jaeger, and G. S. Brown, *Rev. Sci. Instruments*, Vol. 7, September 1936.
23. "A Recording Photoelectric Color Analyzer," by A. C. Hardy, *Jour. Optical Soc. Am.*, Vol. 18, No. 2, pp. 96–117, February 1929.
24. "The Speedomax Power Level Recorder," by W. R. Clark, *Trans. AIEE*, Vol. 59, pp. 957–964, 1940.
    "Polarized Light Servo System," by W. R. Clark, *Trans. AIEE*, Vol. 63, pp. 195–198, April 1944.
25. "Gyroscopic Stabilizer for Tank Guns," by C. R. Hanna and L. B. Lynn, *Elec. Engineering*, Vol. 63, No. 10, October 1944.
26. "Electronic Register Control for Multicolor Printing," by W. D. Cockrell, *Trans. AIEE*, Vol. 65, pp. 617–622, 1946.
27. "Hydraulic Variable Speed Transmissions as Servomotors," by G. C. Newton, Jr., *Jour. Franklin Inst.*, Vol. 243, No. 6, June 1947.
    "Frequency Response Measurement of Hydraulic Power Unit," by M. Russell Hannah, *Trans. ASME*, 1948 (forthcoming).
28. "Automatic Control in Presence of Process Lags," by C. E. Mason and G. A. Philbrick, *Trans. ASME*, May 1940.
29. "Dynamic Behavior and Design of Servomechanisms," by Gordon S. Brown and Albert C. Hall, *Trans. ASME*, pp. 503–524, July 1946.
30. "The Analysis and Design of Servomechanisms," by Herbert Harris, *ASME Paper* 46-F3.
31. "Time Lag in a Control System," by D. R. Hartree, A. Porter, and A. Callender, *Philos. Trans.*, Series A 235, 1935–36, 506.42 R88
    "Time Lag in a Control System, II," by D. R. Hartree, A. Porter, A. Callender, and A. B. Stevenson, *Proc. Royal Soc. London*, Series A Vol. CLXI, 1937.
32. "Frequency Response of Automatic Control Systems," by H. Harris, Jr., *Trans. AIEE*, Vol. 65, pp. 539–545.
    "A Comparison of Two Basic Servomechanisms Types," by H. Harris, *Trans. AIEE*, Vol. 66, pp. 83–93, 1947.
    "The Analysis and Design of Servomechanisms," by H. Harris, *OSRD Report* 454, December 1941.

33. "Parallel Circuits in Servomechanisms," by H. Tyler Marcy, *Trans. AIEE*, Vol. 65, pp. 521–529, 1946.
34. "The Servo Problem as a Transmission Problem," by E. B. Ferrell, *Proc. IRE*, Vol. 33, pp. 763–767, November 1945.
35. "Linear Servo Theory," by Robert E. Graham, *Bell System Tech. Jour.*, Vol. XXV, No. 4, pp. 616–651, October 1946.
36. *Electronic Servo Simulators*, by F. C. Williams and F. J. U. Ritson, Institution of Electrical Engineers Convention, London, May 1947.
    "Analysis of Problems in Dynamics by Electronic Circuits," by J. R. Ragazzini, R. H. Randall, and F. A. Russell, *Proc. IRE*, Vol. 35, pp. 442–452, 1947.
37. "Considerations in Servomechanism Design," by S. W. Herwald, *Trans. AIEE* pp. 871–877, December 1944.
    "Dimensionless Analysis of Servomechanisms by Electrical Analogy, II," by S. W. Herwald and G. D. McCann, *Trans. AIEE*, Vol. 65, pp. 636–639, October 1946.
38. "Selsyn Design and Application," by T. C. Johnson, *Trans. AIEE*, Vol. 64, pp. 703–708, October 1945.
    "Selsyn Instruments for Position Systems," by T. M. Linville and J. S. Woodward, *Elec. Engineering*, June 1934.
    "Electrical Accuracy of Selsyn Generator Control Transformer System," by Harold Chestnut, *Trans. AIEE* Vol. 65, pp. 570–576, August–September Section, 1946.
    Principles of Radar (Chapter XII), by M. I. T. Radar School Staff, McGraw-Hill Book Company, New York, 1946.
39. *Analysis and Design of Translator Chains*, Vols. I and II, by H. Ziebolz, Askania Regulator Company, Chicago, 1946.
40. "High Performance Demodulator for Servomechanisms," by Kenneth E. Schreiner, *Proc. Natl. Elec. Conf.*, Vol. 2, 1946.
41. "The Amplidyne Generator, a Dynamoelectric Amplifier for Power Control," by E. F. W. Anderson, M. A. Edwards, and K. K. Bowman, *G. E. Rev.*, p. 104, March 1940; *Trans. AIEE*, Supplement, December 1940.
    "Industrial Applications of Amplidyne Generators," by D. R. Shoults, M. A. Edwards, and E. E. Crever, *G. E. Rev.*, p. 114, March 1940; *Trans. AIEE*, Supplement, December 1940.
42. "The Application of Lead Networks and Sinusoidal Analysis to Automatic Control Systems," by George Schwartz, *Trans. AIEE*, Vol. 66, pp. 69–77, 1947.
43. "Some Fundamentals of a Theory of the Transductor or Magnetic Amplifier," by A. Uno Lamm, *Trans. AIEE*, Vol. 66, pp. 1078–1085, 1947.
44. *Experimental and Analytical Studies on Oil Gears* M3B1, by Servomechanisms Laboratory, Massachusetts Institute of Technology, 1943. Out of print. (See also U. S. Patent 2,409,190.)
45. "Design Factors Controlling the Dynamic Performance of Instruments," by C. S. Draper and G. P. Bentley. *Trans. ASME*, pp. 411–432. July 1940.
    "General Principles of Instrument Analysis," by C. S. Draper and G. V. Schliestett, *Instruments*, Vol. XII, pp. 137–144, 1939.
46. "Principles Underlying the Rational Solution of Automatic Control Problems," by Sergi D. Mitireff, *Trans. ASME*, Vol. 57, pp. 159–163, May 1935.
47. "Theory of Servo Systems, with Particular Reference to Stabilization," by A. L. Whiteley, *Jour. Inst. Elec. Eng.*, Vol. 93, Part II, pp. 353–367, August 1946.

48. *Transients in Linear Systems*, by M. F. Gardner and J. L. Barnes, John Wiley and Sons, New York, 1942.
49. *Modern Operational Mathematics in Engineering*, by Ruel V. Churchill, McGraw-Hill Book Company, 1944.
50. *Differential Equations for Electrical Engineers*, by Philip Franklin, John Wiley and Sons, New York, 1933.
51. *Electric Circuits*, by the Staff of the Department of Electrical Engineering, Massachusetts Institute of Technology, The Technology Press and John Wiley and Sons, New York, 1940.
52. *Theory of Functions as Applied to Engineering Problems*, by R. Rothe, F. Ollendorf, and K. Pohlhausen, Translation by Alfred Herzenberg, Technology Press, Cambridge, Mass., 1933.
53. *Advanced Rigid Dynamics*, Vol. II, Ch. 6, by E. J. Routh, Macmillan and Company, London, 1930.
54. *Mathematics of Modern Engineering*, by Robert E. Doherty and Ernest G. Keller, John Wiley and Sons, New York, 1936.
55. *Servomechanisms—Charts for Verifying Their Stability and for Finding the Roots of Their Third and Fourth Degree Characteristic Equations*, by Y. J. Liu, Massachusetts Institute of Technology, Cambridge, Mass., 1941.
56. "Method of Successive Approximations of Evaluating the Real and Complex Roots of Cubic and Higher Order Equations," by Shih-Nge Lin, *Jour. Math and Physics*, Vol. 20, No. 3, August 1941.
57. "Comparison of Methods for Evaluating the Complex Roots of Quartic Equations," by H. S. Sharp, *Jour. Math. Physics*, Vol. 20, No. 3, August 1941.
58. "Process Lags in Automatic Control Circuits," by J. G. Ziegler and N. B. Nichols, *Trans. ASME*, July 1943, Vol. 65, No. 5, p. 433.
59. "Stabilized Feedback Amplifiers," by H. S. Black, *Bell System Tech. Jour.*, Vol. 13, 1934. (U. S. Patent 2,102,671, December 1937.)
60. "Regeneration Theory," by H. Nyquist, *Bell System Tech. Jour.*, Vol. 11, January 1932.
61. *Network Analysis and Feedback Amplifier Design*, by H. W. Bode, D. Van Nostrand Company, New York, 1945.
62. *Communication Networks*, Vol. II, by Ernst A. Guillemin, John Wiley and Sons, New York, 1935.
63. *Stabilization of Servo-Mechanisms*, by D. C. Bomberger and B. T. Weber, Restricted Publication of Bell Telephone Laboratories, Inc., December 1941.
64. "The Analysis and an Optimum Synthesis of Linear Servomechanisms," by Donald Herr and Irving Gerst, *Trans. AIEE*, Vol. 66, Technical Preprint 47–165, 1947.
65. *Theory of Servomechanisms*, by Hubert M. James, Nathaniel B. Nichols, Ralph S. Phillips, McGraw-Hill Book Company, New York, 1947.
66. "Bridged-T and Parallel-T Circuits for Measurements at Radio Frequencies," by W. N. Tuttle, *Proc. IRE*, Vol. 28, p. 23, January 1940.
    "A New Type of Selective Circuit and Some Applications," by H. H. Scott, *Proc. IRE*, Vol. 26, p. 226, February 1938.
67. "Transient Response of Television Amplifiers," by A. V. Bedford and G. L. Fredendall, *Proc. IRE*, Vol. 30, pp. 440–457, October 1942.
68. *Theory of Equations*, by J. M. Thomas, McGraw-Hill Book Company, New York, 1938.
69. *Applied Electronics*, Ch. IX, by the Staff of the Department of Electrical Engineering, Massachusetts Institute of Technology, The Technology Press and John Wiley & Sons, New York, 1943.

70. *Mittlebare Regler und Regelanlagen*, von F. V. A. Engel unter Mitwirking von R. C. Oldenbourg, V. D. I. Verlag GMBH, Berlin, 1944. Reproduced by Edwards Bros., Ann Arbor, Mich., 1946.
71. *The Extrapolation, Interpolation, and Smoothing of Stationary Time Series*, by Norbert Wiener, John Wiley and Sons, New York (forthcoming).
72. "Laboratory Aids for Electromechanical System Development," by George C. Newton, Jr., and W. T. White, *Trans. AIEE*, Vol. 66, Technical Preprint 47–52, 1947.
73. "Obtaining Attenuation Frequency Characteristics for Servomechanisms," by Harold Chestnut, *G. E. Rev.*, December 1947.

Index

(The numbers that are followed by asterisks are bibliographical reference numbers, not folios. See the Bibliography.)

Date Due

TJ213 .B7

Brown, Gordon Stanley

Principles of servomechanisms.

DATE	ISSUED TO
	33698

www.ingramcontent.com/pod-product-compliance
Lightning Source LLC
Chambersburg PA
CBHW072006150225
22013CB00003B/98